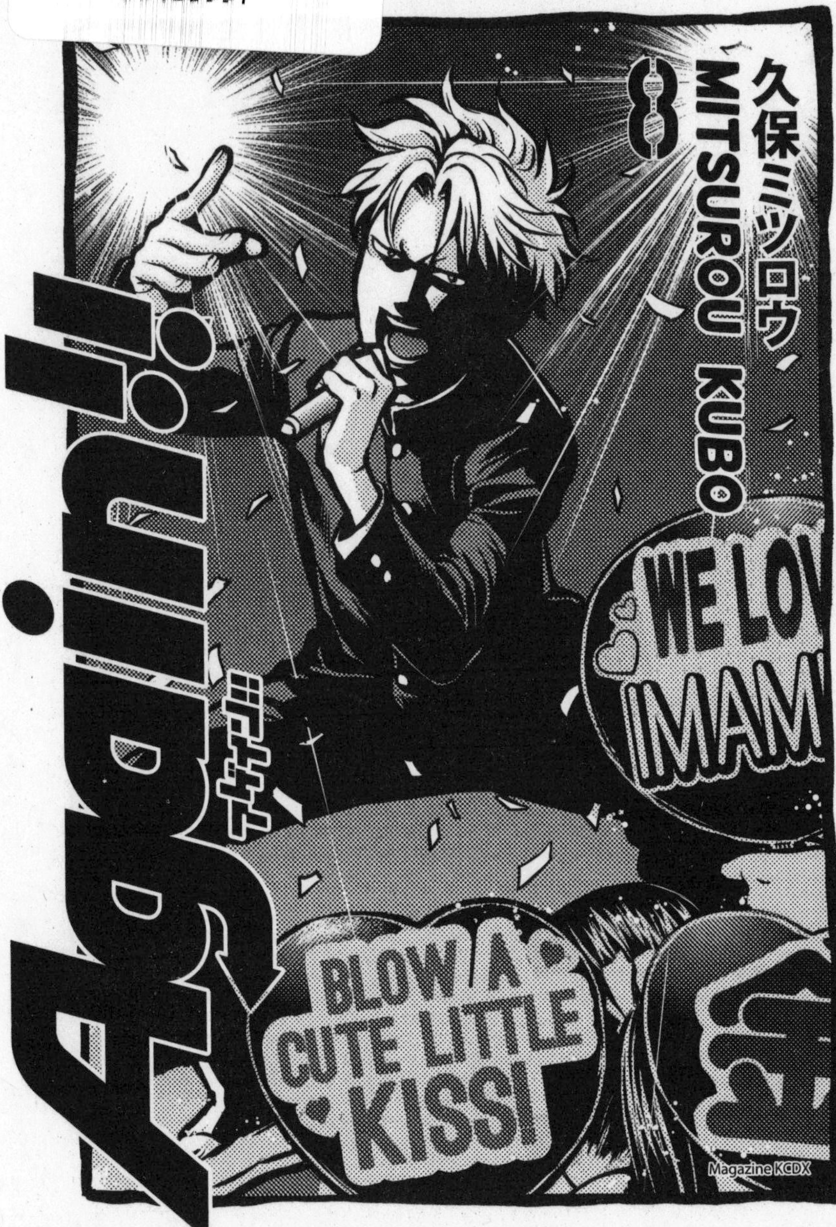
Again!!
8
久保ミツロウ
MITSUROU KUBO
WE LOV
IMAM
BLOW A CUTE LITTLE KISS!
Magazine KCDX

contents

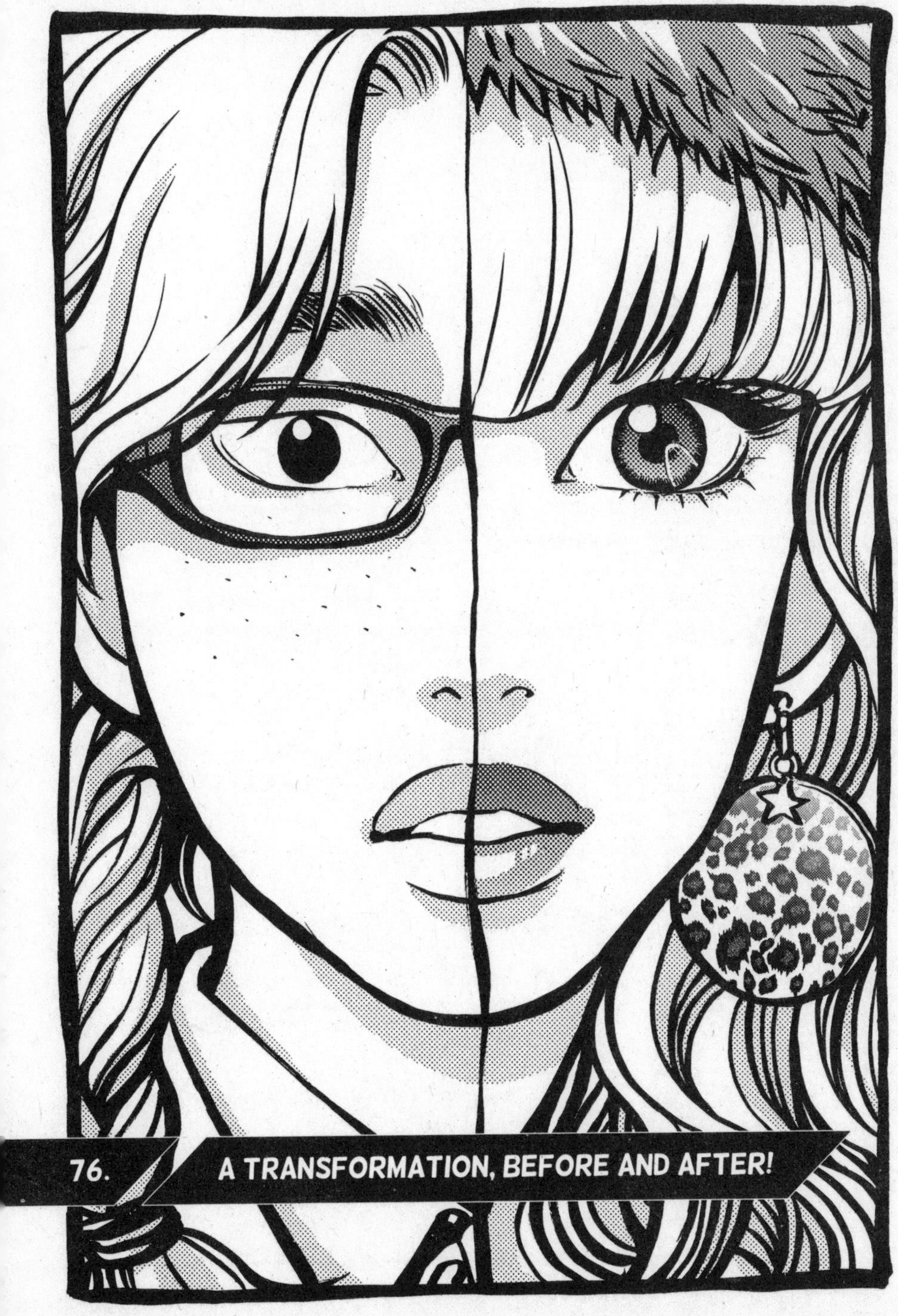
76.
A TRANSFORMATION, BEFORE AND AFTER!

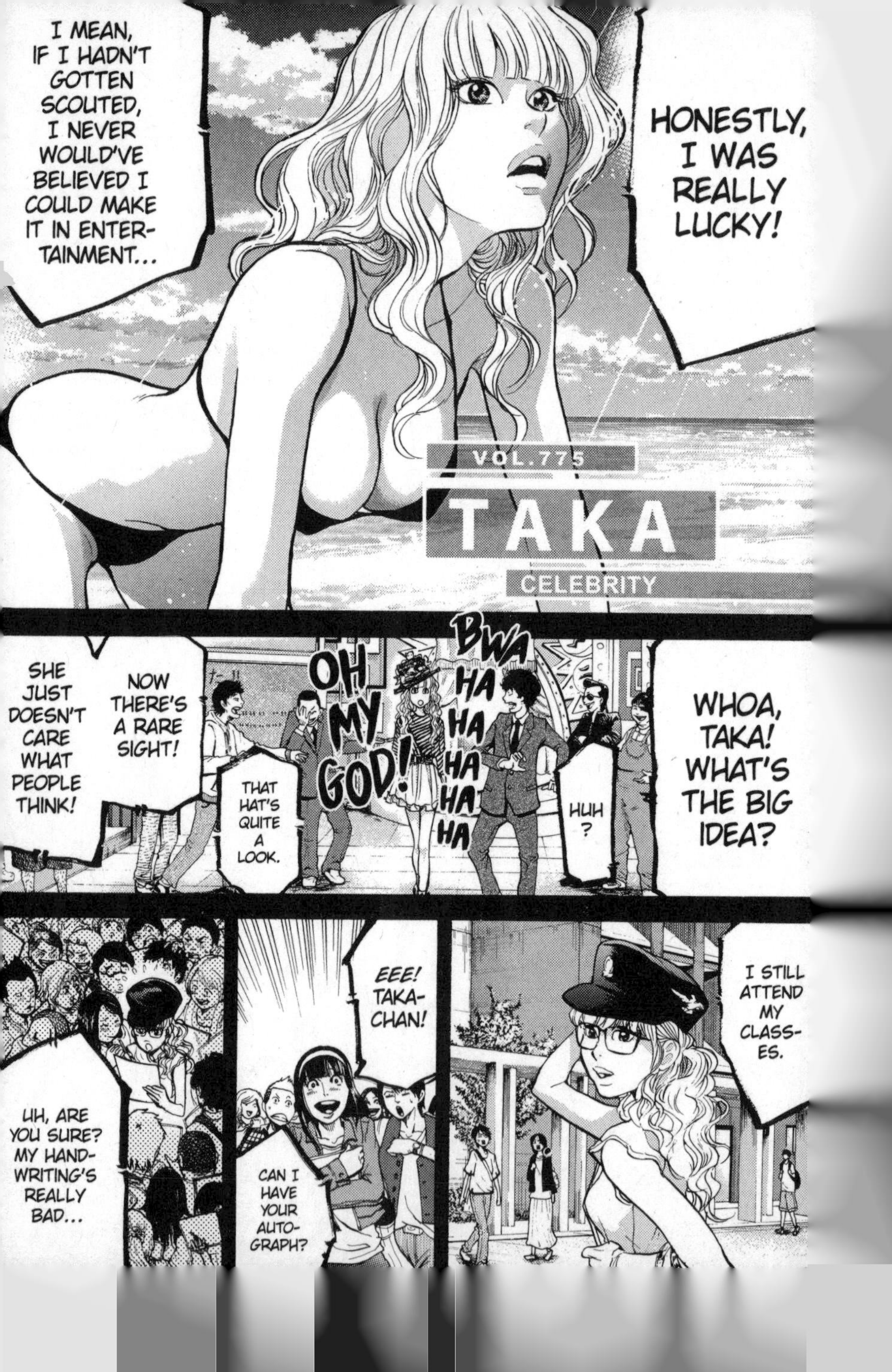
HONESTLY, I WAS REALLY LUCKY!
I MEAN, IF I HADN'T GOTTEN SCOUTED, I NEVER WOULD'VE BELIEVED I COULD MAKE IT IN ENTER-TAINMENT...
VOL.775
TAKA
CELEBRITY
WHOA, TAKA! WHAT'S THE BIG IDEA?
HUH?
BWAHAHAHAHAHA
OH MY GOD!
THAT HAT'S QUITE A LOOK.
NOW THERE'S A RARE SIGHT!
SHE JUST DOESN'T CARE WHAT PEOPLE THINK!
I STILL ATTEND MY CLASS-ES.
EEE! TAKA-CHAN!
CAN I HAVE YOUR AUTO-GRAPH?
UH, ARE YOU SURE? MY HAND-WRITING'S REALLY BAD...

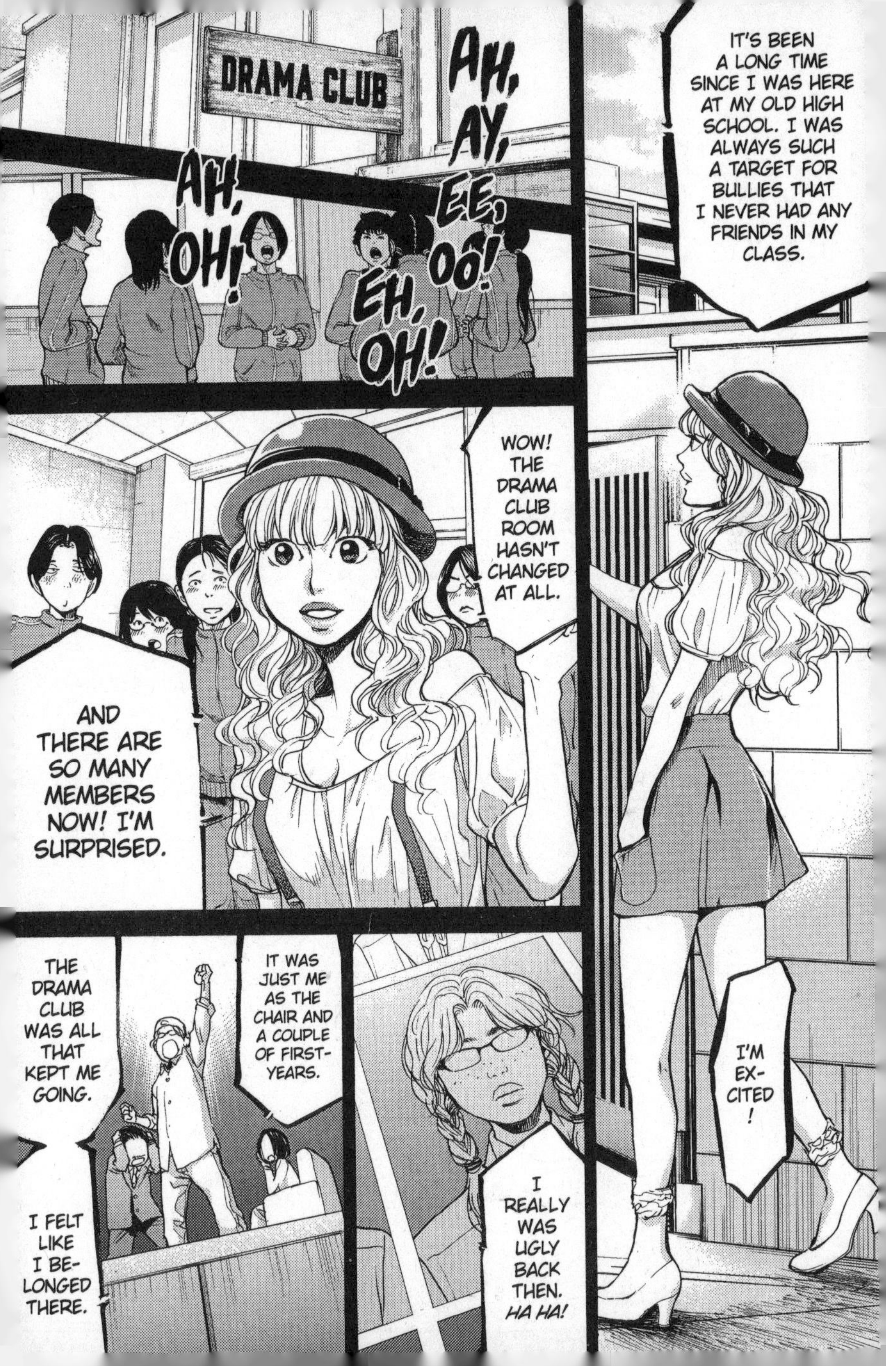
IT'S BEEN A LONG TIME SINCE I WAS HERE AT MY OLD HIGH SCHOOL. I WAS ALWAYS SUCH A TARGET FOR BULLIES THAT I NEVER HAD ANY FRIENDS IN MY CLASS.
I'M EX-CITED!
DRAMA CLUB
AH, AY, EE, OO!
AH, OH!
EH, OH!
WOW! THE DRAMA CLUB ROOM HASN'T CHANGED AT ALL.
AND THERE ARE SO MANY MEMBERS NOW! I'M SURPRISED.
I REALLY WAS UGLY BACK THEN. *HA HA!*
IT WAS JUST ME AS THE CHAIR AND A COUPLE OF FIRST-YEARS.
THE DRAMA CLUB WAS ALL THAT KEPT ME GOING.
I FELT LIKE I BE-LONGED THERE.

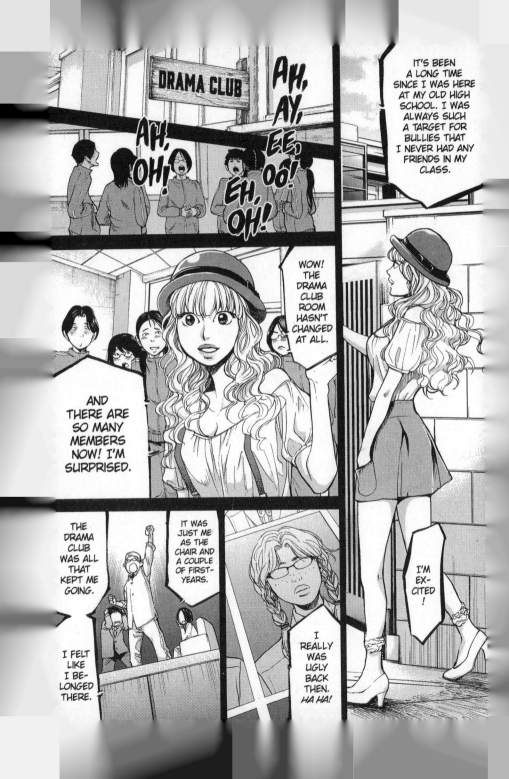

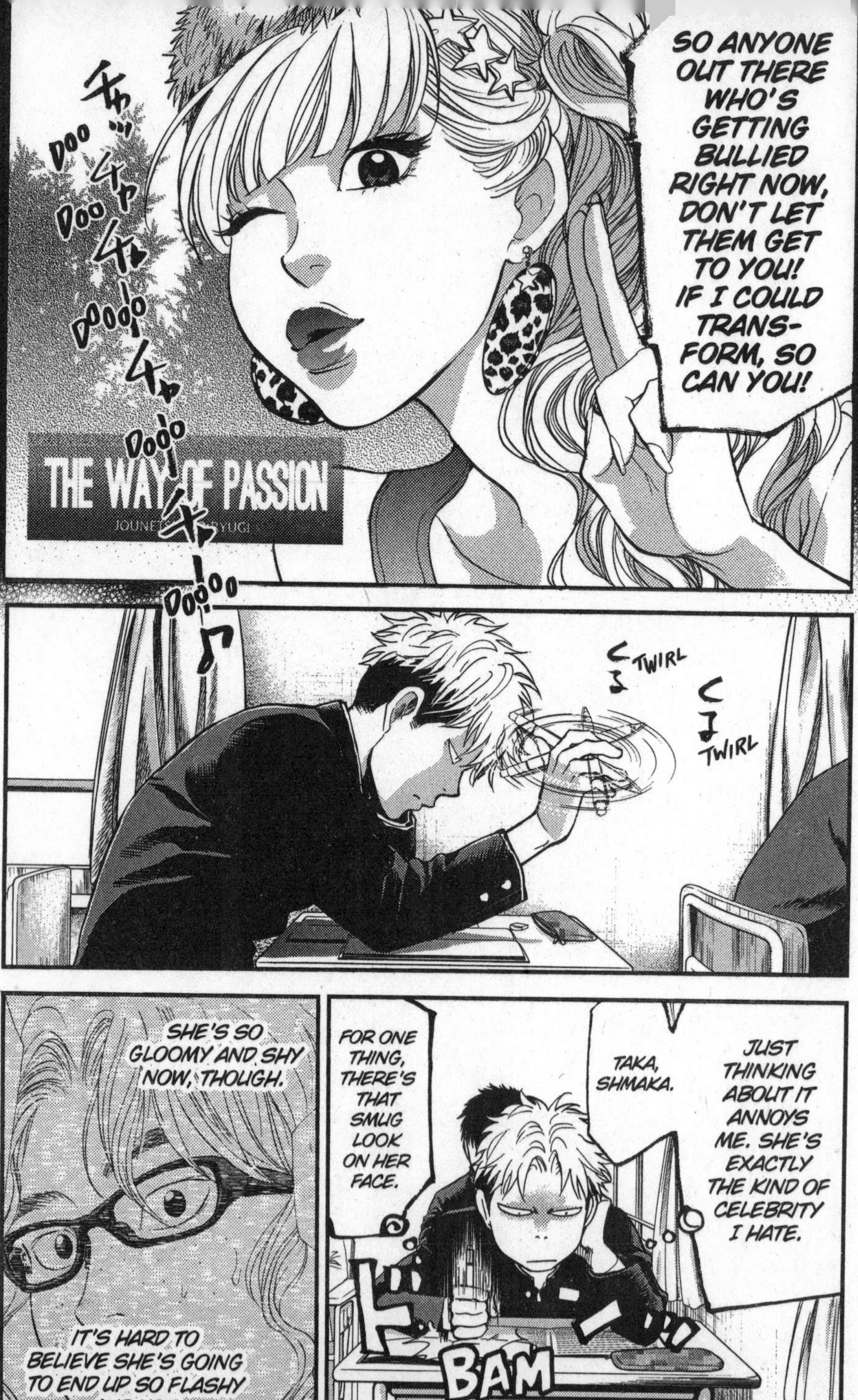
SO ANYONE OUT THERE WHO'S GETTING BULLIED RIGHT NOW, DON'T LET THEM GET TO YOU! IF I COULD TRANS-FORM, SO CAN YOU!
DOO
DOO
DOOOO
DOOOO
DOOOO
THE WAY OF PASSION
TWIRL
TWIRL
JUST THINKING ABOUT IT ANNOYS ME. SHE'S EXACTLY THE KIND OF CELEBRITY I HATE.
TAKA, SHMAKA.
FOR ONE THING, THERE'S THAT SMUG LOOK ON HER FACE.
BAM
SHE'S SO GLOOMY AND SHY NOW, THOUGH.
IT'S HARD TO BELIEVE SHE'S GOING TO END UP SO FLASHY AND HOT.

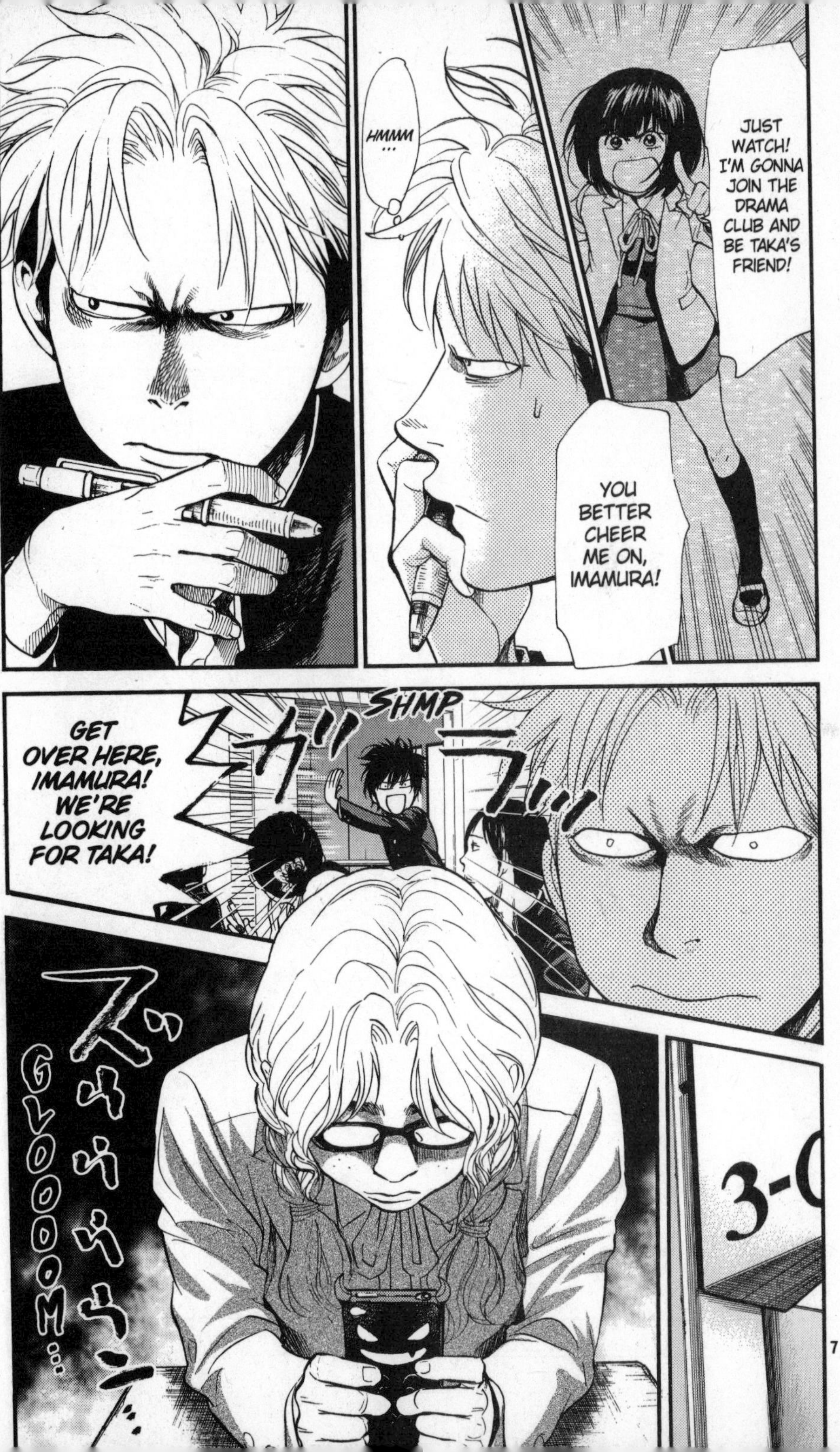
JUST WATCH! I'M GONNA JOIN THE DRAMA CLUB AND BE TAKA'S FRIEND!
YOU BETTER CHEER ME ON, IMAMURA!
HMMM...
SHMP
GET OVER HERE, IMAMURA! WE'RE LOOKING FOR TAKA!
3-C
GLOOOOOM...

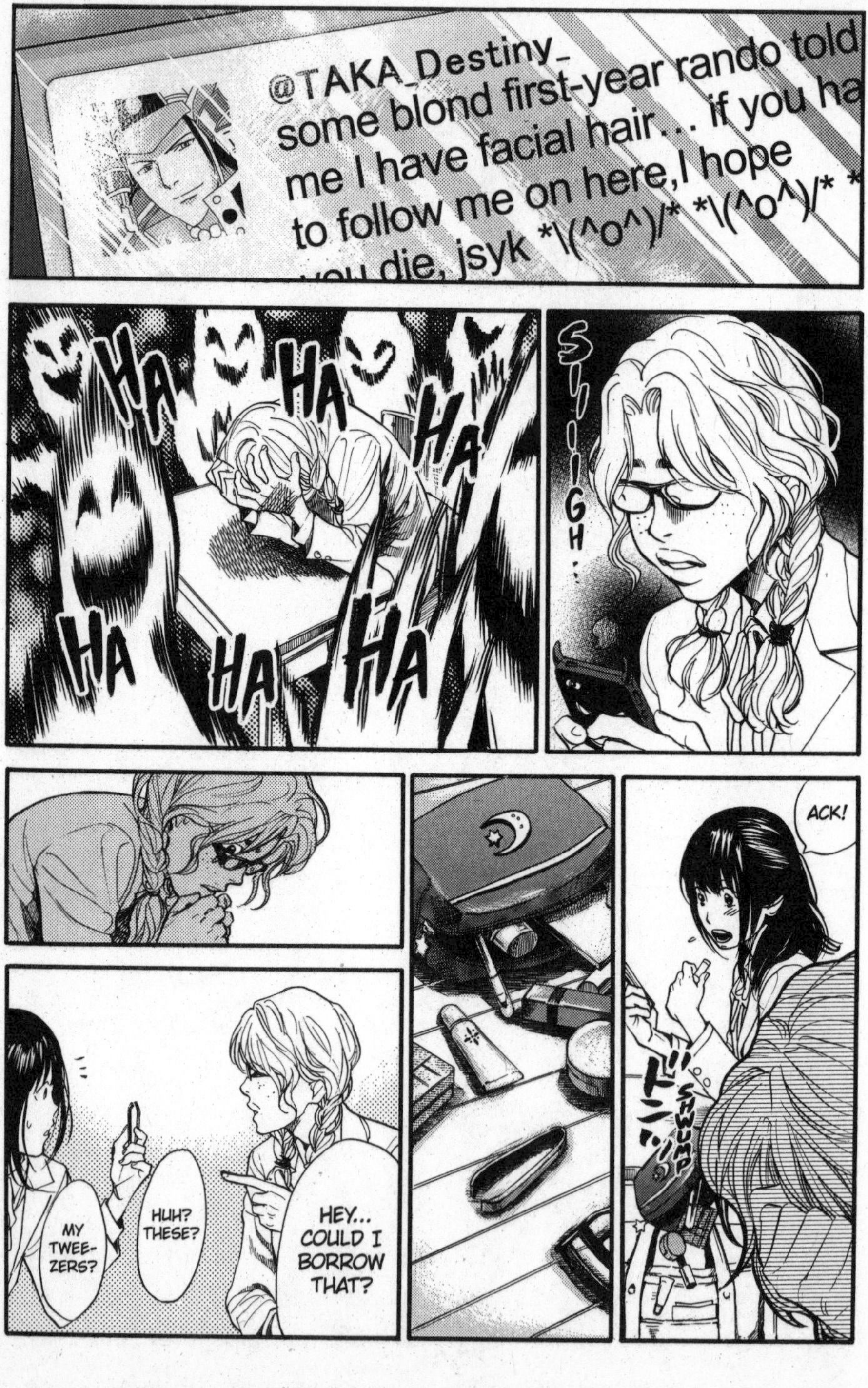
@TAKA_Destiny_
some blond first-year rando told
me I have facial hair. . . if you ha
to follow me on here,I hope
to follow me on here,I hope
you die, jsyk *\(^o^)/* *\(^o^)/* *
SIIIIIGH...
HA HA HA HA HA HA HA
ACK!
SHWUMP
HEY... COULD I BORROW THAT?
HUH? THESE?
MY TWEEZERS?

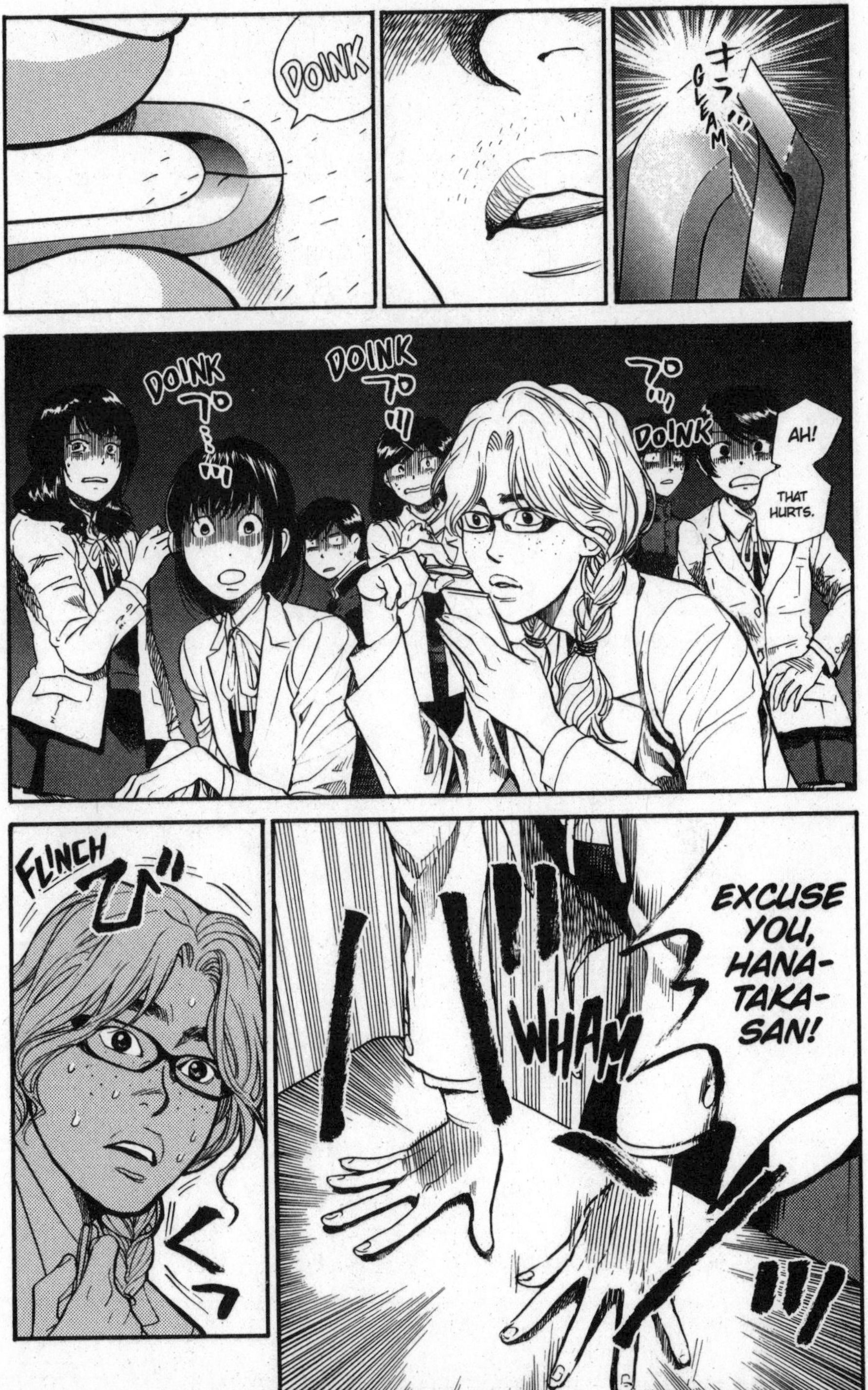
GLEAM
DOINK
AH!
THAT HURTS.
DOINK
DOINK
DOINK
EXCUSE YOU, HANA-TAKA-SAN!
WHAM
FLINCH

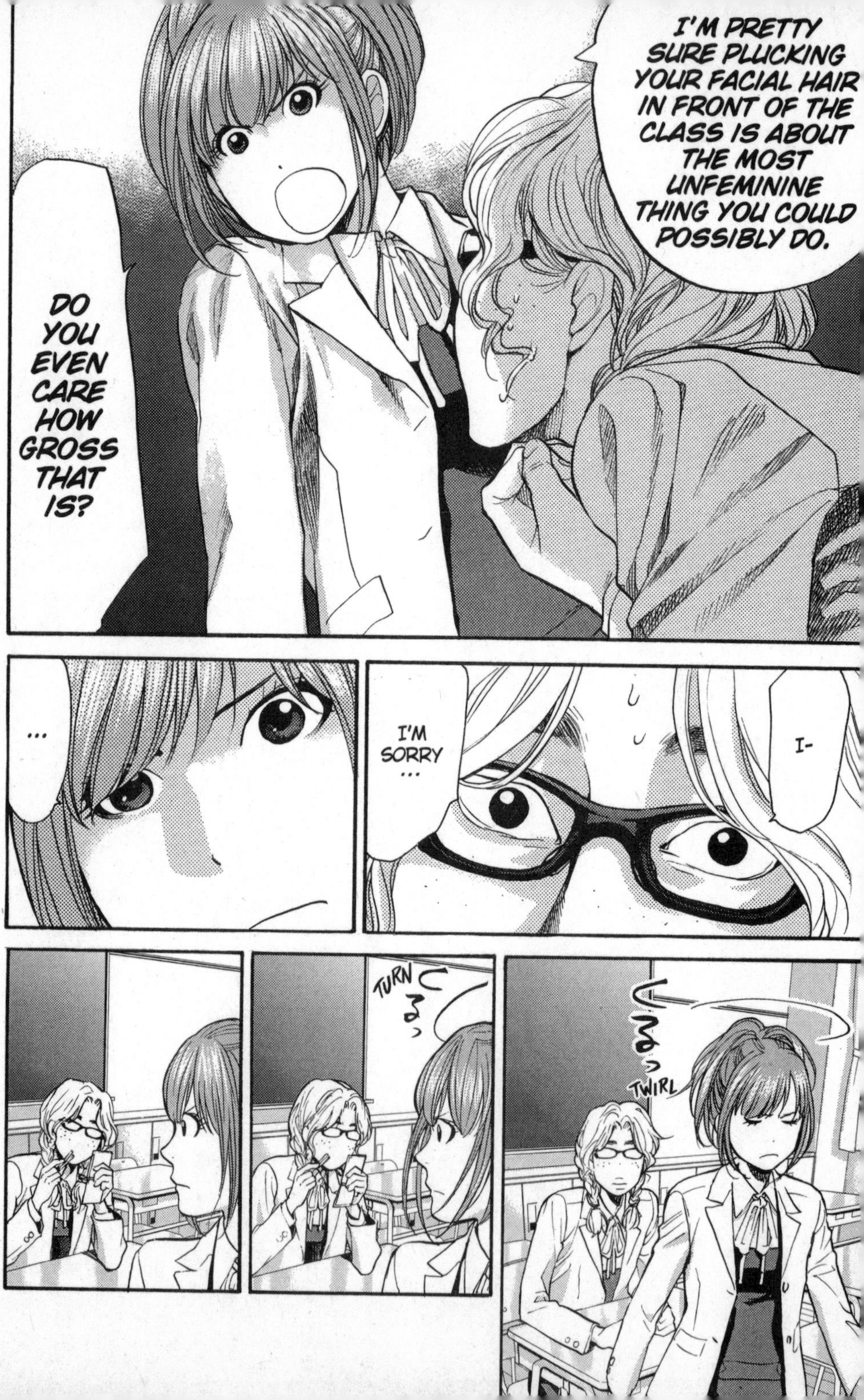
I'M PRETTY SURE PLUCKING YOUR FACIAL HAIR IN FRONT OF THE CLASS IS ABOUT THE MOST UNFEMININE THING YOU COULD POSSIBLY DO.
DO YOU EVEN CARE HOW GROSS THAT IS?
I-
I'M SORRY ...
...
TWIRL
TURN

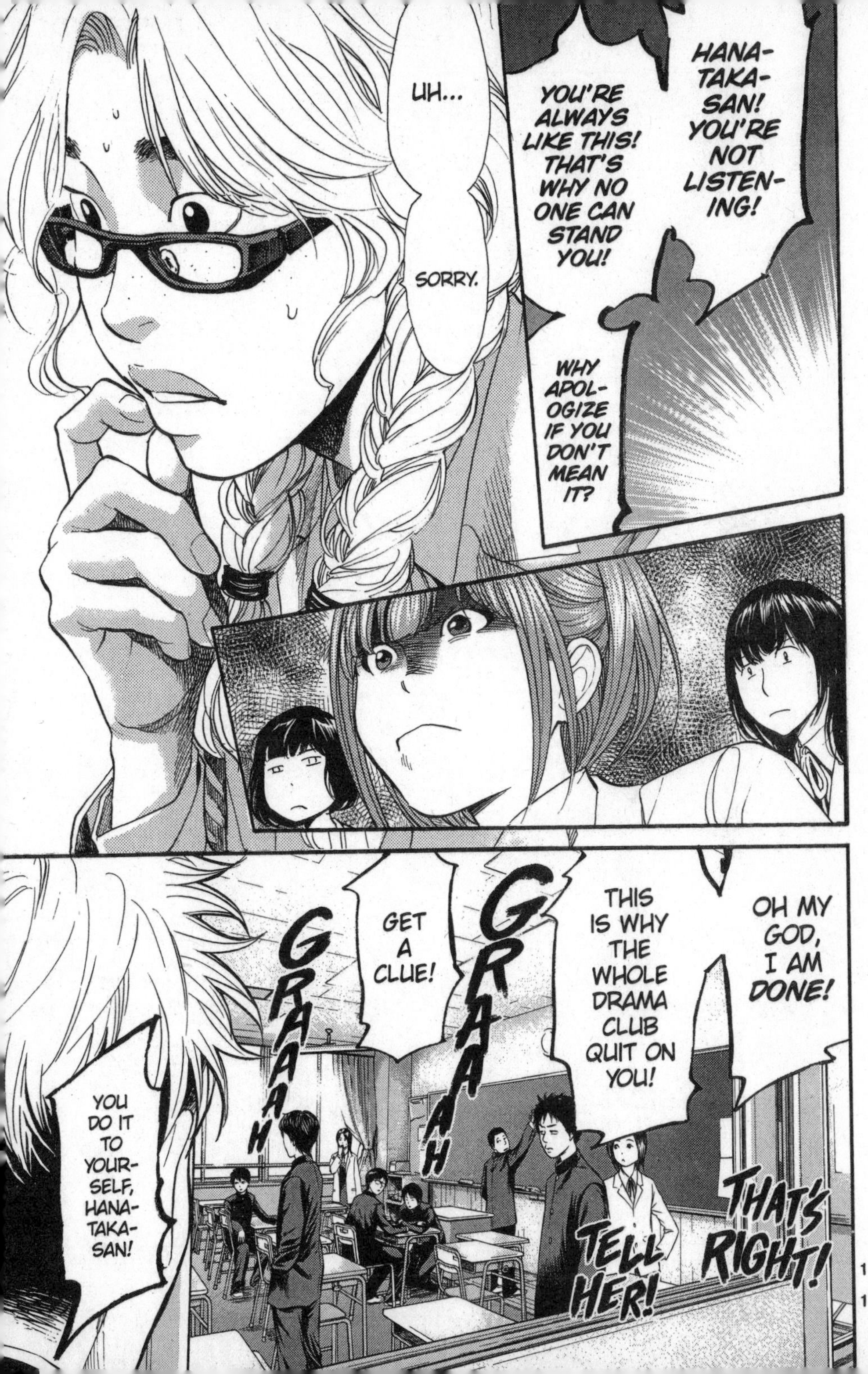
HANA-TAKA-SAN! YOU'RE NOT LISTEN-ING!
YOU'RE ALWAYS LIKE THIS! THAT'S WHY NO ONE CAN STAND YOU!
WHY APOL-OGIZE IF YOU DON'T MEAN IT?
UH...
SORRY.
OH MY GOD, I AM DONE!
THIS IS WHY THE WHOLE DRAMA CLUB QUIT ON YOU!
GRAAAH
GET A CLUE!
GRAAAH
THAT'S RIGHT!
TELL HER!
YOU DO IT TO YOUR-SELF, HANA-TAKA-SAN!

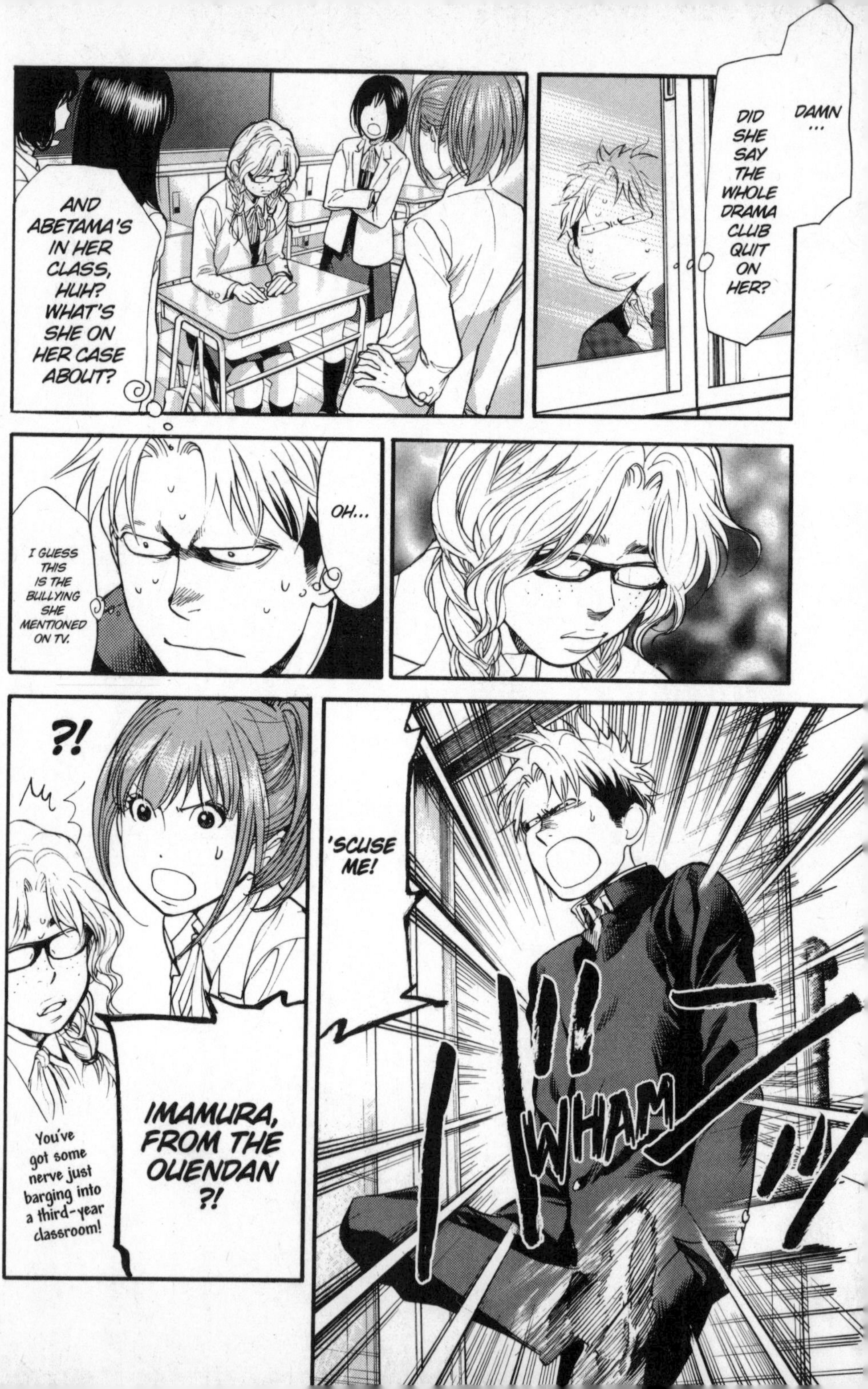

DAMN...
DID SHE SAY THE WHOLE DRAMA CLUB QUIT ON HER?
AND ABETAMA'S IN HER CLASS, HUH? WHAT'S SHE ON HER CASE ABOUT?
OH...
I GUESS THIS IS THE BULLYING SHE MENTIONED ON TV.
'SCUSE ME!
WHAM
?!
IMAMURA, FROM THE OUENDAN ?!
You've got some nerve just barging into a third-year classroom!

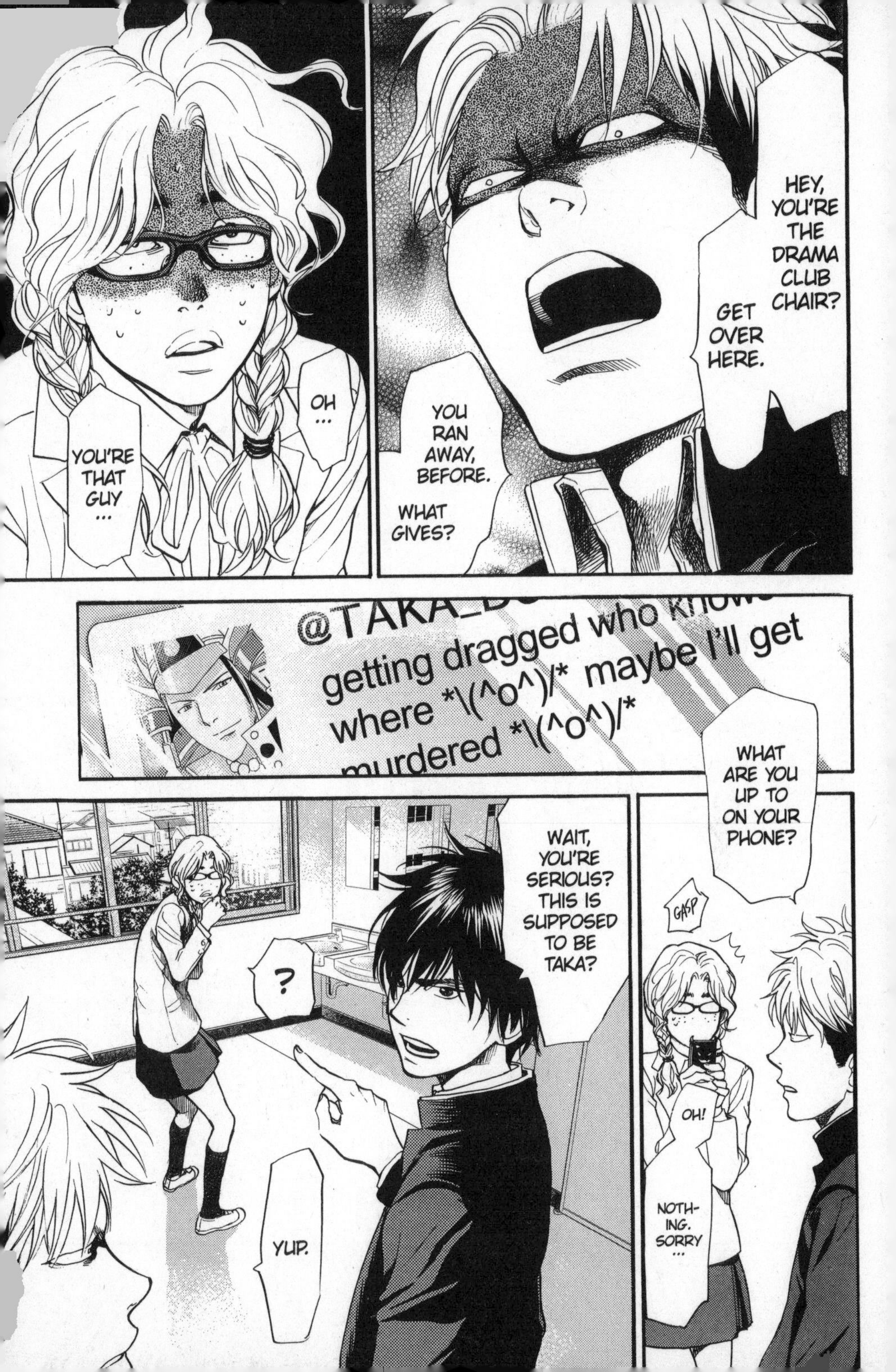
HEY, YOU'RE THE DRAMA CLUB CHAIR?
GET OVER HERE.
YOU RAN AWAY, BEFORE.
WHAT GIVES?
OH ...
YOU'RE THAT GUY ...
@TAKA_
getting dragged who
where *\(^o^)/* maybe I'll get
\(^o^)/
WHAT ARE YOU UP TO ON YOUR PHONE?
GASP
OH!
NOTH-ING. SORRY ...
WAIT, YOU'RE SERIOUS? THIS IS SUPPOSED TO BE TAKA?
?
YUP.

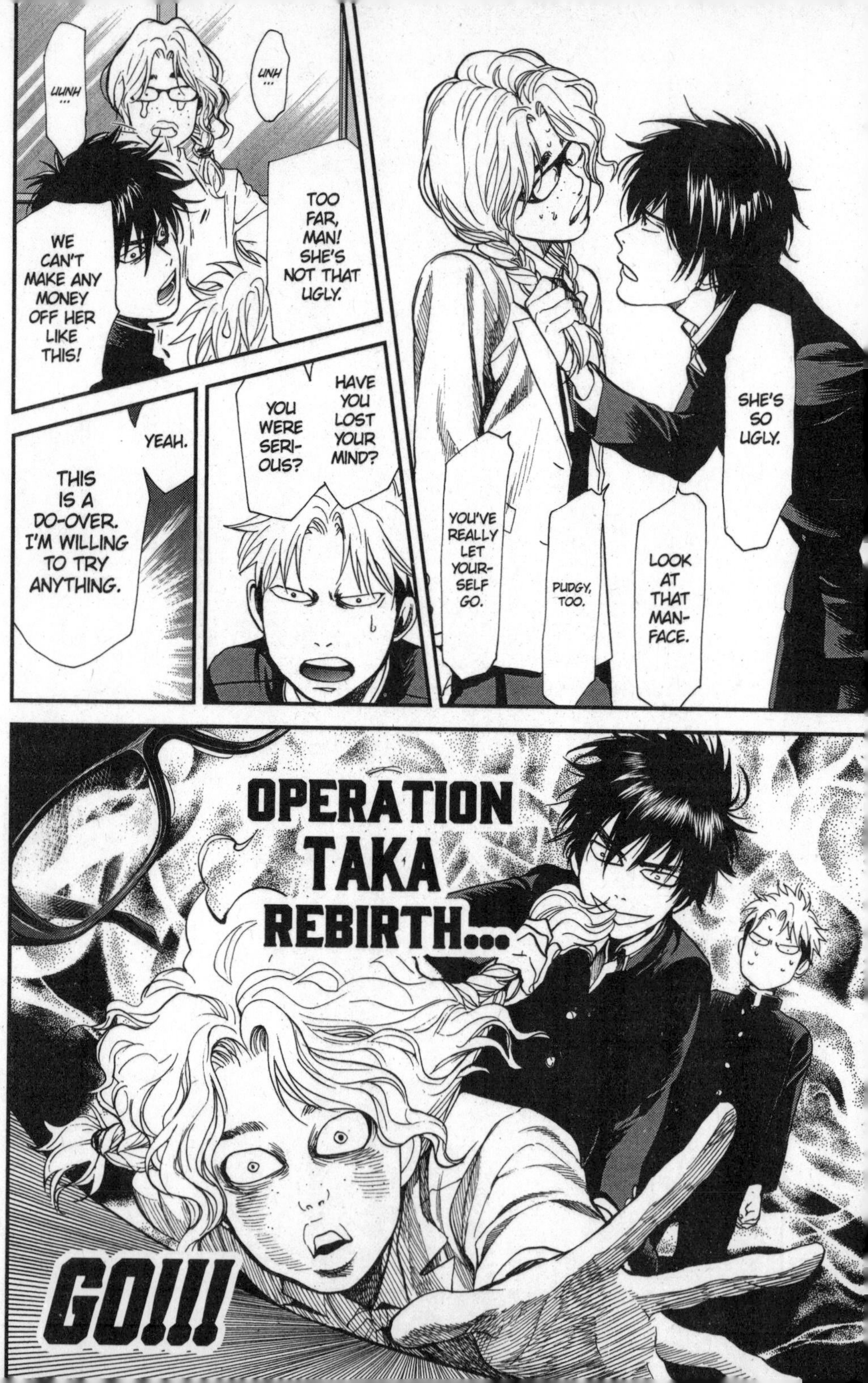

SHE'S SO UGLY.
LOOK AT THAT MAN-FACE.
PUDGY, TOO.
YOU'VE REALLY LET YOURSELF GO.
UNH...
UUNH...
TOO FAR, MAN! SHE'S NOT THAT UGLY.
WE CAN'T MAKE ANY MONEY OFF HER LIKE THIS!
HAVE YOU LOST YOUR MIND?
YOU WERE SERIOUS?
YEAH.
THIS IS A DO-OVER. I'M WILLING TO TRY ANYTHING.
OPERATION TAKA REBIRTH...
GO!!!

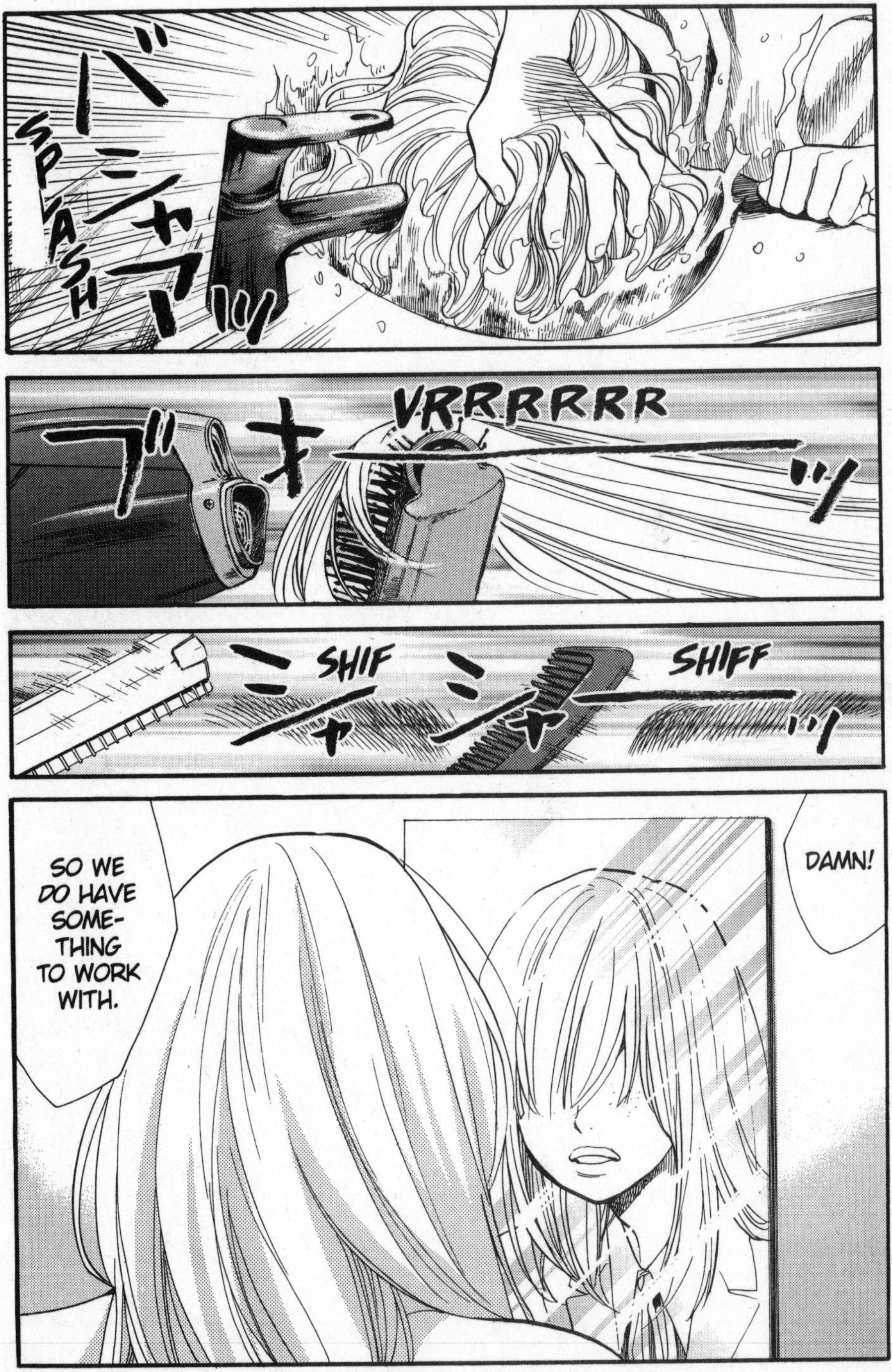
バシャアッ
SPLASH
ブオーッ
VRRRRRR
シャシャーッ
SHIFF
SHIF
DAMN!
SO WE DO HAVE SOME-THING TO WORK WITH.

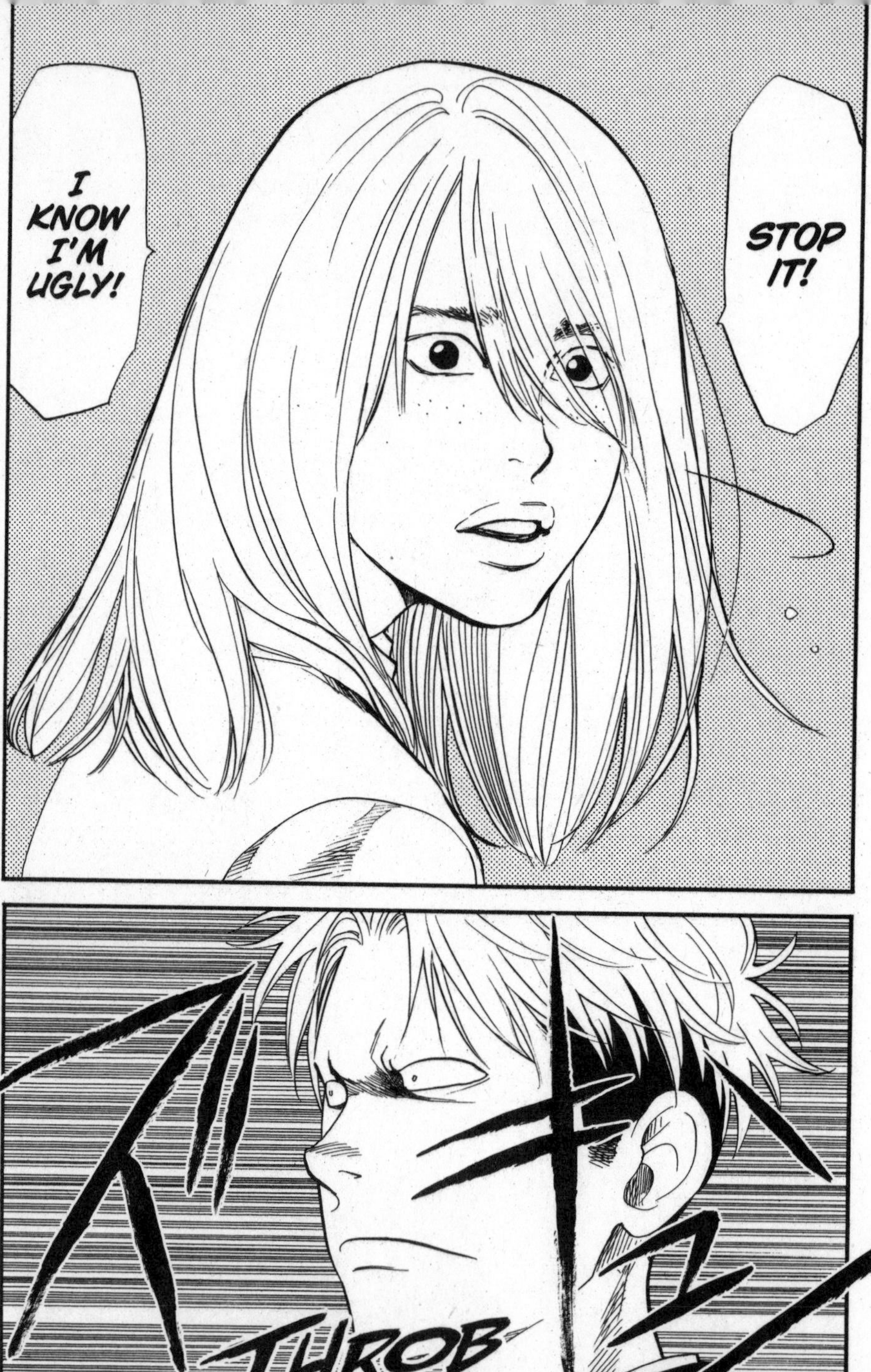
STOP IT!
I KNOW I'M UGLY!
THROB

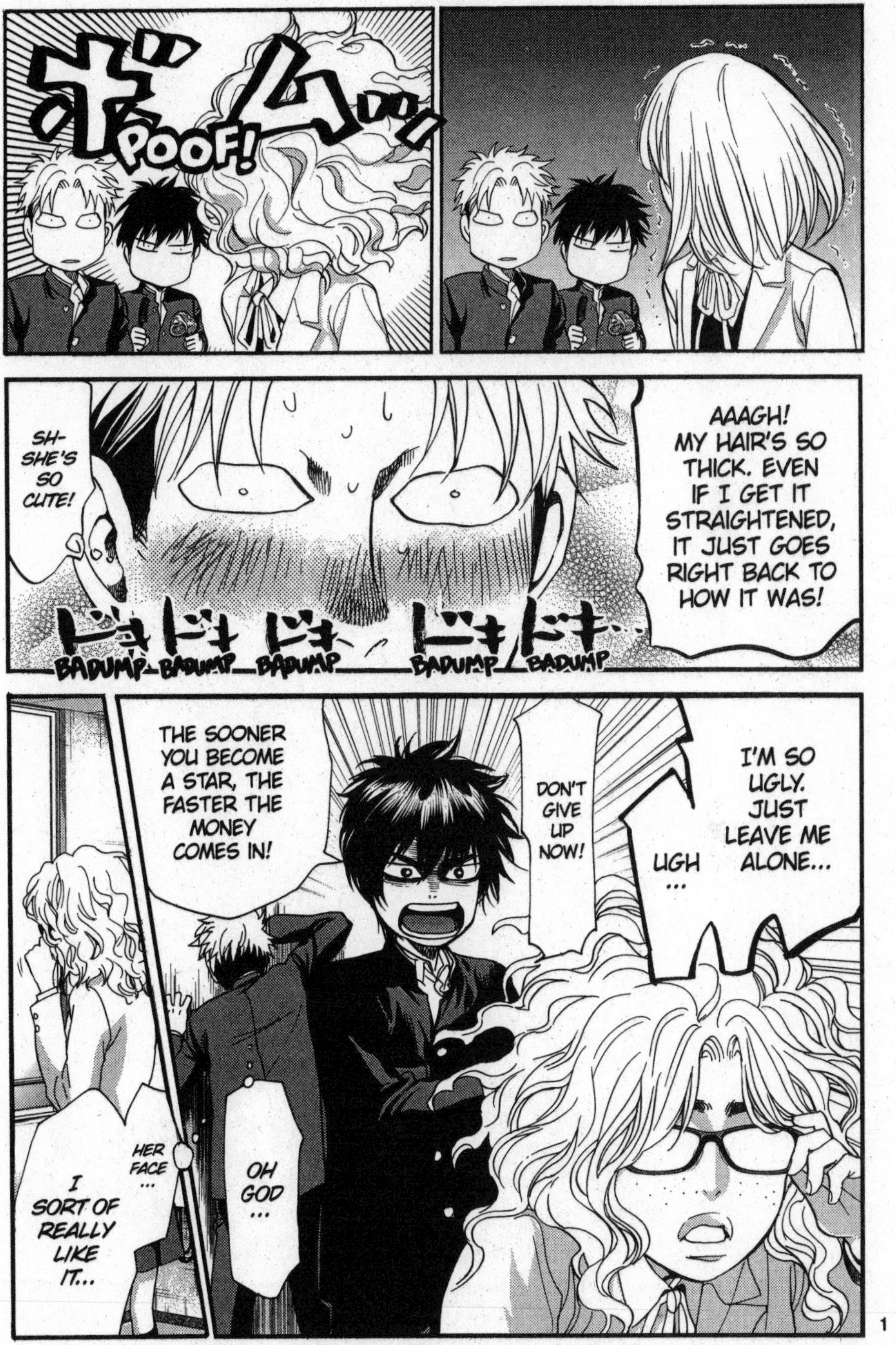
POOF!
AAAGH! MY HAIR'S SO THICK. EVEN IF I GET IT STRAIGHTENED, IT JUST GOES RIGHT BACK TO HOW IT WAS!
SH- SHE'S SO CUTE!
BADUMP BADUMP BADUMP BADUMP BADUMP
I'M SO UGLY. JUST LEAVE ME ALONE...
UGH ...
DON'T GIVE UP NOW!
THE SOONER YOU BECOME A STAR, THE FASTER THE MONEY COMES IN!
OH GOD ...
HER FACE ...
I SORT OF REALLY LIKE IT...

Again!!

アゲイン!!

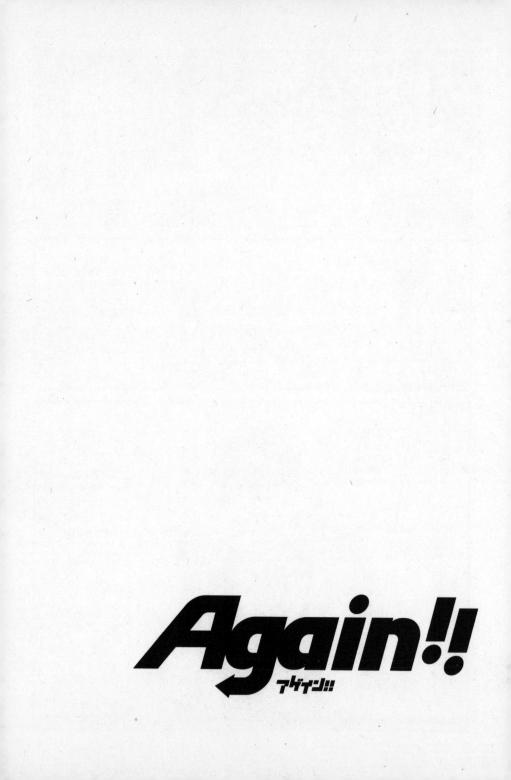

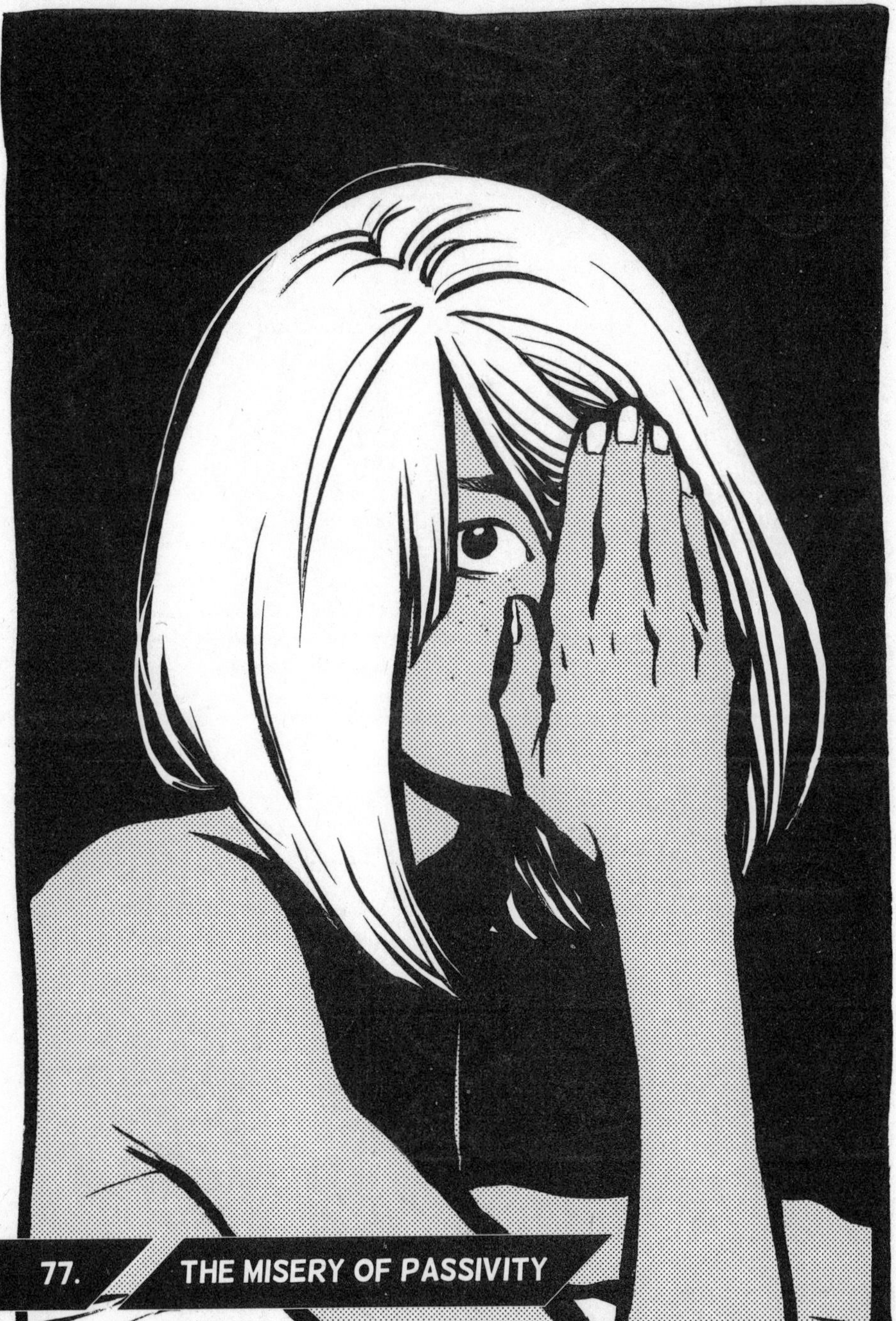

77. THE MISERY OF PASSIVITY

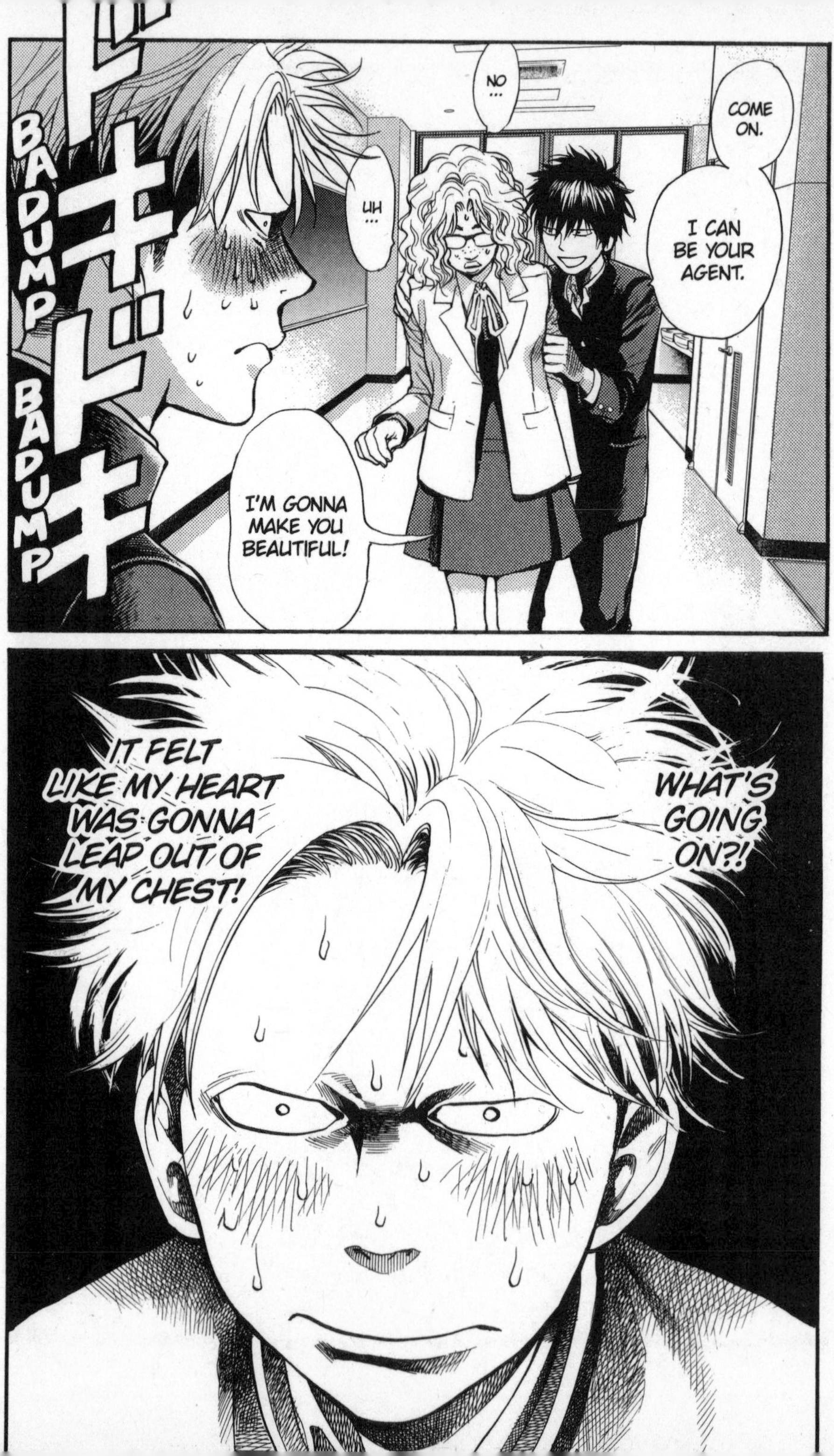
COME ON.
I CAN BE YOUR AGENT.
NO...
UH...
BADUMP BADUMP
I'M GONNA MAKE YOU BEAUTIFUL!
WHAT'S GOING ON?!
IT FELT LIKE MY HEART WAS GONNA LEAP OUT OF MY CHEST!

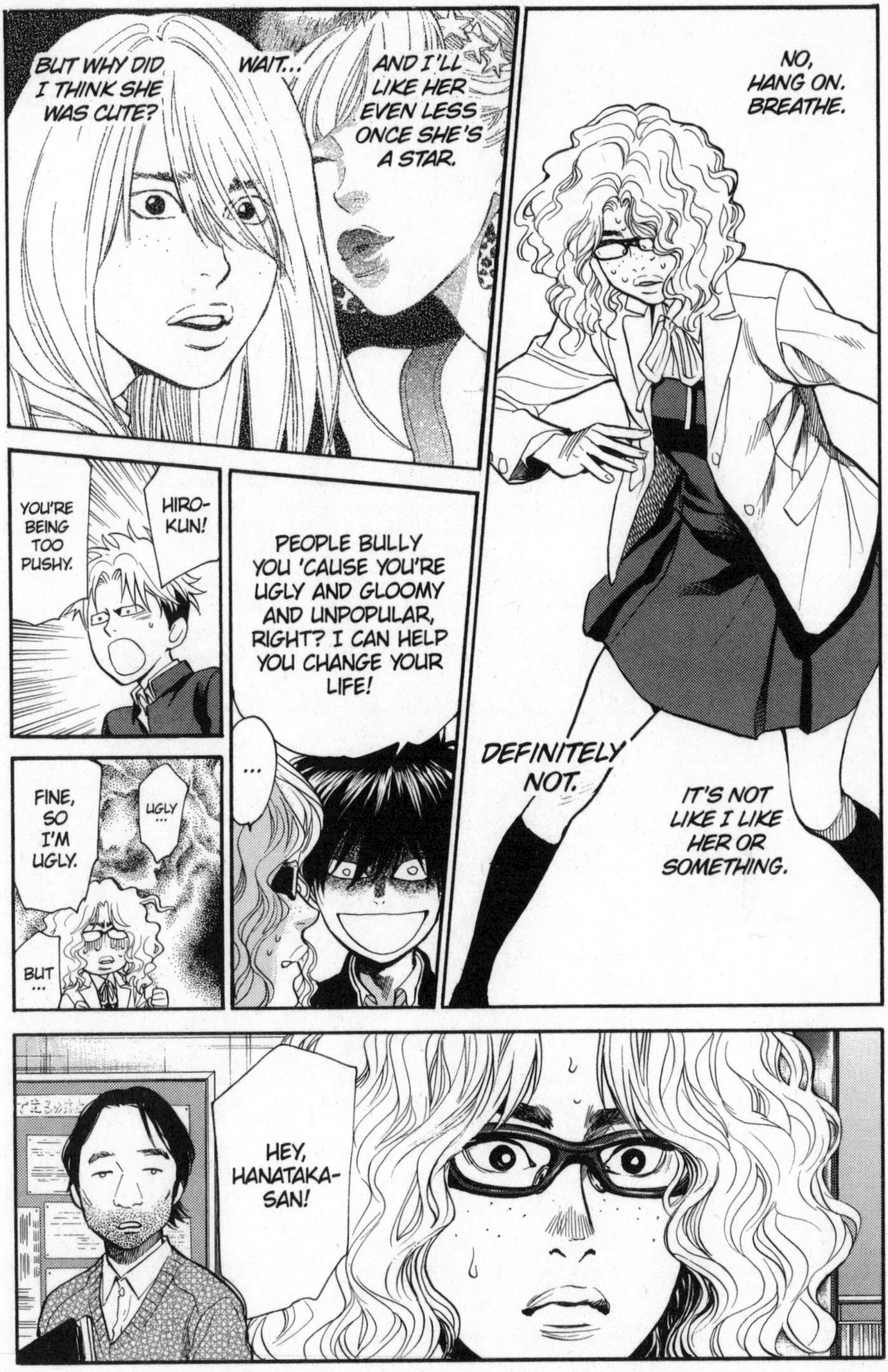
NO, HANG ON. BREATHE.
IT'S NOT LIKE I LIKE HER OR SOMETHING.
DEFINITELY NOT.
AND I'LL LIKE HER EVEN LESS ONCE SHE'S A STAR.
WAIT...
BUT WHY DID I THINK SHE WAS CUTE?
PEOPLE BULLY YOU 'CAUSE YOU'RE UGLY AND GLOOMY AND UNPOPULAR, RIGHT? I CAN HELP YOU CHANGE YOUR LIFE!
...
HIRO-KUN!
YOU'RE BEING TOO PUSHY.
UGLY...
FINE, SO I'M UGLY.
BUT...
HEY, HANATAKA-SAN!

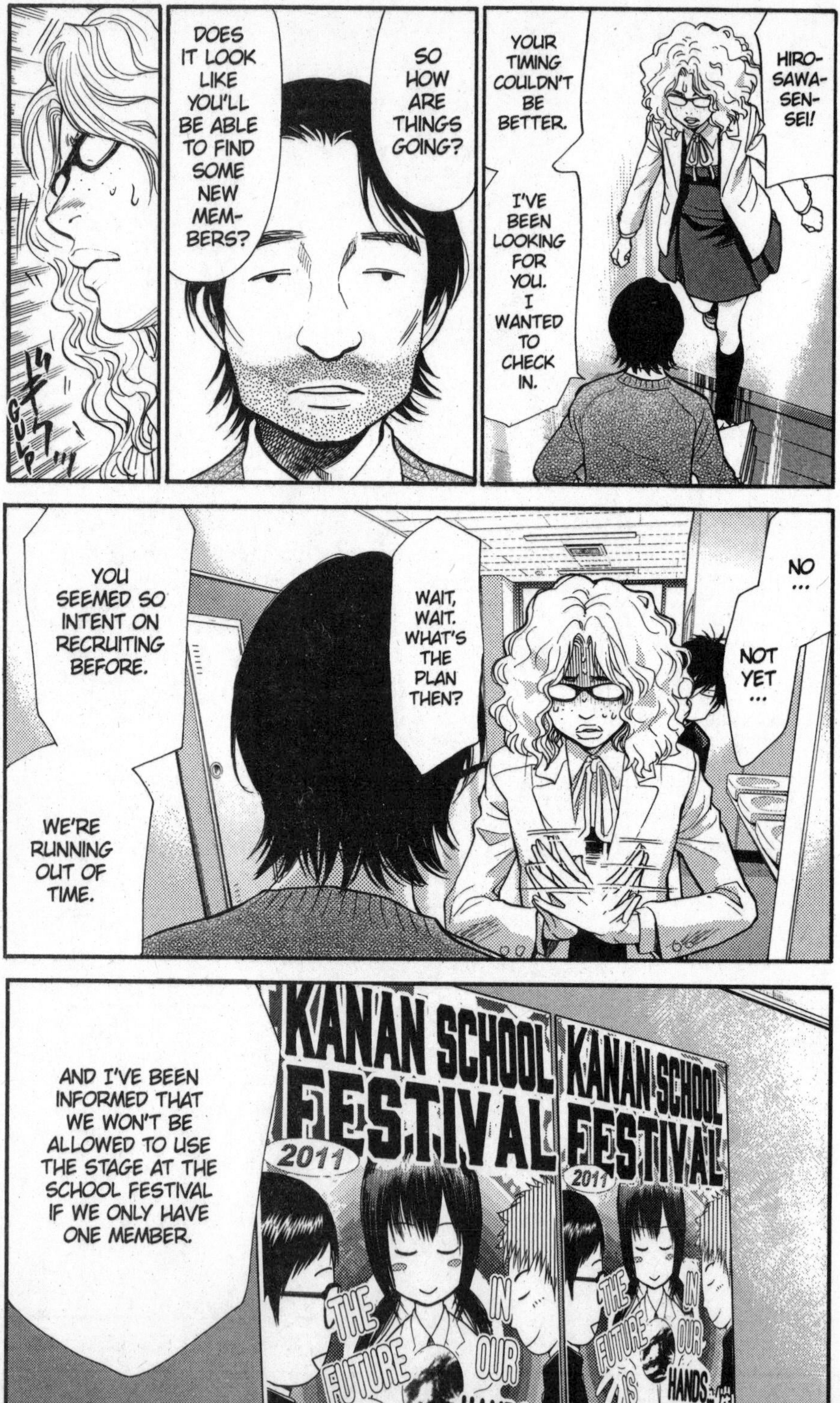
HIRO-SAWA-SEN-SEI!
YOUR TIMING COULDN'T BE BETTER.
I'VE BEEN LOOKING FOR YOU. I WANTED TO CHECK IN.
SO HOW ARE THINGS GOING?
DOES IT LOOK LIKE YOU'LL BE ABLE TO FIND SOME NEW MEM-BERS?
GULP
NO...
NOT YET...
WAIT, WAIT. WHAT'S THE PLAN THEN?
YOU SEEMED SO INTENT ON RECRUITING BEFORE.
WE'RE RUNNING OUT OF TIME.
AND I'VE BEEN INFORMED THAT WE WON'T BE ALLOWED TO USE THE STAGE AT THE SCHOOL FESTIVAL IF WE ONLY HAVE ONE MEMBER.
KANAN SCHOOL FESTIVAL
2011
THE FUTURE IS IN OUR HANDS
KANAN SCHOOL FESTIVAL
2011
THE FUTURE IS IN OUR HANDS

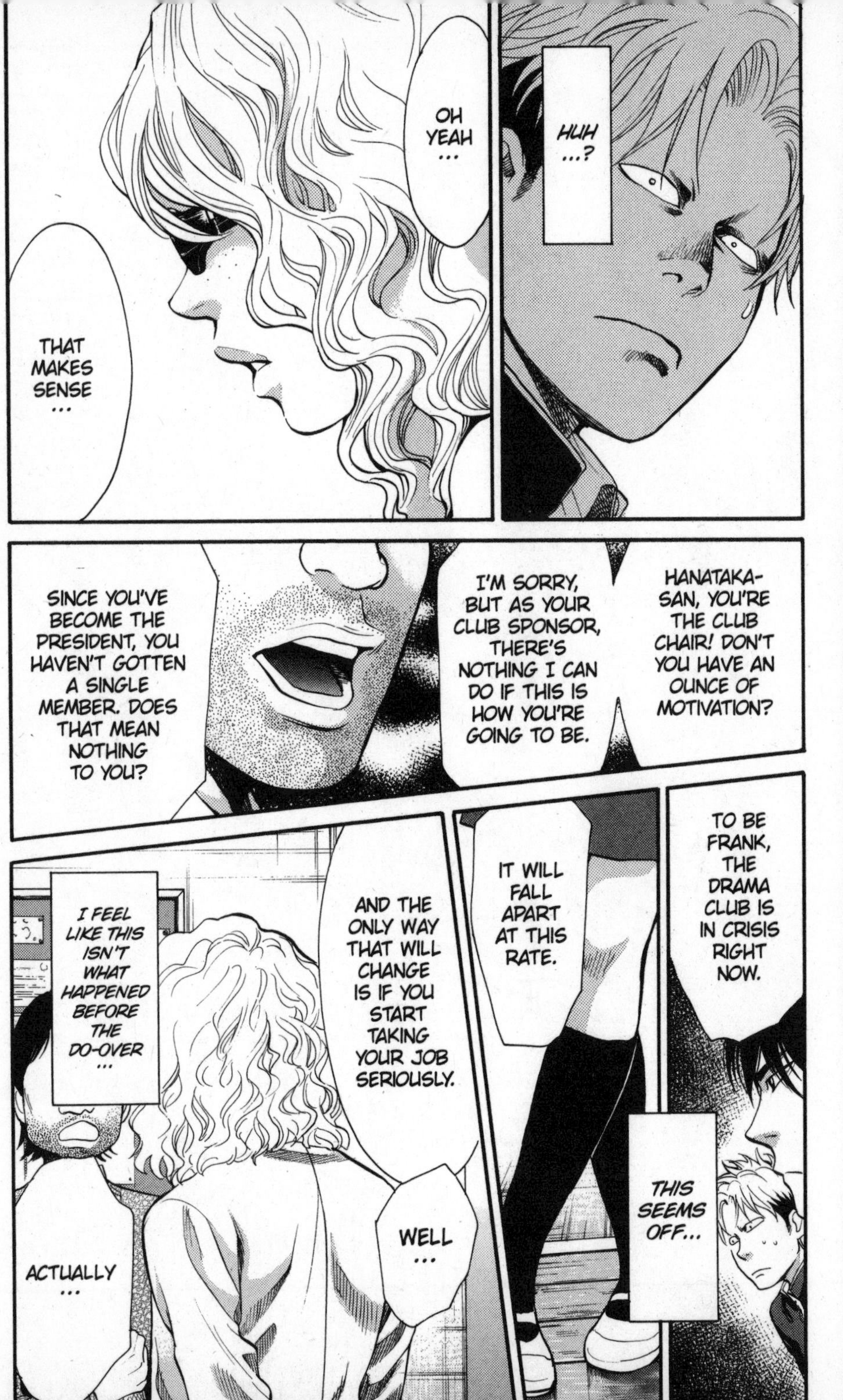
HUH ...?
OH YEAH ...
THAT MAKES SENSE ...
HANATAKA-SAN, YOU'RE THE CLUB CHAIR! DON'T YOU HAVE AN OUNCE OF MOTIVATION?
I'M SORRY, BUT AS YOUR CLUB SPONSOR, THERE'S NOTHING I CAN DO IF THIS IS HOW YOU'RE GOING TO BE.
SINCE YOU'VE BECOME THE PRESIDENT, YOU HAVEN'T GOTTEN A SINGLE MEMBER. DOES THAT MEAN NOTHING TO YOU?
TO BE FRANK, THE DRAMA CLUB IS IN CRISIS RIGHT NOW.
THIS SEEMS OFF...
IT WILL FALL APART AT THIS RATE.
AND THE ONLY WAY THAT WILL CHANGE IS IF YOU START TAKING YOUR JOB SERIOUSLY.
I FEEL LIKE THIS ISN'T WHAT HAPPENED BEFORE THE DO-OVER ...
WELL ...
ACTUALLY ...

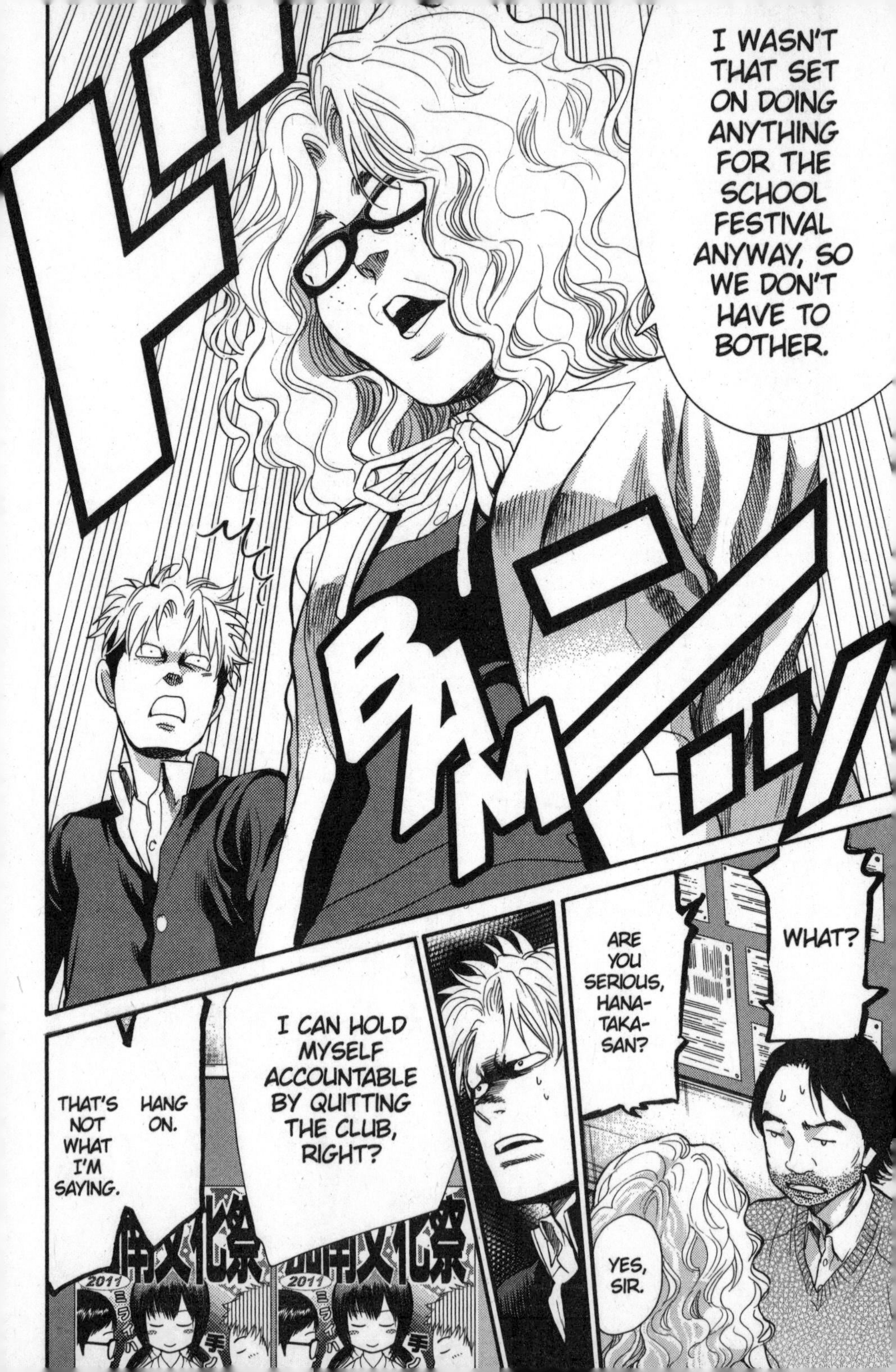
I WASN'T THAT SET ON DOING ANYTHING FOR THE SCHOOL FESTIVAL ANYWAY, SO WE DON'T HAVE TO BOTHER.
BAM!
WHAT?
ARE YOU SERIOUS, HANATAKA-SAN?
YES, SIR.
I CAN HOLD MYSELF ACCOUNTABLE BY QUITTING THE CLUB, RIGHT?
HANG ON.
THAT'S NOT WHAT I'M SAYING.

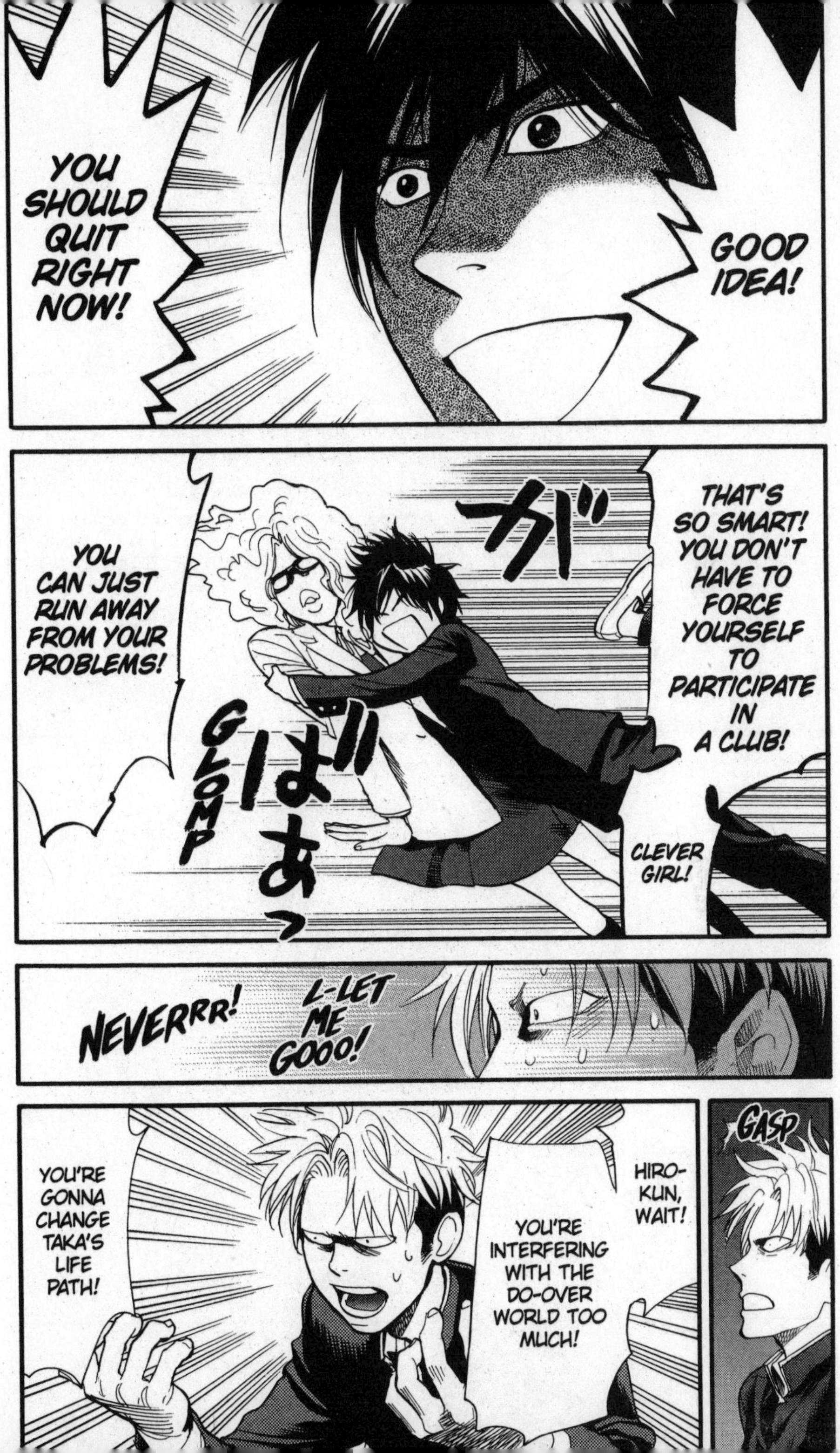
GOOD IDEA!
YOU SHOULD QUIT RIGHT NOW!
THAT'S SO SMART! YOU DON'T HAVE TO FORCE YOURSELF TO PARTICIPATE IN A CLUB!
ガ
CLEVER GIRL!
YOU CAN JUST RUN AWAY FROM YOUR PROBLEMS!
ばあっ
GLOMP
L-LET ME GOOO!
NEVERRR!
GASP
HIRO-KUN, WAIT!
YOU'RE INTERFERING WITH THE DO-OVER WORLD TOO MUCH!
YOU'RE GONNA CHANGE TAKA'S LIFE PATH!

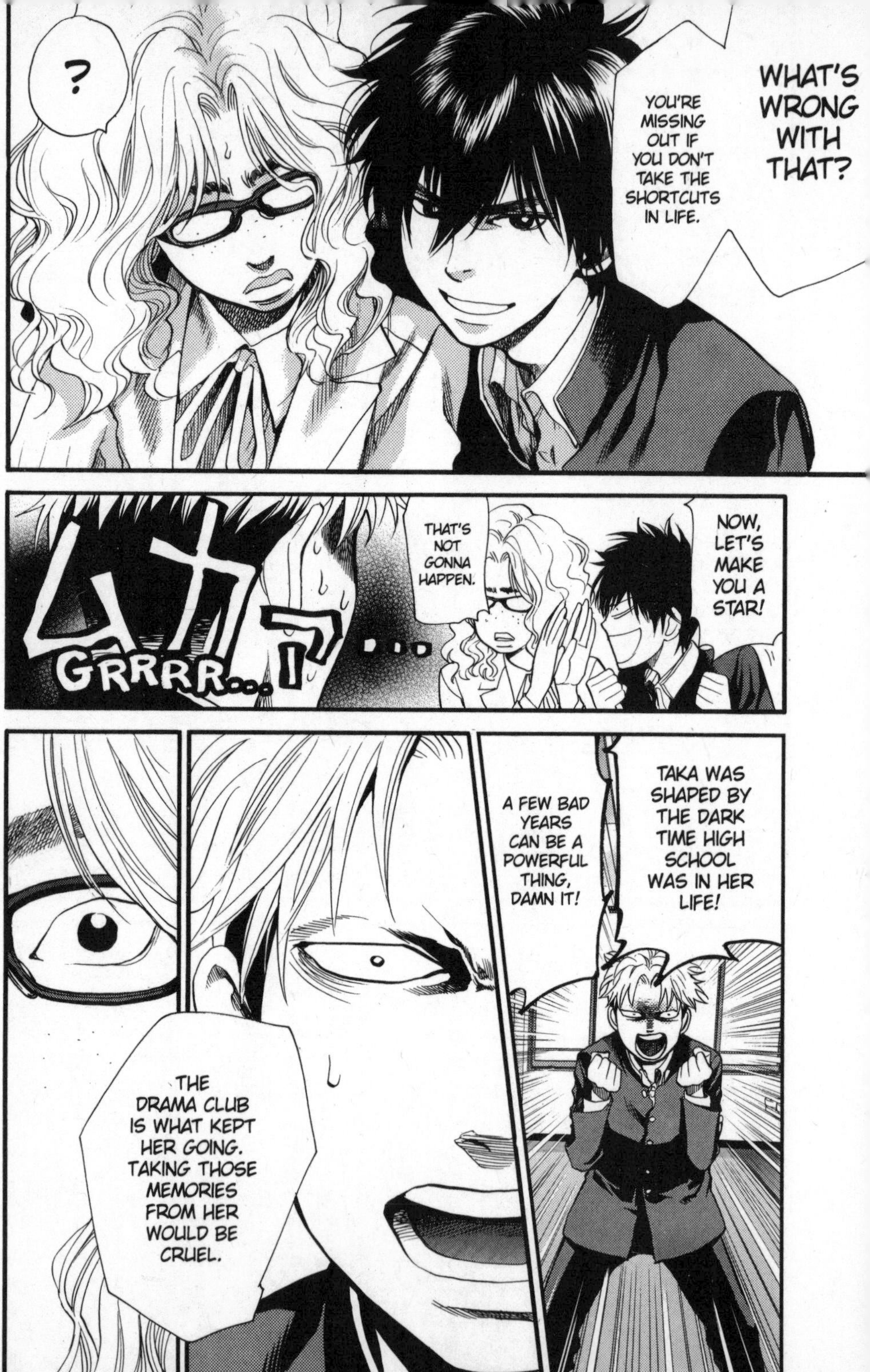
WHAT'S WRONG WITH THAT?
YOU'RE MISSING OUT IF YOU DON'T TAKE THE SHORTCUTS IN LIFE.
?
NOW, LET'S MAKE YOU A STAR!
THAT'S NOT GONNA HAPPEN.
ムカッ...
GRRRR...
TAKA WAS SHAPED BY THE DARK TIME HIGH SCHOOL WAS IN HER LIFE!
A FEW BAD YEARS CAN BE A POWERFUL THING, DAMN IT!
THE DRAMA CLUB IS WHAT KEPT HER GOING. TAKING THOSE MEMORIES FROM HER WOULD BE CRUEL.

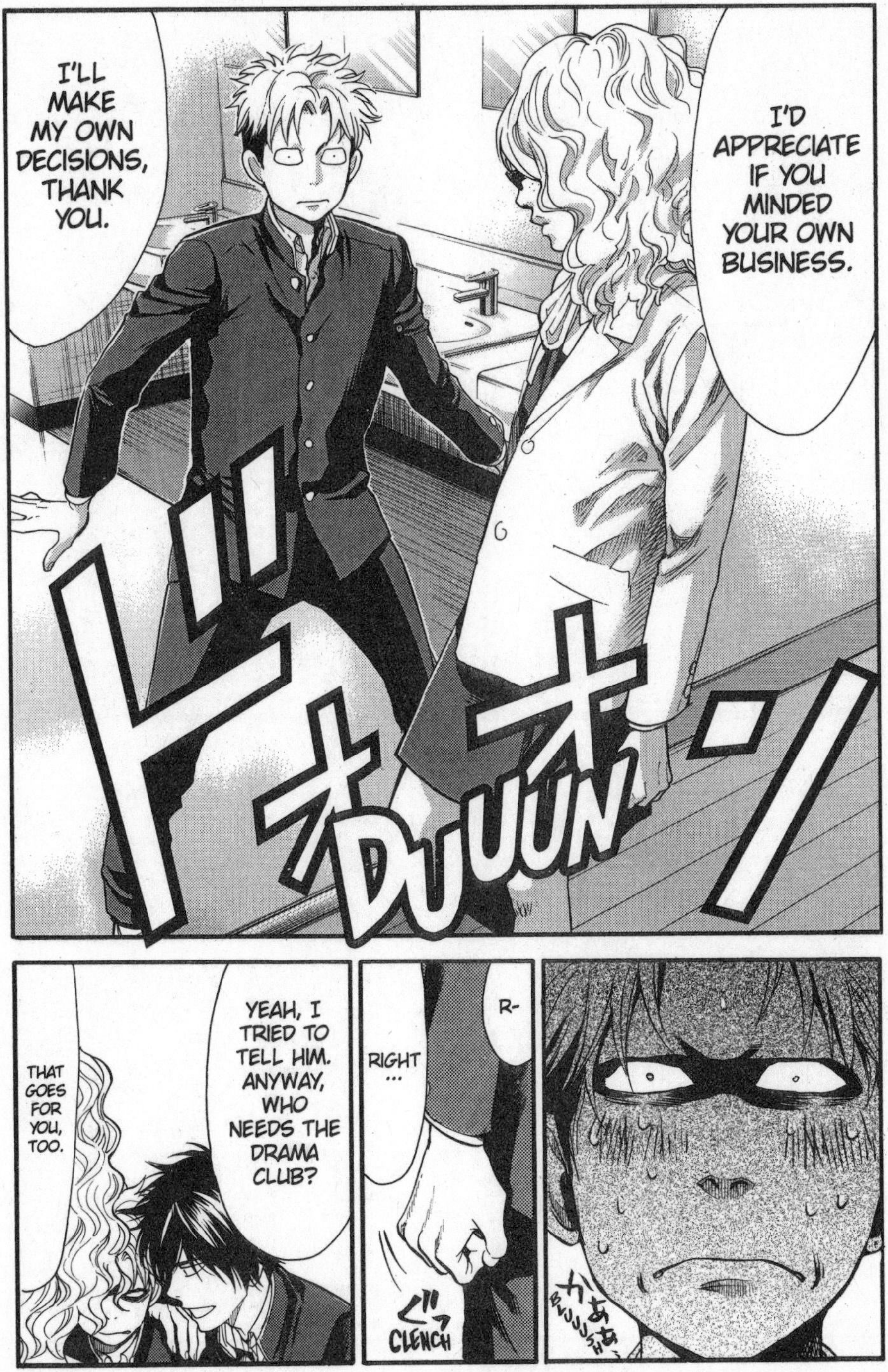
I'D APPRECIATE IF YOU MINDED YOUR OWN BUSINESS.
I'LL MAKE MY OWN DECISIONS, THANK YOU.
ドォーン
DUUUN
BLUUUSH
R-
RIGHT...
ぐっ
CLENCH
YEAH, I TRIED TO TELL HIM. ANYWAY, WHO NEEDS THE DRAMA CLUB?
THAT GOES FOR YOU, TOO.

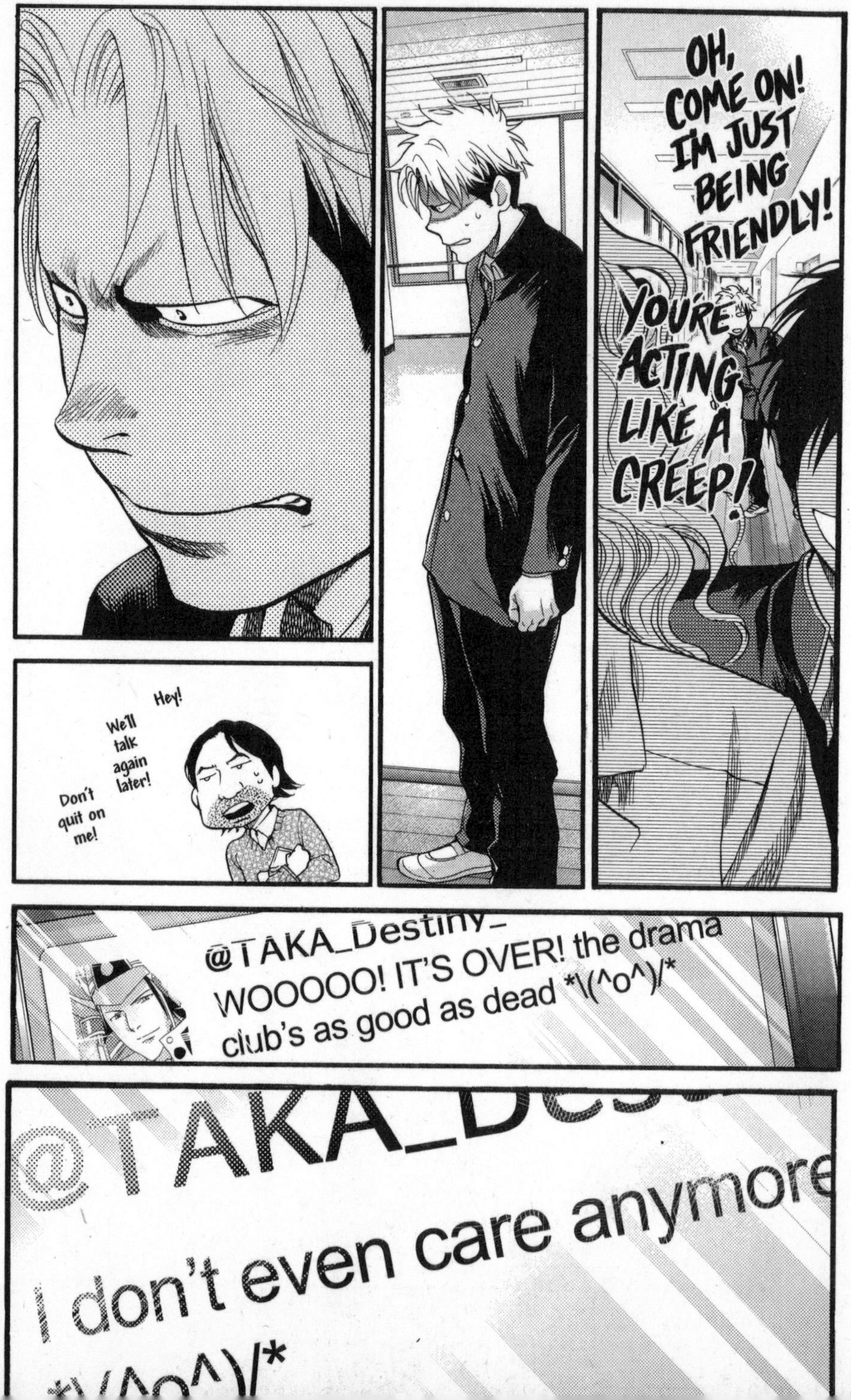
OH, COME ON! I'M JUST BEING FRIENDLY!
YOU'RE ACTING LIKE A CREEP!
Hey!
We'll talk again later!
Don't quit on me!
@TAKA_Destiny_
WOOOOO! IT'S OVER! the drama club's as good as dead *\(^o^)/*
@TAKA_Des
I don't even care anymore
\(^o^)/

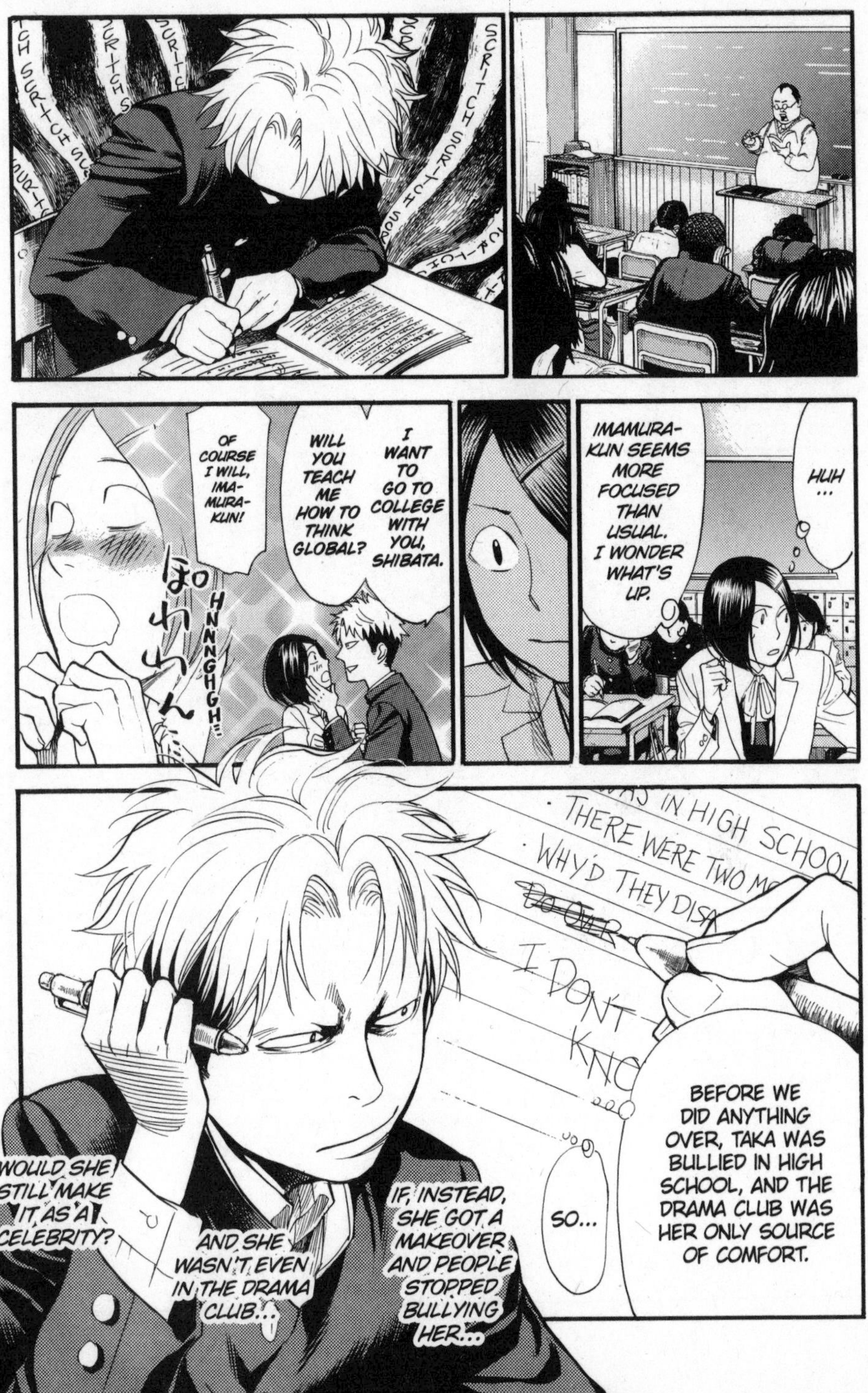
SCRITCH SCRITCH
SCRITCH SCRITCH
SCRITCH
HUH...
IMAMURA-KUN SEEMS MORE FOCUSED THAN USUAL. I WONDER WHAT'S UP.
I WANT TO GO TO COLLEGE WITH YOU, SHIBATA.
WILL YOU TEACH ME HOW TO THINK GLOBAL?
OF COURSE I WILL, IMA-MURA-KUN!
HNNNGHGH
THERE WERE TWO MO
WHY'D THEY DISA
DO OVER
I DON'T KNO
BEFORE WE DID ANYTHING OVER, TAKA WAS BULLIED IN HIGH SCHOOL, AND THE DRAMA CLUB WAS HER ONLY SOURCE OF COMFORT.
SO...
IF, INSTEAD, SHE GOT A MAKEOVER AND PEOPLE STOPPED BULLYING HER...
AND SHE WASN'T EVEN IN THE DRAMA CLUB...
WOULD SHE STILL MAKE IT AS A CELEBRITY?

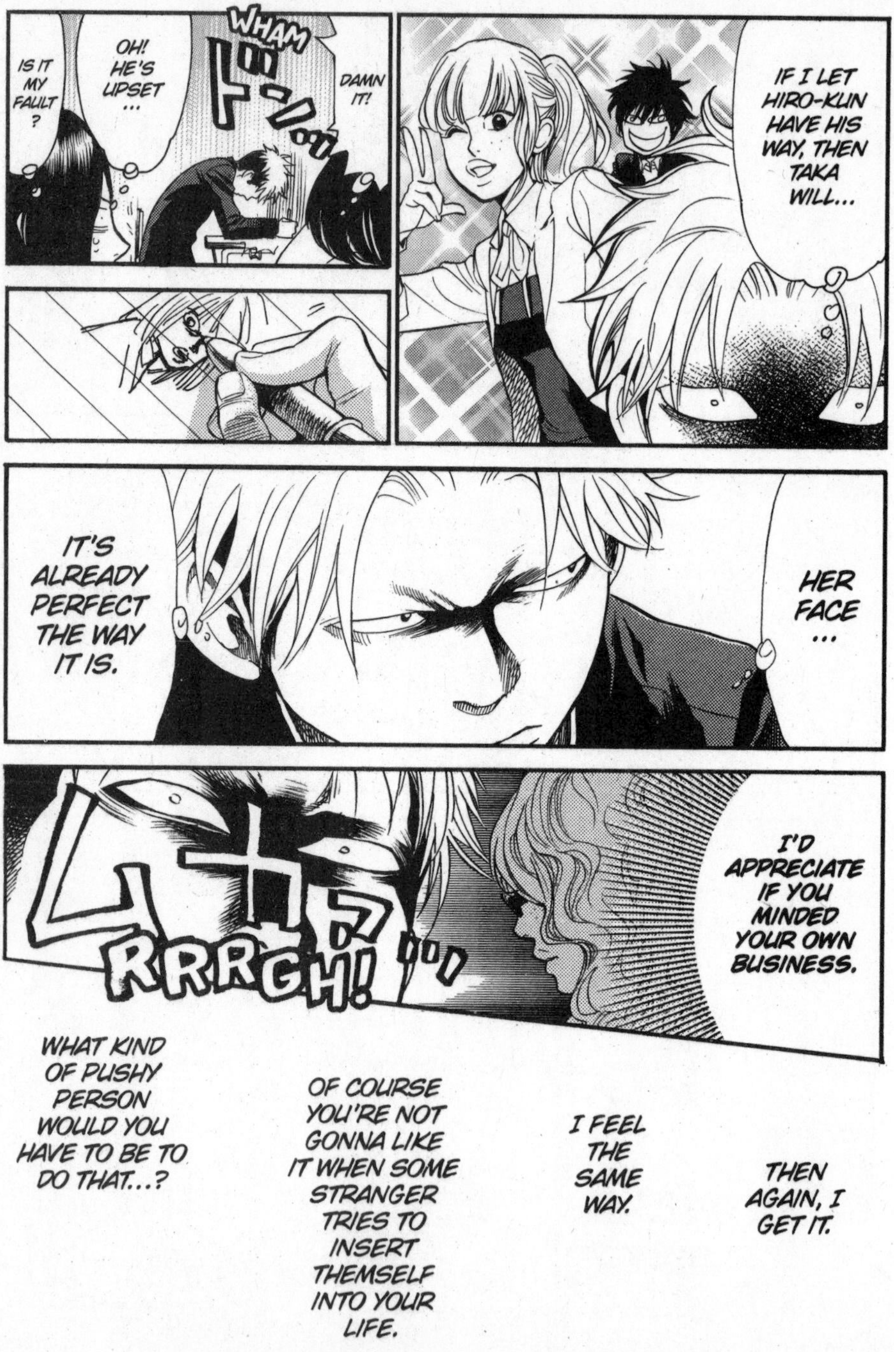
IF I LET HIRO-KUN HAVE HIS WAY, THEN TAKA WILL...
DAMN IT!
WHAM
OH! HE'S UPSET...
IS IT MY FAULT?
HER FACE...
IT'S ALREADY PERFECT THE WAY IT IS.
I'D APPRECIATE IF YOU MINDED YOUR OWN BUSINESS.
RRRGH!
THEN AGAIN, I GET IT.
I FEEL THE SAME WAY.
OF COURSE YOU'RE NOT GONNA LIKE IT WHEN SOME STRANGER TRIES TO INSERT THEMSELF INTO YOUR LIFE.
WHAT KIND OF PUSHY PERSON WOULD YOU HAVE TO BE TO DO THAT...?

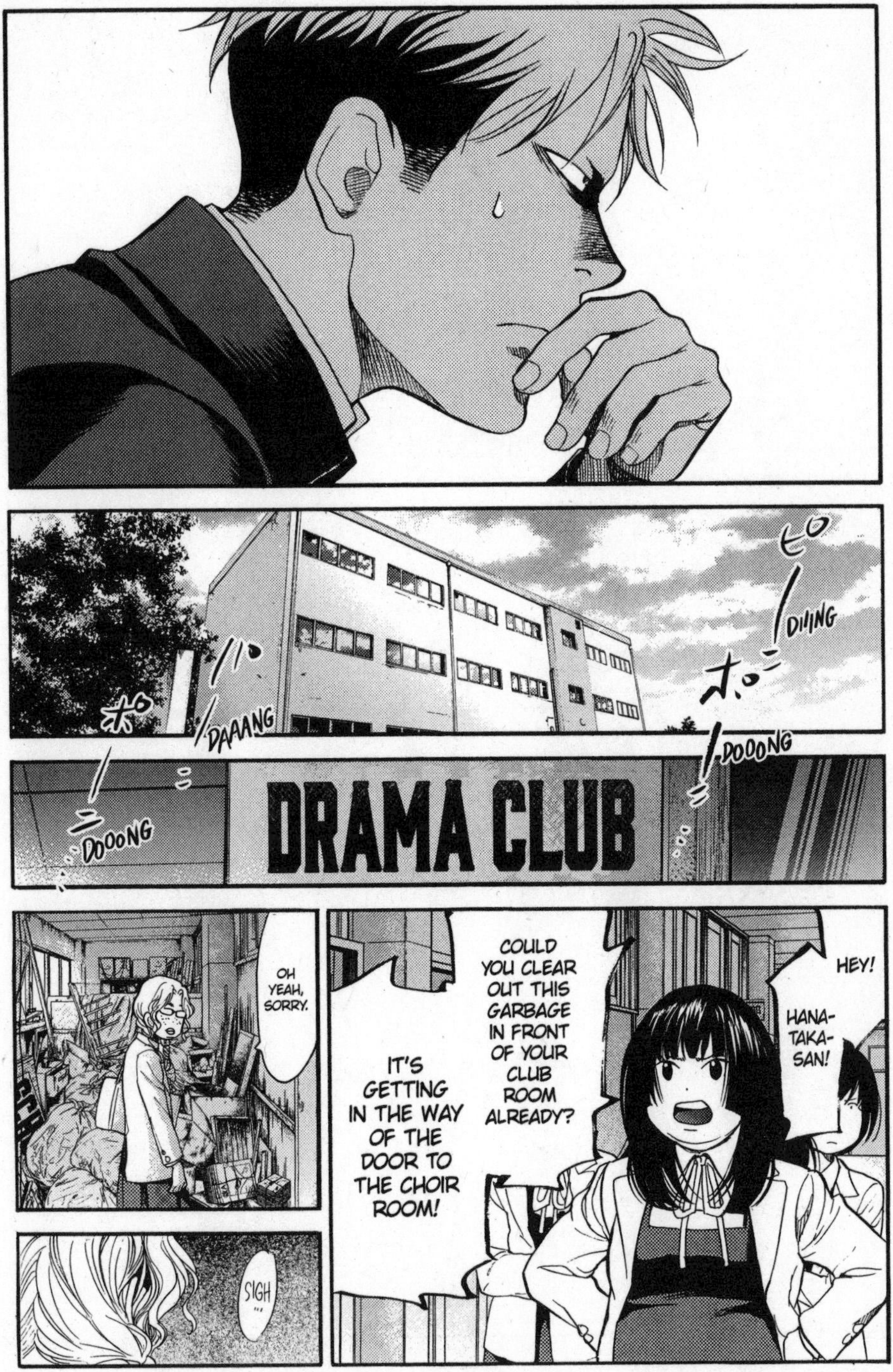
DIIING
DAAANG
DOOONG
DRAMA CLUB
DOOONG
HEY!
HANA-TAKA-SAN!
COULD YOU CLEAR OUT THIS GARBAGE IN FRONT OF YOUR CLUB ROOM ALREADY?
IT'S GETTING IN THE WAY OF THE DOOR TO THE CHOIR ROOM!
OH YEAH, SORRY.
SIGH...

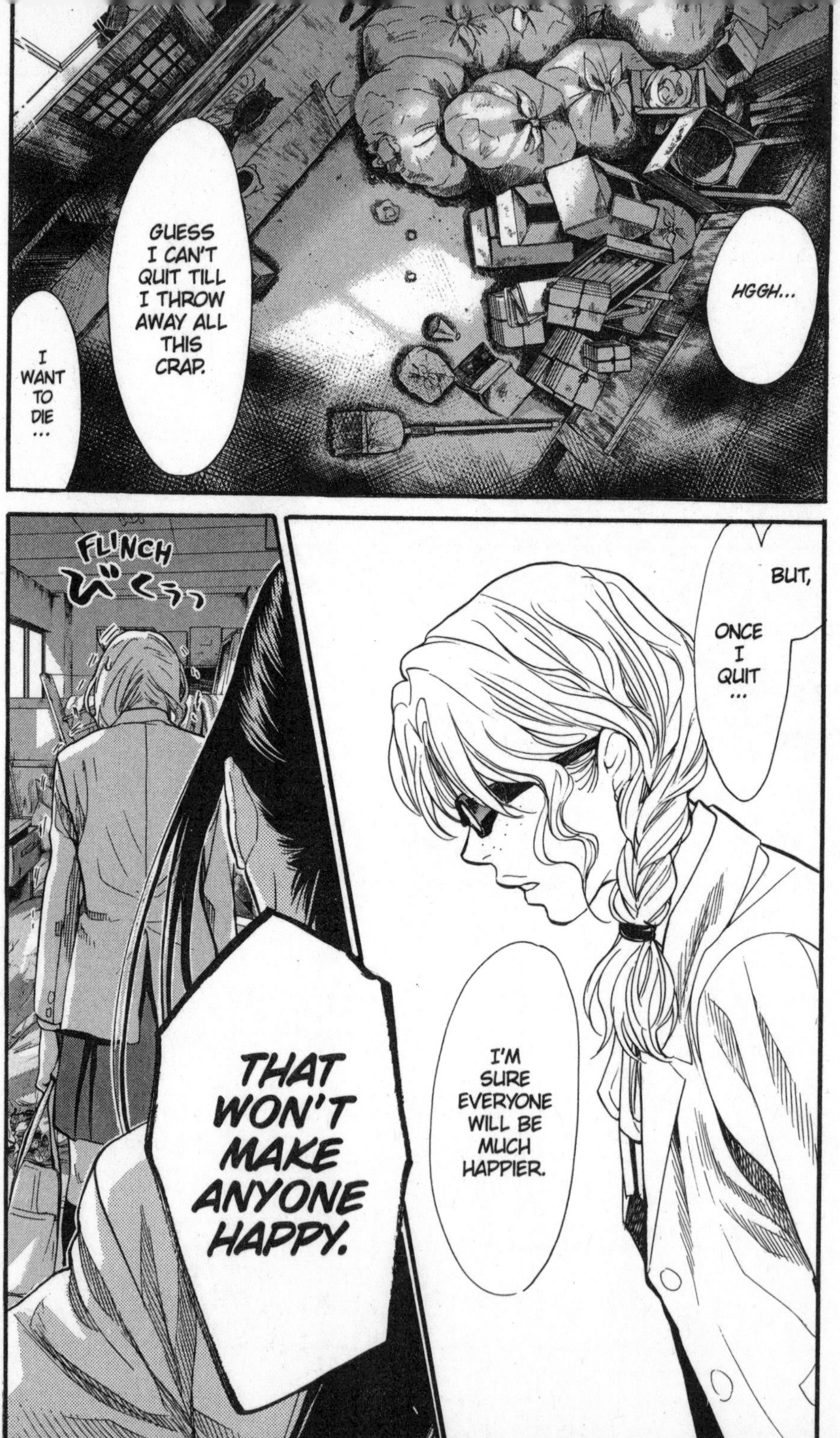
HGGH...
GUESS I CAN'T QUIT TILL I THROW AWAY ALL THIS CRAP.
I WANT TO DIE...
BUT,
ONCE I QUIT...
I'M SURE EVERYONE WILL BE MUCH HAPPIER.
FLINCH
びくっ
THAT WON'T MAKE ANYONE HAPPY.

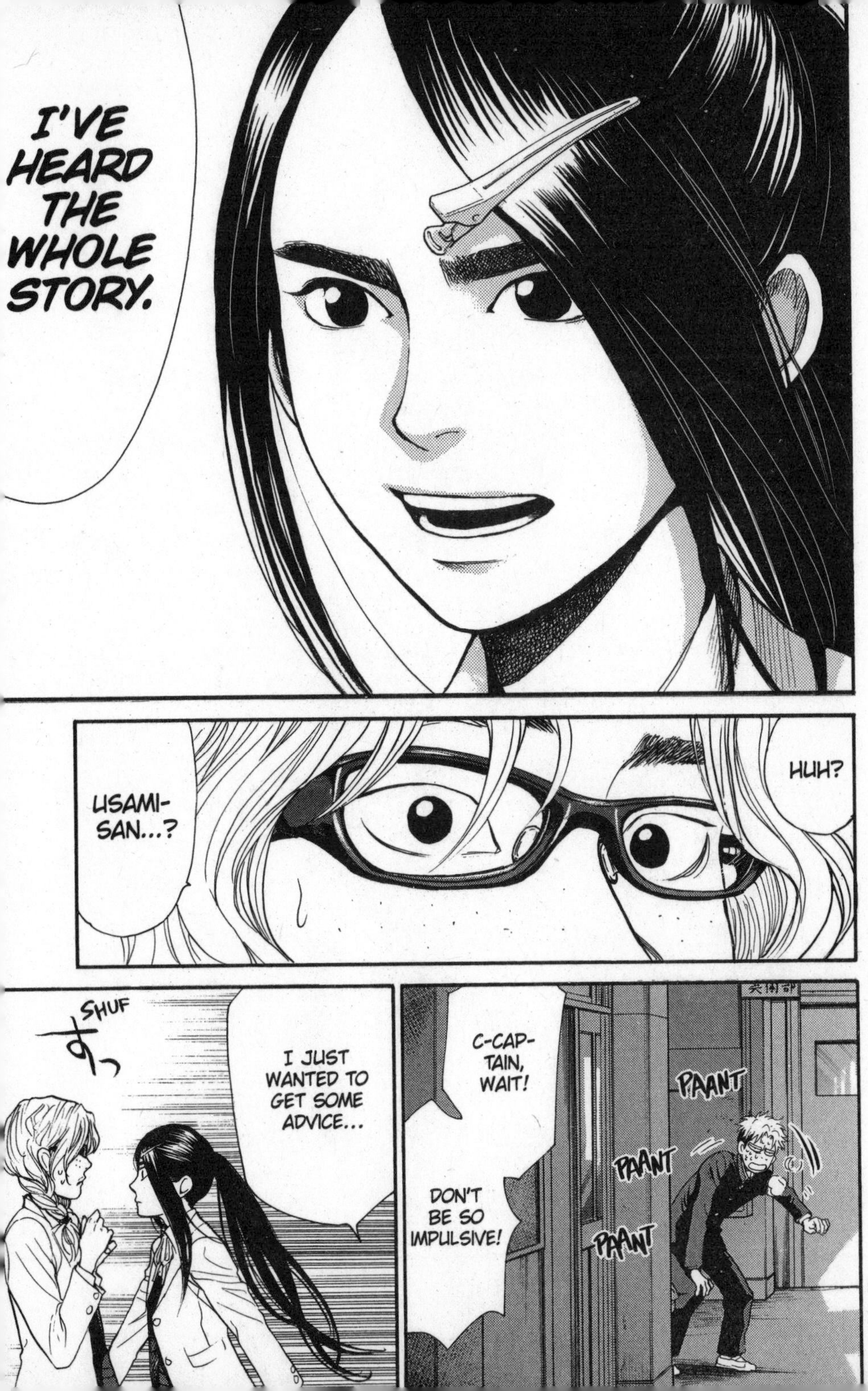
I'VE HEARD THE WHOLE STORY.
HUH?
USAMI-SAN...?
C-CAP-TAIN, WAIT!
PAANT
PAANT
DON'T BE SO IMPULSIVE!
PAANT
I JUST WANTED TO GET SOME ADVICE...
SHUF
すっ

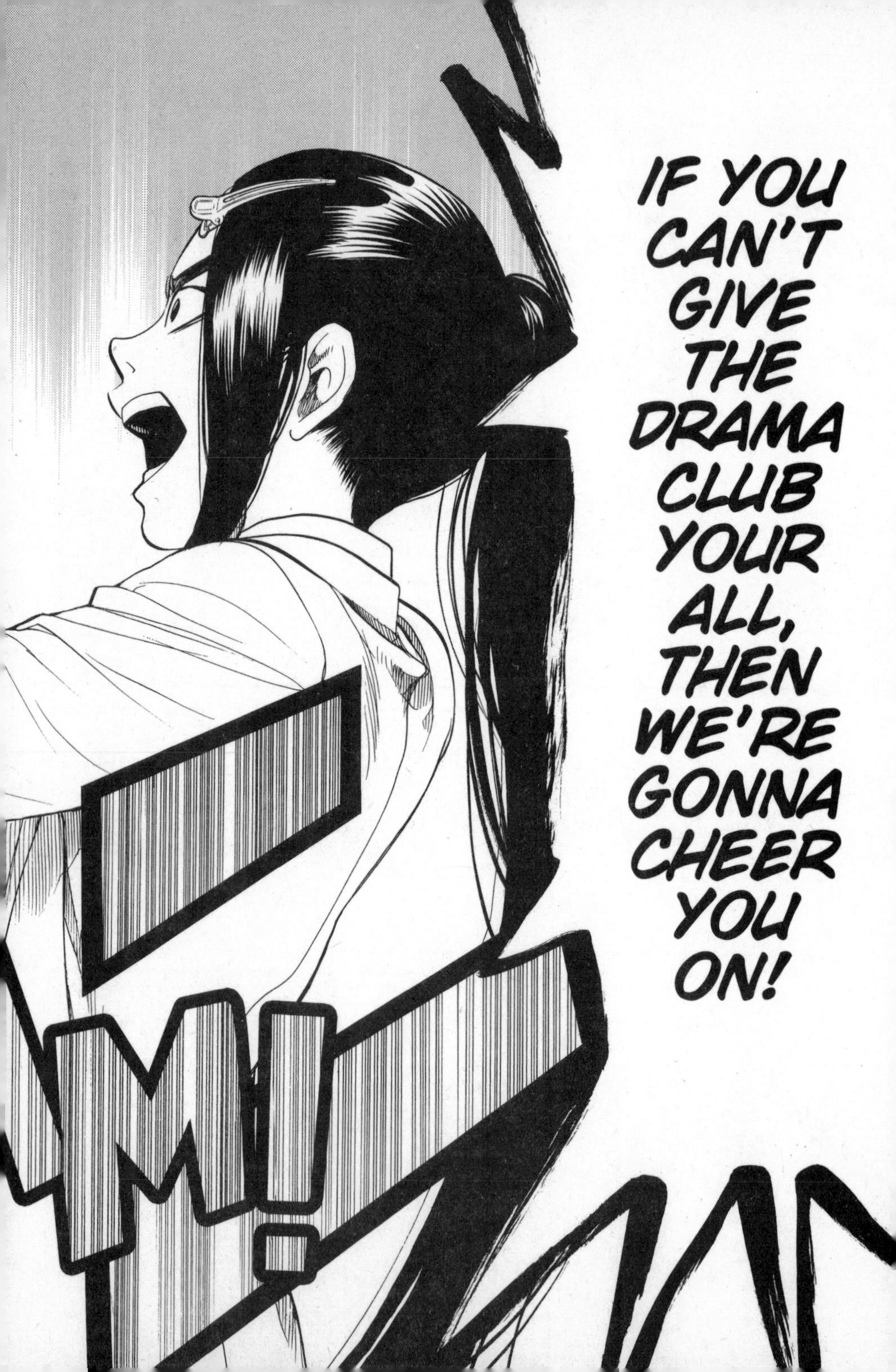
IF YOU CAN'T GIVE THE DRAMA CLUB YOUR ALL, THEN WE'RE GONNA CHEER YOU ON!
M!

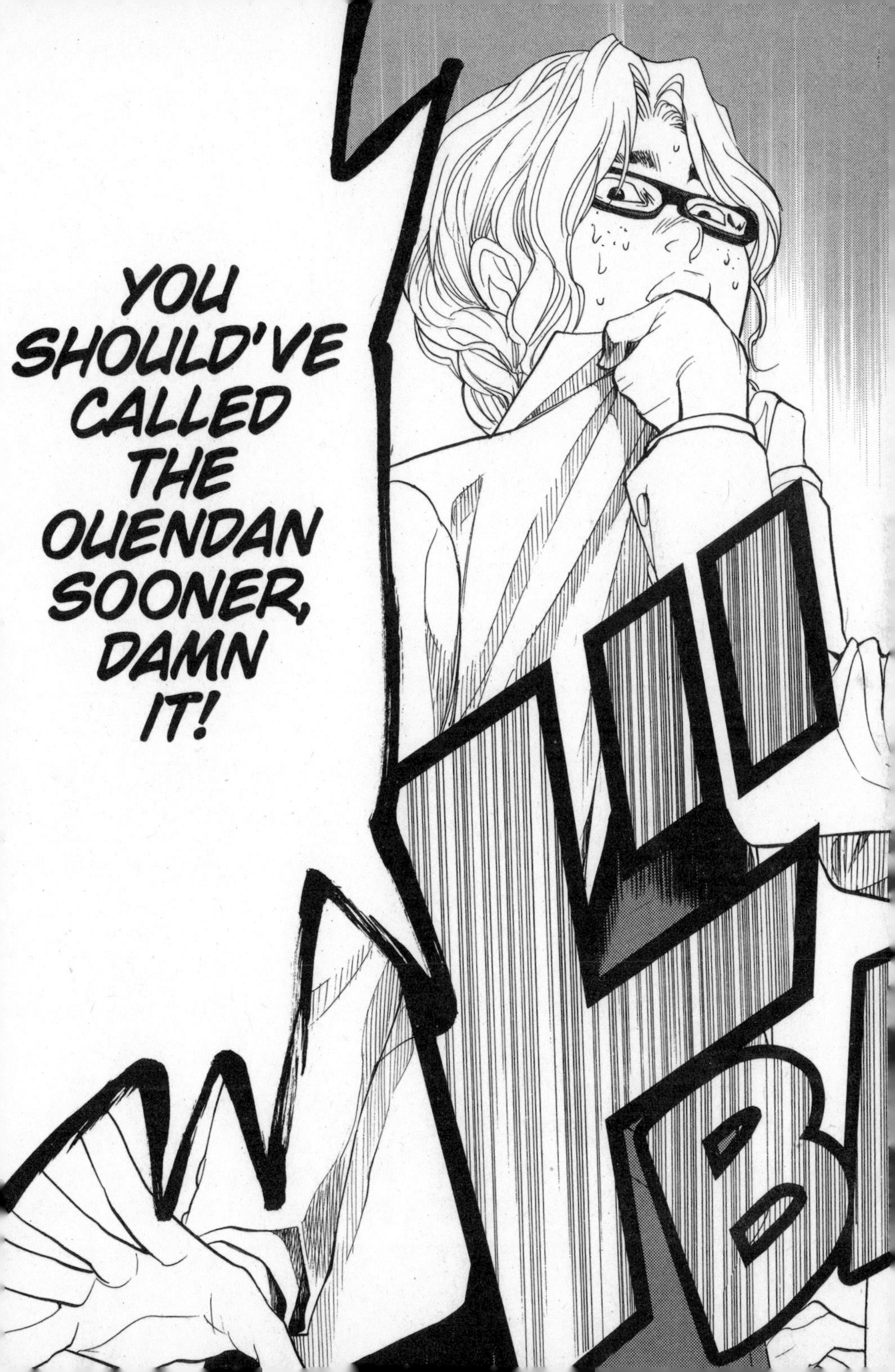
YOU SHOULD'VE CALLED THE OUENDAN SOONER, DAMN IT!

Again!!

アゲイン!!

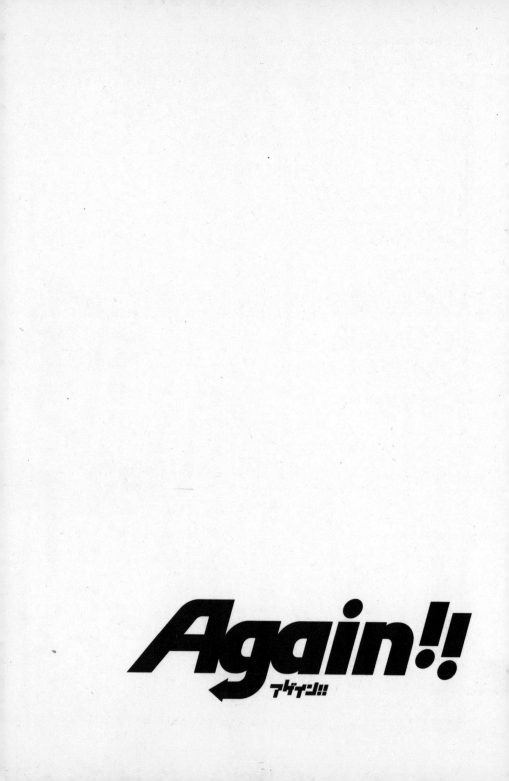

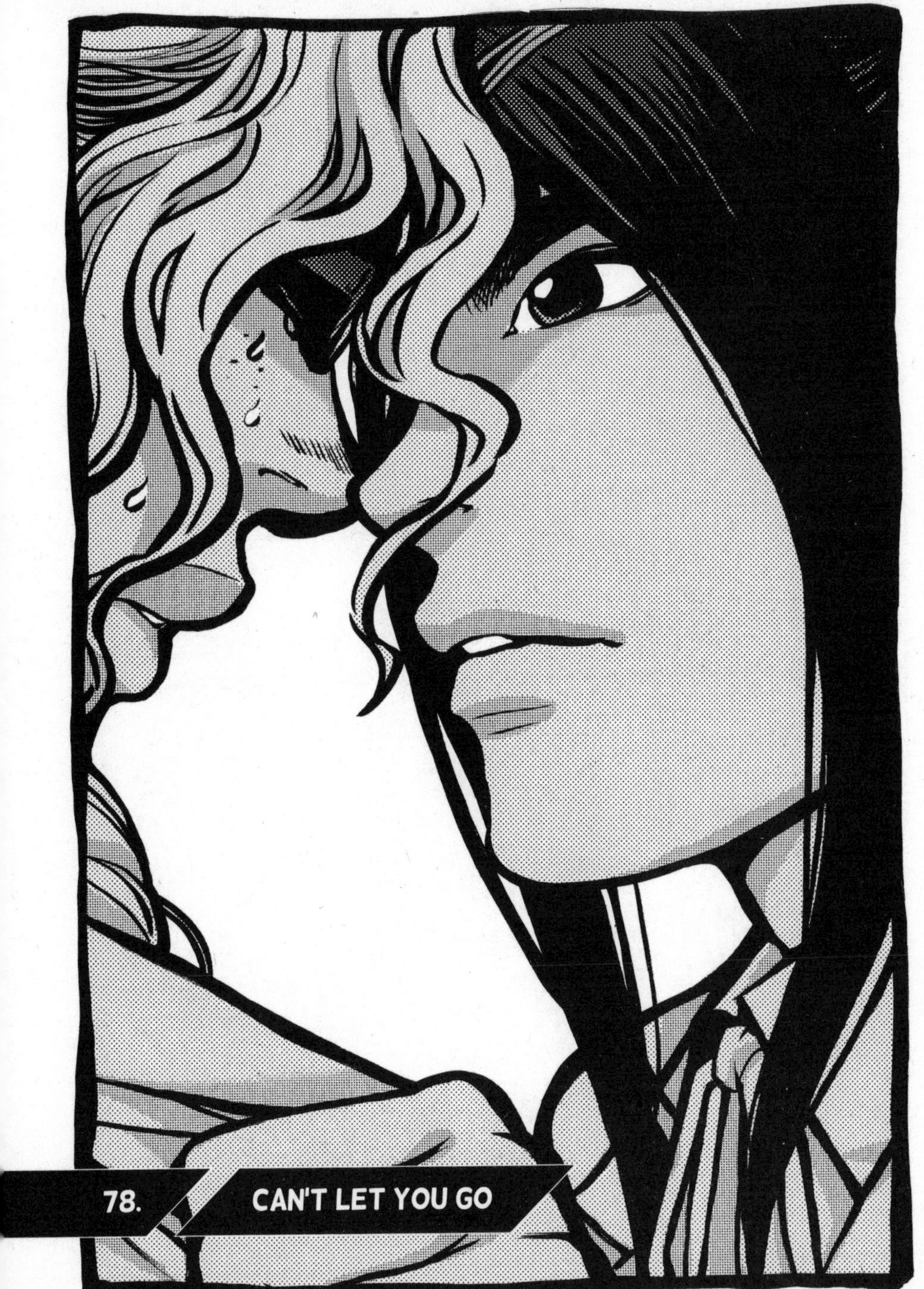

78. CAN'T LET YOU GO

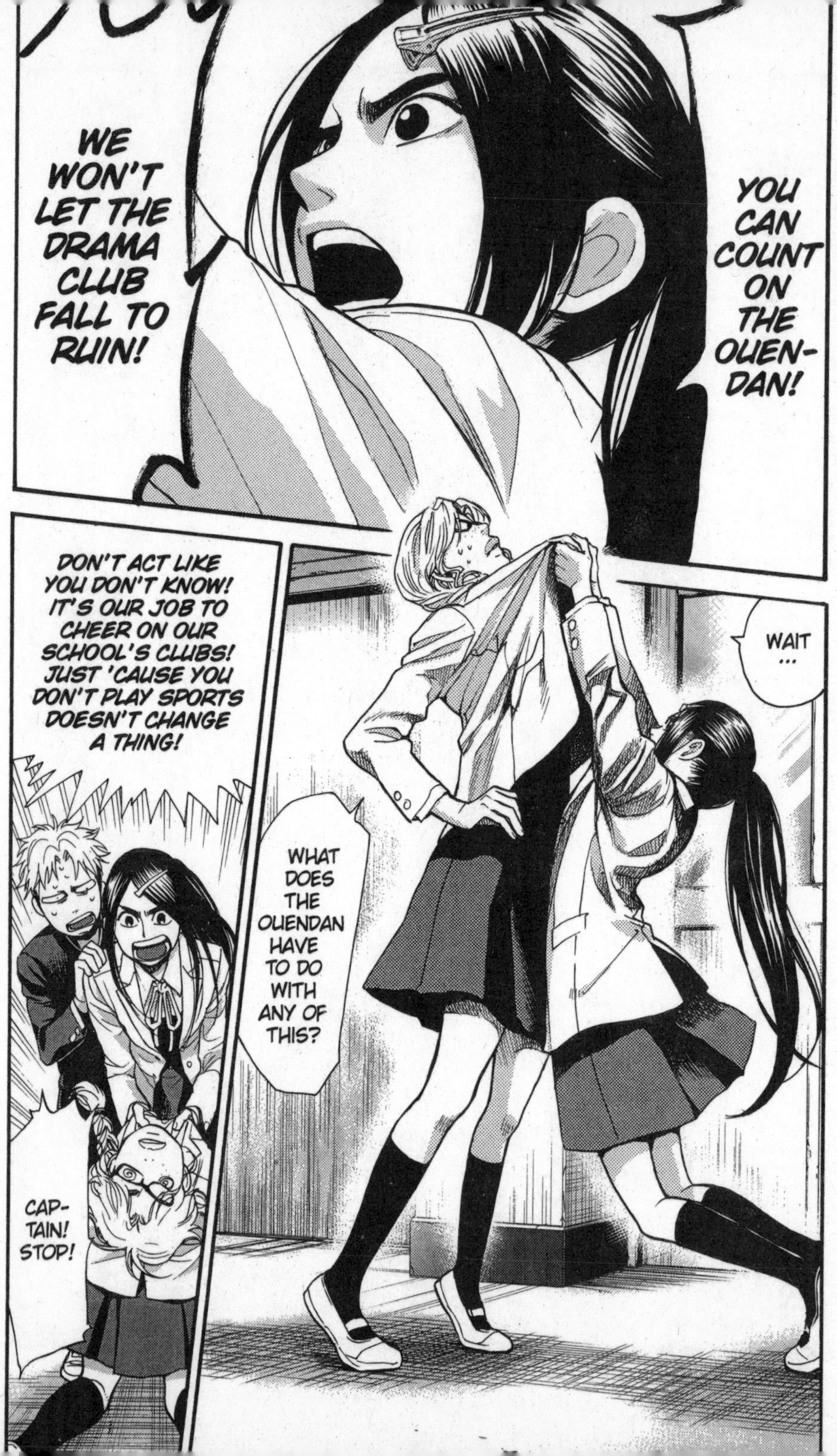
YOU CAN COUNT ON THE OUEN-DAN!
WE WON'T LET THE DRAMA CLUB FALL TO RUIN!
WAIT ...
WHAT DOES THE OUENDAN HAVE TO DO WITH ANY OF THIS?
DON'T ACT LIKE YOU DON'T KNOW! IT'S OUR JOB TO CHEER ON OUR SCHOOL'S CLUBS! JUST 'CAUSE YOU DON'T PLAY SPORTS DOESN'T CHANGE A THING!
CAP-TAIN! STOP!

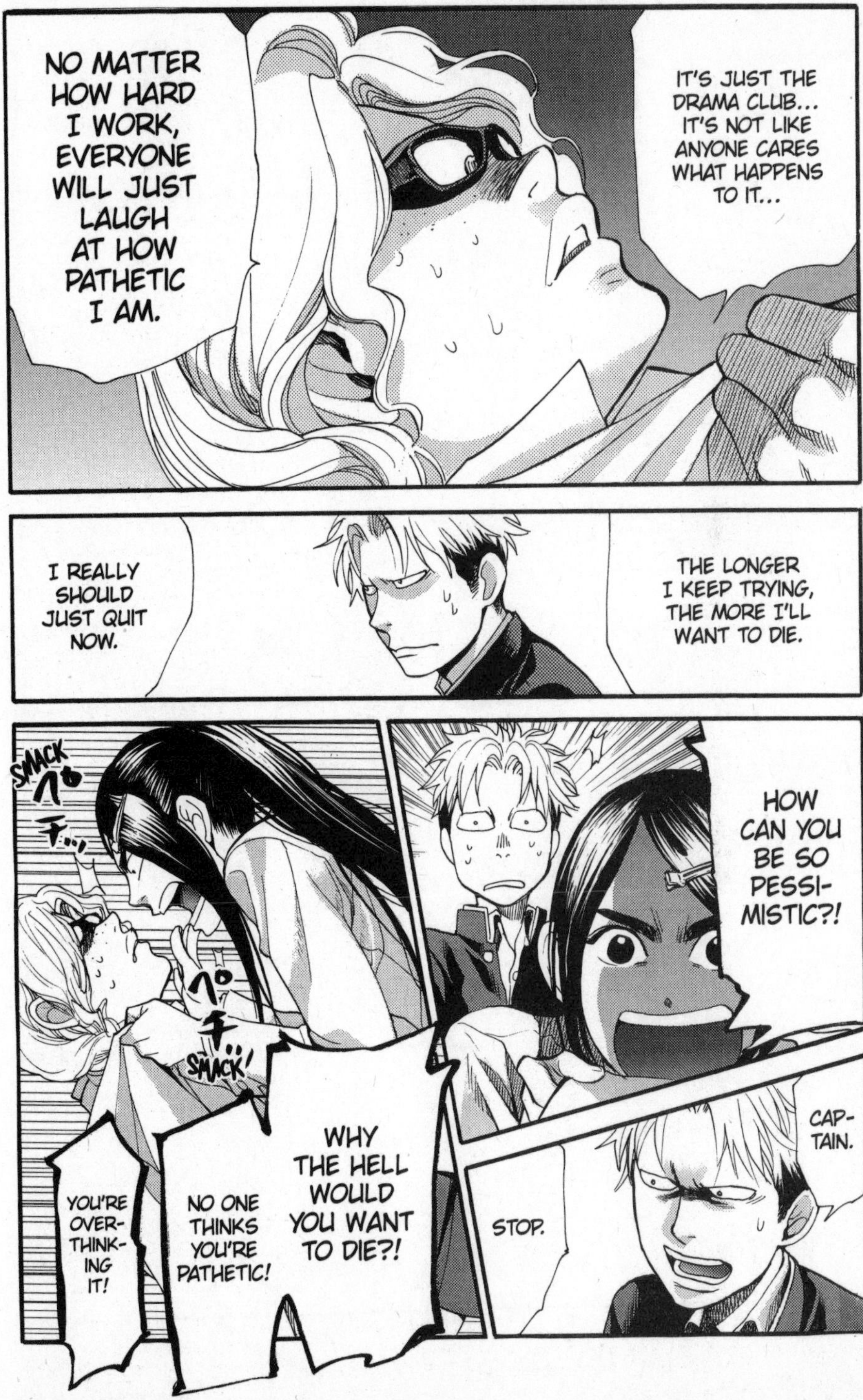

IT'S JUST THE DRAMA CLUB... IT'S NOT LIKE ANYONE CARES WHAT HAPPENS TO IT...
NO MATTER HOW HARD I WORK, EVERYONE WILL JUST LAUGH AT HOW PATHETIC I AM.
THE LONGER I KEEP TRYING, THE MORE I'LL WANT TO DIE.
I REALLY SHOULD JUST QUIT NOW.
HOW CAN YOU BE SO PESSI-MISTIC?!
CAP-TAIN.
STOP.
SMACK
SMACK!
WHY THE HELL WOULD YOU WANT TO DIE?!
NO ONE THINKS YOU'RE PATHETIC!
YOU'RE OVER-THINK-ING IT!

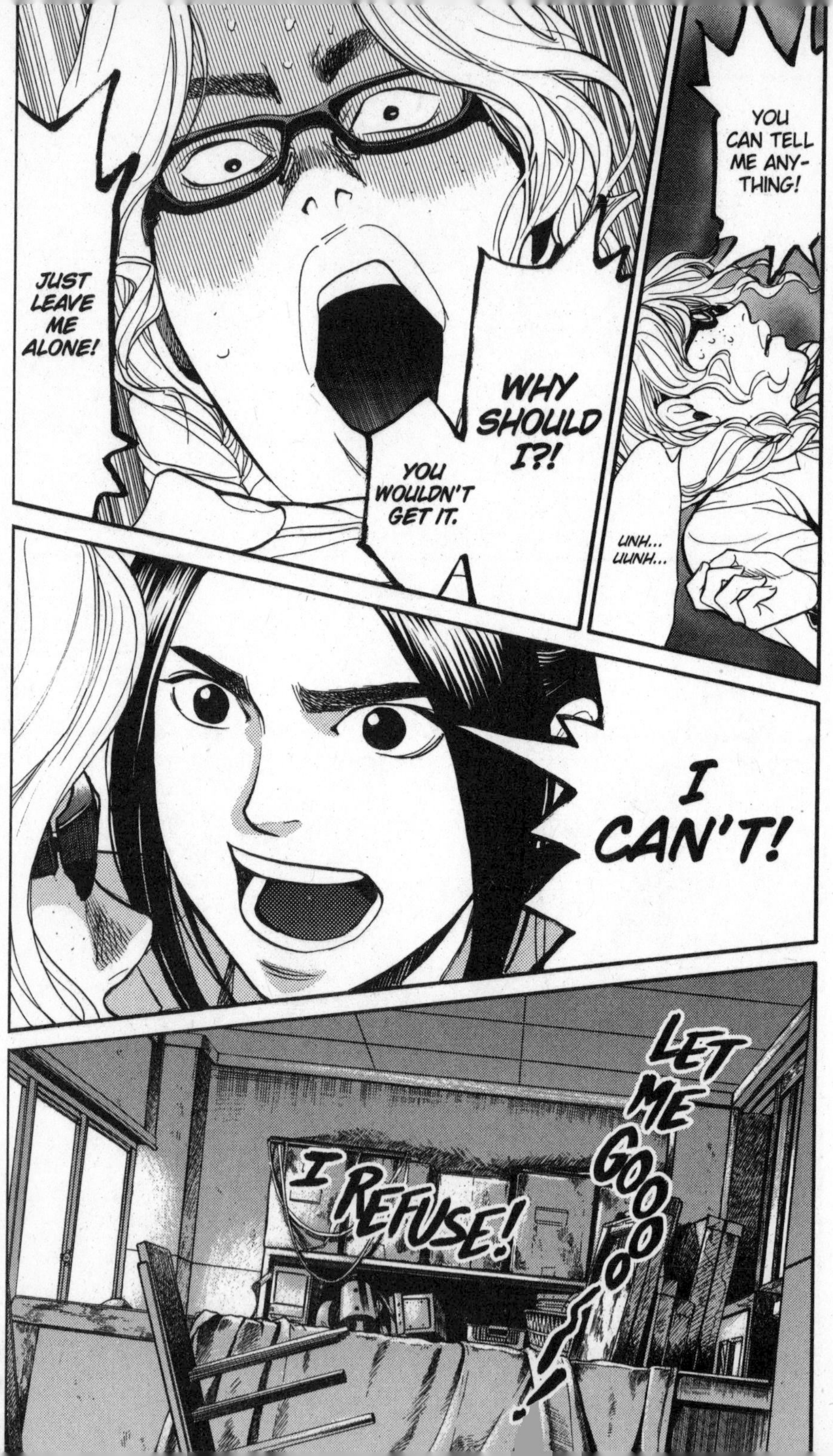
YOU CAN TELL ME ANYTHING!
UNH... UUNH...
WHY SHOULD I?!
YOU WOULDN'T GET IT.
JUST LEAVE ME ALONE!
I CAN'T!
LET ME GOOOO--!
I REFUSE!

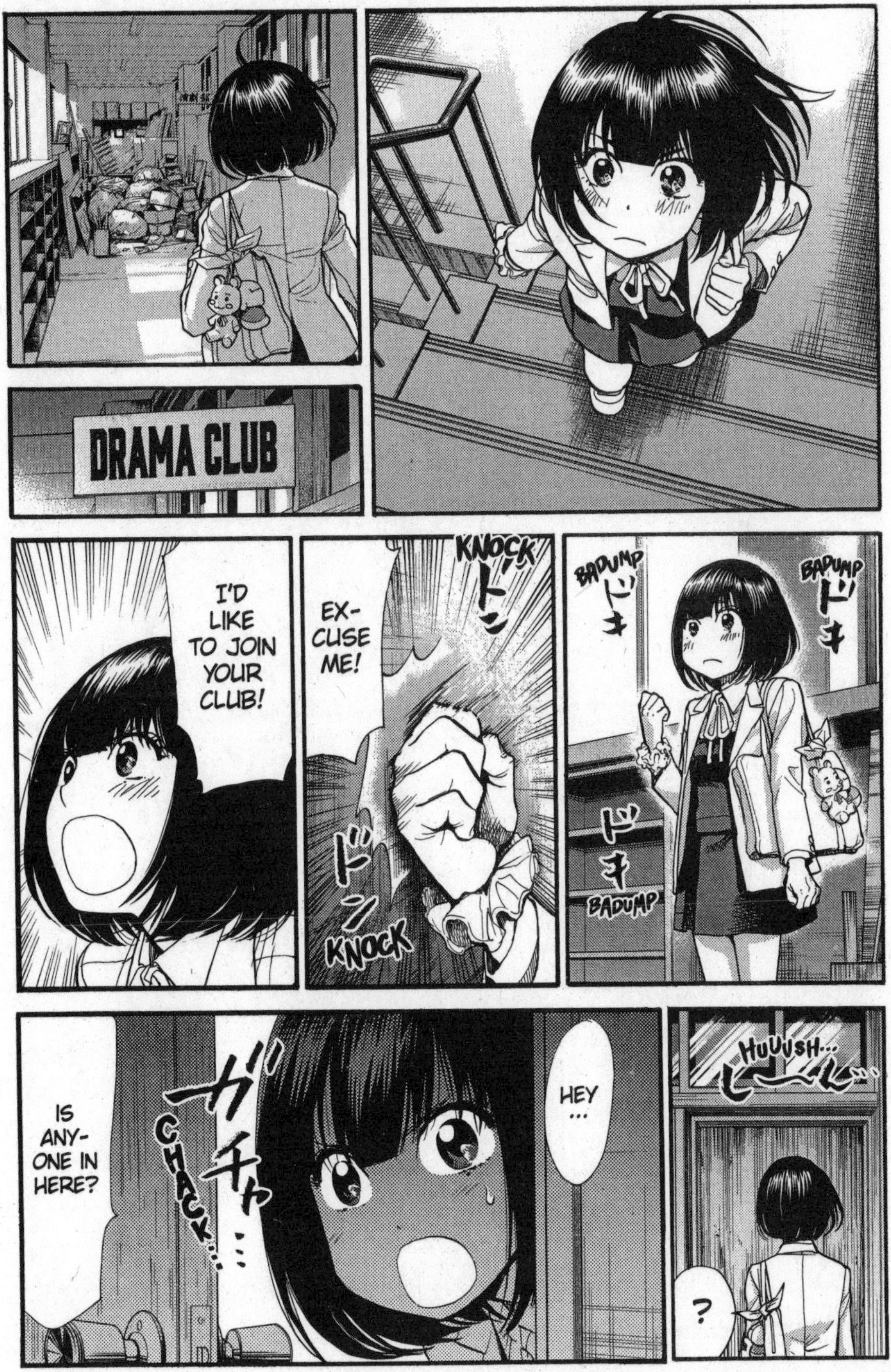
DRAMA CLUB
BADUMP ドキ
BADUMP ドキ
ドキ BADUMP
KNOCK ドン
EX-CUSE ME!
ドン KNOCK
I'D LIKE TO JOIN YOUR CLUB!
HUUUSH... しーん…
?
HEY ...
ガチャ CHACK...
IS ANY-ONE IN HERE?

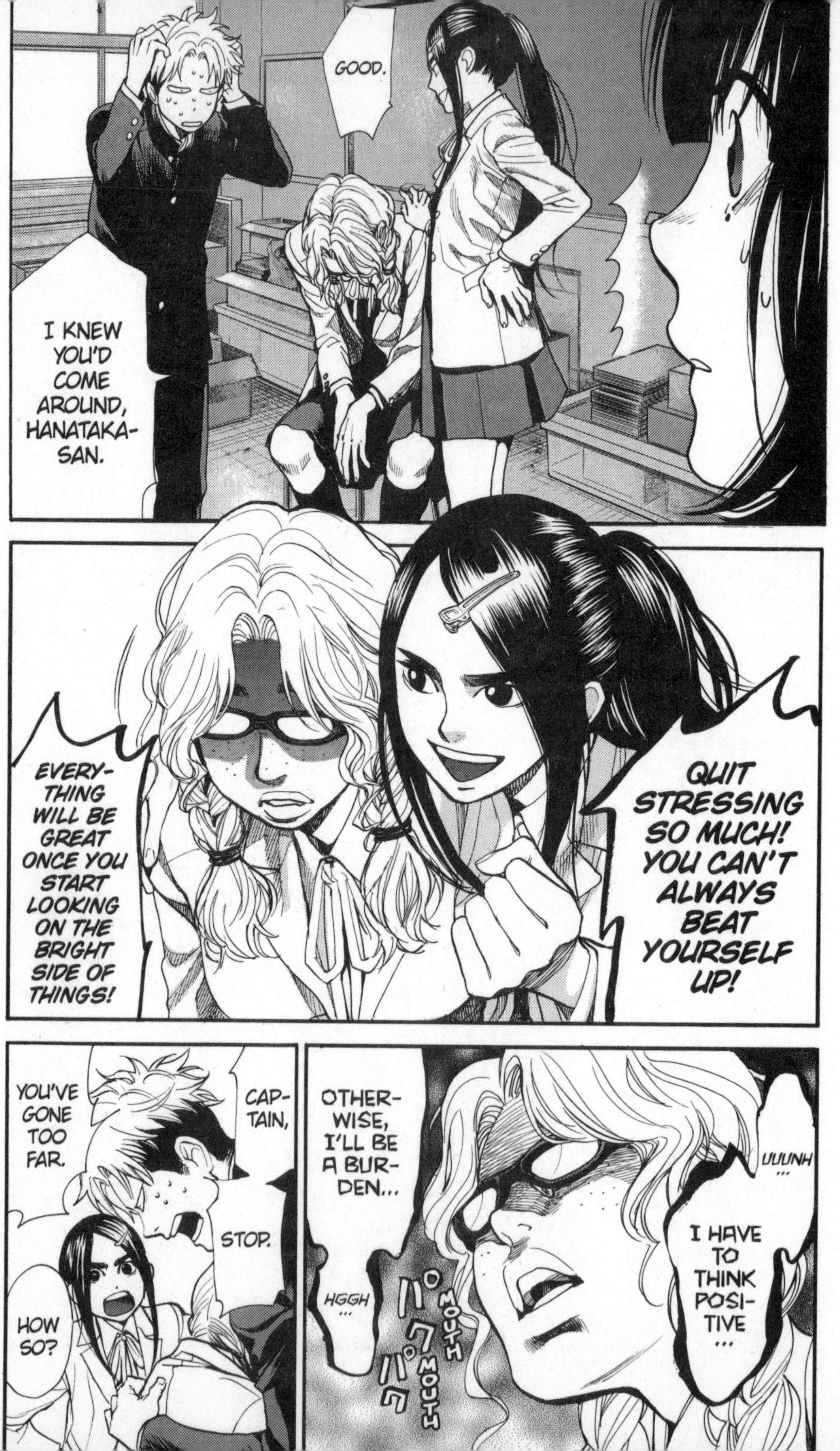
GOOD.
I KNEW YOU'D COME AROUND, HANATAKA-SAN.
QUIT STRESSING SO MUCH! YOU CAN'T ALWAYS BEAT YOURSELF UP!
EVERY-THING WILL BE GREAT ONCE YOU START LOOKING ON THE BRIGHT SIDE OF THINGS!
UUUNH...
I HAVE TO THINK POSI-TIVE...
OTHER-WISE, I'LL BE A BUR-DEN...
HGGH...
MOUTH MOUTH
CAP-TAIN,
YOU'VE GONE TOO FAR.
STOP.
HOW SO?

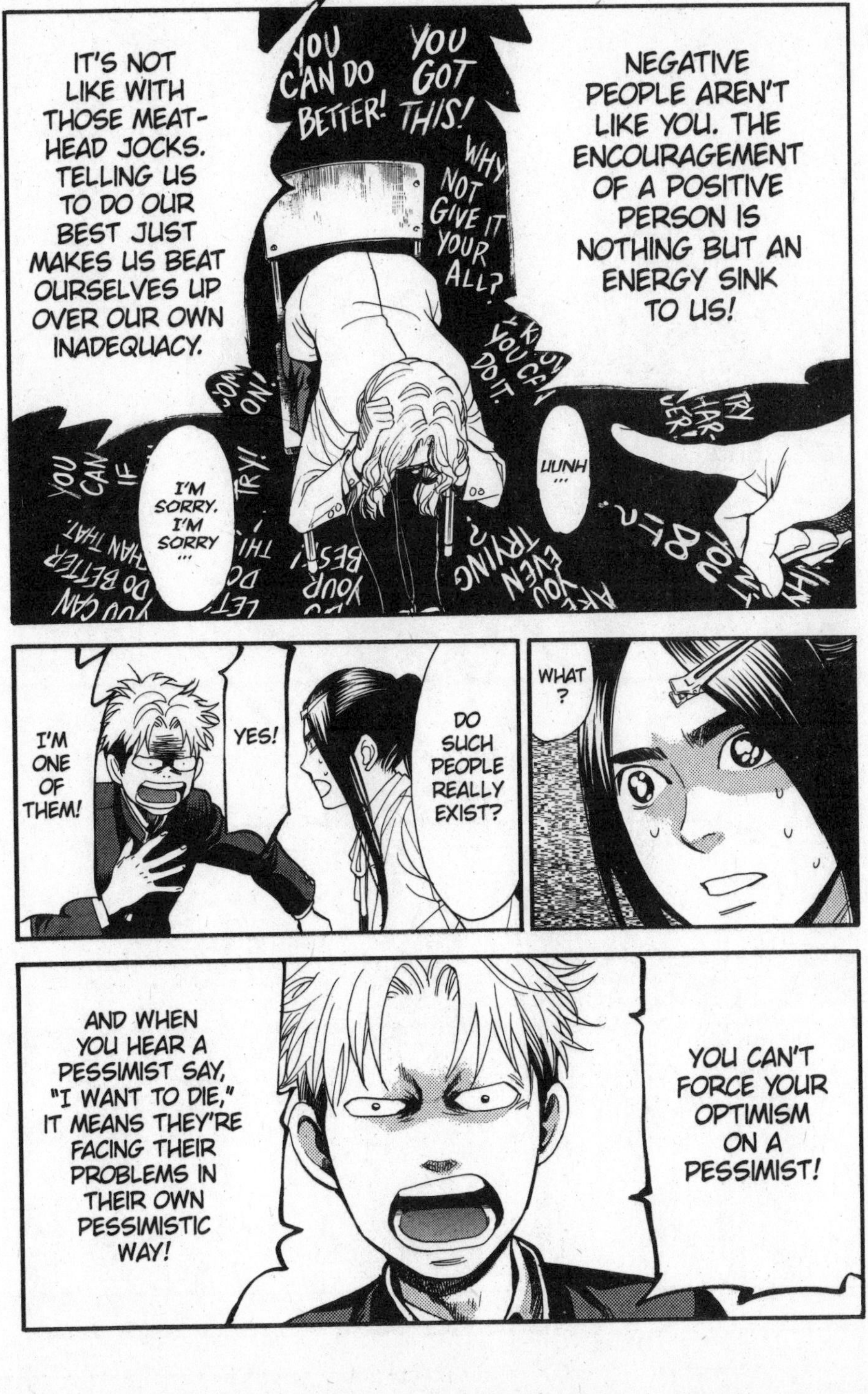
NEGATIVE PEOPLE AREN'T LIKE YOU. THE ENCOURAGEMENT OF A POSITIVE PERSON IS NOTHING BUT AN ENERGY SINK TO US!
YOU GOT THIS!
YOU CAN DO BETTER!
WHY NOT GIVE IT YOUR ALL?
TRY HARDER.
UUNH...
I'M SORRY. I'M SORRY...
IT'S NOT LIKE WITH THOSE MEAT-HEAD JOCKS. TELLING US TO DO OUR BEST JUST MAKES US BEAT OURSELVES UP OVER OUR OWN INADEQUACY.
WHAT?
DO SUCH PEOPLE REALLY EXIST?
YES!
I'M ONE OF THEM!
YOU CAN'T FORCE YOUR OPTIMISM ON A PESSIMIST!
AND WHEN YOU HEAR A PESSIMIST SAY, "I WANT TO DIE," IT MEANS THEY'RE FACING THEIR PROBLEMS IN THEIR OWN PESSIMISTIC WAY!

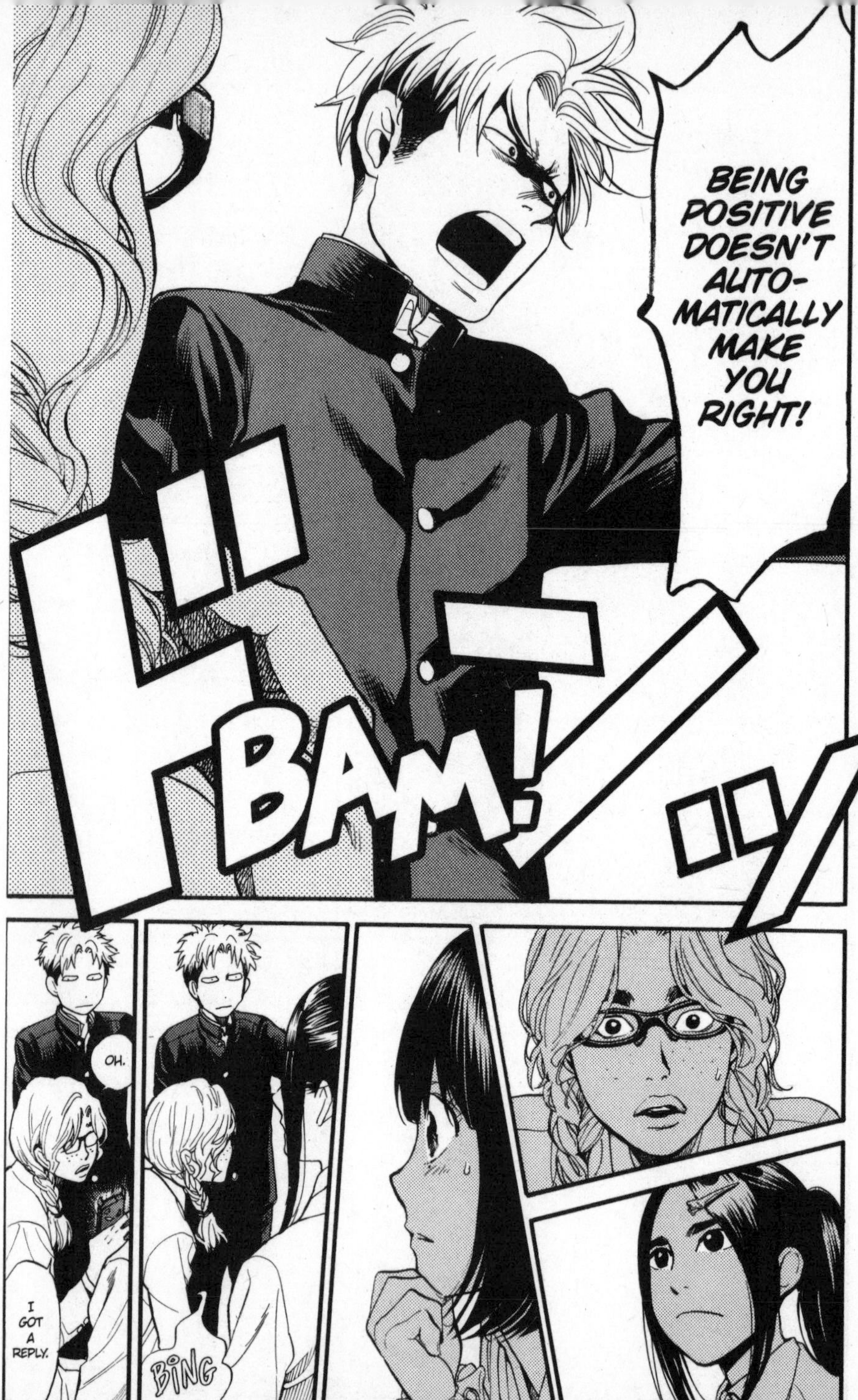
BEING POSITIVE DOESN'T AUTO-MATICALLY MAKE YOU RIGHT!
BAM!
BING
OH.
I GOT A REPLY.

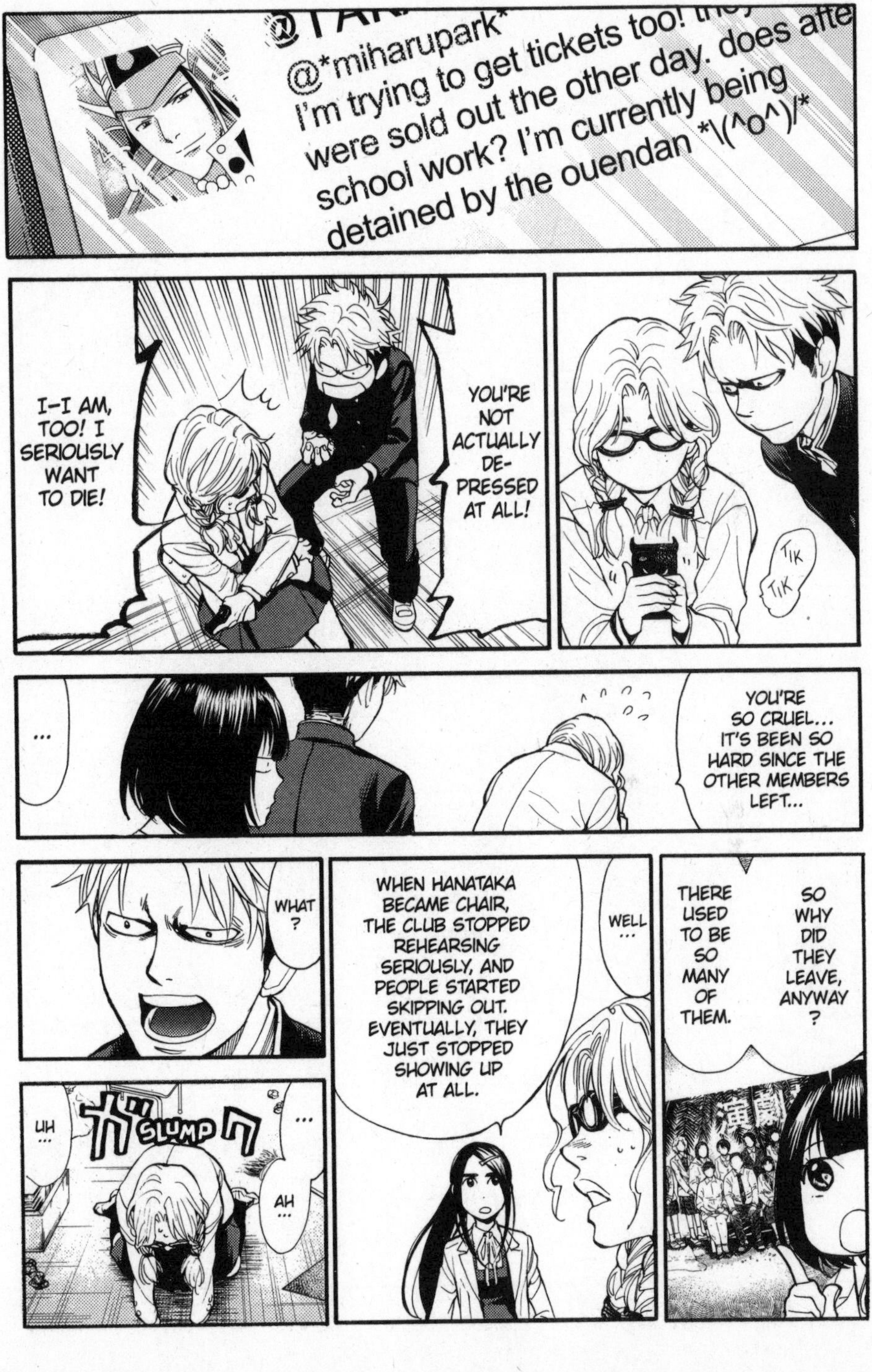
@*miharupark*
I'm trying to get tickets too! they
were sold out the other day. does afte
school work? I'm currently being
detained by the ouendan *\(^o^)/*
TIK
TIK
YOU'RE NOT ACTUALLY DE-PRESSED AT ALL!
I-I AM, TOO! I SERIOUSLY WANT TO DIE!
YOU'RE SO CRUEL... IT'S BEEN SO HARD SINCE THE OTHER MEMBERS LEFT...
...
SO WHY DID THEY LEAVE, ANYWAY?
THERE USED TO BE SO MANY OF THEM.
WELL...
WHEN HANATAKA BECAME CHAIR, THE CLUB STOPPED REHEARSING SERIOUSLY, AND PEOPLE STARTED SKIPPING OUT. EVENTUALLY, THEY JUST STOPPED SHOWING UP AT ALL.
WHAT?
...
SLUMP
UH...
AH...

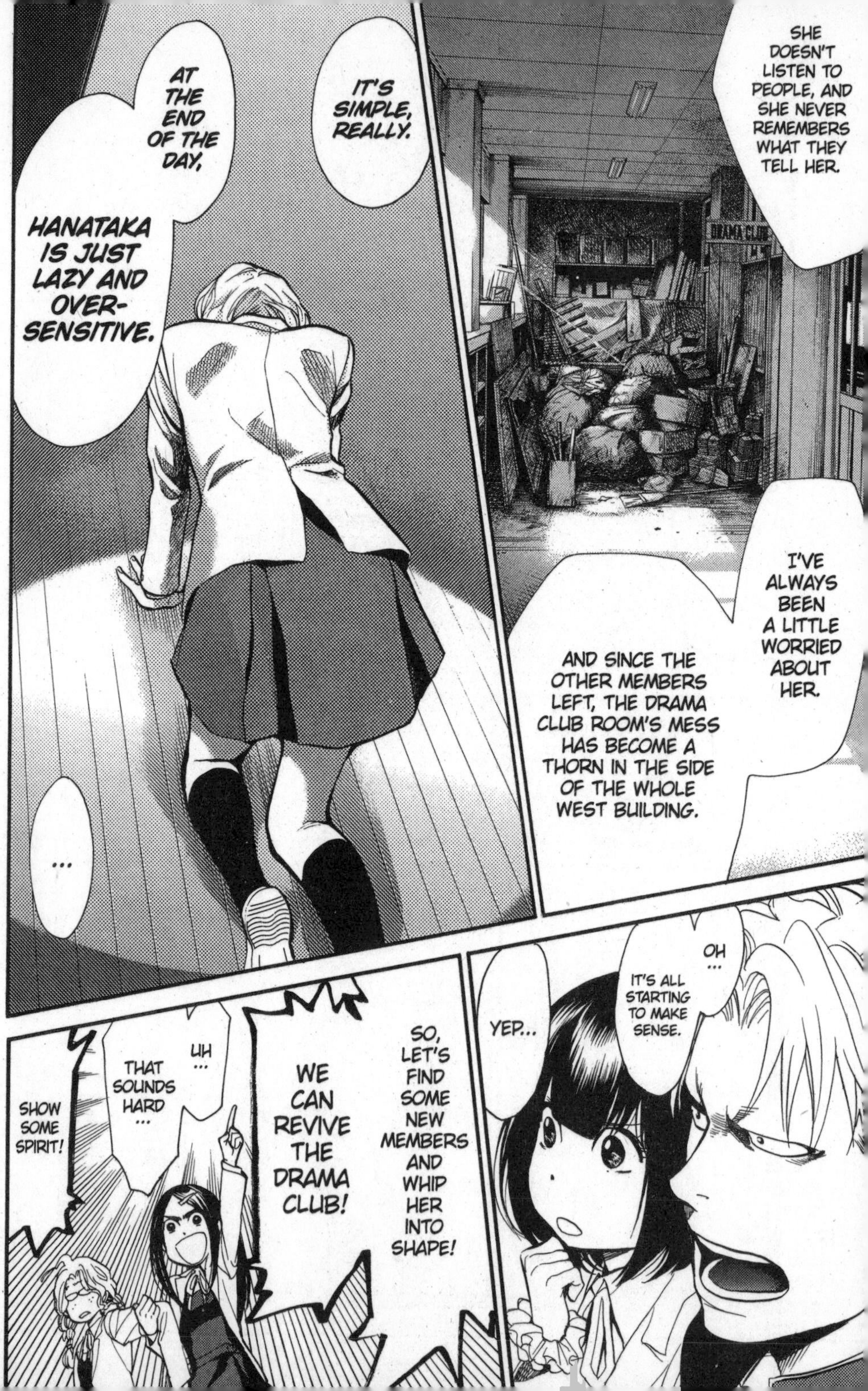
SHE DOESN'T LISTEN TO PEOPLE, AND SHE NEVER REMEMBERS WHAT THEY TELL HER.
DRAMA CLUB
I'VE ALWAYS BEEN A LITTLE WORRIED ABOUT HER.
AND SINCE THE OTHER MEMBERS LEFT, THE DRAMA CLUB ROOM'S MESS HAS BECOME A THORN IN THE SIDE OF THE WHOLE WEST BUILDING.
IT'S SIMPLE, REALLY.
AT THE END OF THE DAY,
HANATAKA IS JUST LAZY AND OVER-SENSITIVE.
...
OH ...
IT'S ALL STARTING TO MAKE SENSE.
YEP...
SO, LET'S FIND SOME NEW MEMBERS AND WHIP HER INTO SHAPE!
WE CAN REVIVE THE DRAMA CLUB!
UH ...
THAT SOUNDS HARD ...
SHOW SOME SPIRIT!

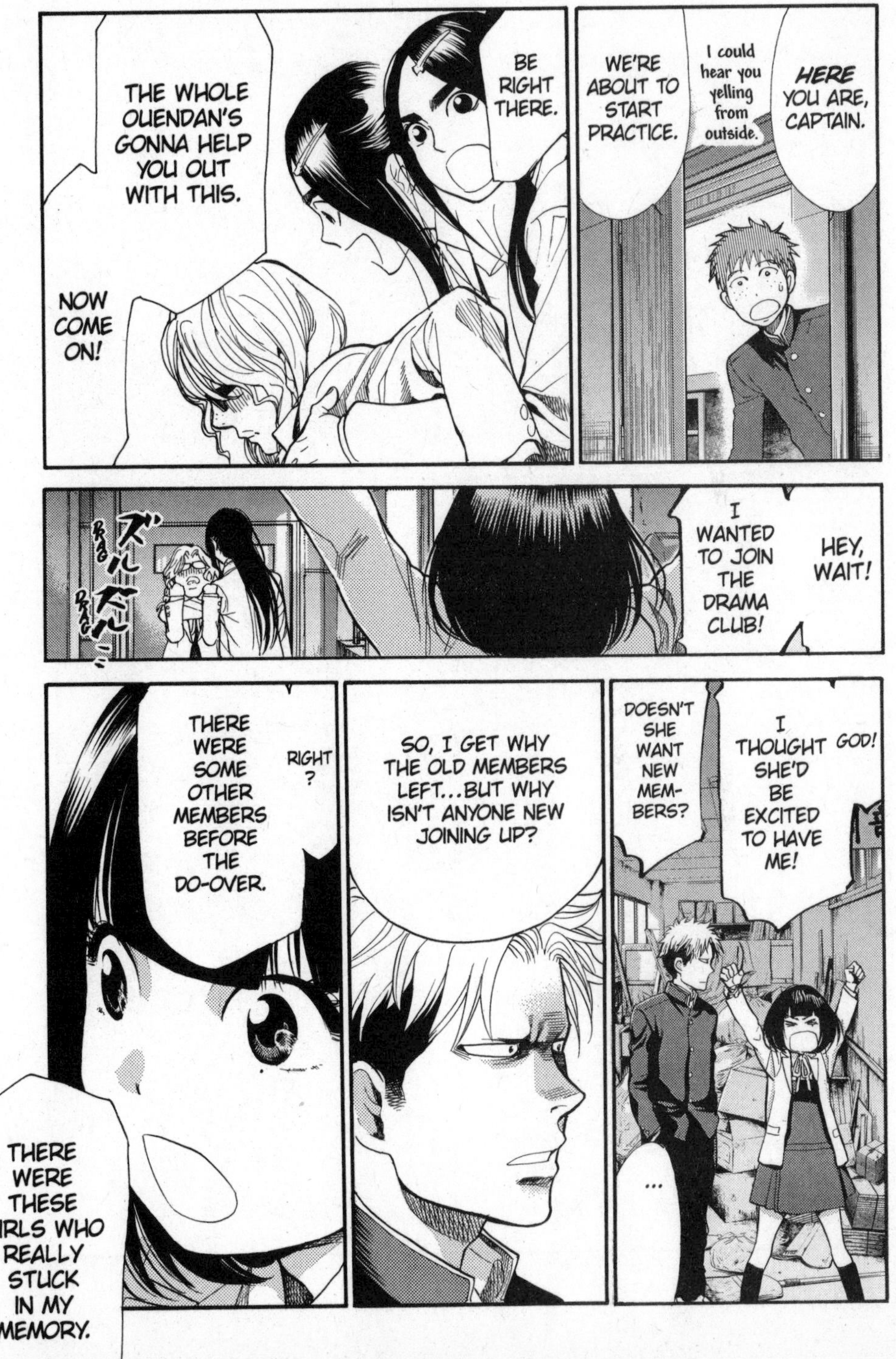
HERE YOU ARE, CAPTAIN.
I could hear you yelling from outside.
WE'RE ABOUT TO START PRACTICE.
BE RIGHT THERE.
THE WHOLE OUENDAN'S GONNA HELP YOU OUT WITH THIS.
NOW COME ON!
HEY, WAIT!
I WANTED TO JOIN THE DRAMA CLUB!
ズルズル
DRAG DRAG
GOD!
I THOUGHT SHE'D BE EXCITED TO HAVE ME!
DOESN'T SHE WANT NEW MEM-BERS?
...
SO, I GET WHY THE OLD MEMBERS LEFT...BUT WHY ISN'T ANYONE NEW JOINING UP?
RIGHT?
THERE WERE SOME OTHER MEMBERS BEFORE THE DO-OVER.
THERE WERE THESE GIRLS WHO REALLY STUCK IN MY MEMORY.

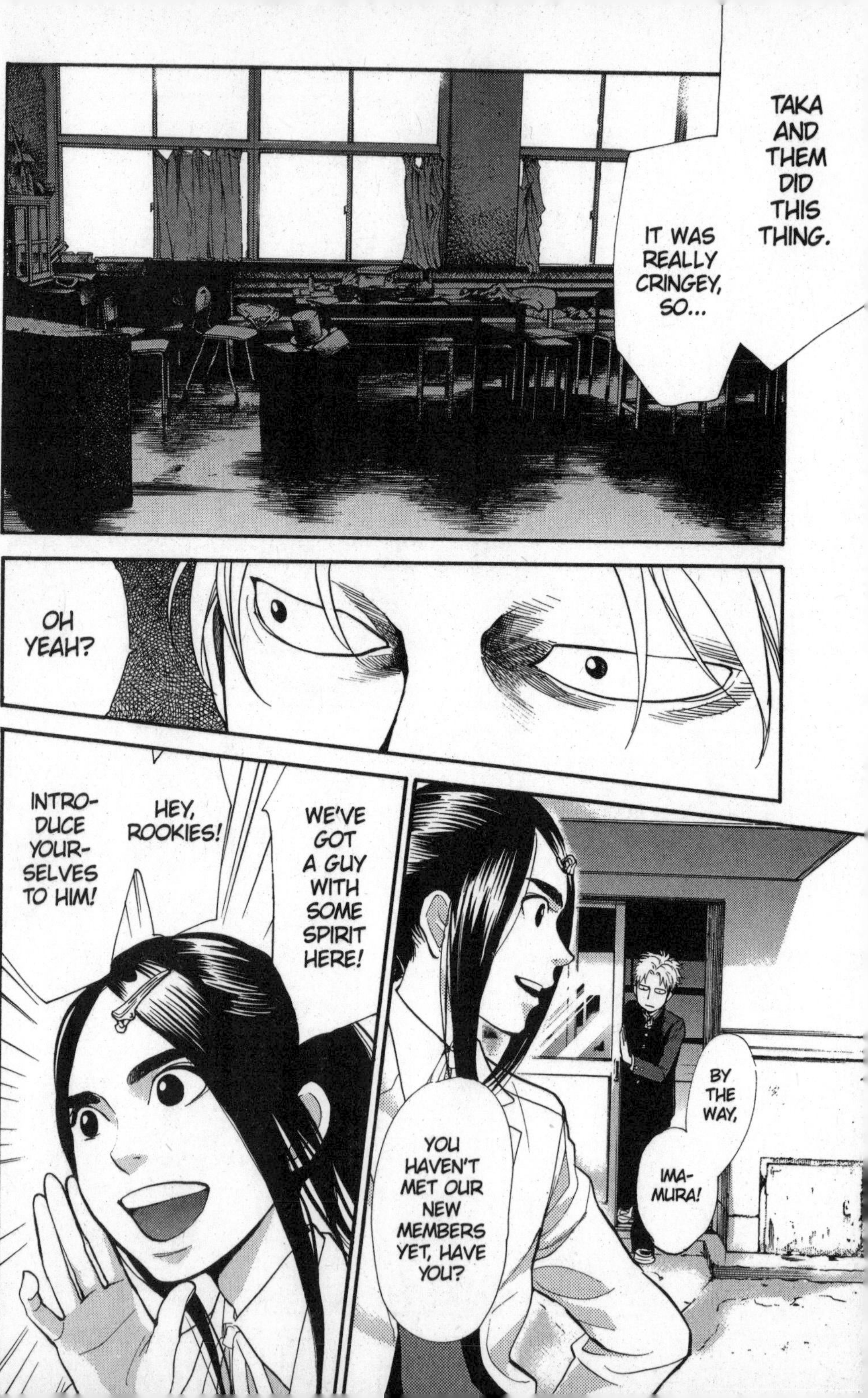
TAKA AND THEM DID THIS THING.
IT WAS REALLY CRINGEY, SO...
OH YEAH?
BY THE WAY,
IMA-MURA!
YOU HAVEN'T MET OUR NEW MEMBERS YET, HAVE YOU?
WE'VE GOT A GUY WITH SOME SPIRIT HERE!
HEY, ROOKIES!
INTRO-DUCE YOUR-SELVES TO HIM!

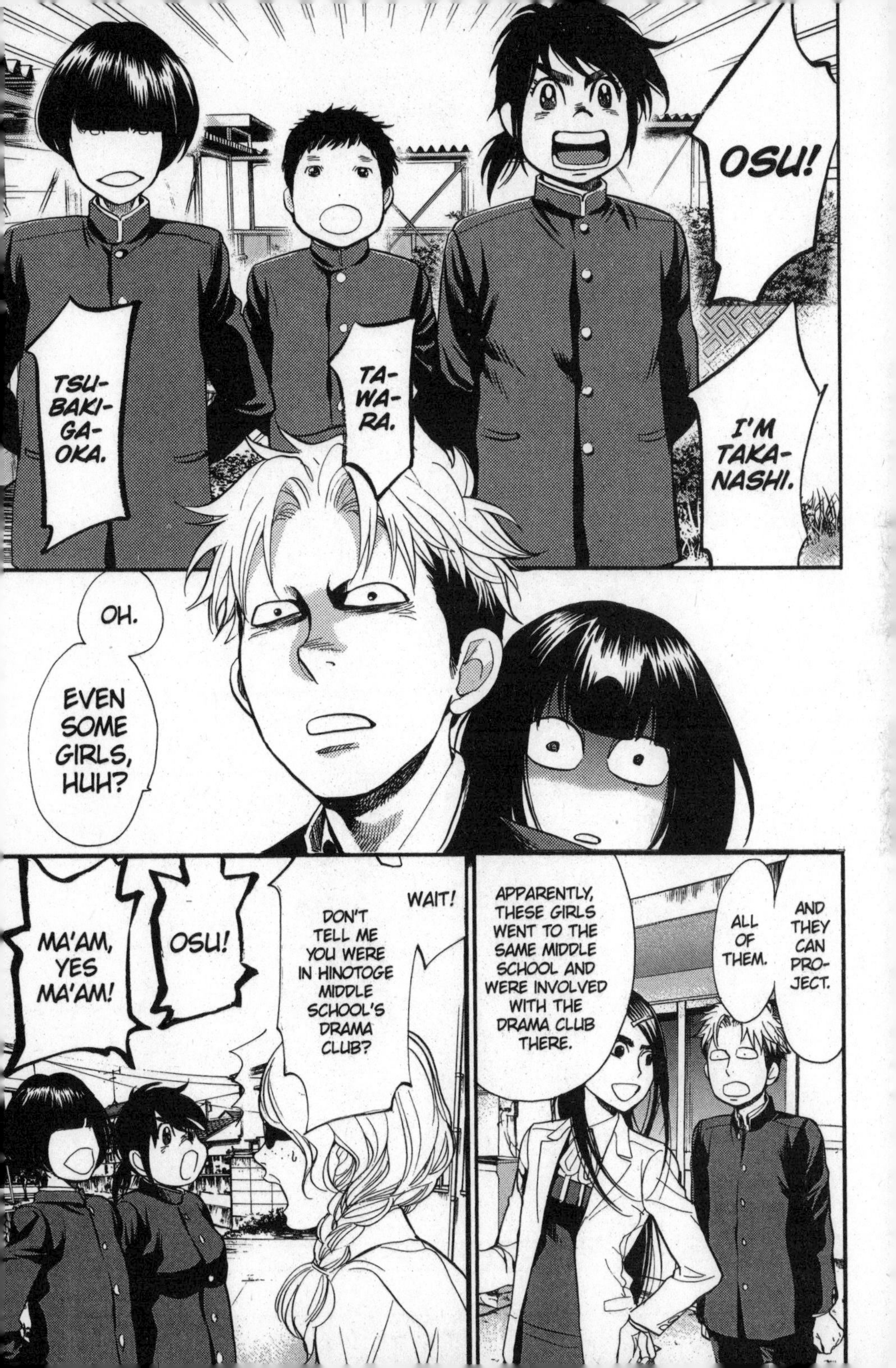
OSU!
I'M TAKANASHI.
TAWARA.
TSUBAKI-GA-OKA.
OH.
EVEN SOME GIRLS, HUH?
AND THEY CAN PROJECT.
ALL OF THEM.
APPARENTLY, THESE GIRLS WENT TO THE SAME MIDDLE SCHOOL AND WERE INVOLVED WITH THE DRAMA CLUB THERE.
WAIT!
DON'T TELL ME YOU WERE IN HINOTOGE MIDDLE SCHOOL'S DRAMA CLUB?
OSU!
MA'AM, YES MA'AM!

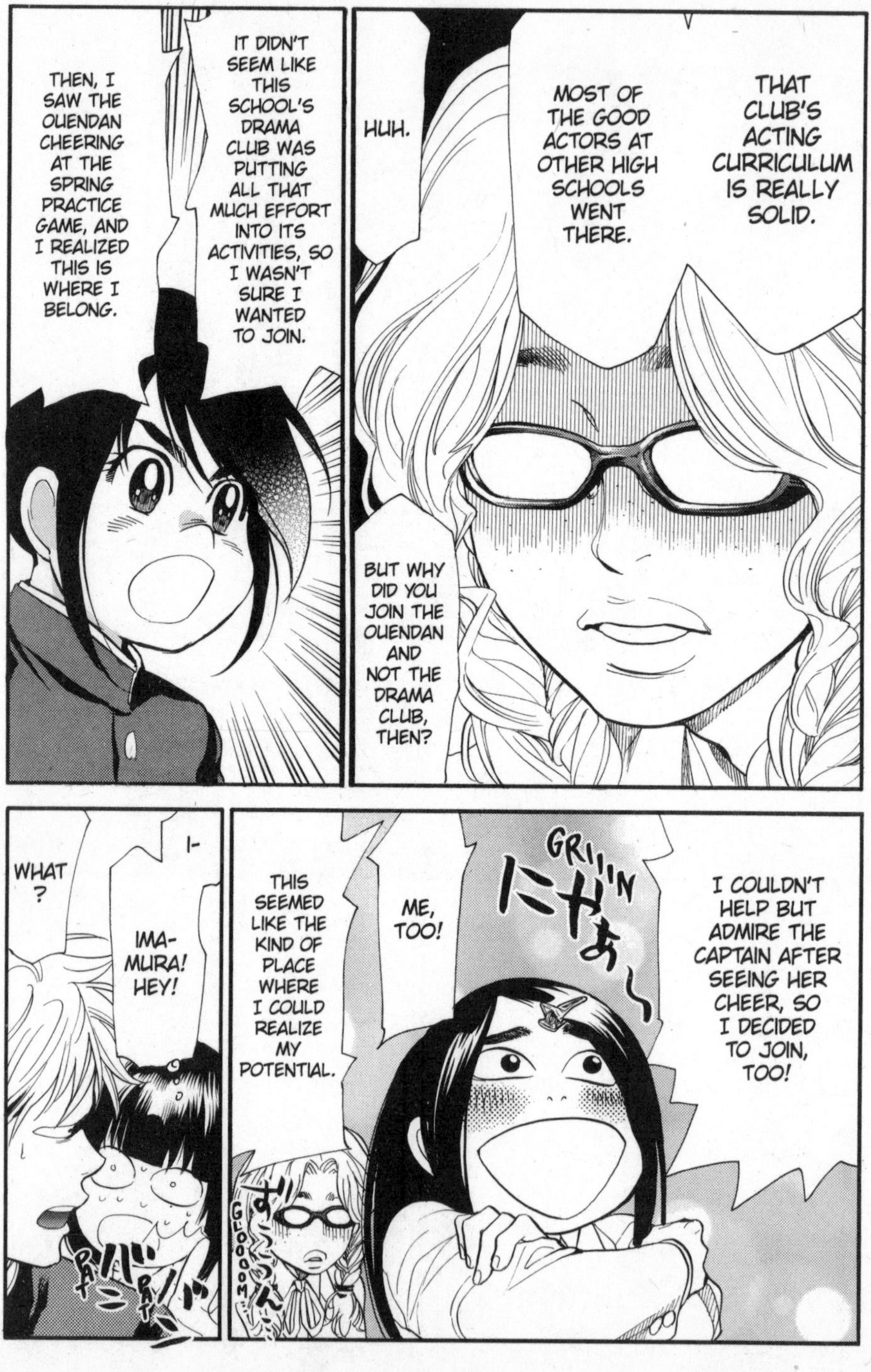

THAT CLUB'S ACTING CURRICULUM IS REALLY SOLID.
MOST OF THE GOOD ACTORS AT OTHER HIGH SCHOOLS WENT THERE.
HUH.
BUT WHY DID YOU JOIN THE OUENDAN AND NOT THE DRAMA CLUB, THEN?
IT DIDN'T SEEM LIKE THIS SCHOOL'S DRAMA CLUB WAS PUTTING ALL THAT MUCH EFFORT INTO ITS ACTIVITIES, SO I WASN'T SURE I WANTED TO JOIN.
THEN, I SAW THE OUENDAN CHEERING AT THE SPRING PRACTICE GAME, AND I REALIZED THIS IS WHERE I BELONG.
I COULDN'T HELP BUT ADMIRE THE CAPTAIN AFTER SEEING HER CHEER, SO I DECIDED TO JOIN, TOO!
GRIIN
にやぁ〜
ME, TOO!
THIS SEEMED LIKE THE KIND OF PLACE WHERE I COULD REALIZE MY POTENTIAL.
ずーん
GLOOOOM...
I-
IMA-MURA! HEY!
WHAT?
PAT PAT

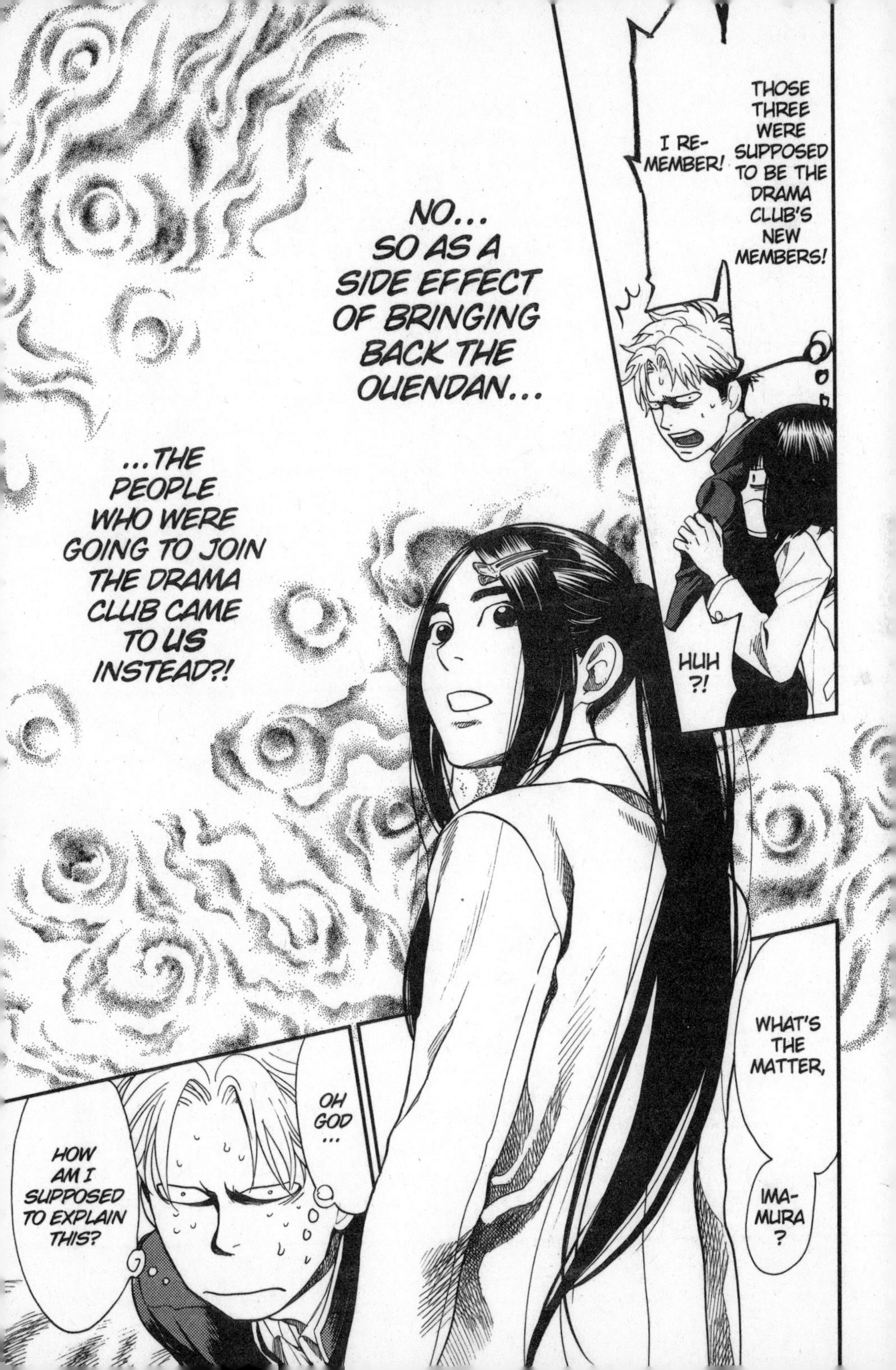
I RE-MEMBER!
THOSE THREE WERE SUPPOSED TO BE THE DRAMA CLUB'S NEW MEMBERS!
HUH?!
NO... SO AS A SIDE EFFECT OF BRINGING BACK THE OUENDAN...
...THE PEOPLE WHO WERE GOING TO JOIN THE DRAMA CLUB CAME TO US INSTEAD?!
WHAT'S THE MATTER,
IMA-MURA?
OH GOD...
HOW AM I SUPPOSED TO EXPLAIN THIS?

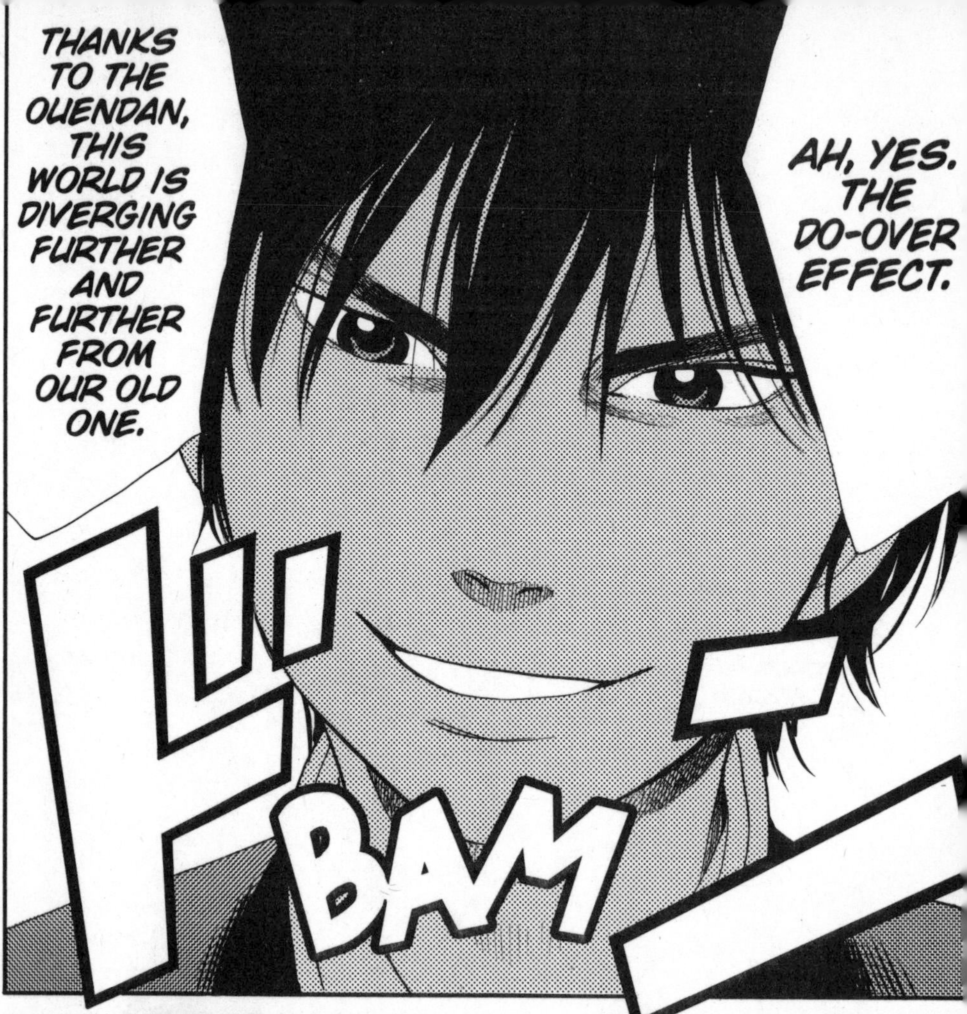
AH, YES. THE DO-OVER EFFECT.
THANKS TO THE OUENDAN, THIS WORLD IS DIVERGING FURTHER AND FURTHER FROM OUR OLD ONE.
BAM
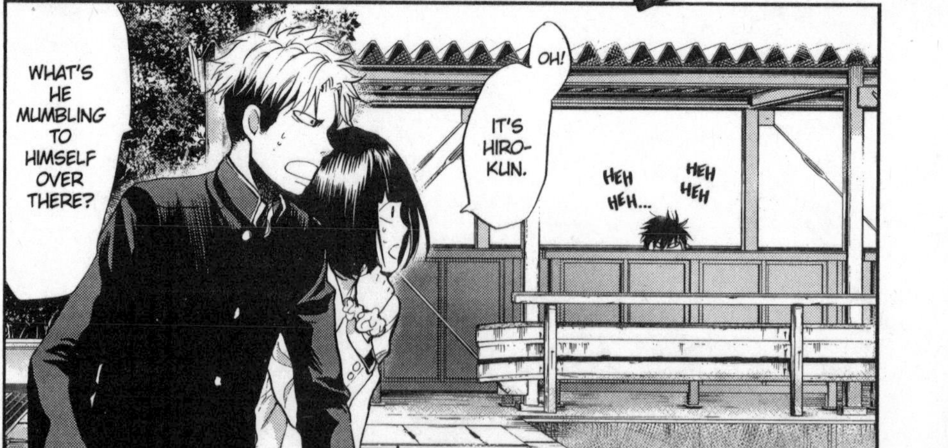
HEH HEH
HEH HEH...
OH!
IT'S HIRO-KUN.
WHAT'S HE MUMBLING TO HIMSELF OVER THERE?

Again!!

アゲイン!!

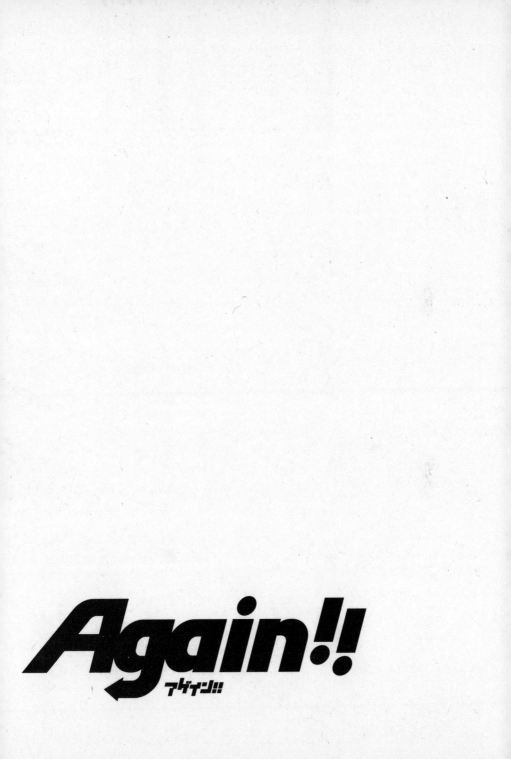

Again!!

アゲイン!!

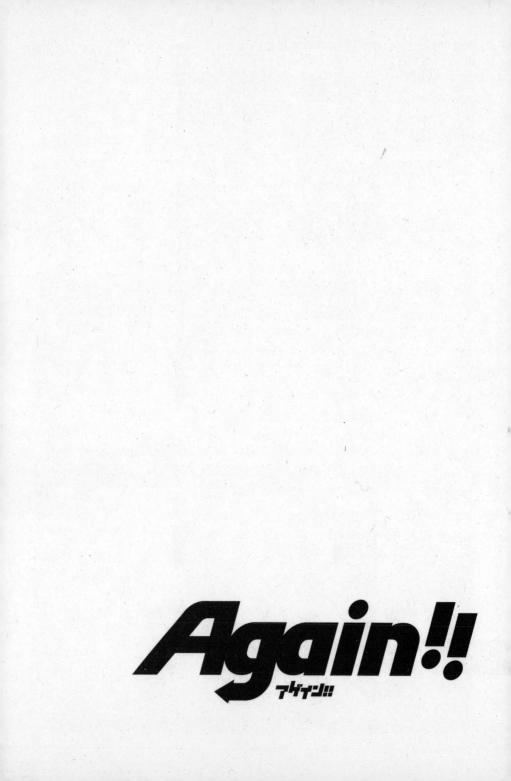

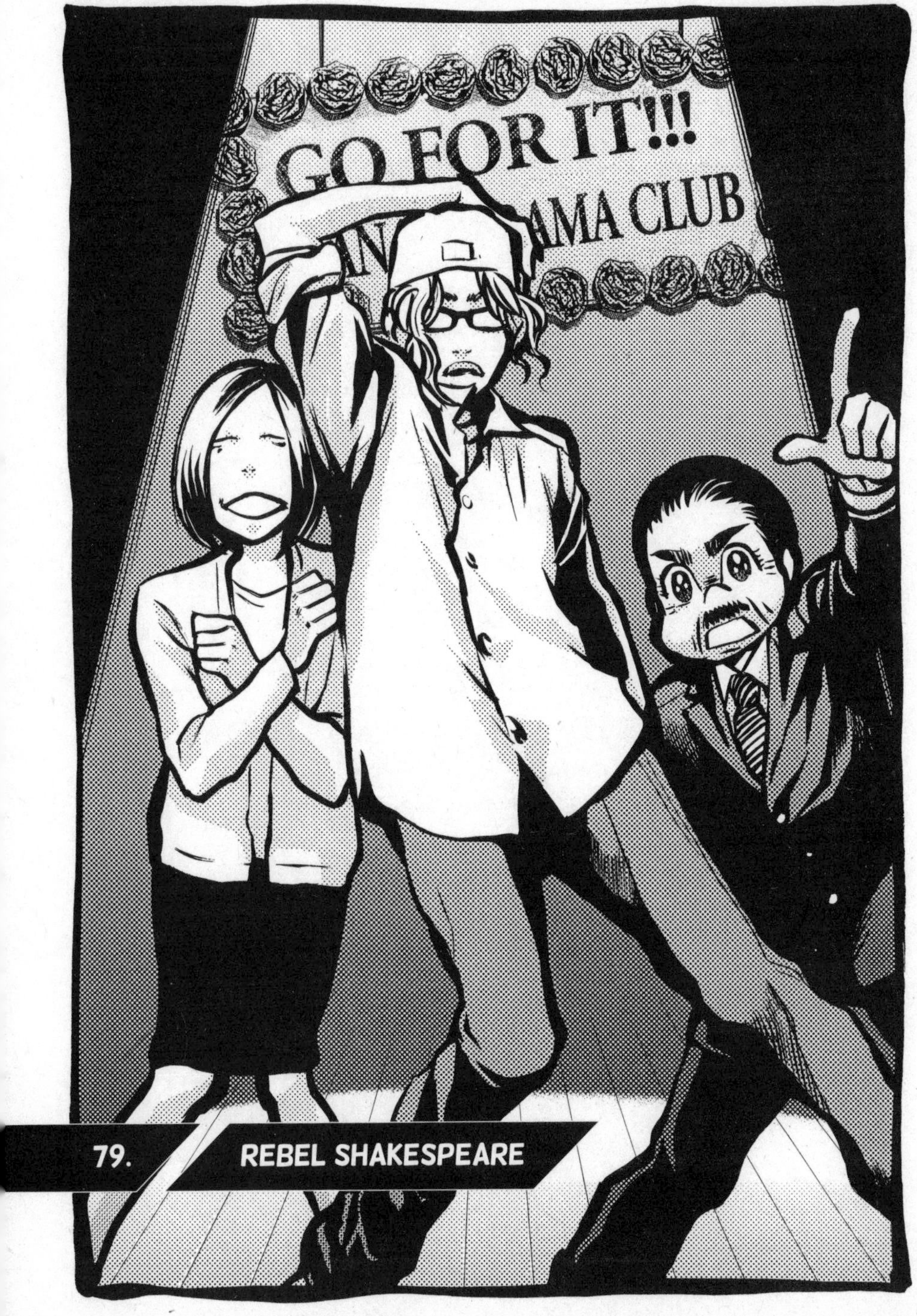
GO FOR IT!!!
AMA CLUB

79. REBEL SHAKESPEARE

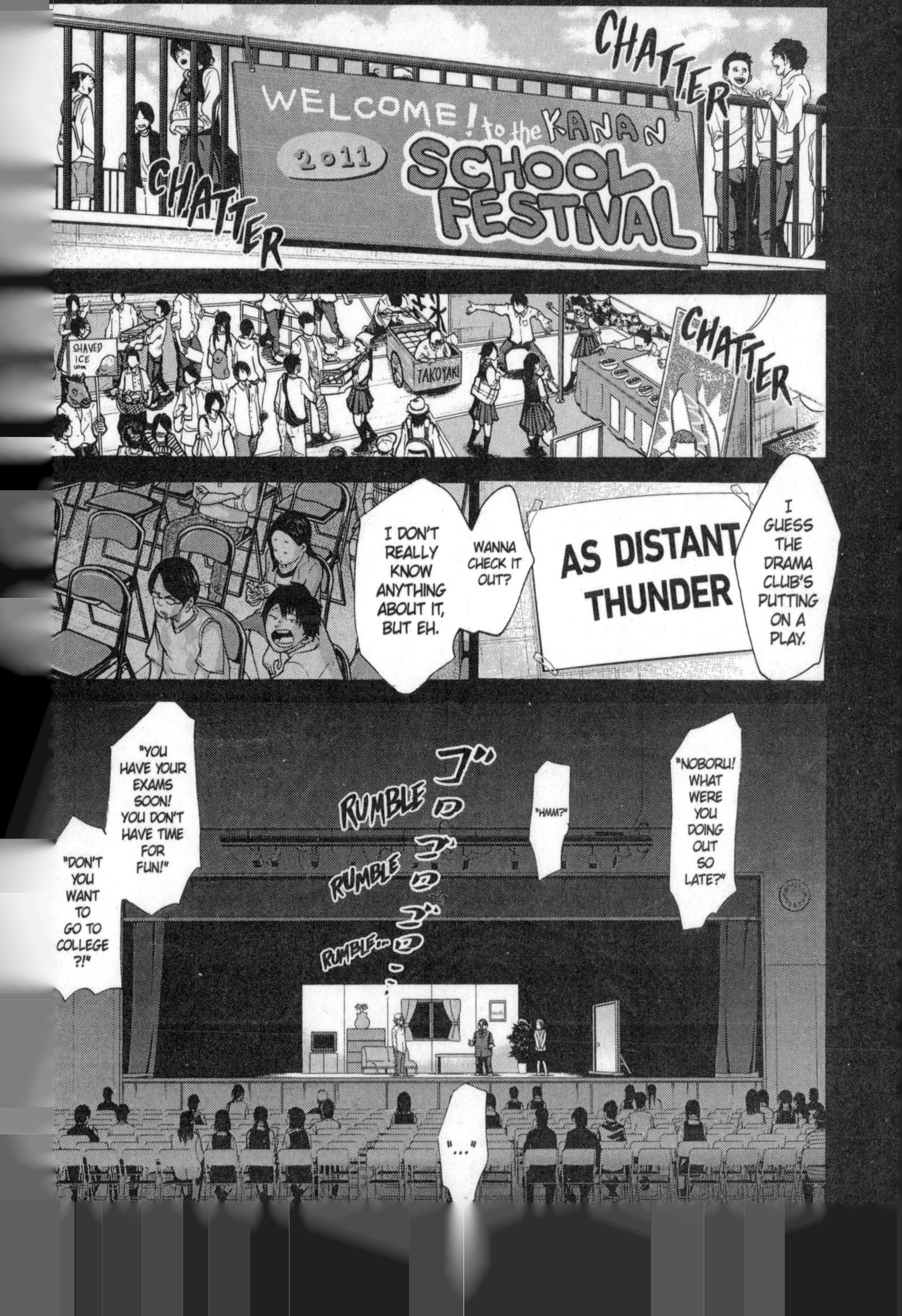
CHATTER
WELCOME! to the KANAN 2011 SCHOOL FESTIVAL
CHATTER
CHATTER
TAKOYAKI
SHAVED ICE
I GUESS THE DRAMA CLUB'S PUTTING ON A PLAY.
AS DISTANT THUNDER
WANNA CHECK IT OUT?
I DON'T REALLY KNOW ANYTHING ABOUT IT, BUT EH.
"NOBORU! WHAT WERE YOU DOING OUT SO LATE?"
"HMM?"
ゴロ RUMBLE
ゴロ RUMBLE
ゴロ… RUMBLE…
"YOU HAVE YOUR EXAMS SOON! YOU DON'T HAVE TIME FOR FUN!"
"DON'T YOU WANT TO GO TO COLLEGE?!"
"..."

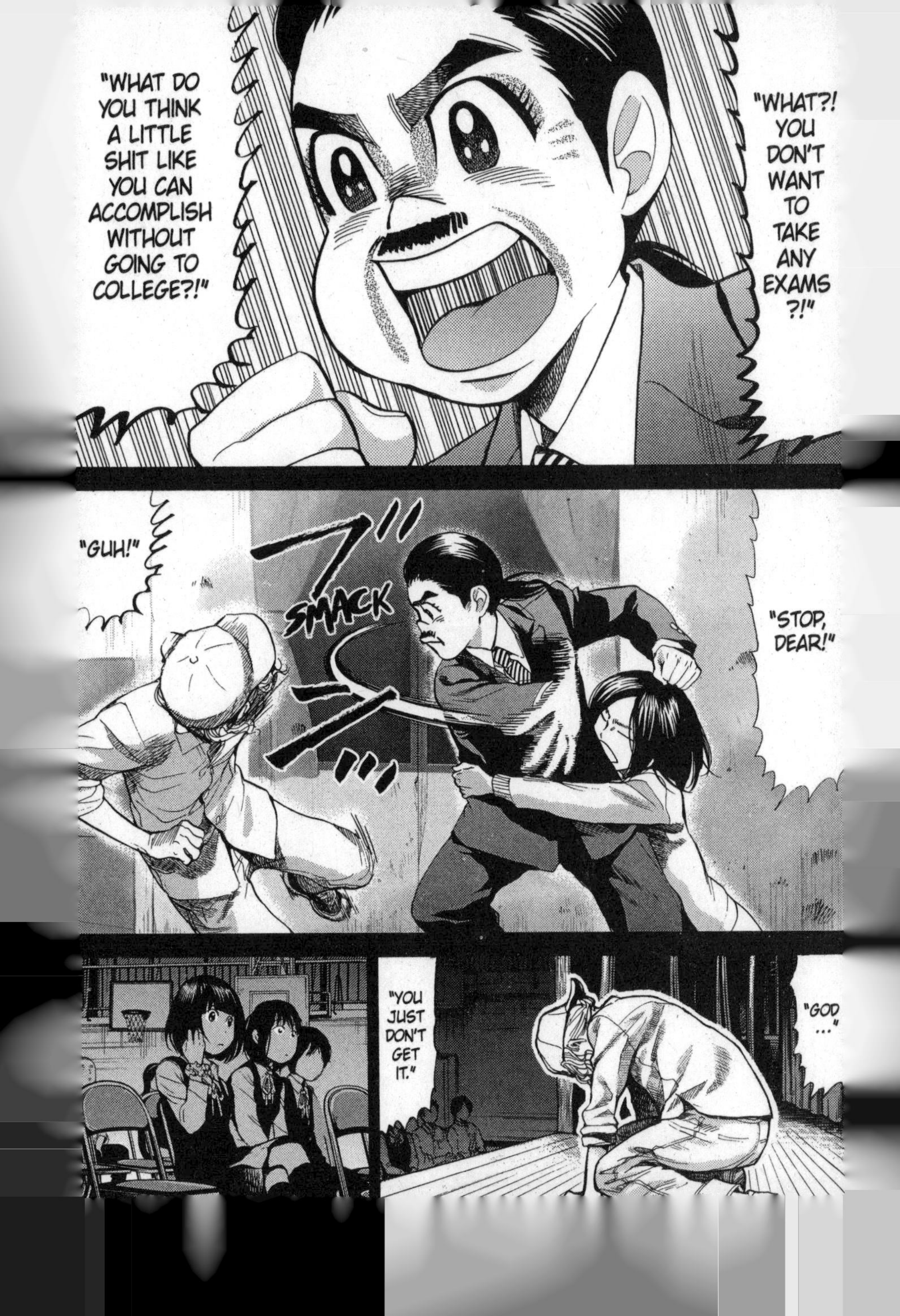
"WHAT?! YOU DON'T WANT TO TAKE ANY EXAMS ?!"
"WHAT DO YOU THINK A LITTLE SHIT LIKE YOU CAN ACCOMPLISH WITHOUT GOING TO COLLEGE?!"
SMACK
"GUH!"
"STOP, DEAR!"
"GOD ..."
"YOU JUST DON'T GET IT."

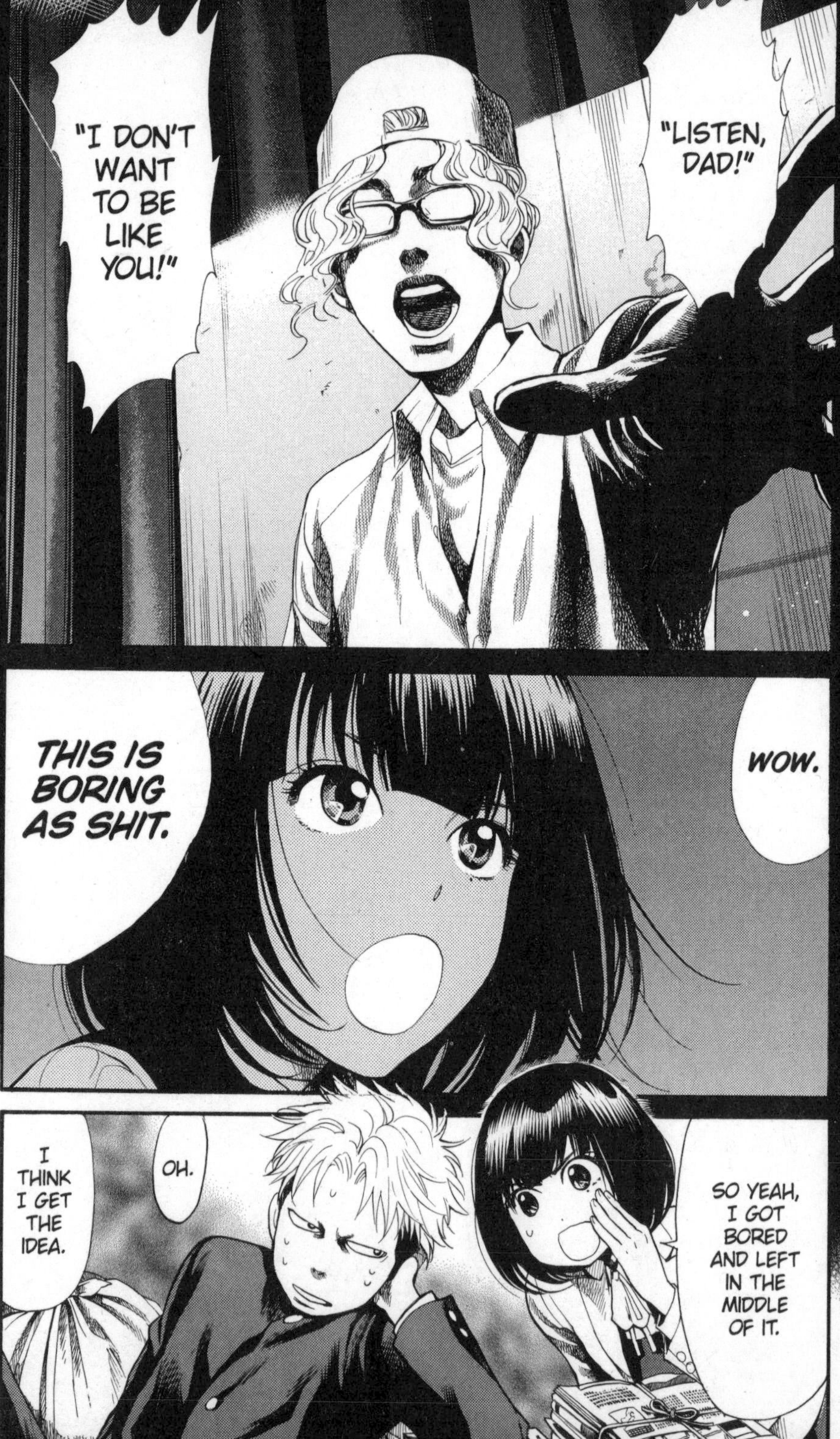
"LISTEN, DAD!"
"I DON'T WANT TO BE LIKE YOU!"
WOW.
THIS IS BORING AS SHIT.
SO YEAH, I GOT BORED AND LEFT IN THE MIDDLE OF IT.
OH.
I THINK I GET THE IDEA.

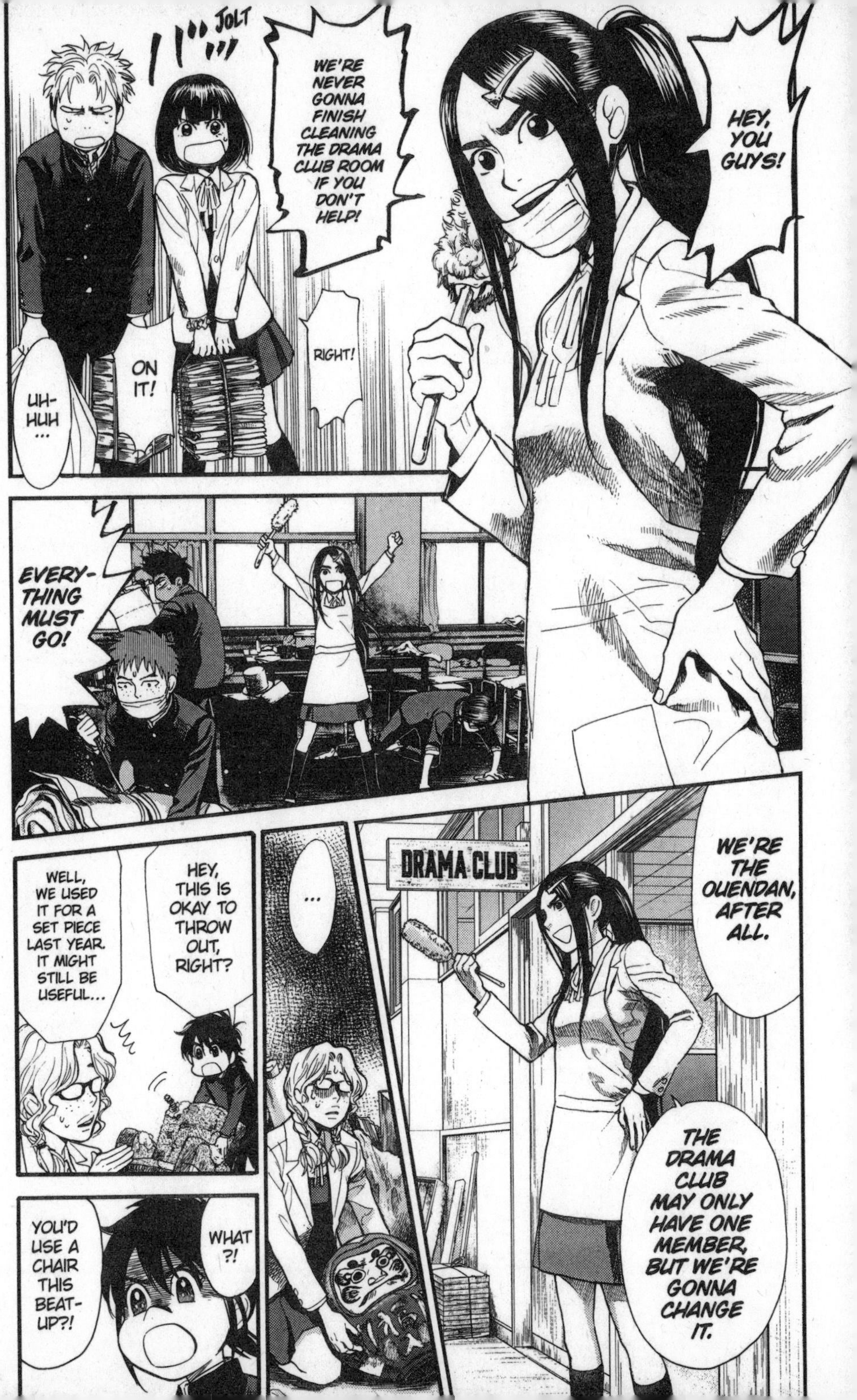
HEY, YOU GUYS!
WE'RE NEVER GONNA FINISH CLEANING THE DRAMA CLUB ROOM IF YOU DON'T HELP!
JOLT
RIGHT!
ON IT!
UH-HUH...
EVERY-THING MUST GO!
DRAMA CLUB
WE'RE THE OUENDAN, AFTER ALL.
THE DRAMA CLUB MAY ONLY HAVE ONE MEMBER, BUT WE'RE GONNA CHANGE IT.
...
HEY, THIS IS OKAY TO THROW OUT, RIGHT?
WELL, WE USED IT FOR A SET PIECE LAST YEAR. IT MIGHT STILL BE USEFUL...
WHAT?!
YOU'D USE A CHAIR THIS BEAT-UP?!

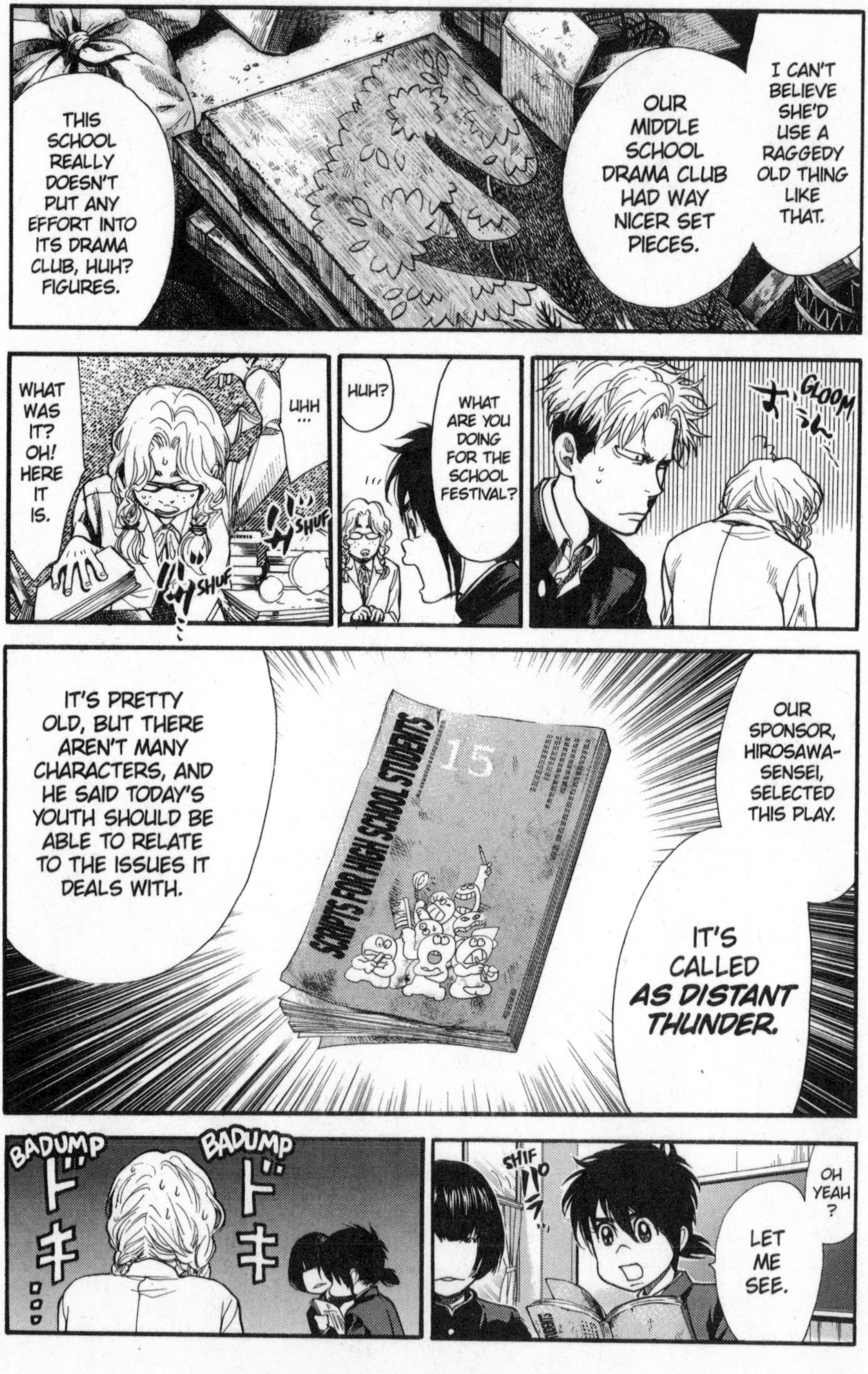

I CAN'T BELIEVE SHE'D USE A RAGGEDY OLD THING LIKE THAT.
OUR MIDDLE SCHOOL DRAMA CLUB HAD WAY NICER SET PIECES.
THIS SCHOOL REALLY DOESN'T PUT ANY EFFORT INTO ITS DRAMA CLUB, HUH? FIGURES.
GLOOM
WHAT ARE YOU DOING FOR THE SCHOOL FESTIVAL?
HUH?
UHH ...
WHAT WAS IT? OH! HERE IT IS.
SHUF
SHUF
OUR SPONSOR, HIROSAWA-SENSEI, SELECTED THIS PLAY.
SCRIPTS FOR HIGH SCHOOL STUDENTS
15
IT'S PRETTY OLD, BUT THERE AREN'T MANY CHARACTERS, AND HE SAID TODAY'S YOUTH SHOULD BE ABLE TO RELATE TO THE ISSUES IT DEALS WITH.
IT'S CALLED ***AS DISTANT THUNDER.***
OH YEAH?
LET ME SEE.
SHIF
BADUMP
ドキ
BADUMP
ドキ

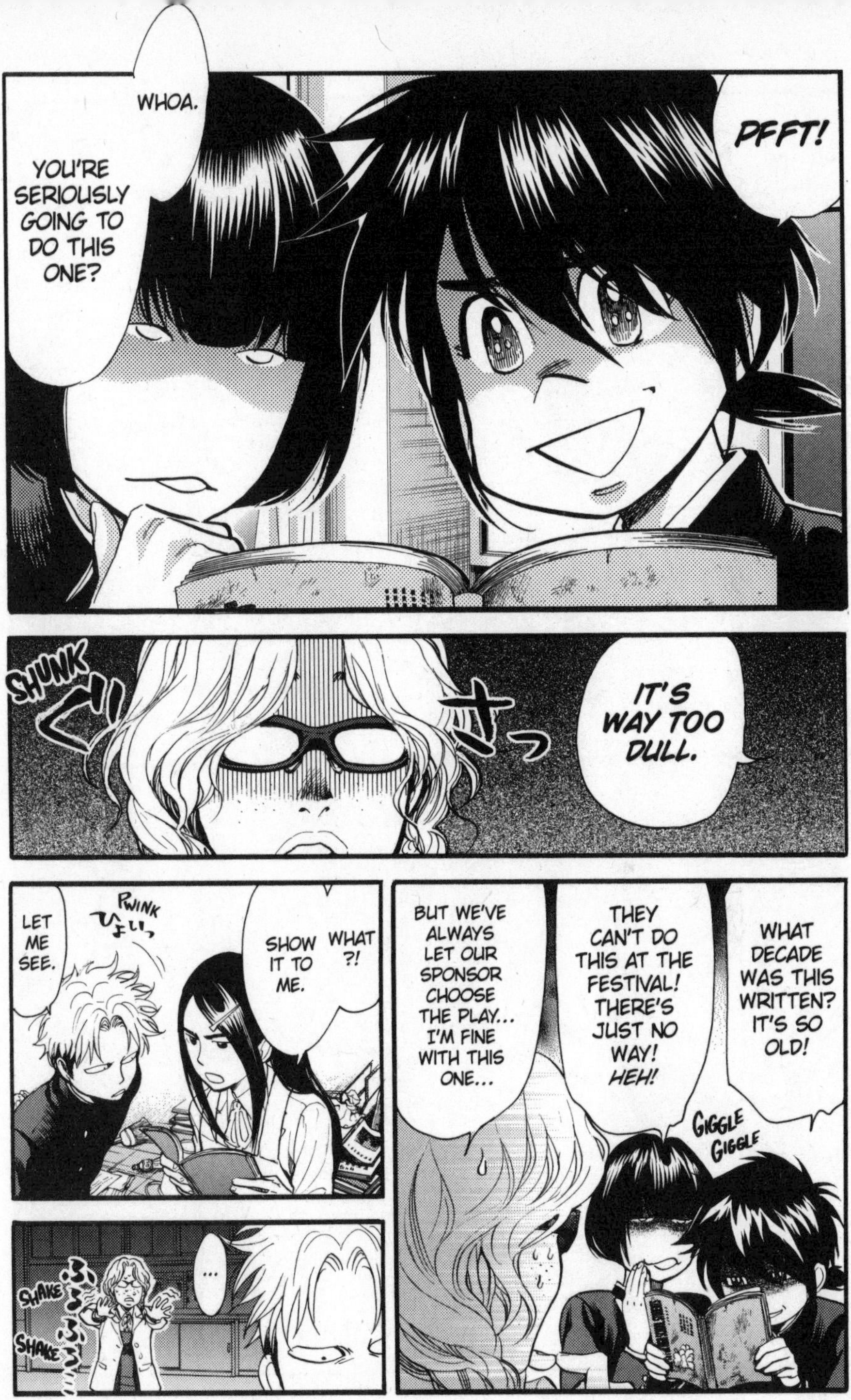
PFFT!
WHOA.
YOU'RE SERIOUSLY GOING TO DO THIS ONE?
IT'S WAY TOO DULL.
SHUNK
WHAT DECADE WAS THIS WRITTEN? IT'S SO OLD!
THEY CAN'T DO THIS AT THE FESTIVAL! THERE'S JUST NO WAY! HEH!
BUT WE'VE ALWAYS LET OUR SPONSOR CHOOSE THE PLAY... I'M FINE WITH THIS ONE...
GIGGLE GIGGLE
WHAT?!
SHOW IT TO ME.
PWINK
LET ME SEE.
...
SHAKE
SHAKE

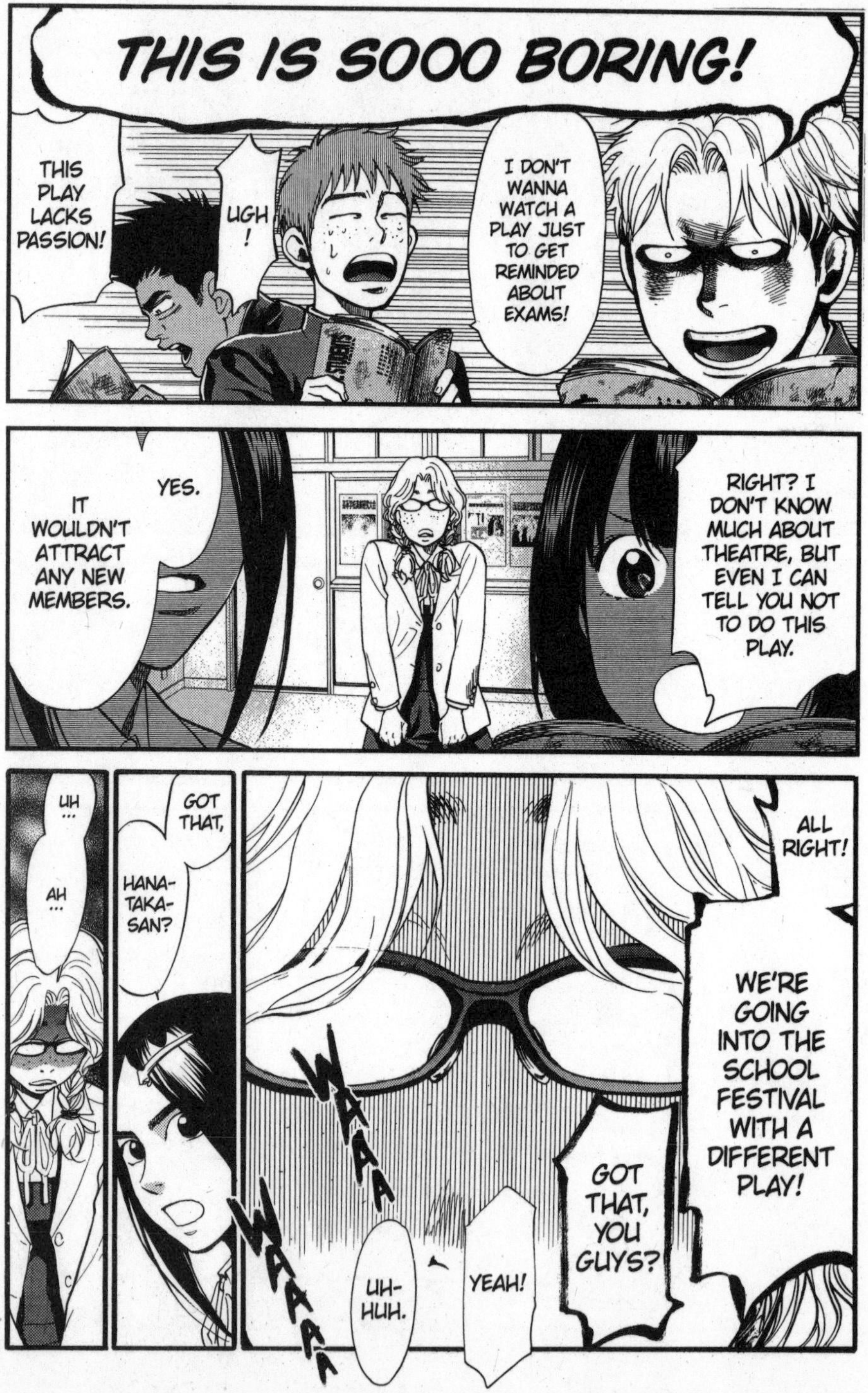
THIS IS SOOO BORING!
I DON'T WANNA WATCH A PLAY JUST TO GET REMINDED ABOUT EXAMS!
UGH!
THIS PLAY LACKS PASSION!
RIGHT? I DON'T KNOW MUCH ABOUT THEATRE, BUT EVEN I CAN TELL YOU NOT TO DO THIS PLAY.
YES.
IT WOULDN'T ATTRACT ANY NEW MEMBERS.
ALL RIGHT!
WE'RE GOING INTO THE SCHOOL FESTIVAL WITH A DIFFERENT PLAY!
GOT THAT, YOU GUYS?
YEAH!
UH-HUH.
WAAA
WAAAA
GOT THAT, HANATAKA-SAN?
UH...
AH...

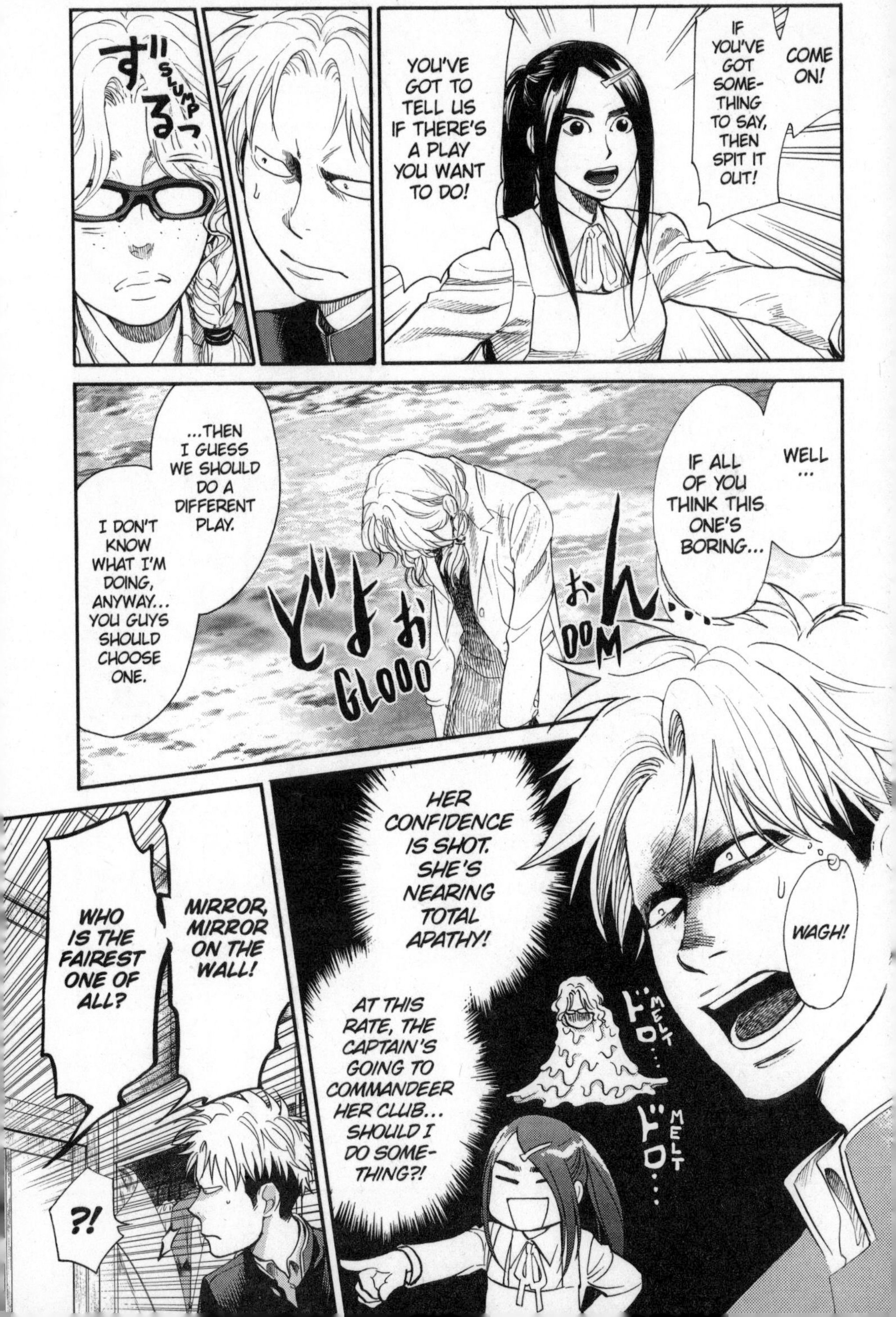
COME ON!
IF YOU'VE GOT SOME-THING TO SAY, THEN SPIT IT OUT!
YOU'VE GOT TO TELL US IF THERE'S A PLAY YOU WANT TO DO!
するっ
SLUMP
WELL...
IF ALL OF YOU THINK THIS ONE'S BORING...
...THEN I GUESS WE SHOULD DO A DIFFERENT PLAY.
I DON'T KNOW WHAT I'M DOING, ANYWAY... YOU GUYS SHOULD CHOOSE ONE.
どよおおん…
GLOOO
OOM
WAGH!
HER CONFIDENCE IS SHOT. SHE'S NEARING TOTAL APATHY!
ドロ…
MELT
ドロ…
MELT
AT THIS RATE, THE CAPTAIN'S GOING TO COMMANDEER HER CLUB... SHOULD I DO SOME-THING?!
MIRROR, MIRROR ON THE WALL!
WHO IS THE FAIREST ONE OF ALL?
?!

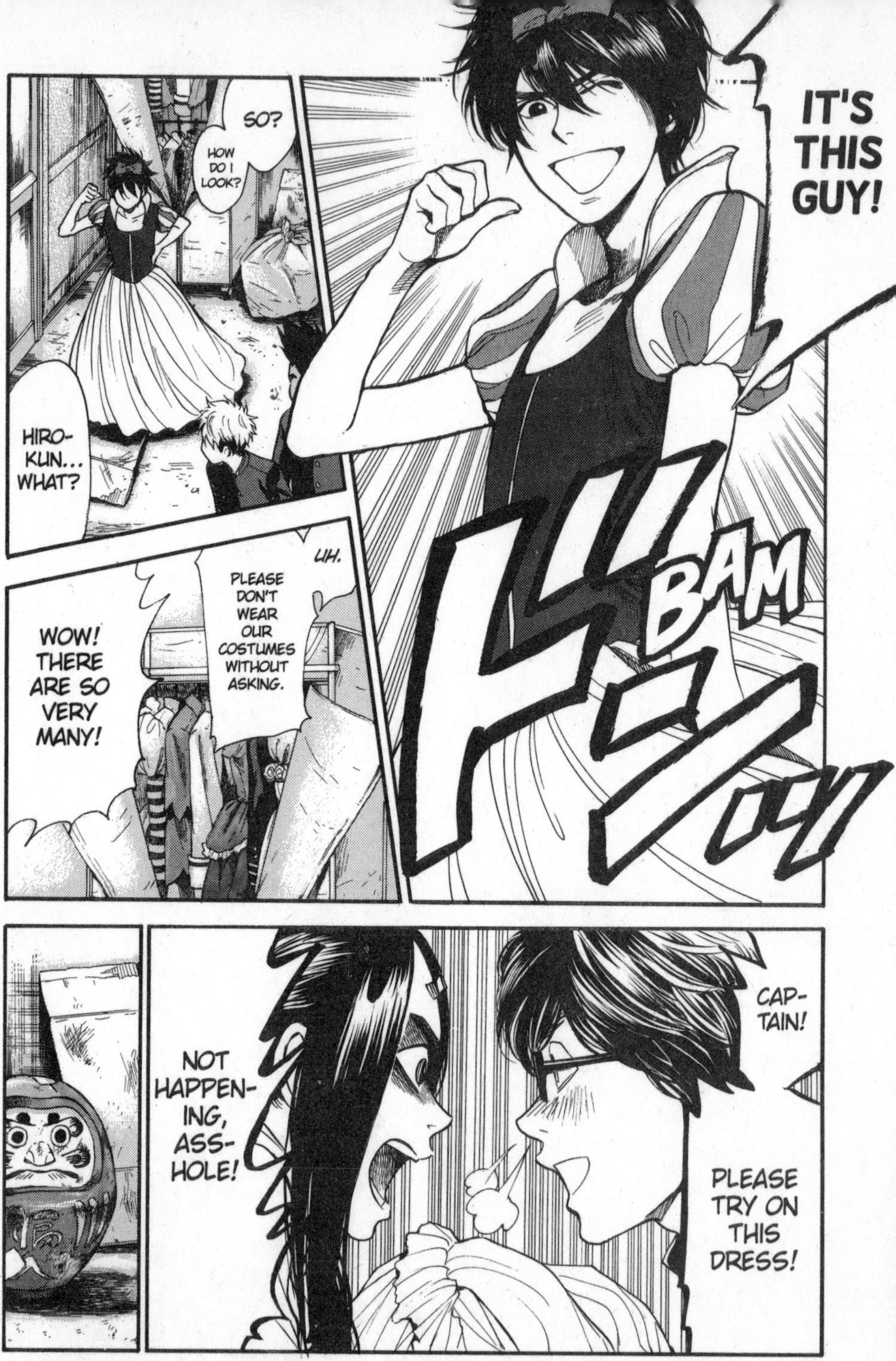
IT'S THIS GUY!
BAM
SO?
HOW DO I LOOK?
HIRO-KUN... WHAT?
UH.
PLEASE DON'T WEAR OUR COSTUMES WITHOUT ASKING.
WOW! THERE ARE SO VERY MANY!
CAP-TAIN!
PLEASE TRY ON THIS DRESS!
NOT HAPPEN-ING, ASS-HOLE!

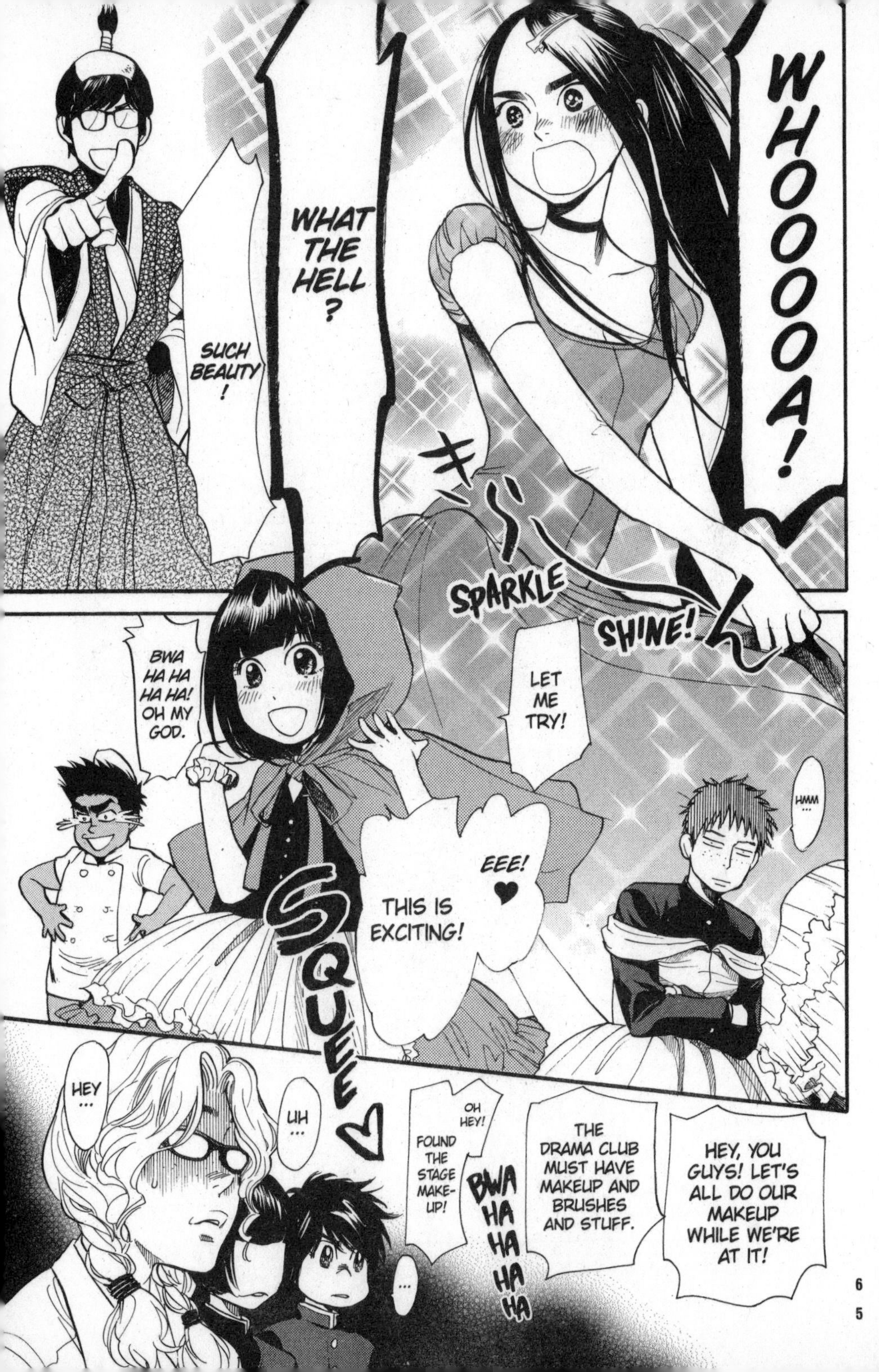

WHOOOOOA!
WHAT THE HELL?
SPARKLE
SHINE!
SUCH BEAUTY!
HMM...
LET ME TRY!
EEE! ♥
THIS IS EXCITING!
SQUEEE ♥
BWA HA HA HA HA! OH MY GOD.
HEY, YOU GUYS! LET'S ALL DO OUR MAKEUP WHILE WE'RE AT IT!
THE DRAMA CLUB MUST HAVE MAKEUP AND BRUSHES AND STUFF.
BWA HA HA HA HA HA
OH HEY!
FOUND THE STAGE MAKE-UP!
UH...
HEY...
...

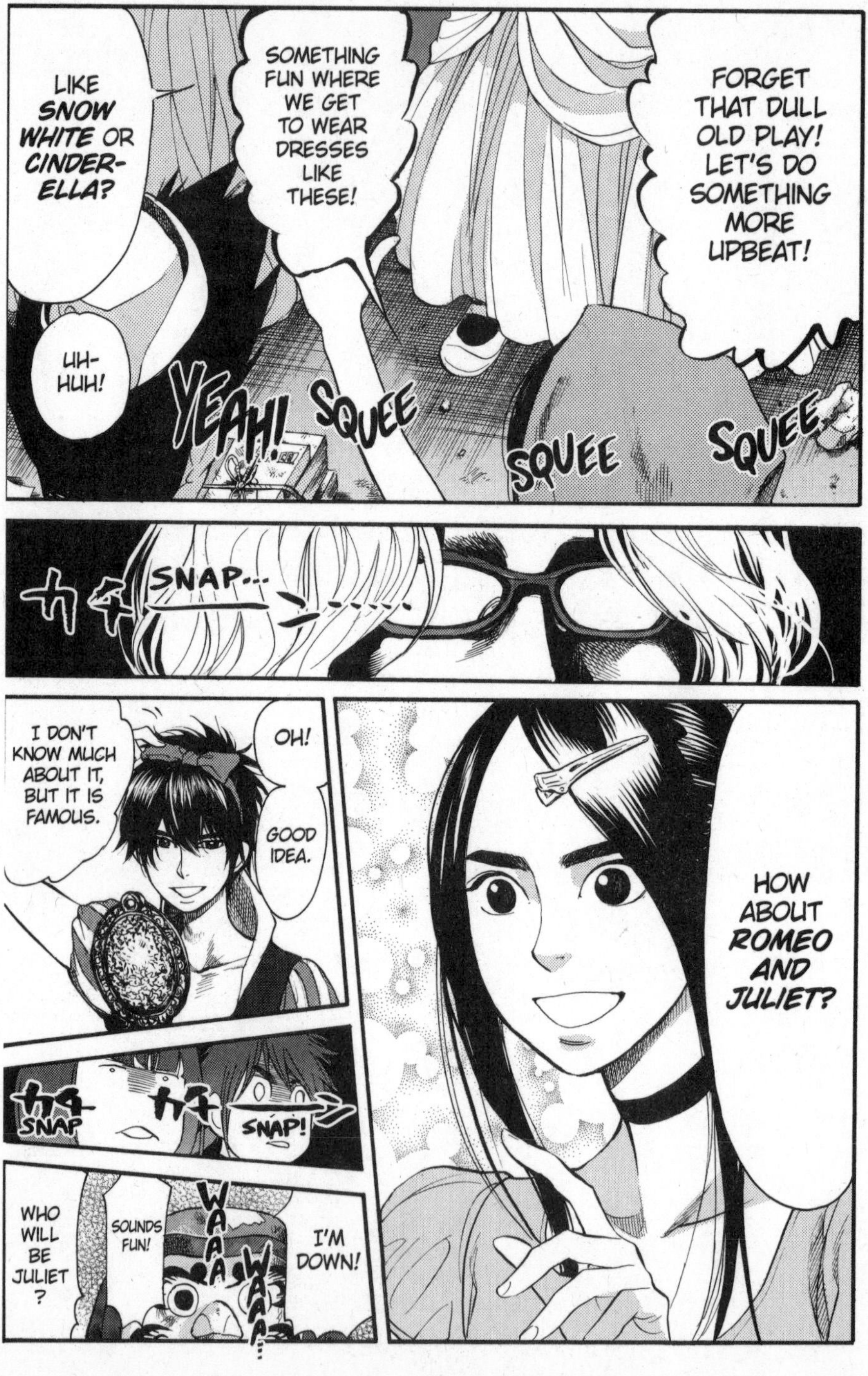
FORGET THAT DULL OLD PLAY! LET'S DO SOMETHING MORE UPBEAT!
SOMETHING FUN WHERE WE GET TO WEAR DRESSES LIKE THESE!
LIKE SNOW WHITE OR CINDERELLA?
UH-HUH!
SQUEE
SQUEE
SQUEE
YEAH!
SNAP...
HOW ABOUT ROMEO AND JULIET?
OH! GOOD IDEA.
I DON'T KNOW MUCH ABOUT IT, BUT IT IS FAMOUS.
SNAP!
SNAP
I'M DOWN!
SOUNDS FUN!
WHO WILL BE JULIET?
WAAA
WAAA...

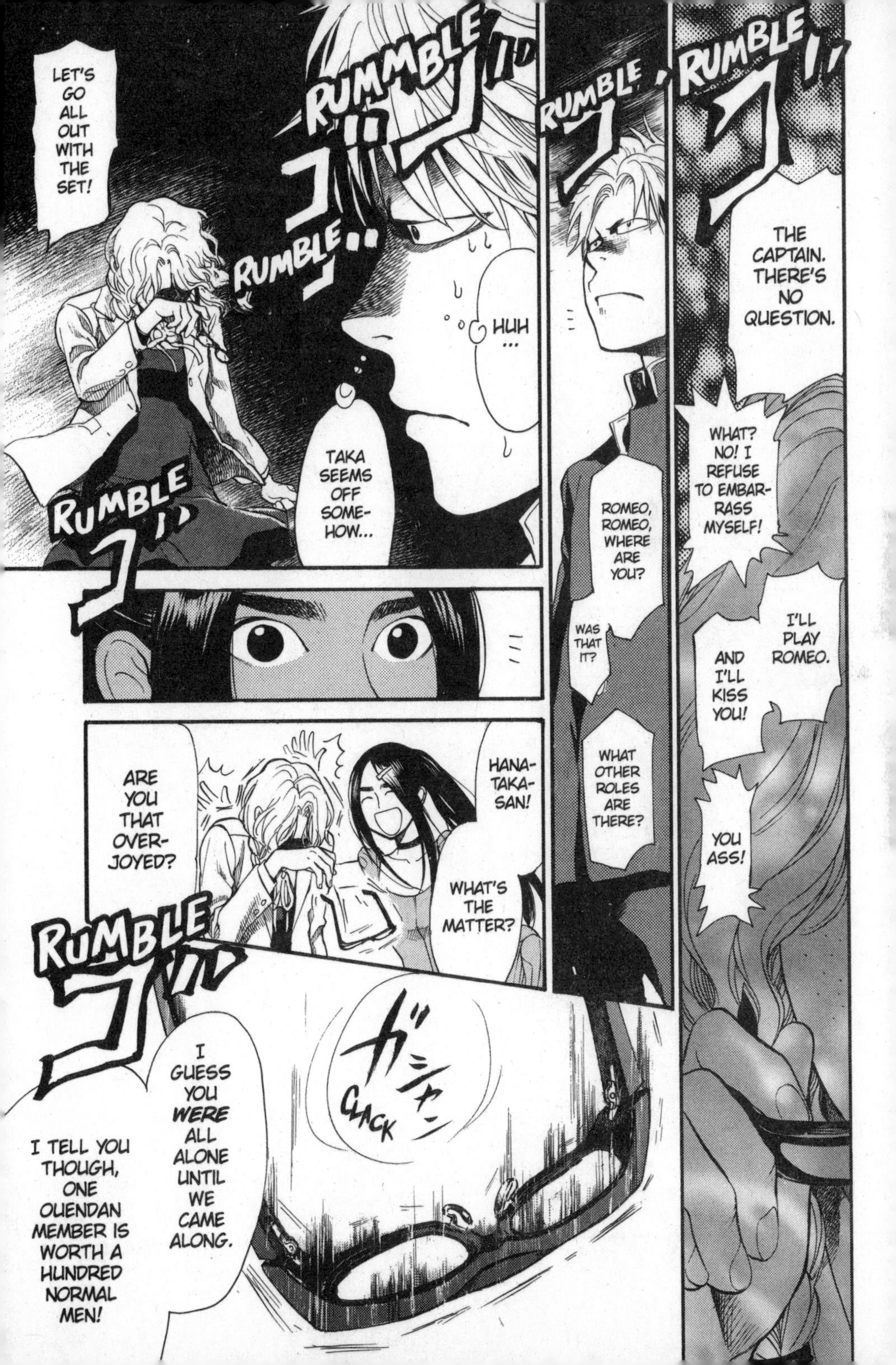
RUMBLE, RUMBLE
THE CAPTAIN. THERE'S NO QUESTION.
WHAT? NO! I REFUSE TO EMBARRASS MYSELF!
I'LL PLAY ROMEO.
AND I'LL KISS YOU!
YOU ASS!
ROMEO, ROMEO, WHERE ARE YOU?
WAS THAT IT?
WHAT OTHER ROLES ARE THERE?
RUMMBLE
LET'S GO ALL OUT WITH THE SET!
RUMBLE..
HUH...
TAKA SEEMS OFF SOMEHOW...
RUMBLE
HANA-TAKA-SAN!
ARE YOU THAT OVERJOYED?
WHAT'S THE MATTER?
RUMBLE
CLACK
I GUESS YOU *WERE* ALL ALONE UNTIL WE CAME ALONG.
I TELL YOU THOUGH, ONE OUENDAN MEMBER IS WORTH A HUNDRED NORMAL MEN!

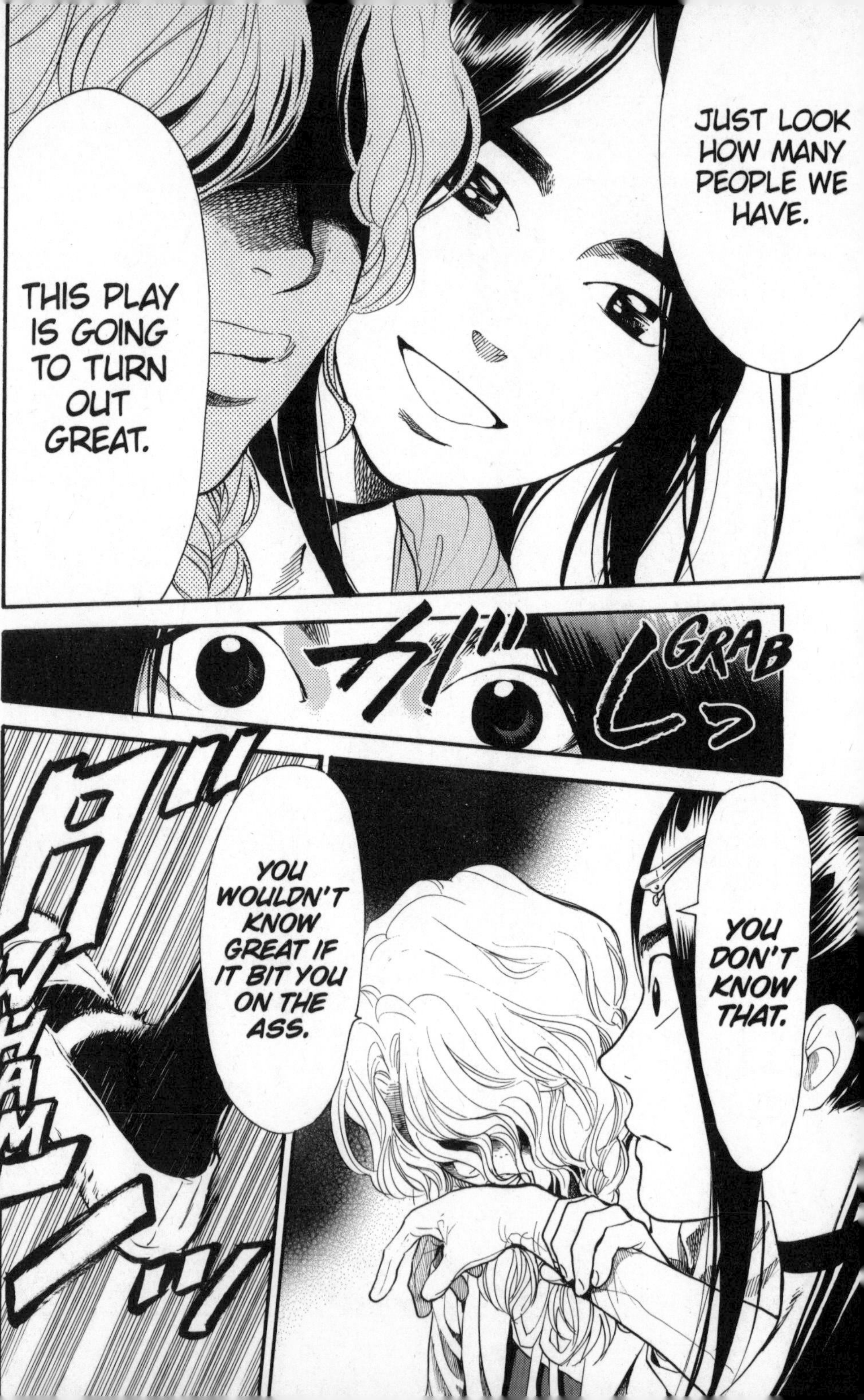
JUST LOOK HOW MANY PEOPLE WE HAVE.
THIS PLAY IS GOING TO TURN OUT GREAT.
GRAB
YOU DON'T KNOW THAT.
YOU WOULDN'T KNOW GREAT IF IT BIT YOU ON THE ASS.
WHAM!!

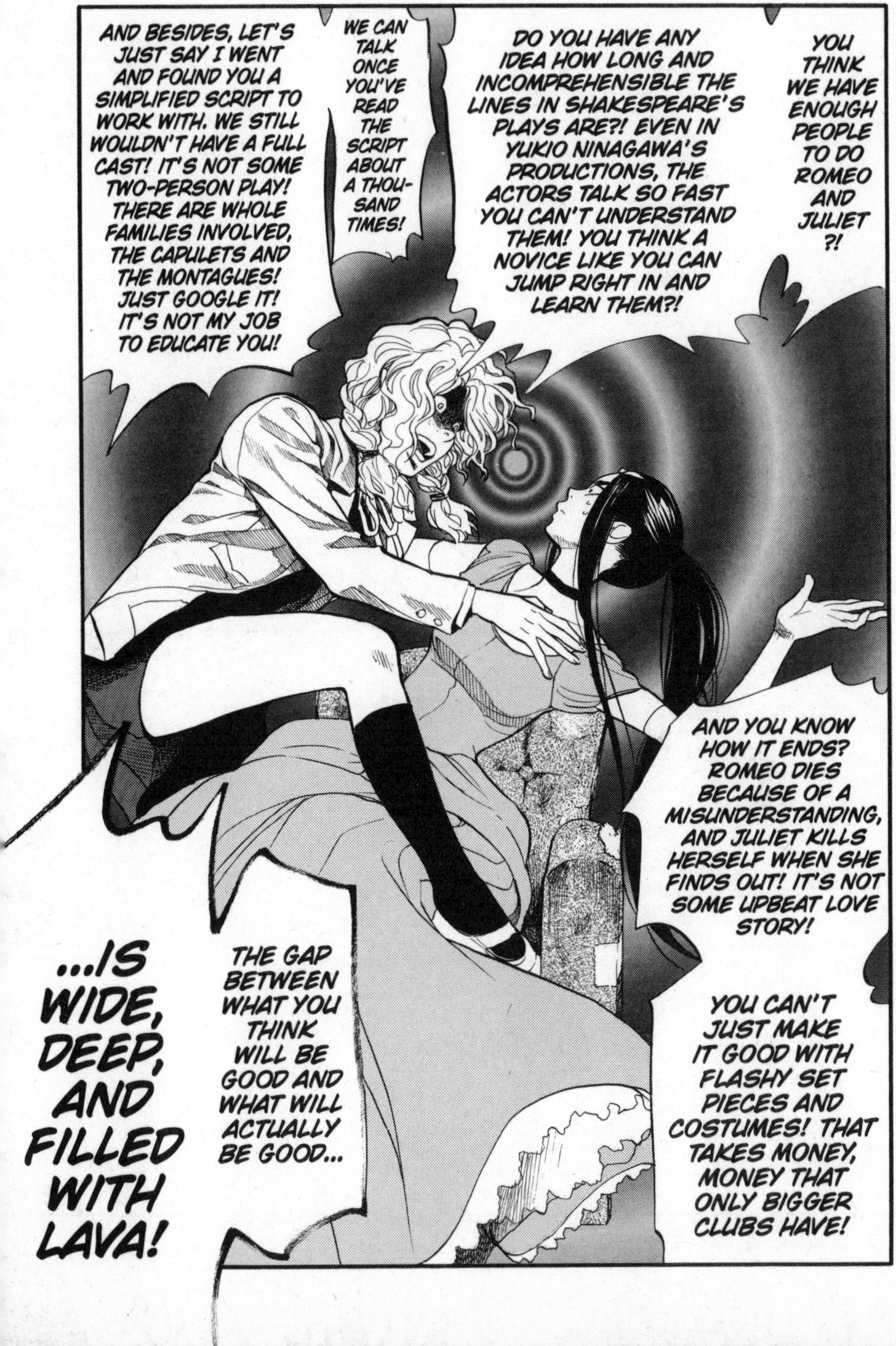

YOU THINK WE HAVE ENOUGH PEOPLE TO DO ROMEO AND JULIET?!
DO YOU HAVE ANY IDEA HOW LONG AND INCOMPREHENSIBLE THE LINES IN SHAKESPEARE'S PLAYS ARE?! EVEN IN YUKIO NINAGAWA'S PRODUCTIONS, THE ACTORS TALK SO FAST YOU CAN'T UNDERSTAND THEM! YOU THINK A NOVICE LIKE YOU CAN JUMP RIGHT IN AND LEARN THEM?!
WE CAN TALK ONCE YOU'VE READ THE SCRIPT ABOUT A THOUSAND TIMES!
AND BESIDES, LET'S JUST SAY I WENT AND FOUND YOU A SIMPLIFIED SCRIPT TO WORK WITH. WE STILL WOULDN'T HAVE A FULL CAST! IT'S NOT SOME TWO-PERSON PLAY! THERE ARE WHOLE FAMILIES INVOLVED, THE CAPULETS AND THE MONTAGUES! JUST GOOGLE IT! IT'S NOT MY JOB TO EDUCATE YOU!
AND YOU KNOW HOW IT ENDS? ROMEO DIES BECAUSE OF A MISUNDERSTANDING, AND JULIET KILLS HERSELF WHEN SHE FINDS OUT! IT'S NOT SOME UPBEAT LOVE STORY!
YOU CAN'T JUST MAKE IT GOOD WITH FLASHY SET PIECES AND COSTUMES! THAT TAKES MONEY, MONEY THAT ONLY BIGGER CLUBS HAVE!
THE GAP BETWEEN WHAT YOU THINK WILL BE GOOD AND WHAT WILL ACTUALLY BE GOOD...
...IS WIDE, DEEP, AND FILLED WITH LAVA!

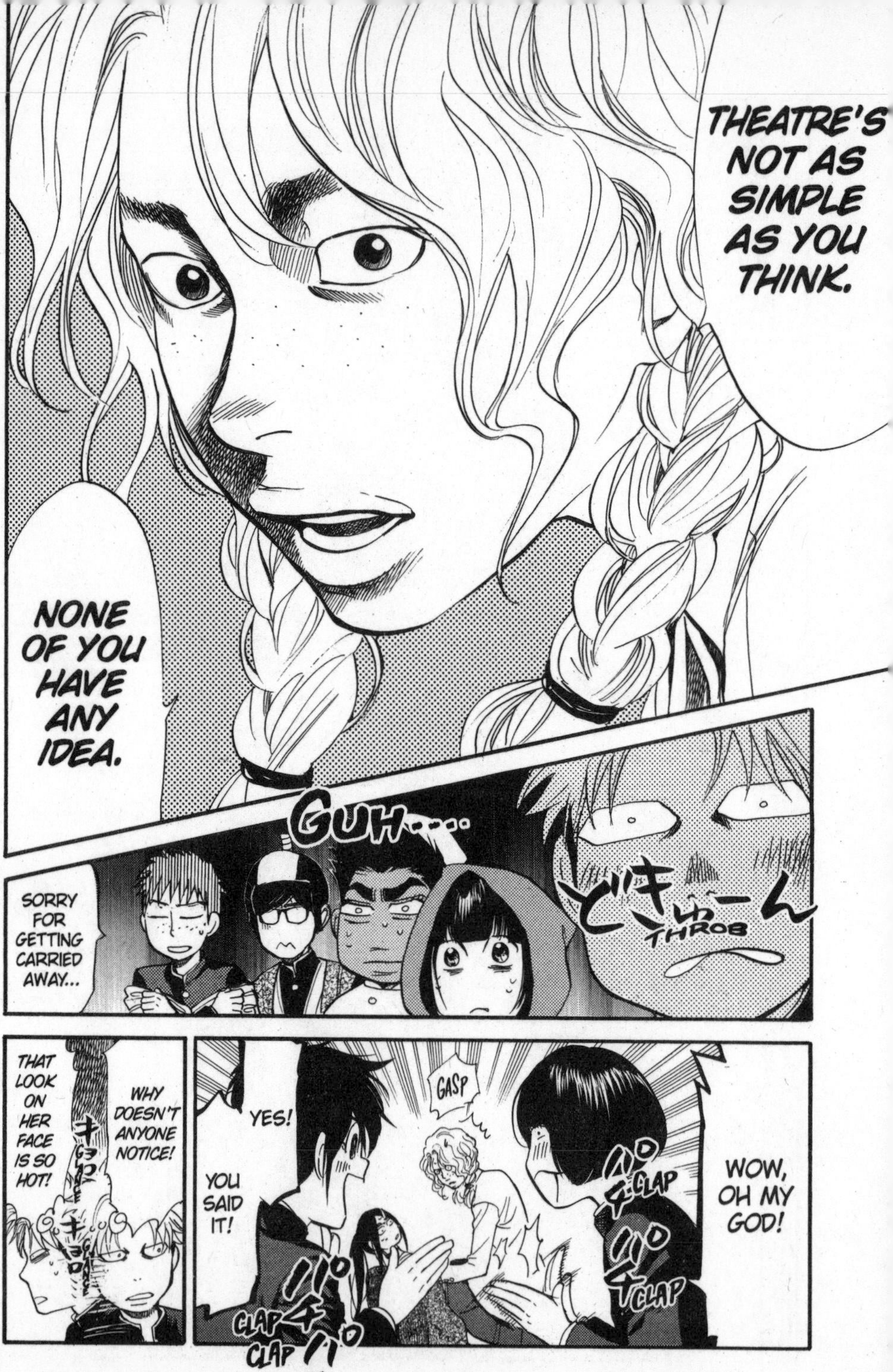
THEATRE'S NOT AS SIMPLE AS YOU THINK.
NONE OF YOU HAVE ANY IDEA.
GUH....
THROB
SORRY FOR GETTING CARRIED AWAY...
WOW, OH MY GOD!
CLAP
CLAP
GASP
YES!
YOU SAID IT!
CLAP
CLAP
WHY DOESN'T ANYONE NOTICE!
THAT LOOK ON HER FACE IS SO HOT!

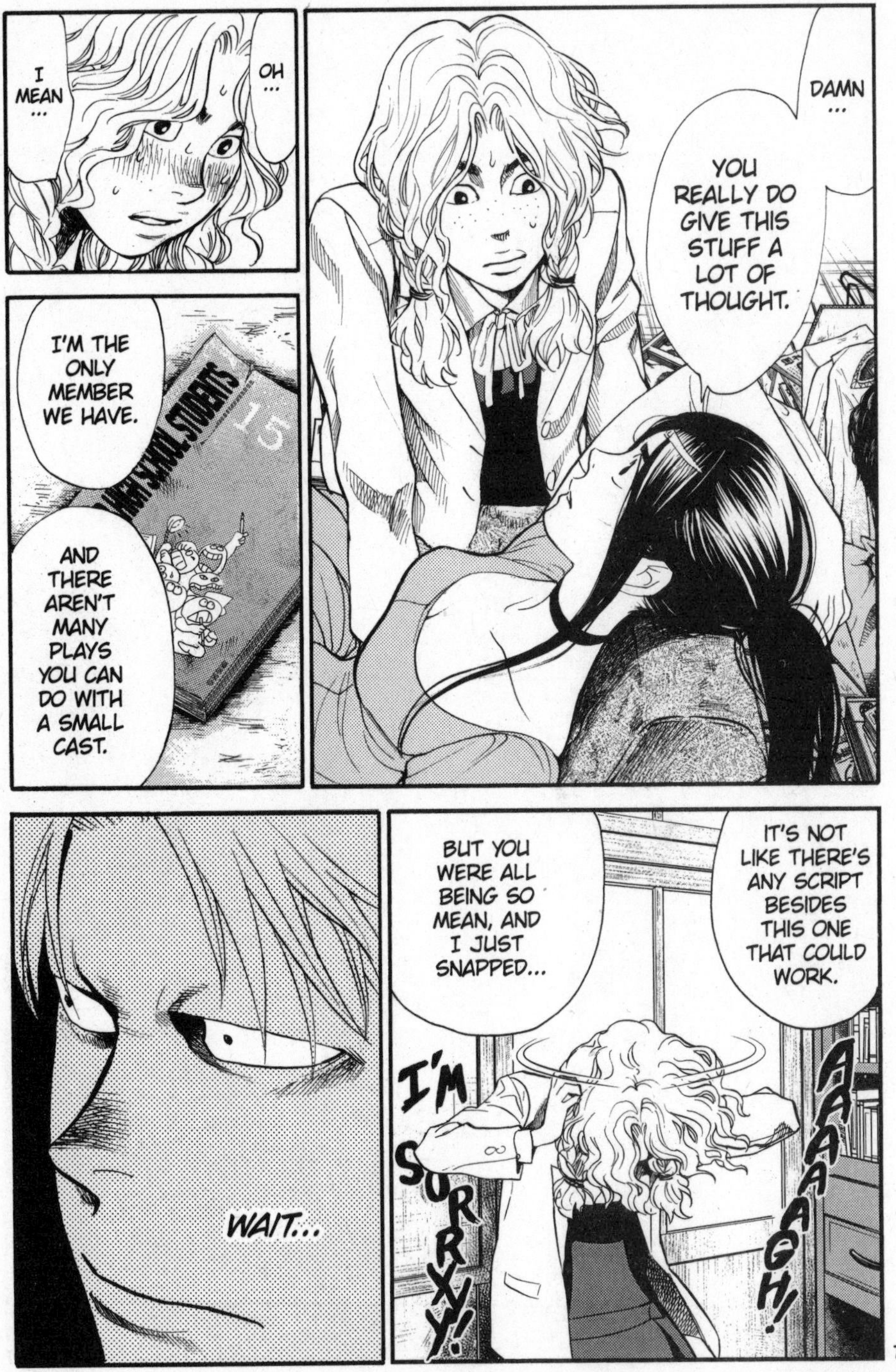
DAMN...
YOU REALLY DO GIVE THIS STUFF A LOT OF THOUGHT.
OH...
I MEAN...
HIGH SCHOOL STUDENTS
15
I'M THE ONLY MEMBER WE HAVE.
AND THERE AREN'T MANY PLAYS YOU CAN DO WITH A SMALL CAST.
IT'S NOT LIKE THERE'S ANY SCRIPT BESIDES THIS ONE THAT COULD WORK.
BUT YOU WERE ALL BEING SO MEAN, AND I JUST SNAPPED...
AAAAAAGH!
I'M SORRY!
WAIT...

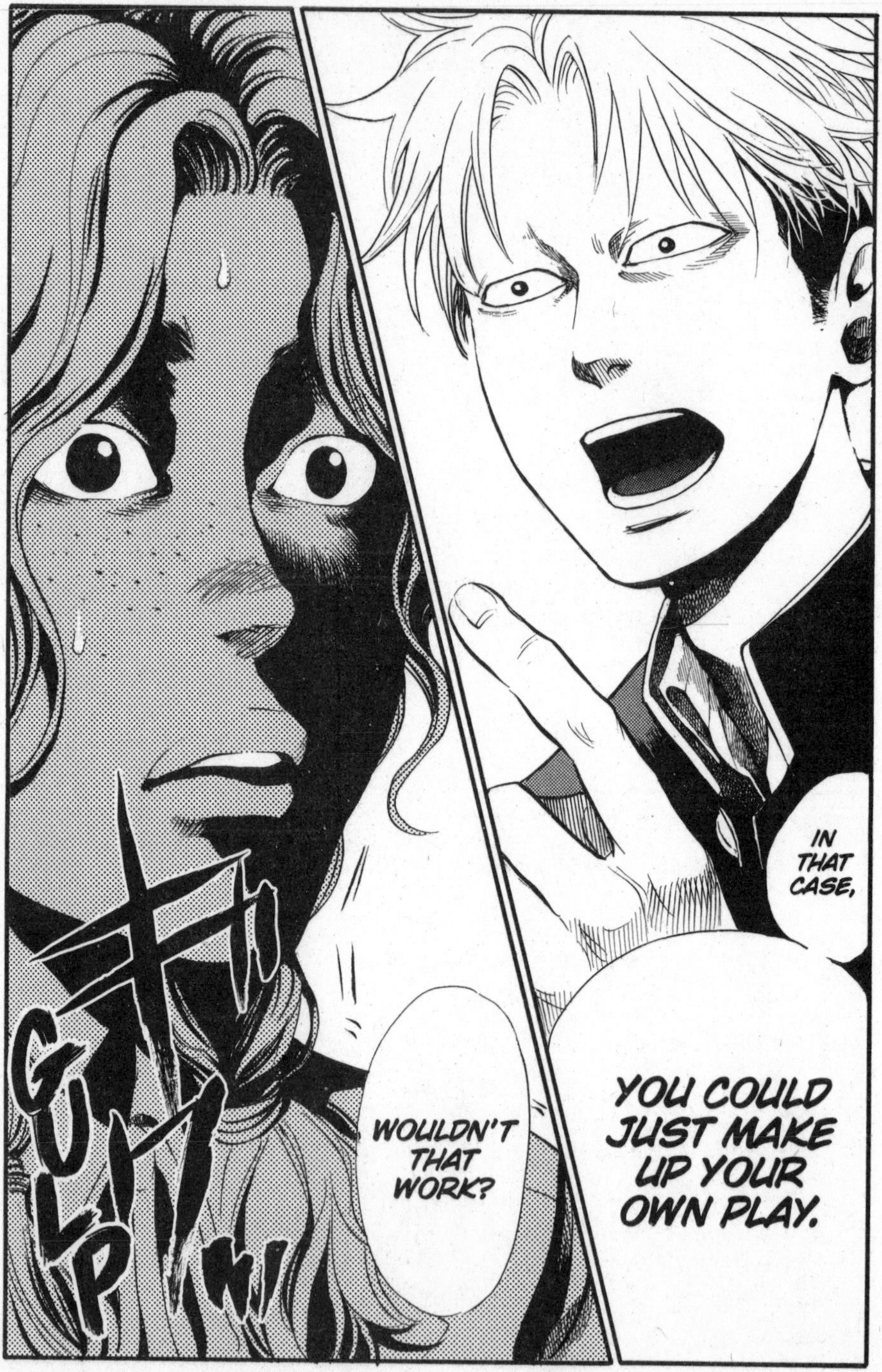
IN THAT CASE,
YOU COULD JUST MAKE UP YOUR OWN PLAY.
WOULDN'T THAT WORK?
GULP!

80. SONG AND DANCE! THE DREAM PLAY!

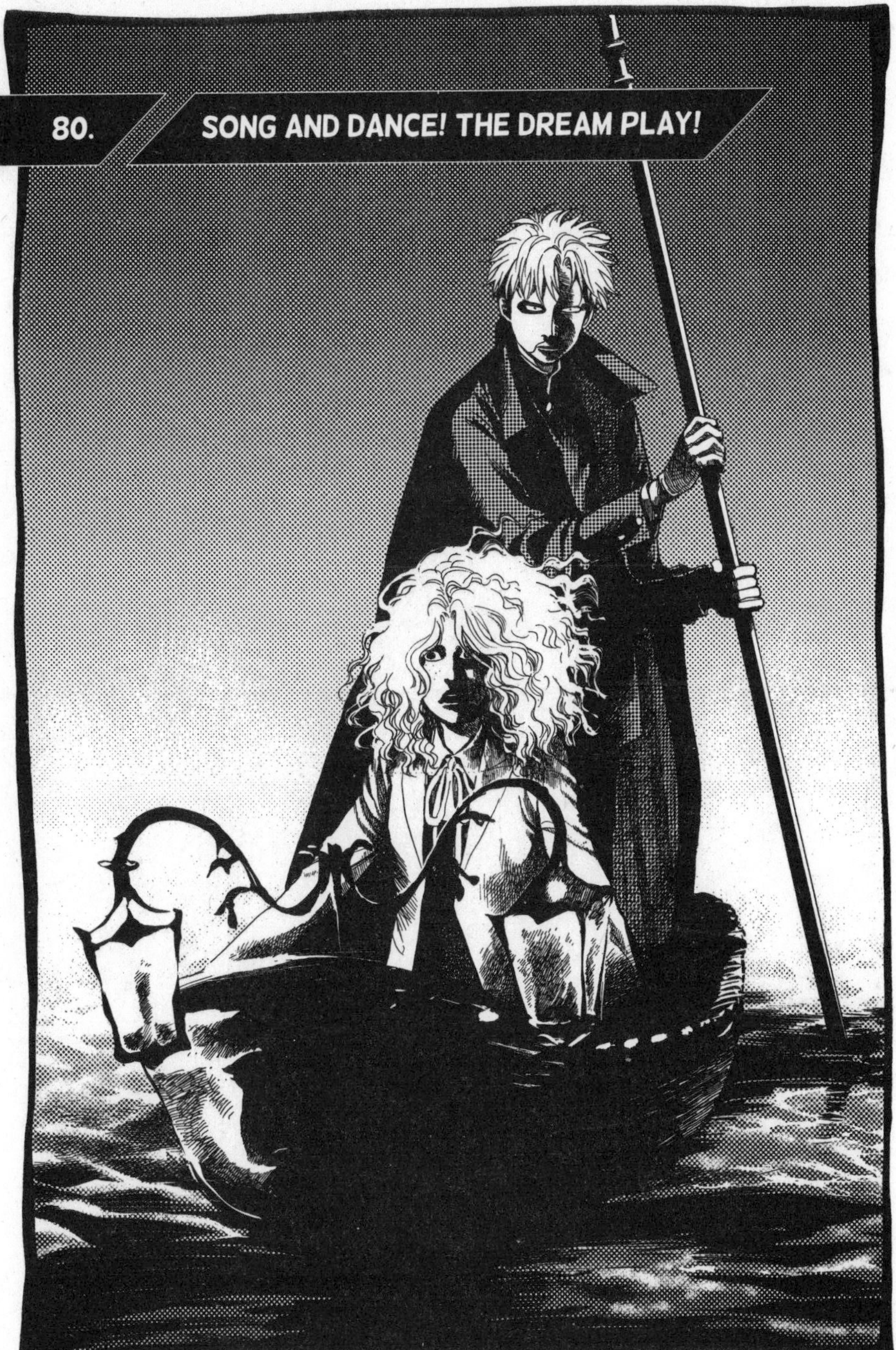

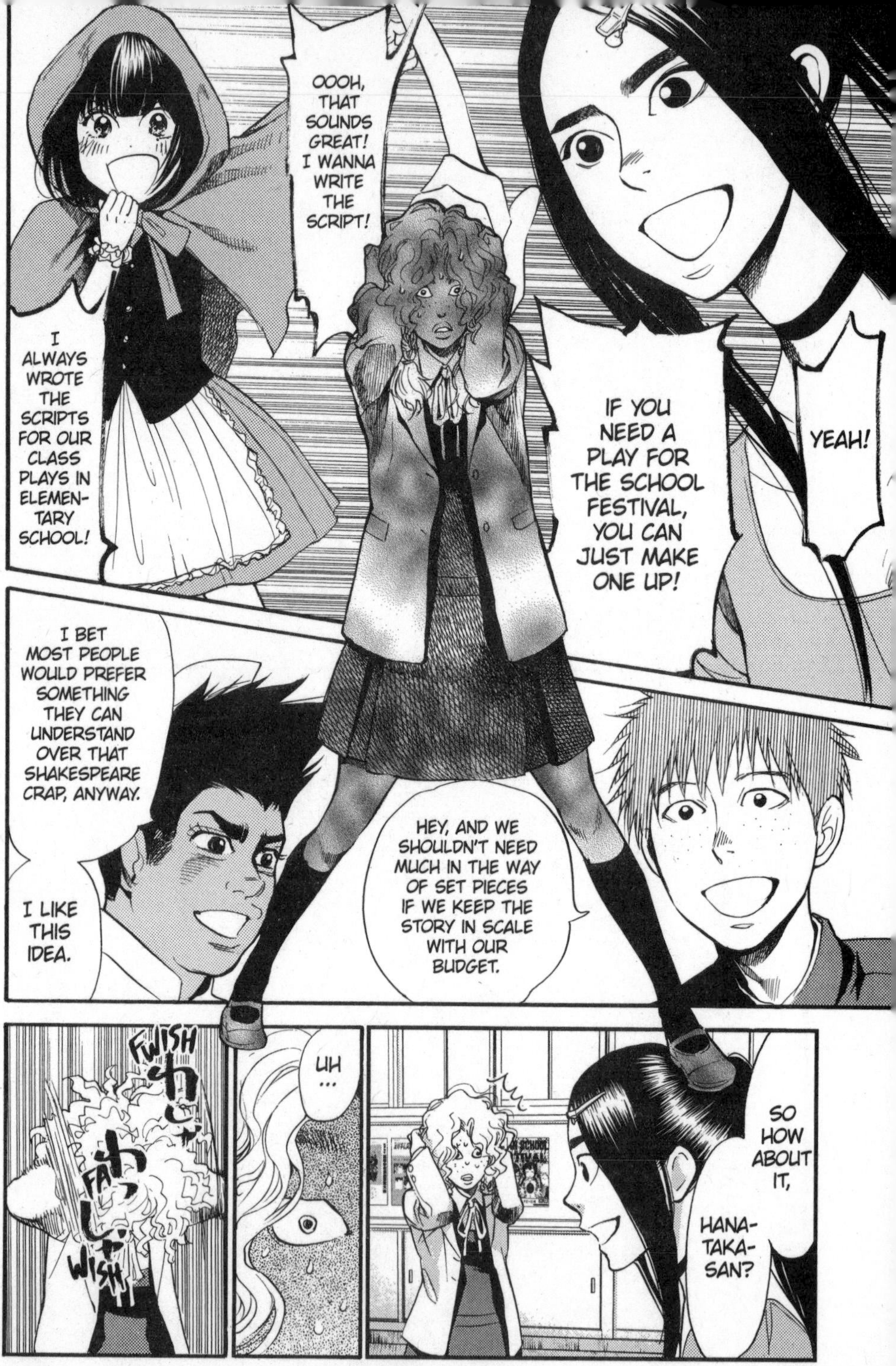
YEAH!
IF YOU NEED A PLAY FOR THE SCHOOL FESTIVAL, YOU CAN JUST MAKE ONE UP!
OOOH, THAT SOUNDS GREAT! I WANNA WRITE THE SCRIPT!
I ALWAYS WROTE THE SCRIPTS FOR OUR CLASS PLAYS IN ELEMENTARY SCHOOL!
HEY, AND WE SHOULDN'T NEED MUCH IN THE WAY OF SET PIECES IF WE KEEP THE STORY IN SCALE WITH OUR BUDGET.
I BET MOST PEOPLE WOULD PREFER SOMETHING THEY CAN UNDERSTAND OVER THAT SHAKESPEARE CRAP, ANYWAY.
I LIKE THIS IDEA.
SO HOW ABOUT IT, HANA-TAKA-SAN?
UH ...
FWISH
FA WISH

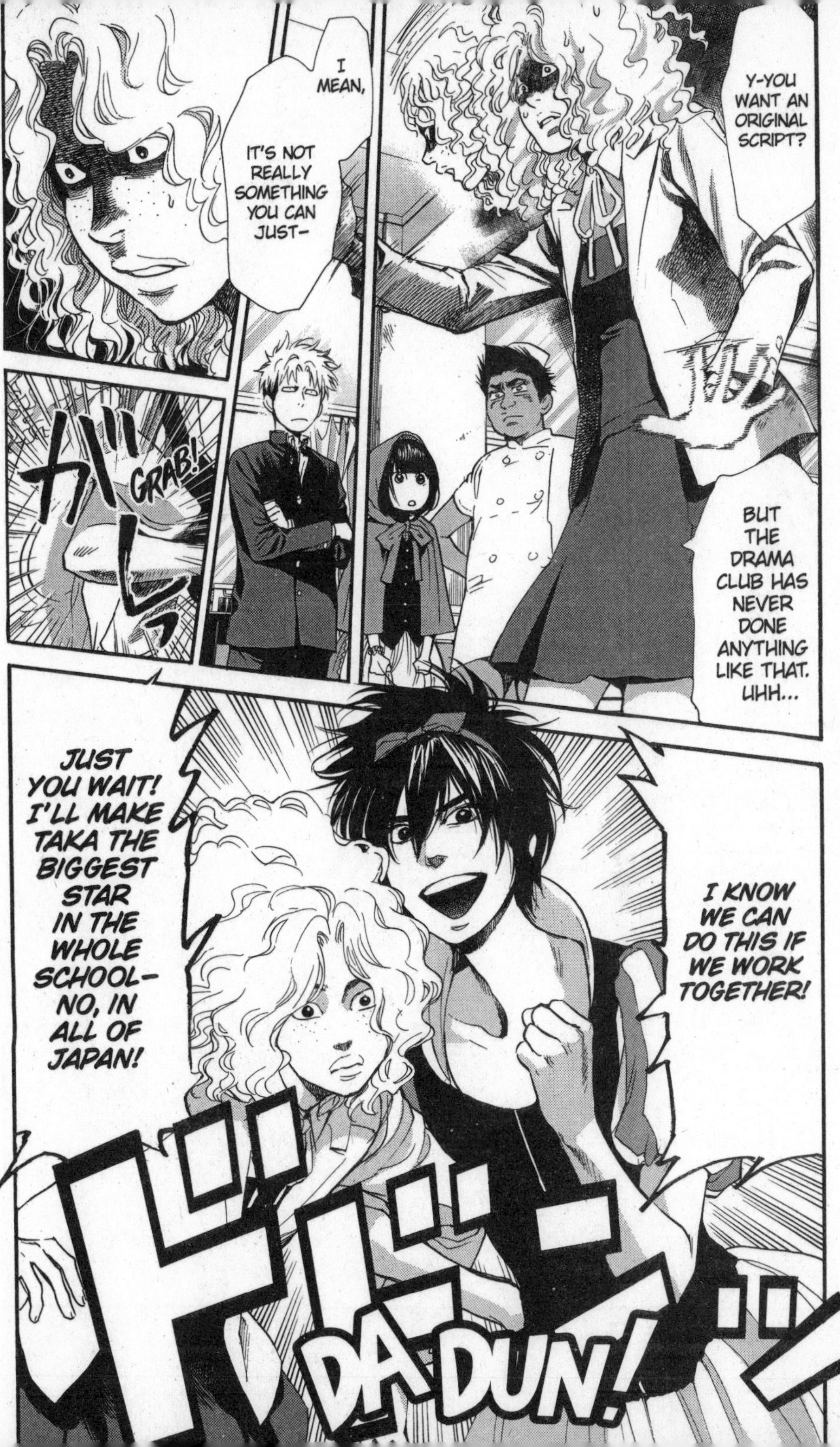
Y-YOU WANT AN ORIGINAL SCRIPT?
BUT THE DRAMA CLUB HAS NEVER DONE ANYTHING LIKE THAT. UHH...
I MEAN,
IT'S NOT REALLY SOMETHING YOU CAN JUST-
GRAB!
I KNOW WE CAN DO THIS IF WE WORK TOGETHER!
JUST YOU WAIT! I'LL MAKE TAKA THE BIGGEST STAR IN THE WHOLE SCHOOL- NO, IN ALL OF JAPAN!
DA-DUN!

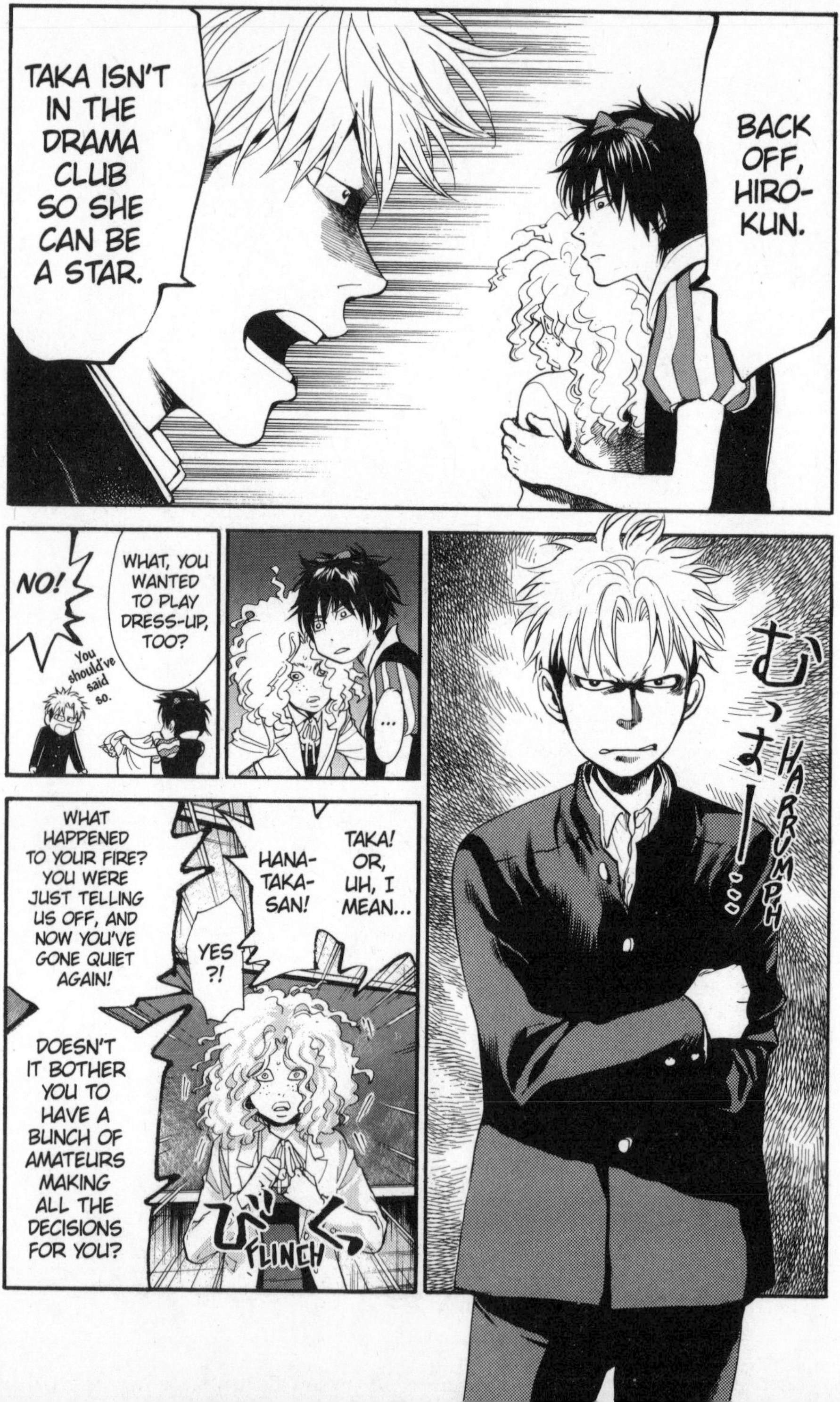

BACK OFF, HIRO-KUN.
TAKA ISN'T IN THE DRAMA CLUB SO SHE CAN BE A STAR.
むっすー
HARRUMPH
...
WHAT, YOU WANTED TO PLAY DRESS-UP, TOO?
NO!
You should've said so.
TAKA! OR, UH, I MEAN...
HANA-TAKA-SAN!
WHAT HAPPENED TO YOUR FIRE? YOU WERE JUST TELLING US OFF, AND NOW YOU'VE GONE QUIET AGAIN!
YES?!
DOESN'T IT BOTHER YOU TO HAVE A BUNCH OF AMATEURS MAKING ALL THE DECISIONS FOR YOU?
びくっ
FLINCH

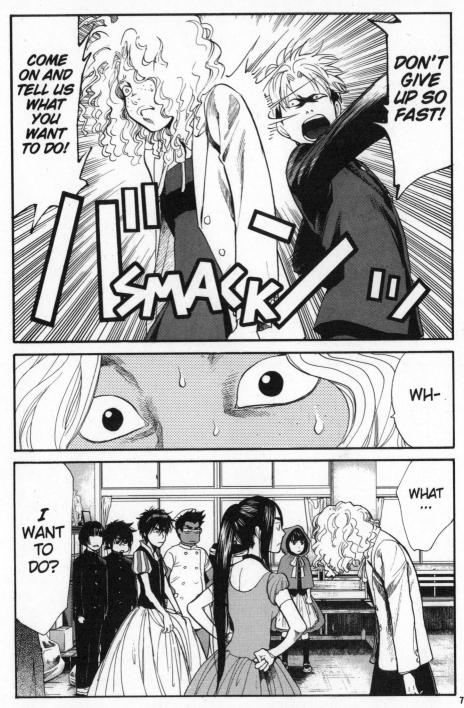

DON'T GIVE UP SO FAST!
COME ON AND TELL US WHAT YOU WANT TO DO!
SMACK
WH-
WHAT ...
I WANT TO DO?

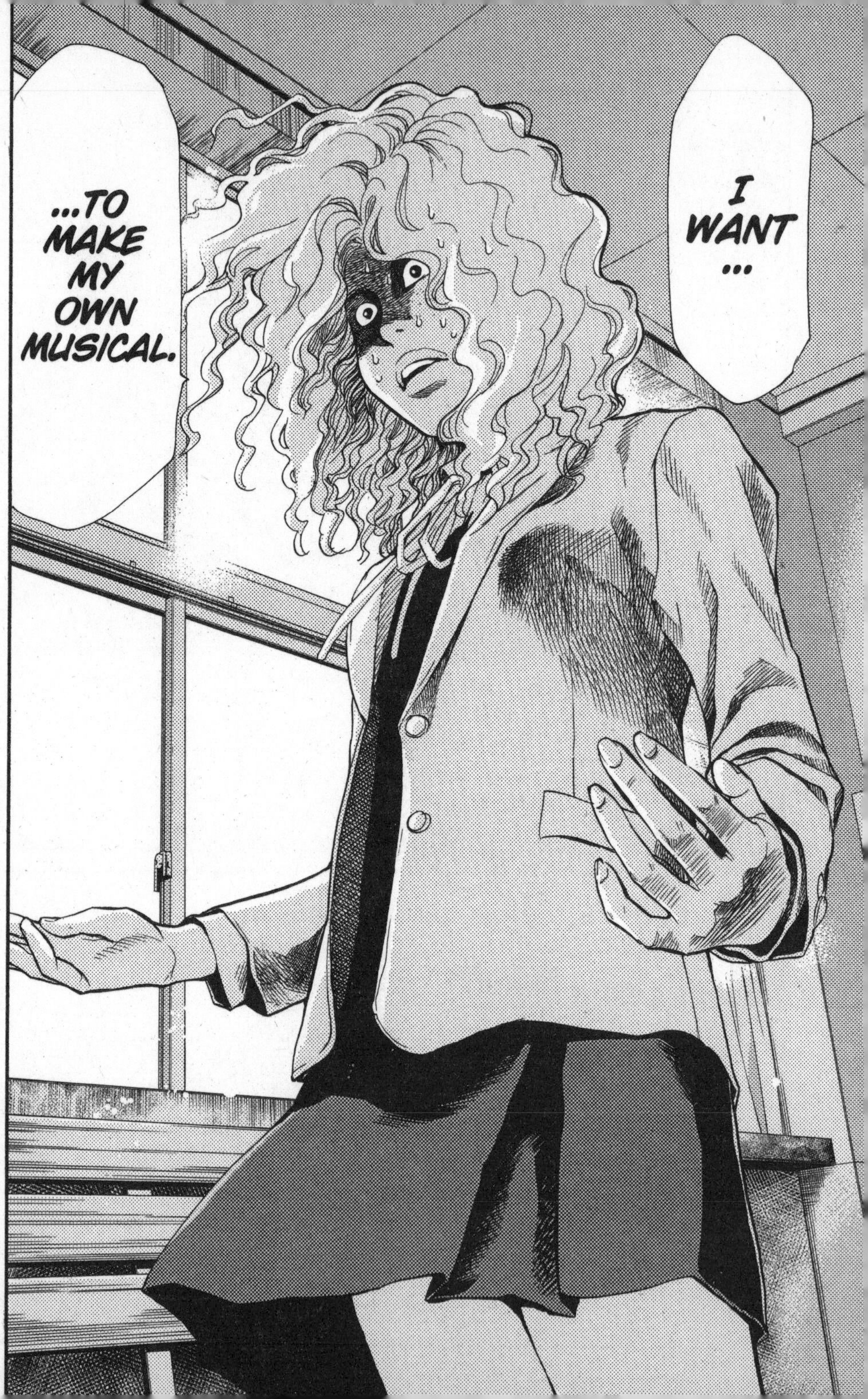
I WANT ...
...TO MAKE MY OWN MUSICAL.

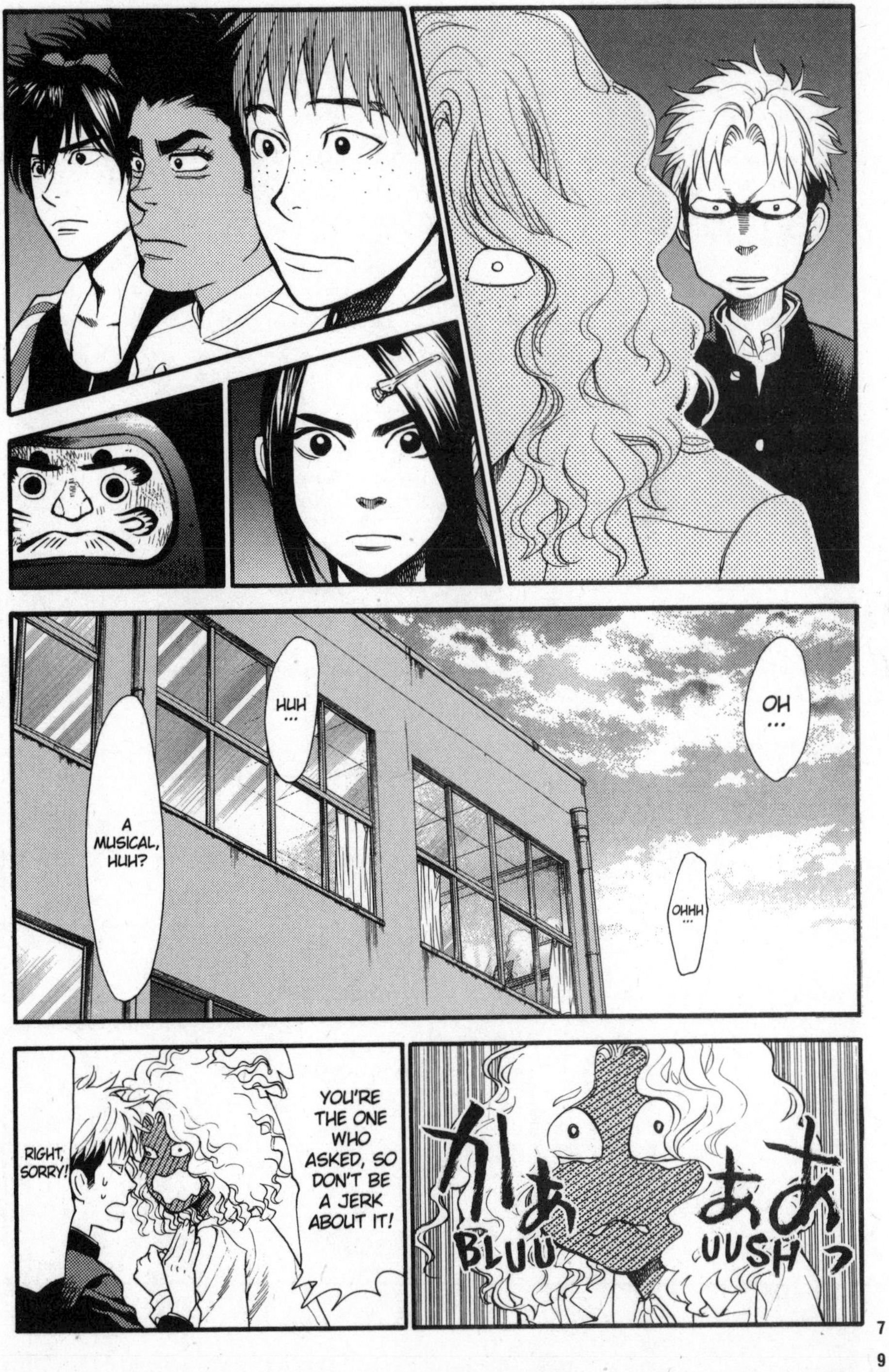

OH...
OHHH...
HUH...
A MUSICAL, HUH?
かあああっ
BLUUUUSH
YOU'RE THE ONE WHO ASKED, SO DON'T BE A JERK ABOUT IT!
RIGHT, SORRY!

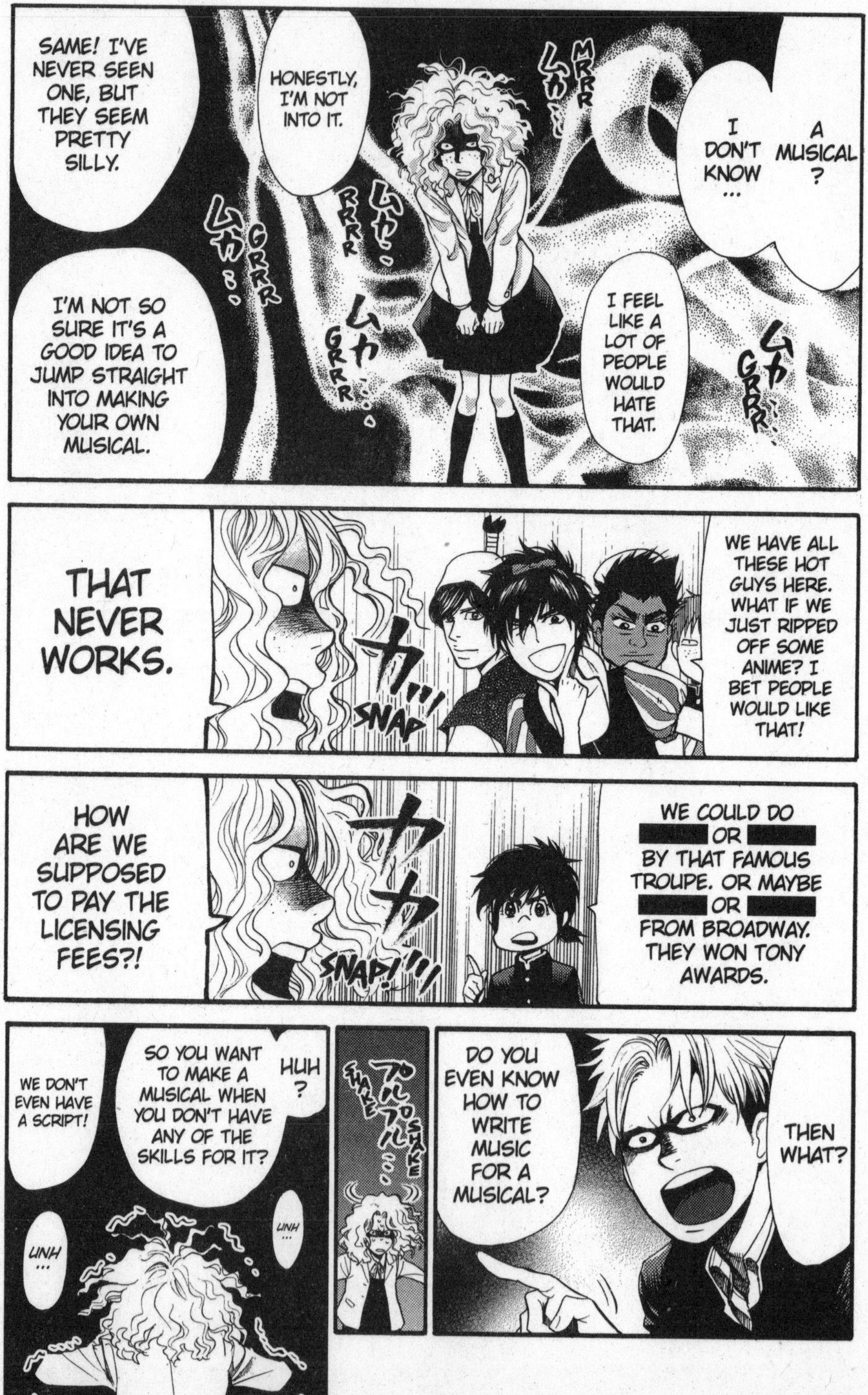
A MUSICAL?
I DON'T KNOW...
MRRR
HONESTLY, I'M NOT INTO IT.
SAME! I'VE NEVER SEEN ONE, BUT THEY SEEM PRETTY SILLY.
RRRR
GRRR
I FEEL LIKE A LOT OF PEOPLE WOULD HATE THAT.
GRRR...
GRRR...
I'M NOT SO SURE IT'S A GOOD IDEA TO JUMP STRAIGHT INTO MAKING YOUR OWN MUSICAL.
WE HAVE ALL THESE HOT GUYS HERE. WHAT IF WE JUST RIPPED OFF SOME ANIME? I BET PEOPLE WOULD LIKE THAT!
SNAP
THAT NEVER WORKS.
WE COULD DO [redacted] OR [redacted] BY THAT FAMOUS TROUPE. OR MAYBE [redacted] OR [redacted] FROM BROADWAY. THEY WON TONY AWARDS.
SNAP!
HOW ARE WE SUPPOSED TO PAY THE LICENSING FEES?!
THEN WHAT?
DO YOU EVEN KNOW HOW TO WRITE MUSIC FOR A MUSICAL?
SHAKE SHAKE
HUH?
SO YOU WANT TO MAKE A MUSICAL WHEN YOU DON'T HAVE ANY OF THE SKILLS FOR IT?
WE DON'T EVEN HAVE A SCRIPT!
UNH...
UNH...

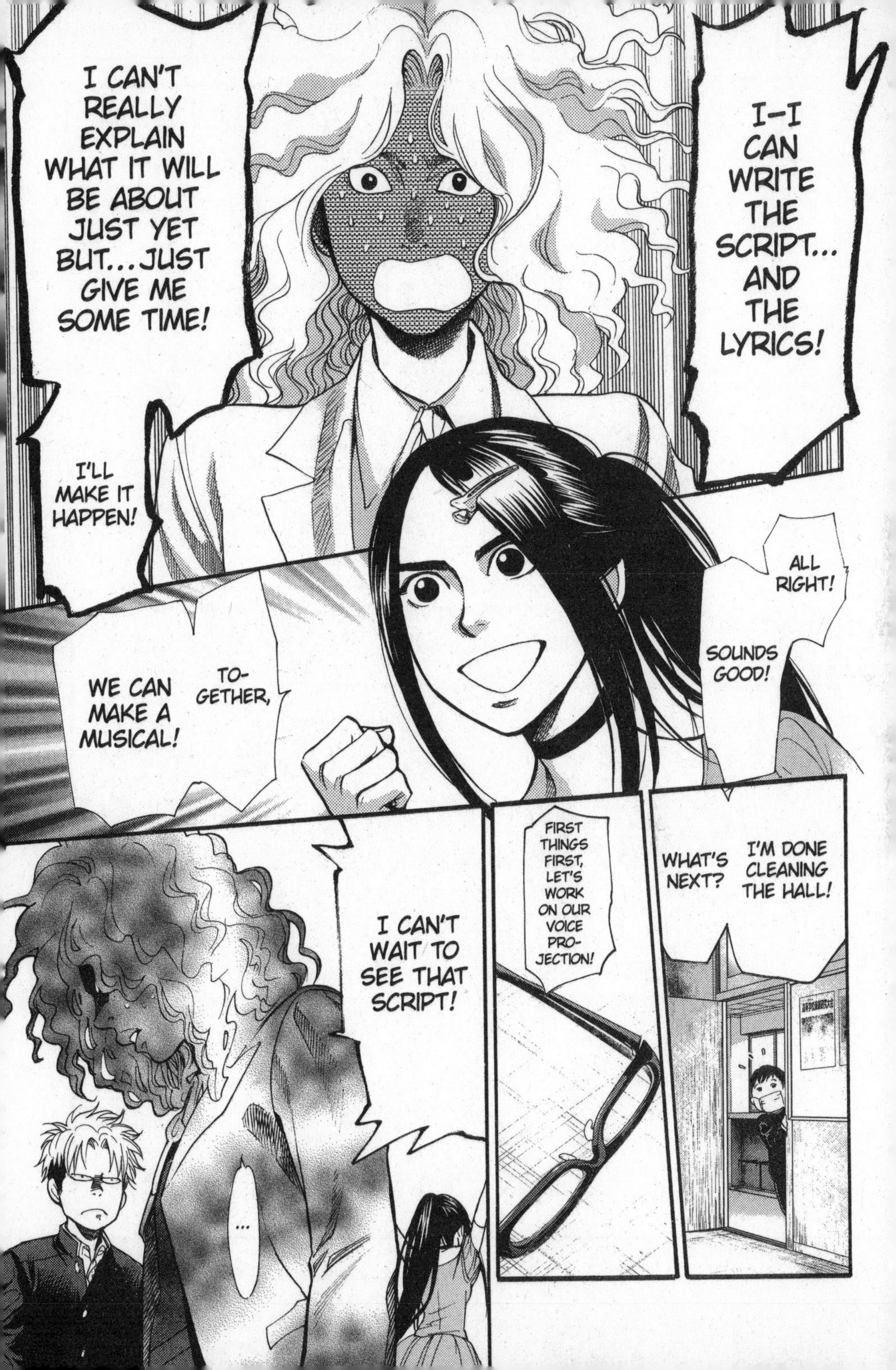
I-I CAN WRITE THE SCRIPT... AND THE LYRICS!
I CAN'T REALLY EXPLAIN WHAT IT WILL BE ABOUT JUST YET BUT...JUST GIVE ME SOME TIME!
I'LL MAKE IT HAPPEN!
ALL RIGHT!
SOUNDS GOOD!
TO-GETHER,
WE CAN MAKE A MUSICAL!
I'M DONE CLEANING THE HALL!
WHAT'S NEXT?
FIRST THINGS FIRST, LET'S WORK ON OUR VOICE PRO-JECTION!
I CAN'T WAIT TO SEE THAT SCRIPT!
...

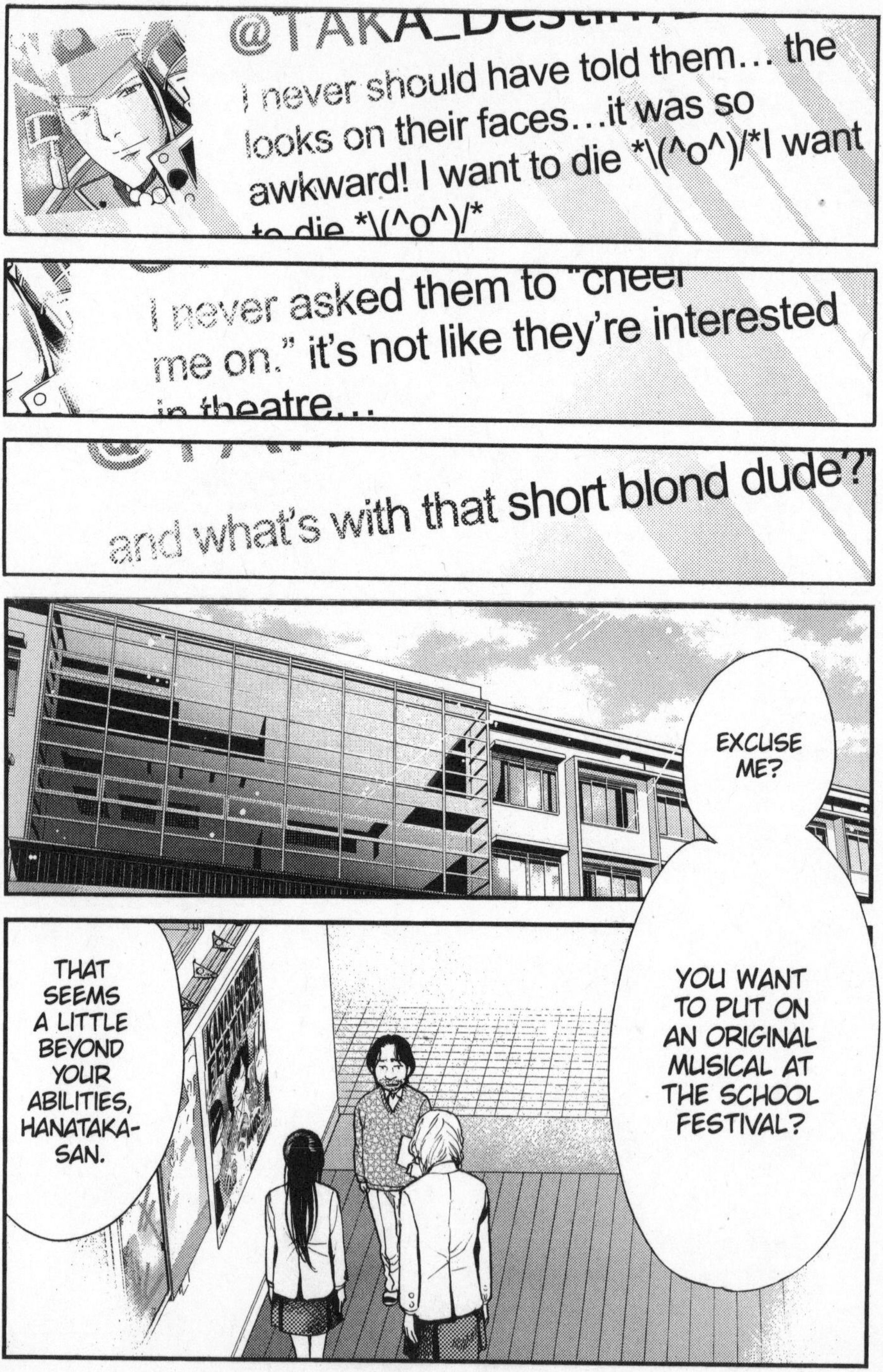
I never should have told them… the looks on their faces…it was so awkward! I want to die *\(^o^)/*I want to die *\(^o^)/*
I never asked them to "cheer me on." it's not like they're interested in theatre…
and what's with that short blond dude?
EXCUSE ME?
YOU WANT TO PUT ON AN ORIGINAL MUSICAL AT THE SCHOOL FESTIVAL?
THAT SEEMS A LITTLE BEYOND YOUR ABILITIES, HANATAKA-SAN.

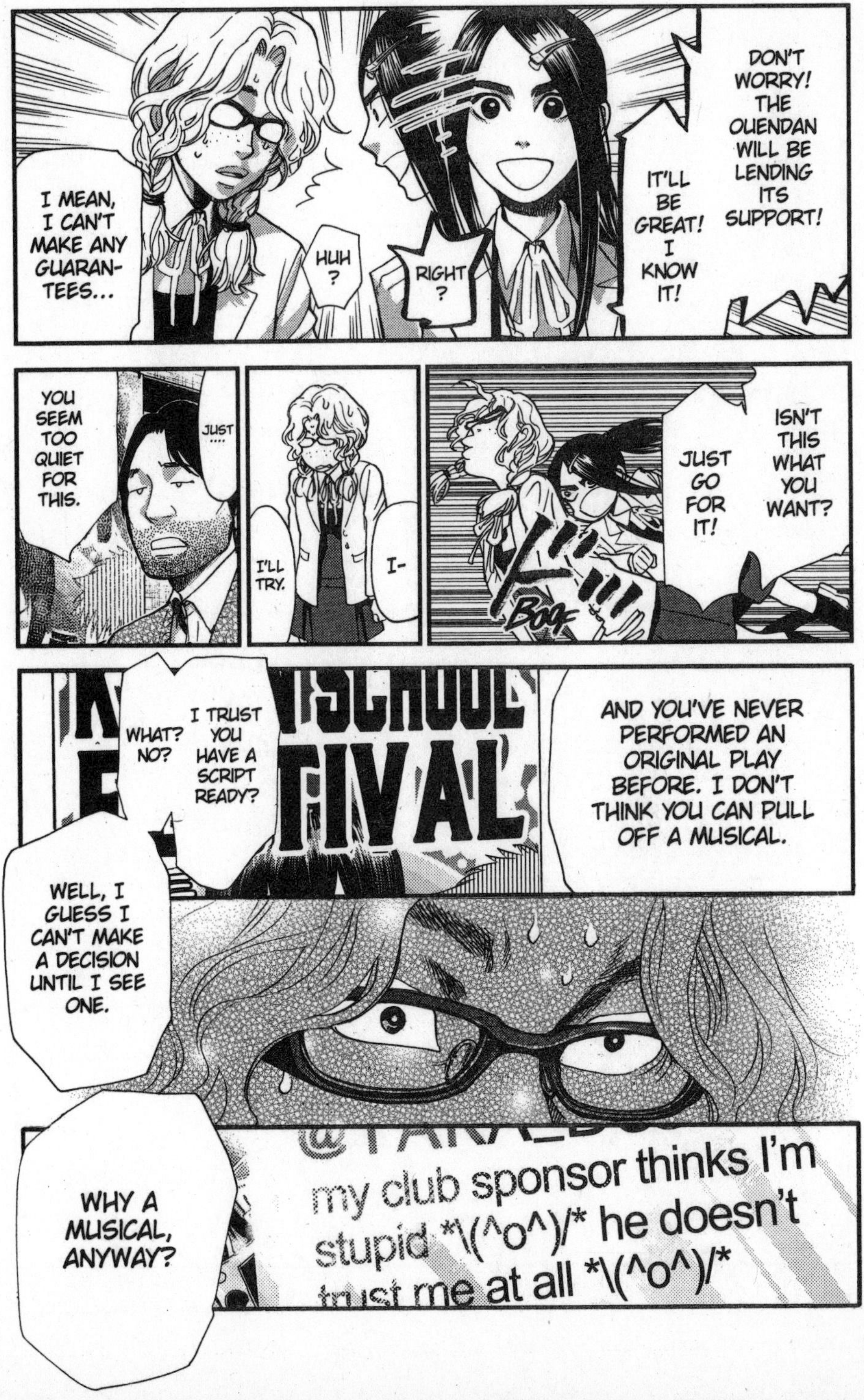
DON'T WORRY! THE OUENDAN WILL BE LENDING ITS SUPPORT!
IT'LL BE GREAT! I KNOW IT!
RIGHT?
HUH?
I MEAN, I CAN'T MAKE ANY GUARAN-TEES...
ISN'T THIS WHAT YOU WANT?
JUST GO FOR IT!
BOGF
I-
I'LL TRY.
JUST....
YOU SEEM TOO QUIET FOR THIS.
AND YOU'VE NEVER PERFORMED AN ORIGINAL PLAY BEFORE. I DON'T THINK YOU CAN PULL OFF A MUSICAL.
I TRUST YOU HAVE A SCRIPT READY?
WHAT? NO?
WELL, I GUESS I CAN'T MAKE A DECISION UNTIL I SEE ONE.
my club sponsor thinks I'm stupid *\(^o^)/* he doesn't trust me at all *\(^o^)/*
WHY A MUSICAL, ANYWAY?

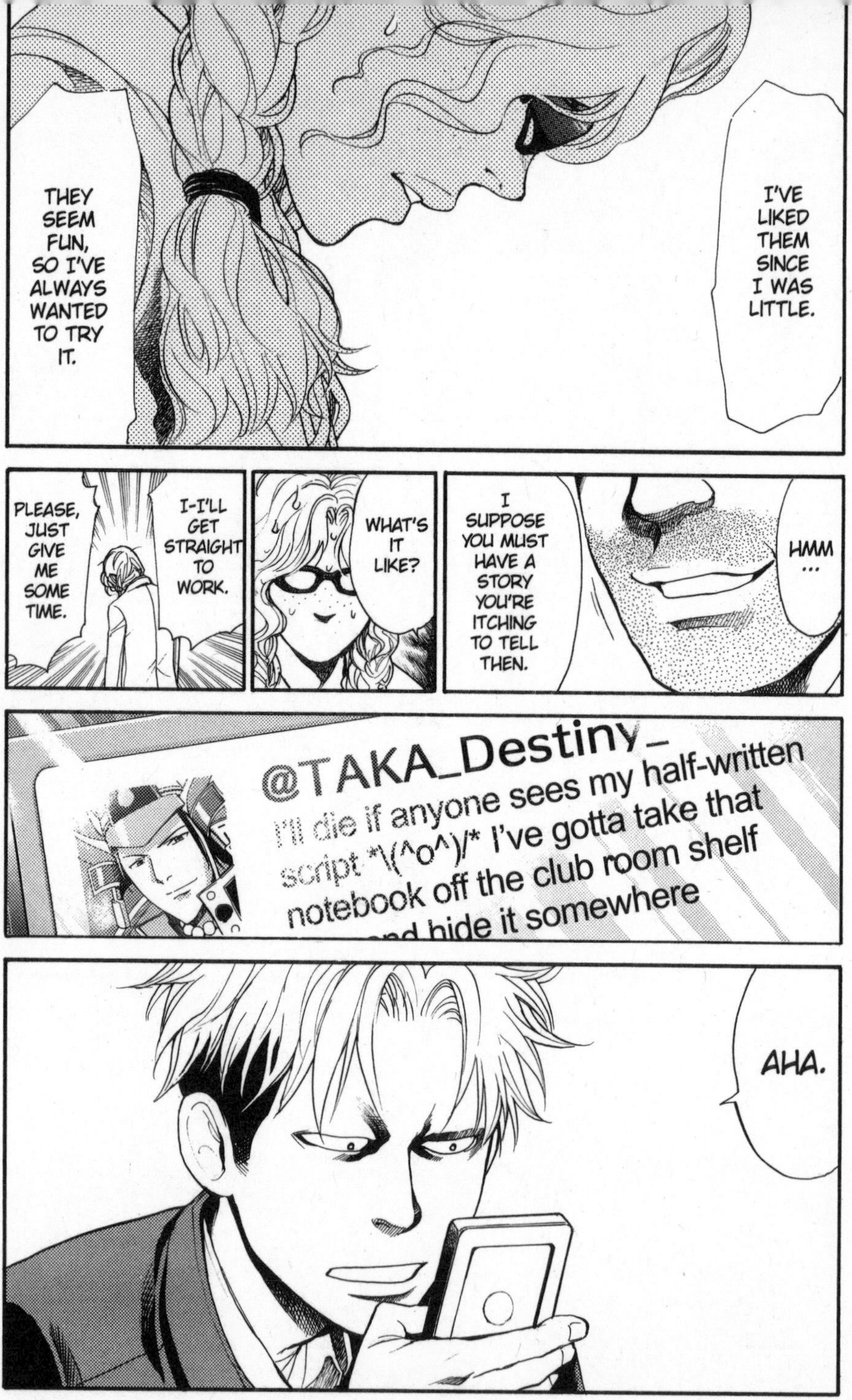
I'VE LIKED THEM SINCE I WAS LITTLE.
THEY SEEM FUN, SO I'VE ALWAYS WANTED TO TRY IT.
HMM...
I SUPPOSE YOU MUST HAVE A STORY YOU'RE ITCHING TO TELL THEN.
WHAT'S IT LIKE?
I-I'LL GET STRAIGHT TO WORK.
PLEASE, JUST GIVE ME SOME TIME.
@TAKA_Destiny_
I'll die if anyone sees my half-written script *\(^o^)/* I've gotta take that notebook off the club room shelf
hide it somewhere
AHA.

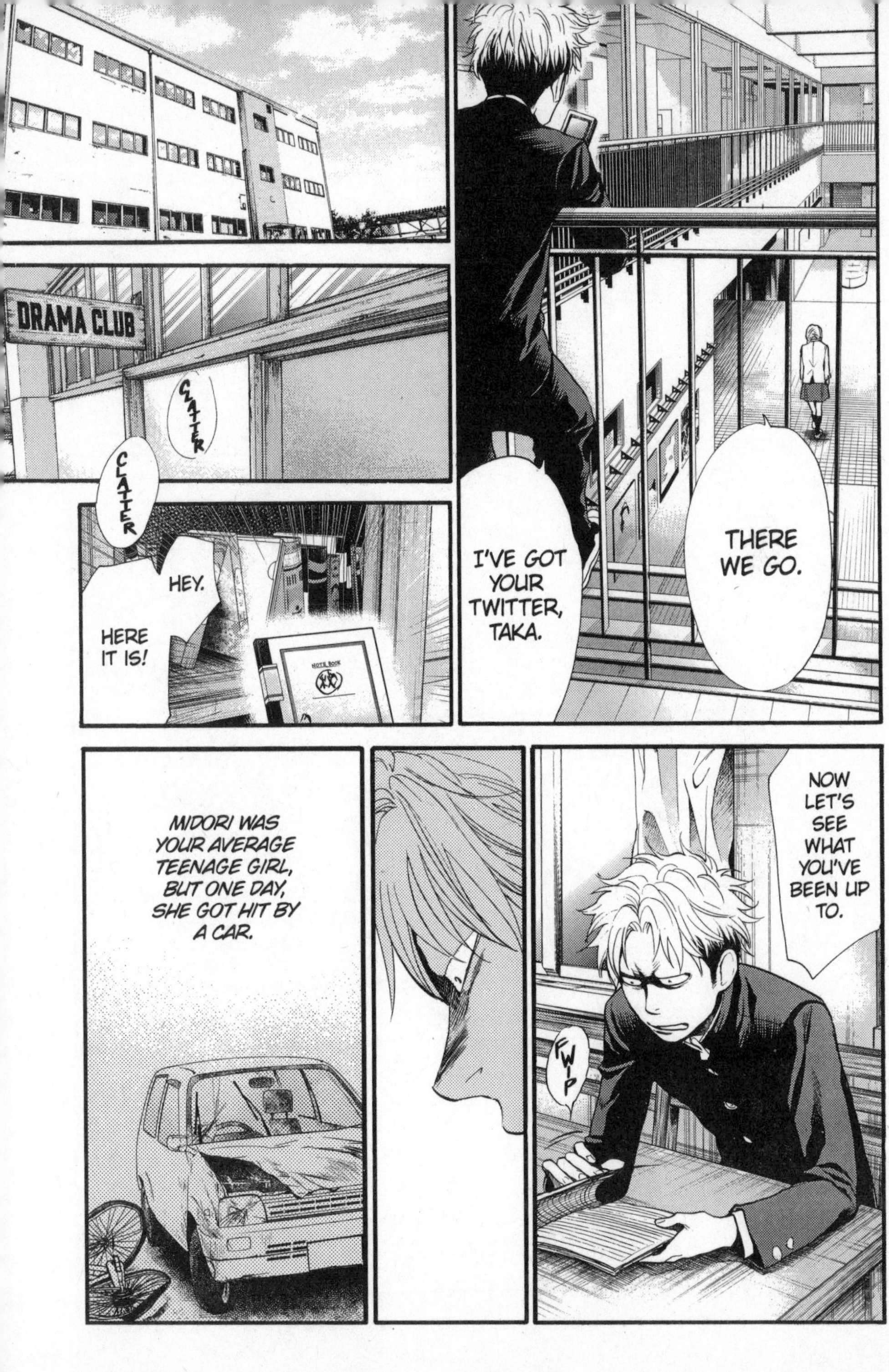
THERE WE GO.
I'VE GOT YOUR TWITTER, TAKA.
DRAMA CLUB
CLATTER
CLATTER
HEY.
HERE IT IS!
NOTE BOOK
NOW LET'S SEE WHAT YOU'VE BEEN UP TO.
FWIP
MIDORI WAS YOUR AVERAGE TEENAGE GIRL, BUT ONE DAY, SHE GOT HIT BY A CAR.

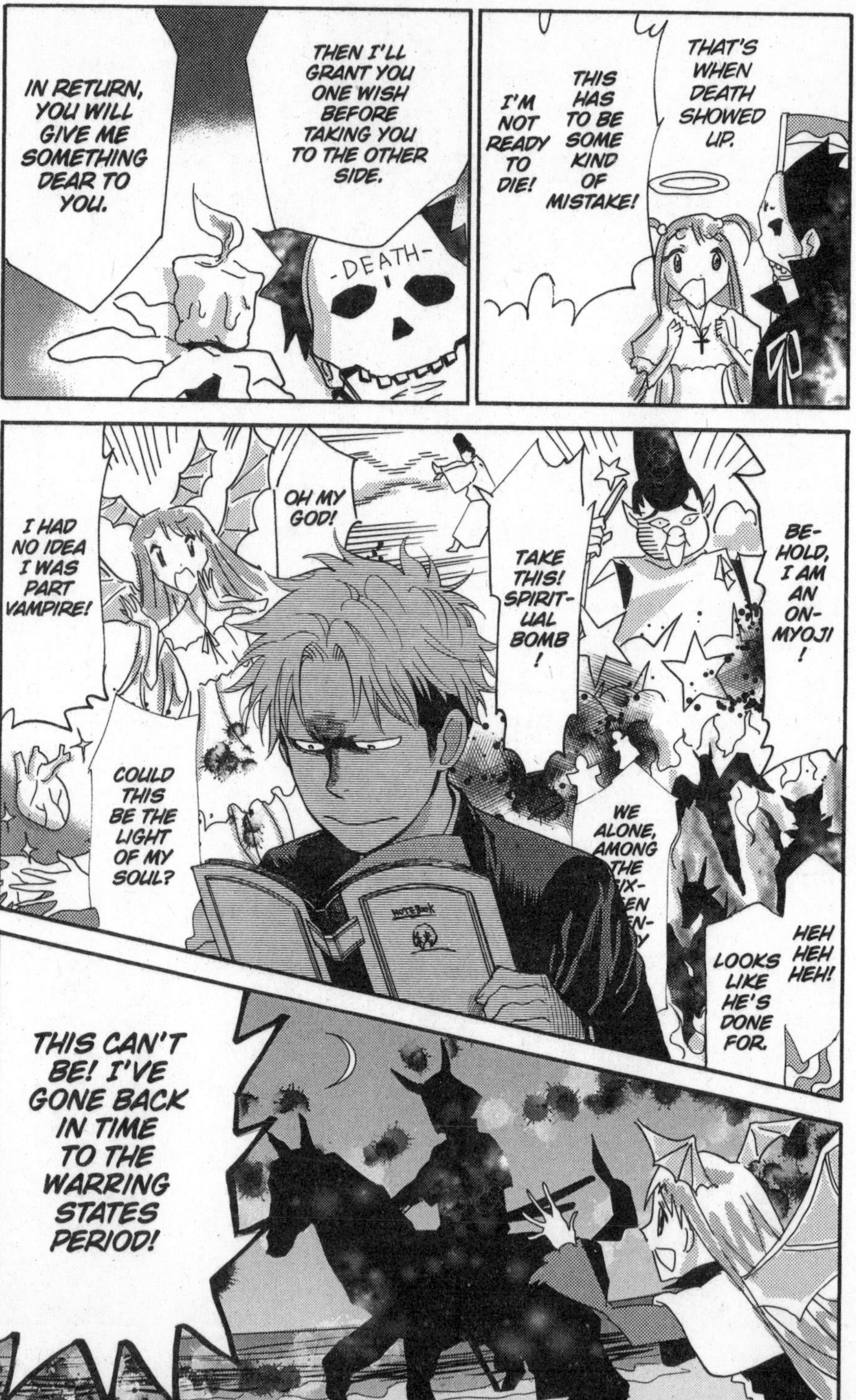
THAT'S WHEN DEATH SHOWED UP.
THIS HAS TO BE SOME KIND OF MISTAKE!
I'M NOT READY TO DIE!
THEN I'LL GRANT YOU ONE WISH BEFORE TAKING YOU TO THE OTHER SIDE.
-DEATH-
IN RETURN, YOU WILL GIVE ME SOMETHING DEAR TO YOU.
BE-HOLD, I AM AN ON-MYOJI!
TAKE THIS! SPIRIT-UAL BOMB!
OH MY GOD!
I HAD NO IDEA I WAS PART VAMPIRE!
WE ALONE, AMONG THE
COULD THIS BE THE LIGHT OF MY SOUL?
HEH HEH HEH!
LOOKS LIKE HE'S DONE FOR.
THIS CAN'T BE! I'VE GONE BACK IN TIME TO THE WARRING STATES PERIOD!

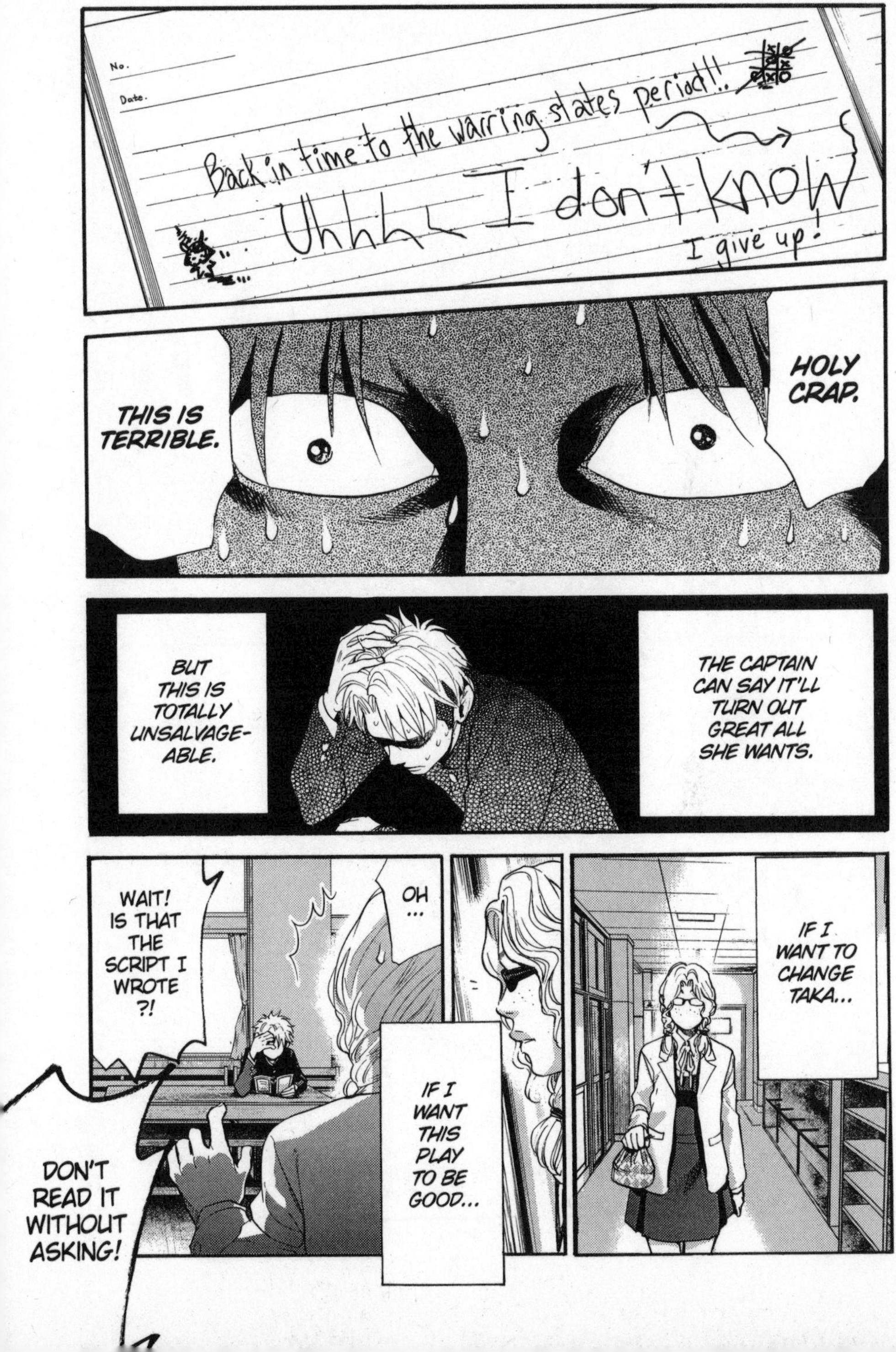
No.
Date.
Back in time to the warring states period!!
Uhhh~ I don't know
I give up!
HOLY CRAP.
THIS IS TERRIBLE.
THE CAPTAIN CAN SAY IT'LL TURN OUT GREAT ALL SHE WANTS.
BUT THIS IS TOTALLY UNSALVAGE-ABLE.
IF I WANT TO CHANGE TAKA...
OH ...
IF I WANT THIS PLAY TO BE GOOD...
WAIT! IS THAT THE SCRIPT I WROTE ?!
DON'T READ IT WITHOUT ASKING!

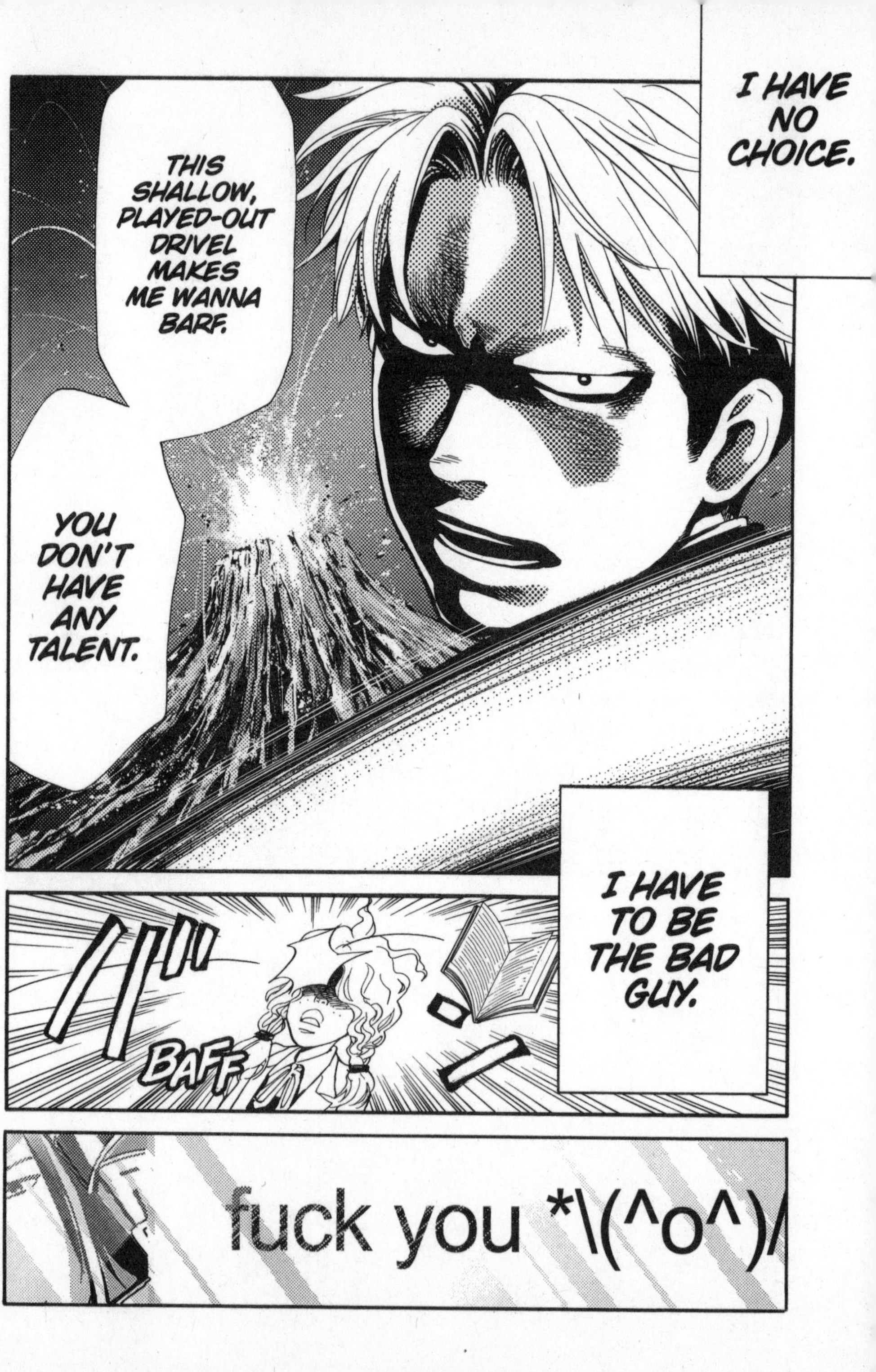
I HAVE NO CHOICE.
THIS SHALLOW, PLAYED-OUT DRIVEL MAKES ME WANNA BARF.
YOU DON'T HAVE ANY TALENT.
I HAVE TO BE THE BAD GUY.
BAFF
fuck you *\(^o^)/

81. STUDENTS OF THE WORLD, HEAR ME!

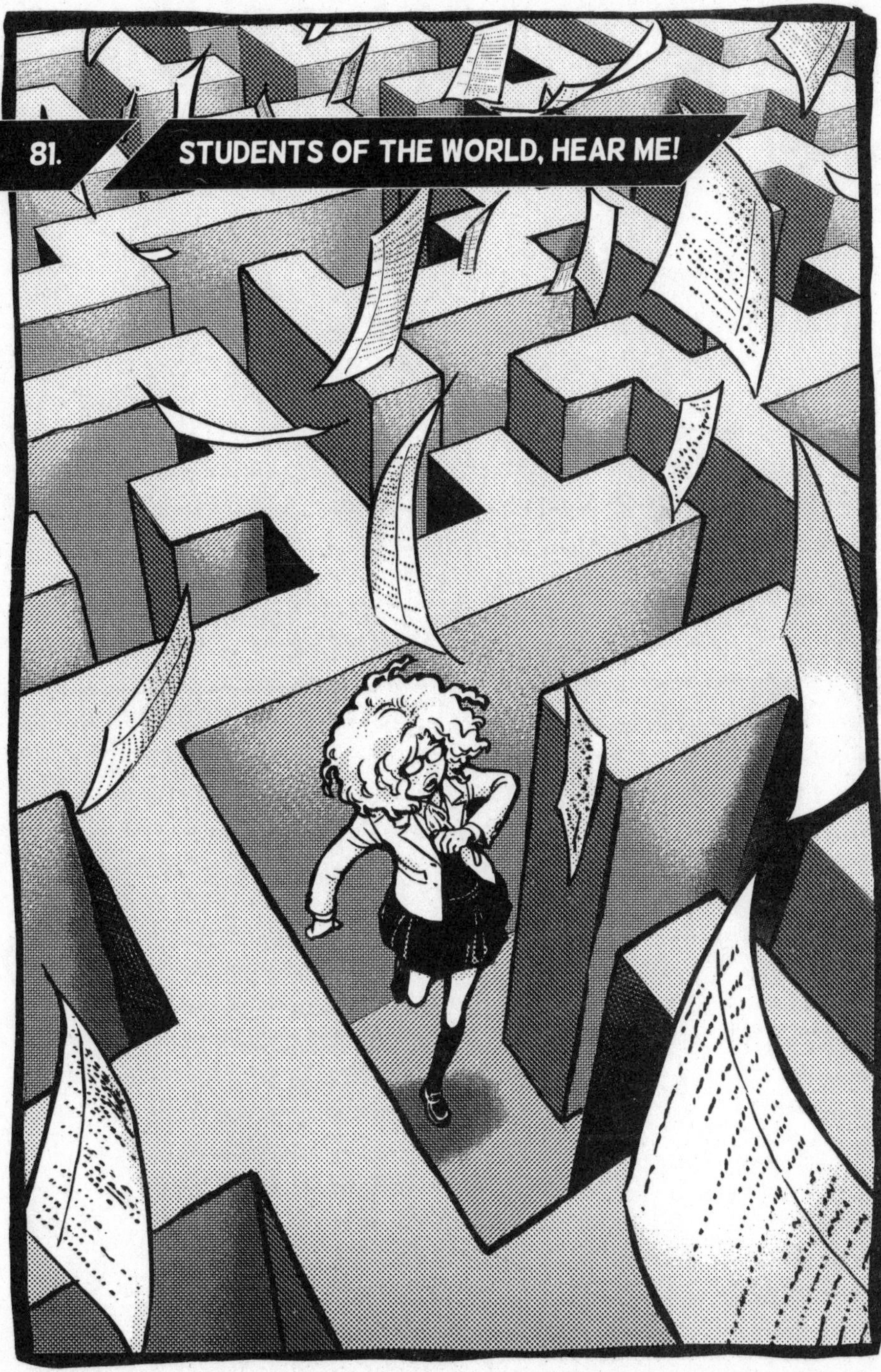

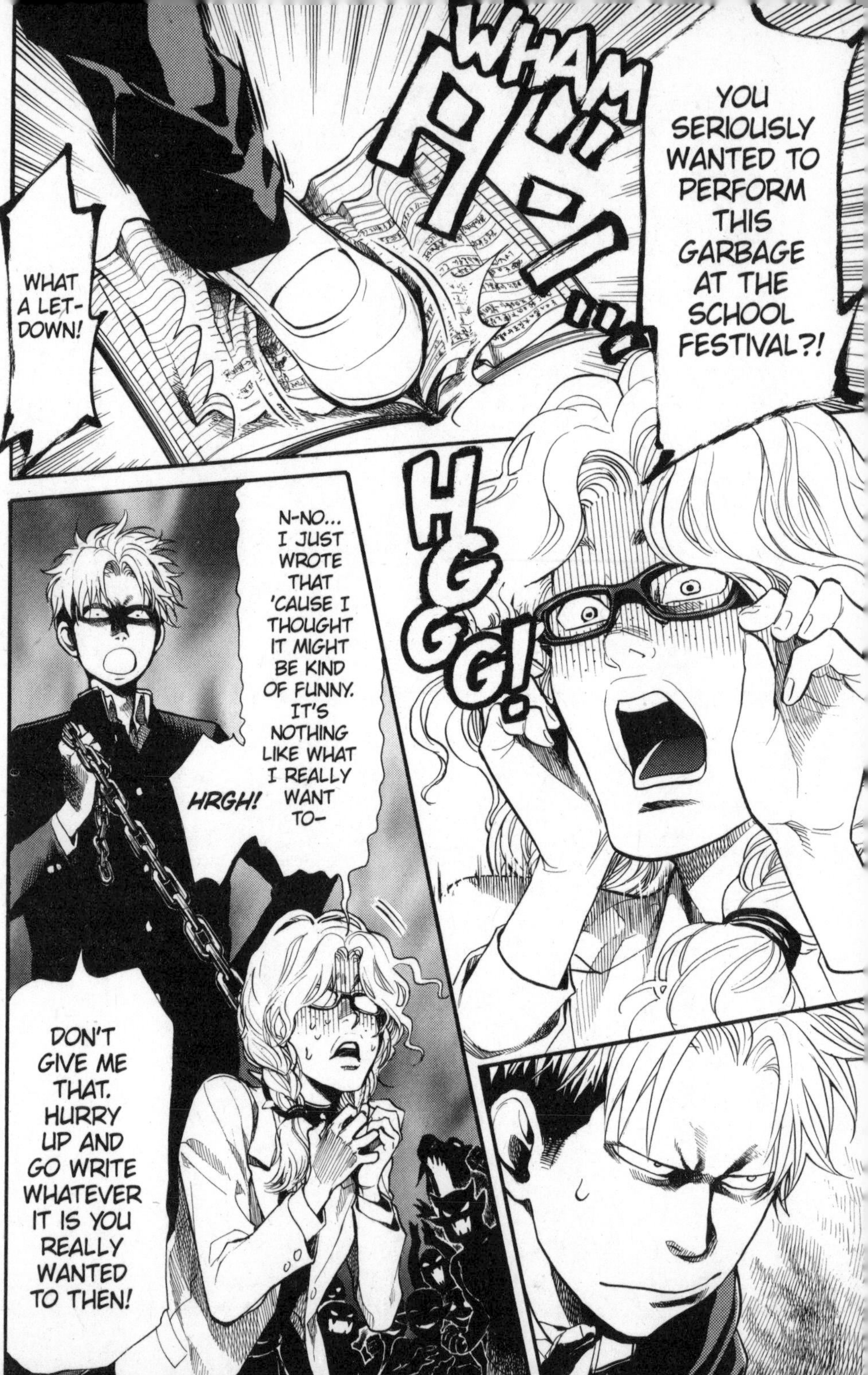
WHAM
YOU SERIOUSLY WANTED TO PERFORM THIS GARBAGE AT THE SCHOOL FESTIVAL?!
WHAT A LET-DOWN!
HGGG!
N-NO... I JUST WROTE THAT 'CAUSE I THOUGHT IT MIGHT BE KIND OF FUNNY. IT'S NOTHING LIKE WHAT I REALLY WANT TO-
HRGH!
DON'T GIVE ME THAT. HURRY UP AND GO WRITE WHATEVER IT IS YOU REALLY WANTED TO THEN!

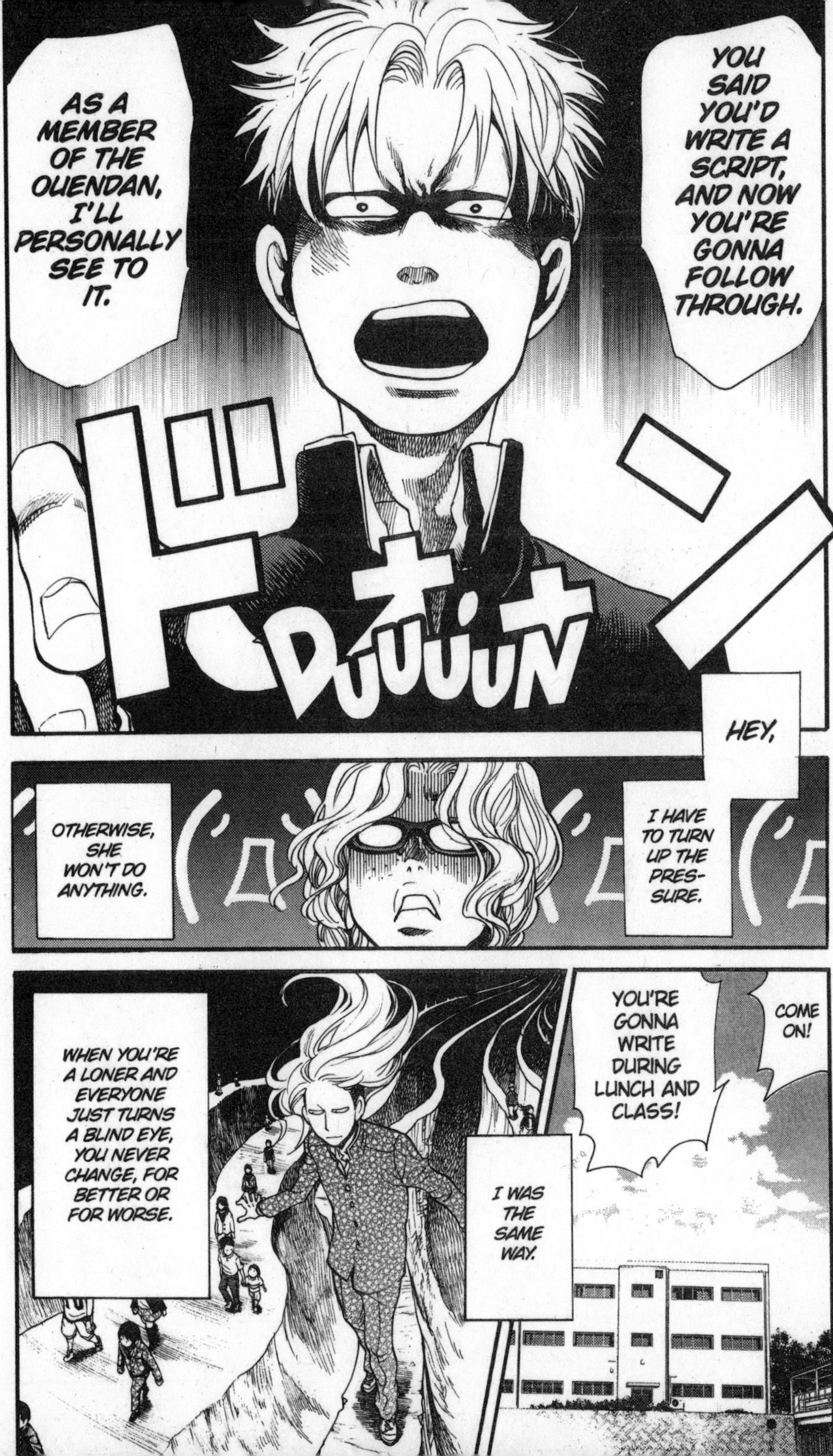
YOU SAID YOU'D WRITE A SCRIPT, AND NOW YOU'RE GONNA FOLLOW THROUGH.
AS A MEMBER OF THE OUENDAN, I'LL PERSONALLY SEE TO IT.
DUUUUN
HEY,
I HAVE TO TURN UP THE PRES-SURE.
OTHERWISE, SHE WON'T DO ANYTHING.
COME ON!
YOU'RE GONNA WRITE DURING LUNCH AND CLASS!
I WAS THE SAME WAY.
WHEN YOU'RE A LONER AND EVERYONE JUST TURNS A BLIND EYE, YOU NEVER CHANGE, FOR BETTER OR FOR WORSE.

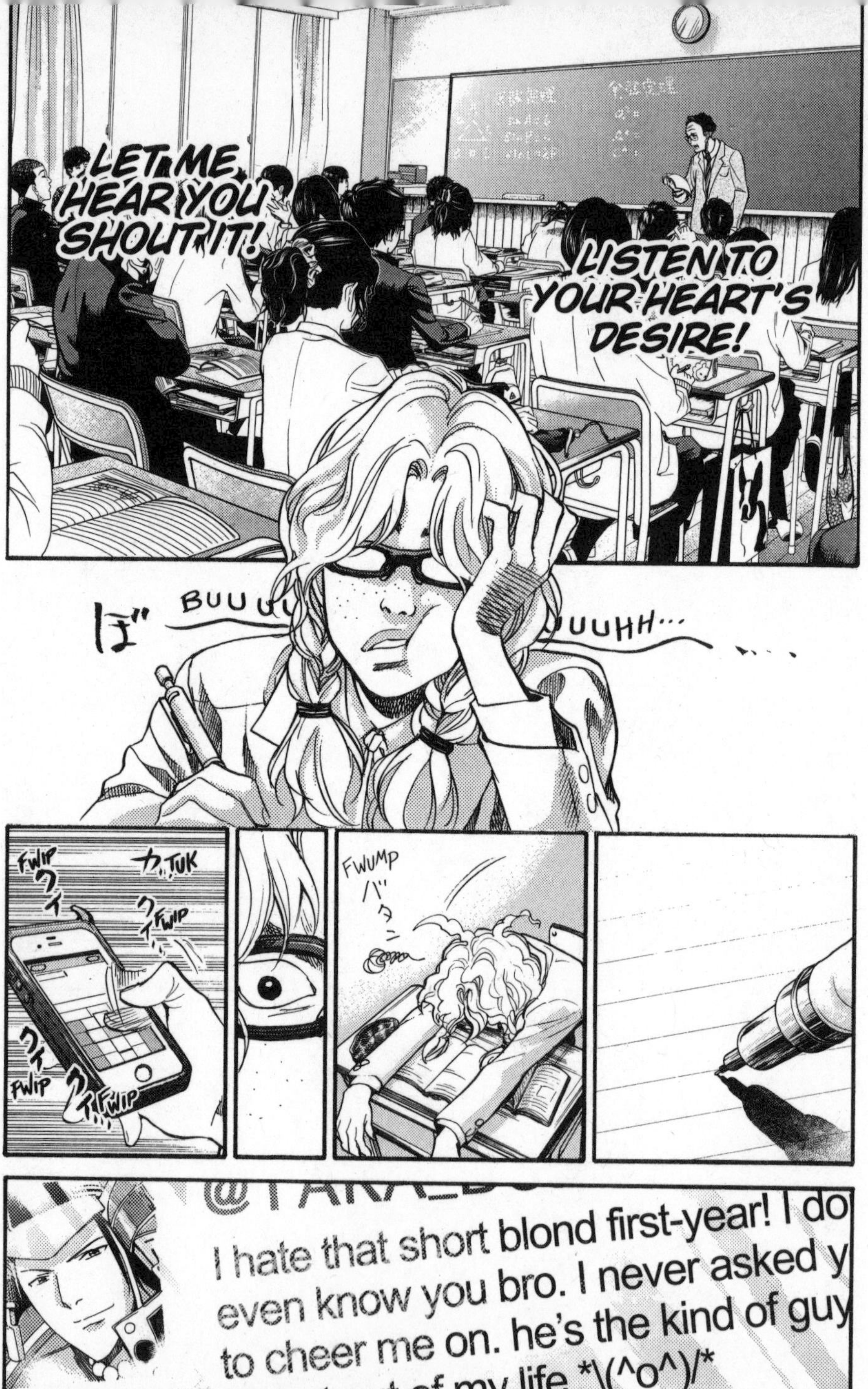
LISTEN TO YOUR HEART'S DESIRE!
LET ME HEAR YOU SHOUT IT!
BUUUU
UUUHH...
FWUMP
バタン
FWIP
TUK
FWIP
FWIP
FWIP
I hate that short blond first-year! I do
even know you bro. I never asked y
to cheer me on. he's the kind of guy
I want out of my life *\(^o^)/*

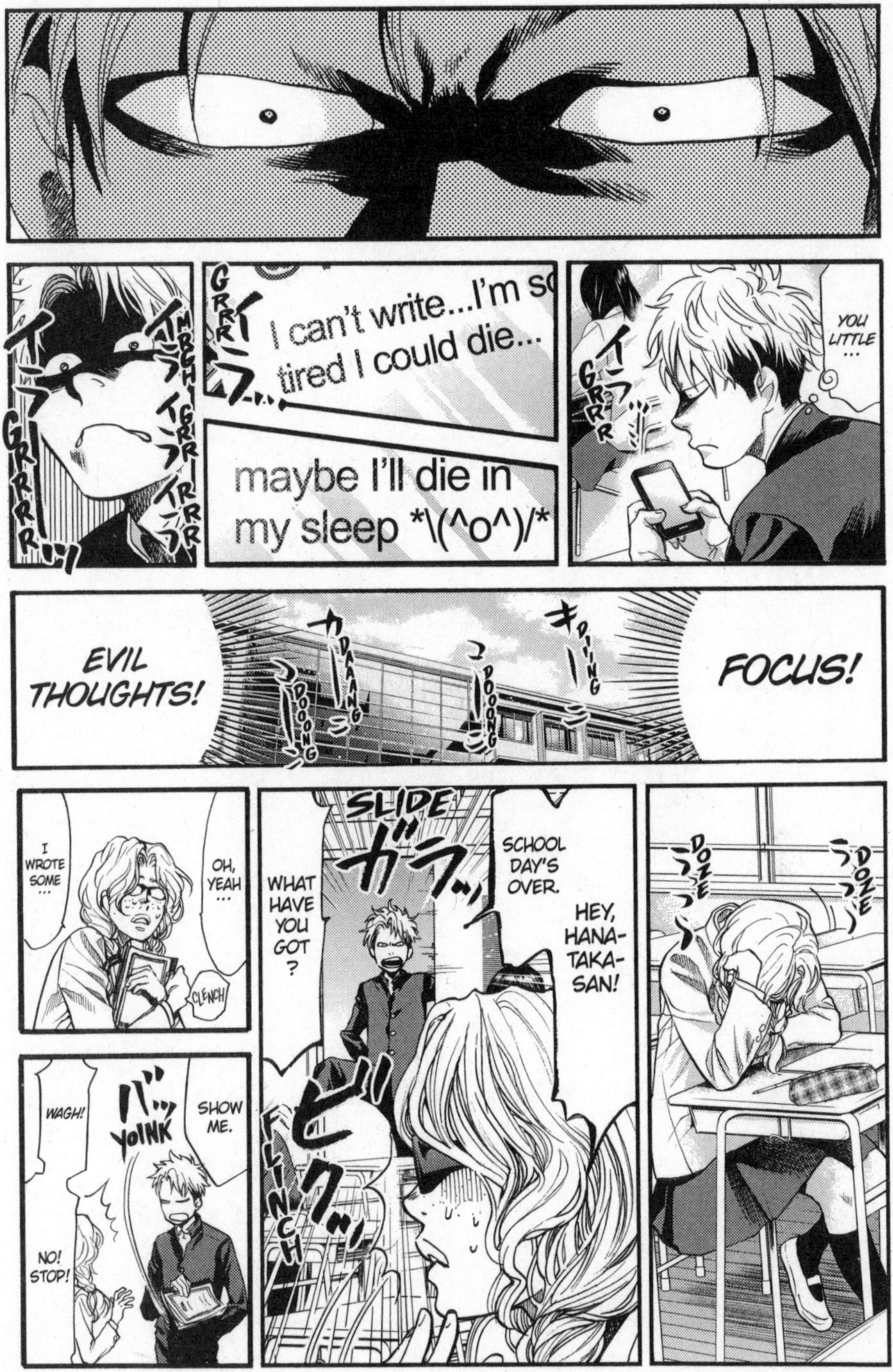
YOU LITTLE ...
GRRR
I can't write...I'm so tired I could die...
GRRR
maybe I'll die in my sleep *\(^o^)/*
MBGH
GRRR
GRRRR
FOCUS!
DING
DOOONG
DAAANG
DOOONG
EVIL THOUGHTS!
DOZE
DOZE
SCHOOL DAY'S OVER.
HEY, HANA-TAKA-SAN!
SLIDE
FLINCH
WHAT HAVE YOU GOT?
OH, YEAH ...
I WROTE SOME ...
CLENCH
SHOW ME.
YOINK
WAGH!
NO! STOP!

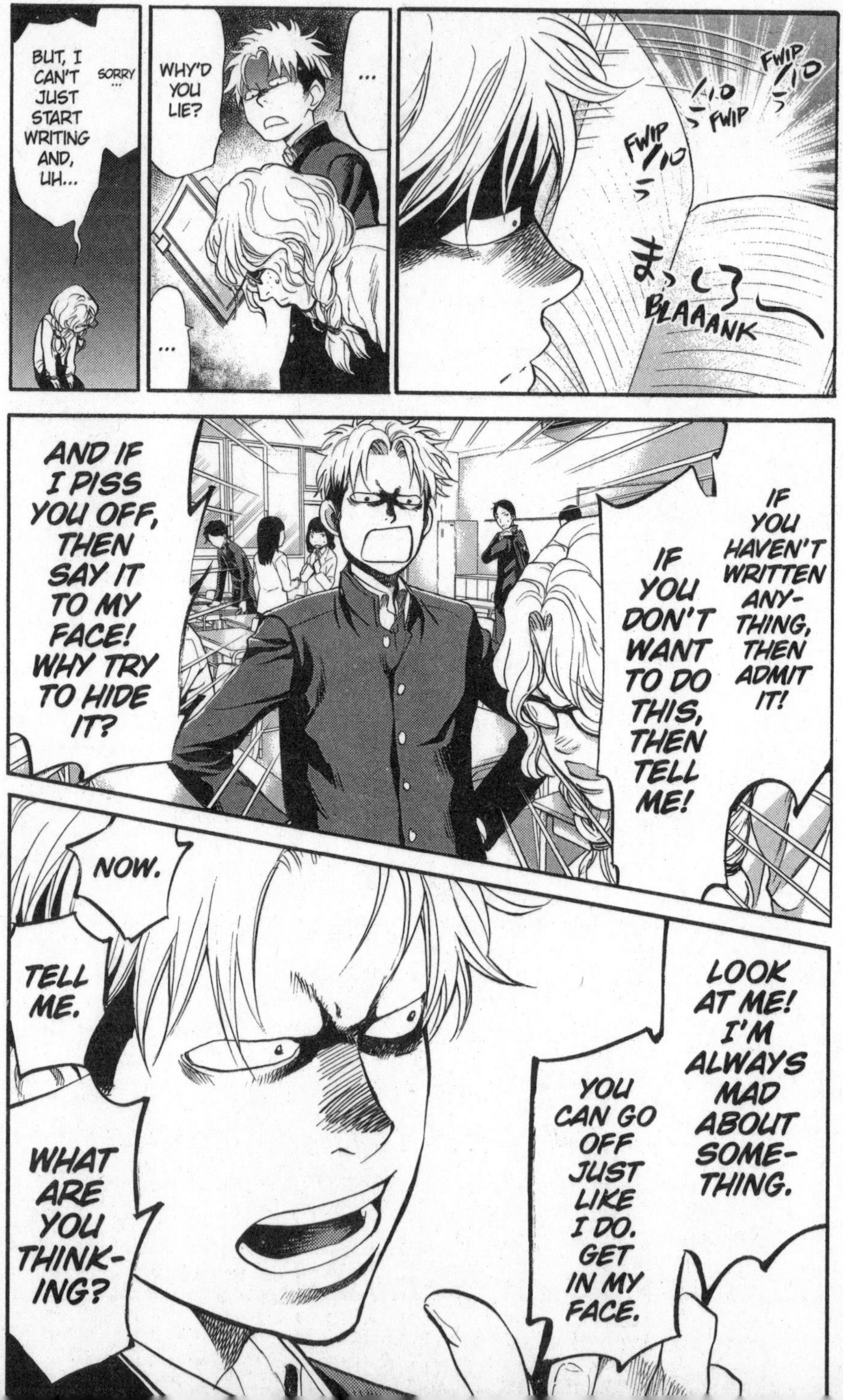
FWIP
FWIP
FWIP
まっしろ
BLAAANK
...
WHY'D YOU LIE?
...
SORRY...
BUT, I CAN'T JUST START WRITING AND, UH...
IF YOU HAVEN'T WRITTEN ANYTHING, THEN ADMIT IT!
IF YOU DON'T WANT TO DO THIS, THEN TELL ME!
AND IF I PISS YOU OFF, THEN SAY IT TO MY FACE! WHY TRY TO HIDE IT?
LOOK AT ME! I'M ALWAYS MAD ABOUT SOMETHING.
YOU CAN GO OFF JUST LIKE I DO. GET IN MY FACE.
NOW.
TELL ME.
WHAT ARE YOU THINKING?

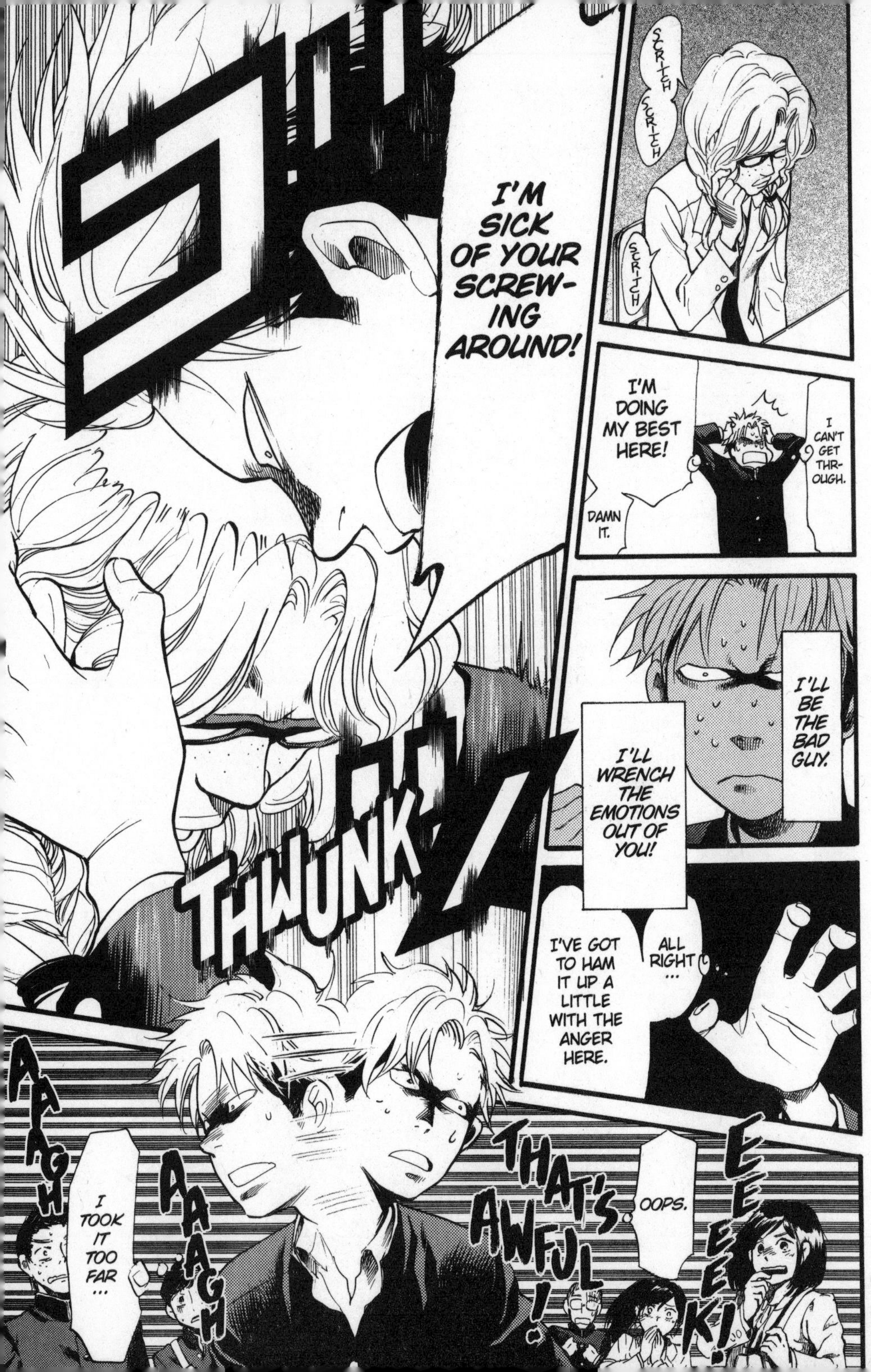
SCRITCH SCRITCH
SCRITCH
I CAN'T GET THROUGH.
I'M DOING MY BEST HERE!
DAMN IT.
I'LL BE THE BAD GUY.
I'LL WRENCH THE EMOTIONS OUT OF YOU!
ALL RIGHT ...
I'VE GOT TO HAM IT UP A LITTLE WITH THE ANGER HERE.
I'M SICK OF YOUR SCREWING AROUND!
THWUNK
EEEEK!
OOPS.
THAT'S AWFUL!
AAAGH
I TOOK IT TOO FAR ...
AAAGH

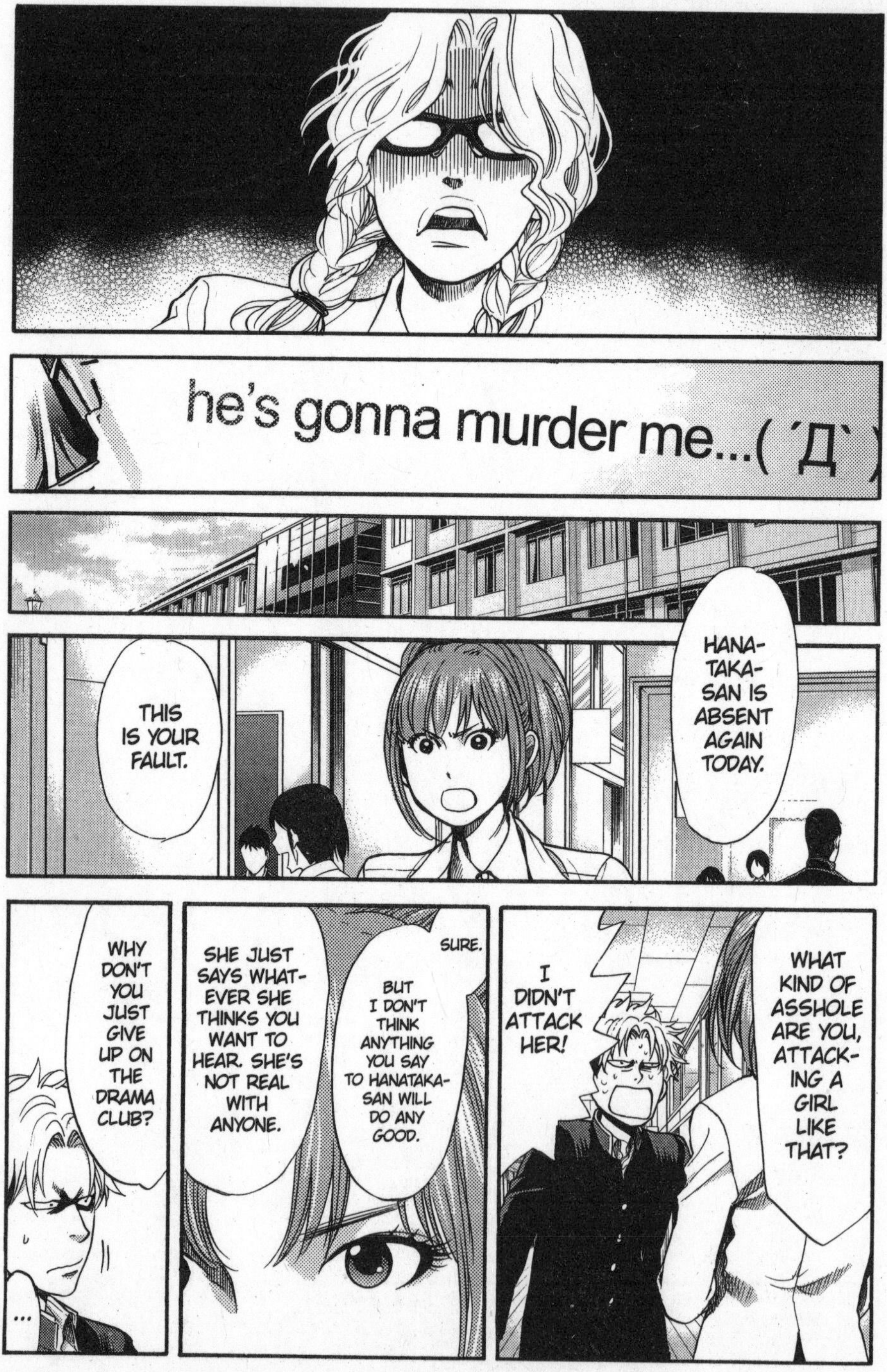
he's gonna murder me...(´Д`)
HANA-TAKA-SAN IS ABSENT AGAIN TODAY.
THIS IS YOUR FAULT.
WHAT KIND OF ASSHOLE ARE YOU, ATTACK-ING A GIRL LIKE THAT?
I DIDN'T ATTACK HER!
SURE.
BUT I DON'T THINK ANYTHING YOU SAY TO HANATAKA-SAN WILL DO ANY GOOD.
SHE JUST SAYS WHAT-EVER SHE THINKS YOU WANT TO HEAR. SHE'S NOT REAL WITH ANYONE.
WHY DON'T YOU JUST GIVE UP ON THE DRAMA CLUB?
...

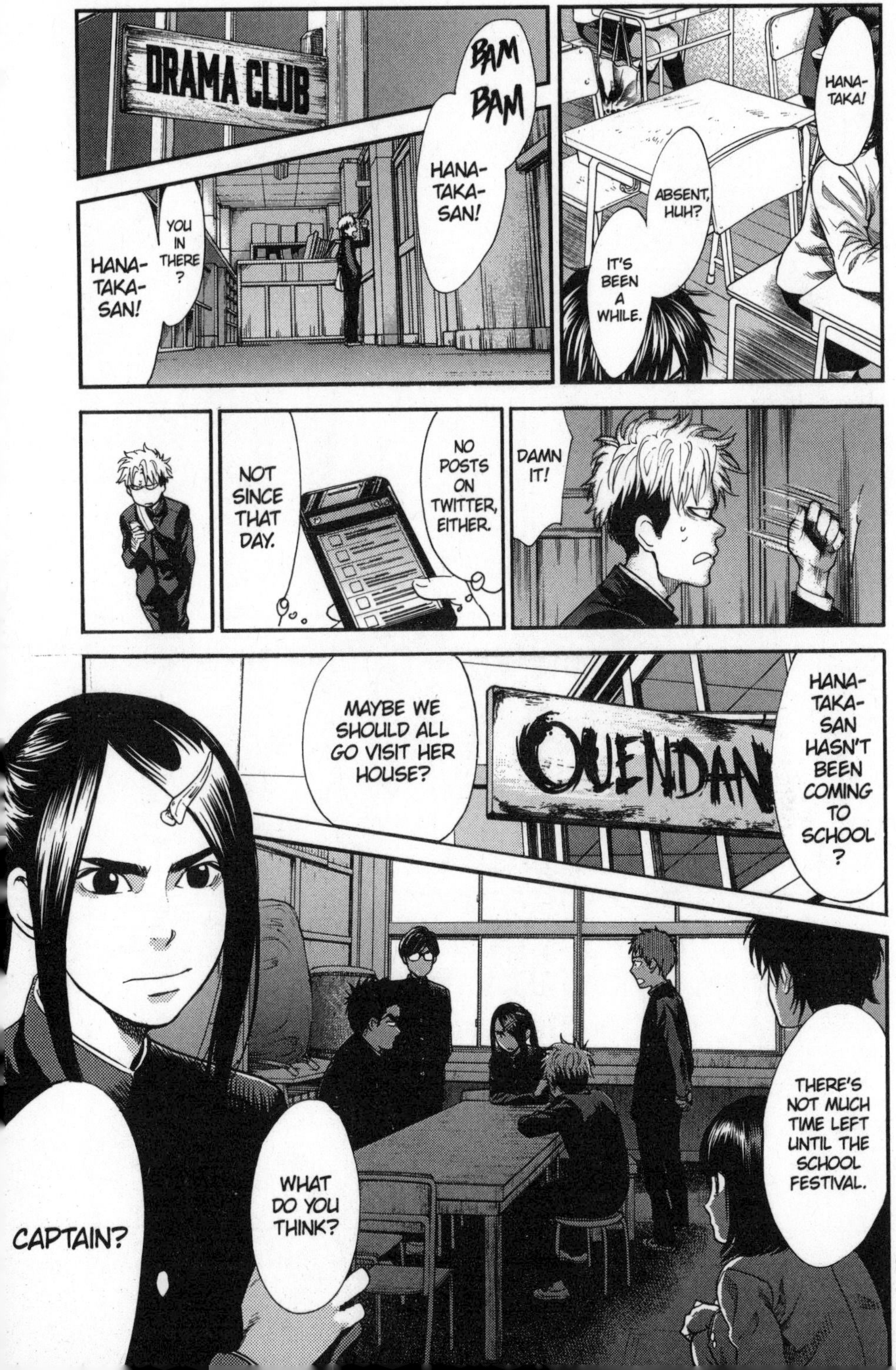
HANA-TAKA!
ABSENT, HUH?
IT'S BEEN A WHILE.
DRAMA CLUB
BAM BAM
HANA-TAKA-SAN!
YOU IN THERE?
HANA-TAKA-SAN!
DAMN IT!
NO POSTS ON TWITTER, EITHER.
NOT SINCE THAT DAY.
HANA-TAKA-SAN HASN'T BEEN COMING TO SCHOOL?
OUENDAN
MAYBE WE SHOULD ALL GO VISIT HER HOUSE?
THERE'S NOT MUCH TIME LEFT UNTIL THE SCHOOL FESTIVAL.
WHAT DO YOU THINK?
CAPTAIN?

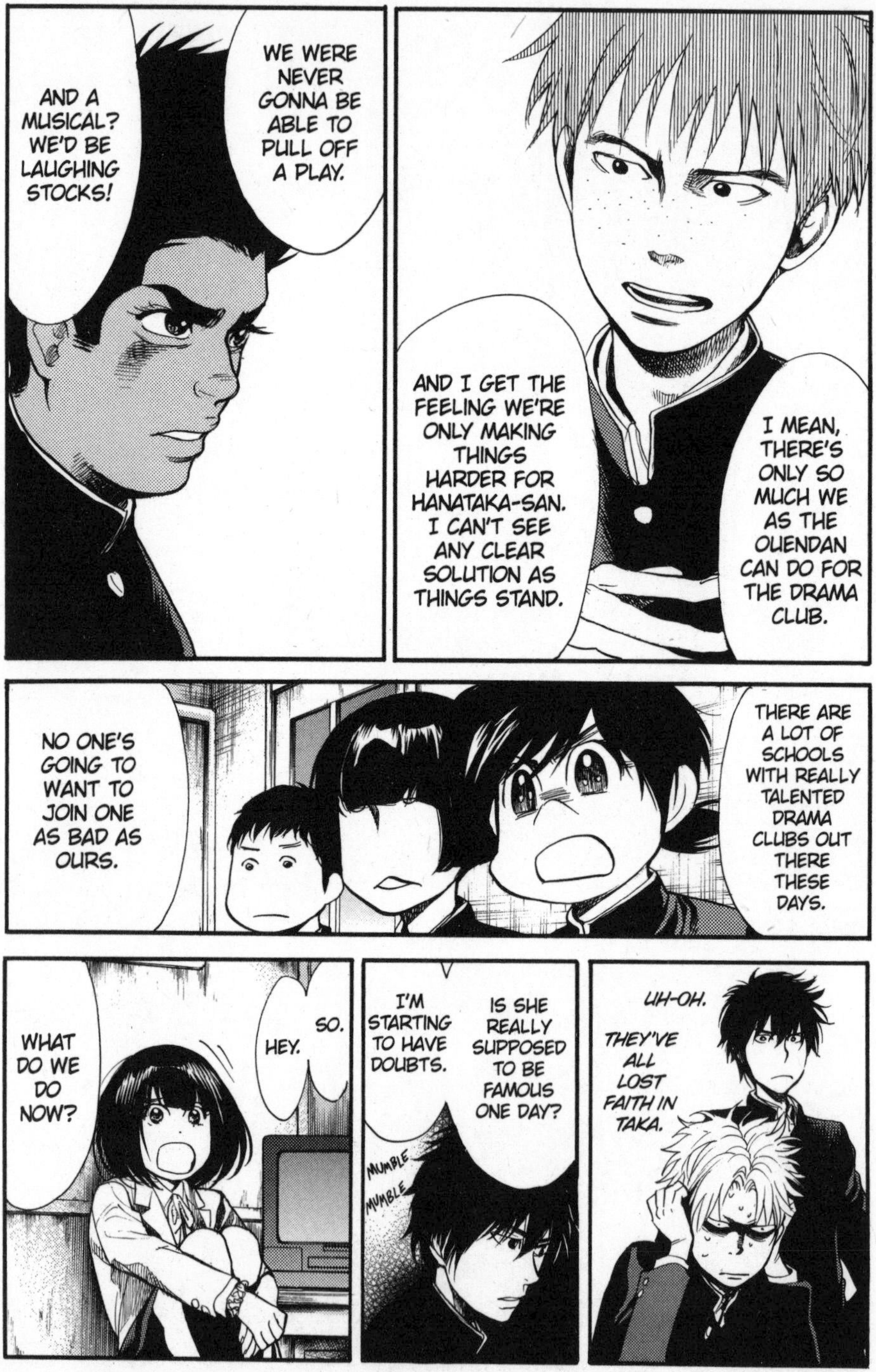
I MEAN, THERE'S ONLY SO MUCH WE AS THE OUENDAN CAN DO FOR THE DRAMA CLUB.
AND I GET THE FEELING WE'RE ONLY MAKING THINGS HARDER FOR HANATAKA-SAN. I CAN'T SEE ANY CLEAR SOLUTION AS THINGS STAND.
WE WERE NEVER GONNA BE ABLE TO PULL OFF A PLAY.
AND A MUSICAL? WE'D BE LAUGHING STOCKS!
THERE ARE A LOT OF SCHOOLS WITH REALLY TALENTED DRAMA CLUBS OUT THERE THESE DAYS.
NO ONE'S GOING TO WANT TO JOIN ONE AS BAD AS OURS.
UH-OH.
THEY'VE ALL LOST FAITH IN TAKA.
IS SHE REALLY SUPPOSED TO BE FAMOUS ONE DAY?
I'M STARTING TO HAVE DOUBTS.
MUMBLE
MUMBLE
SO.
HEY.
WHAT DO WE DO NOW?

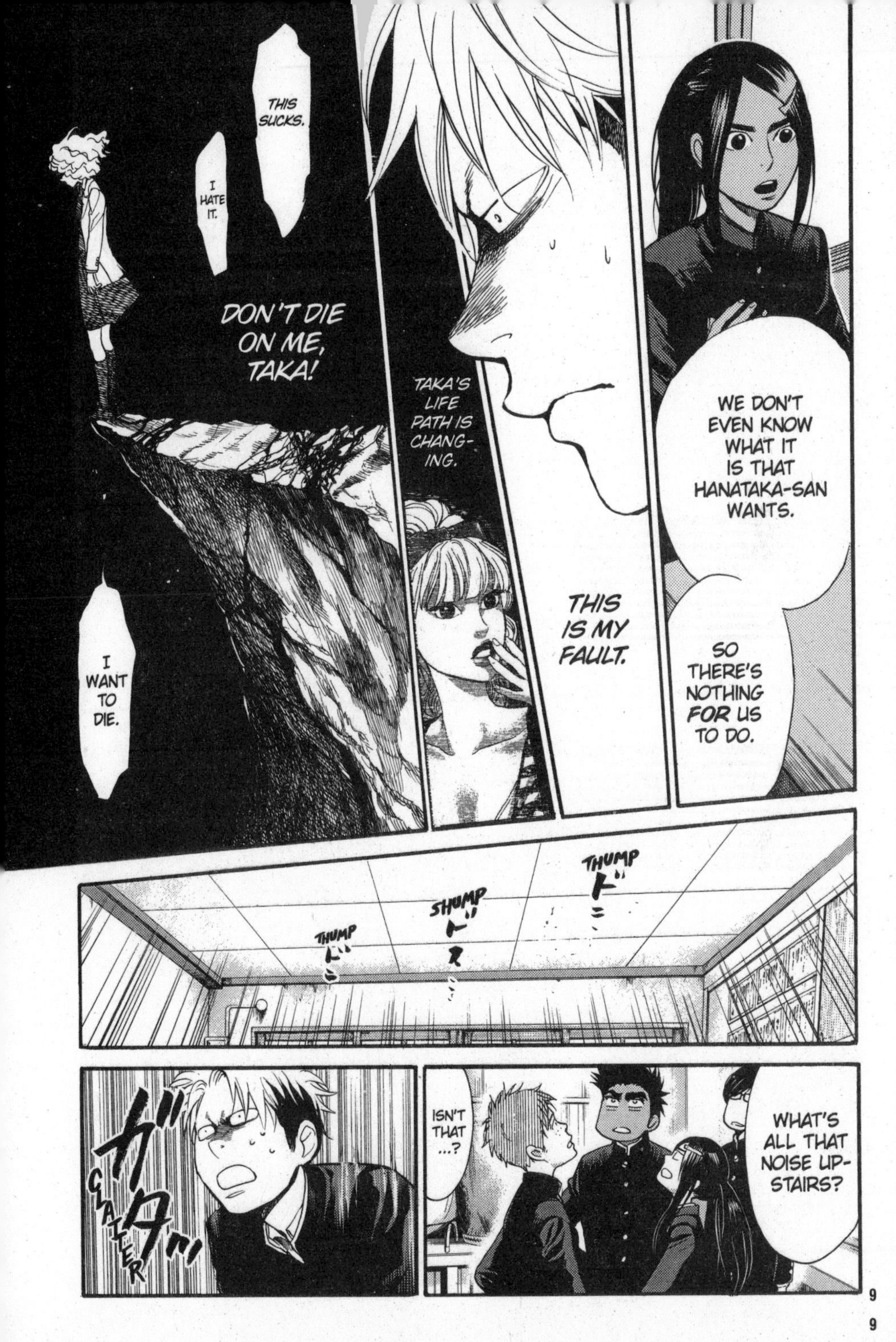
WE DON'T EVEN KNOW WHAT IT IS THAT HANATAKA-SAN WANTS.
SO THERE'S NOTHING FOR US TO DO.
THIS IS MY FAULT.
TAKA'S LIFE PATH IS CHANG-ING.
THIS SUCKS.
I HATE IT.
DON'T DIE ON ME, TAKA!
I WANT TO DIE.
THUMP
SHUMP
THUMP
WHAT'S ALL THAT NOISE UP-STAIRS?
ISN'T THAT ...?
CLATTER

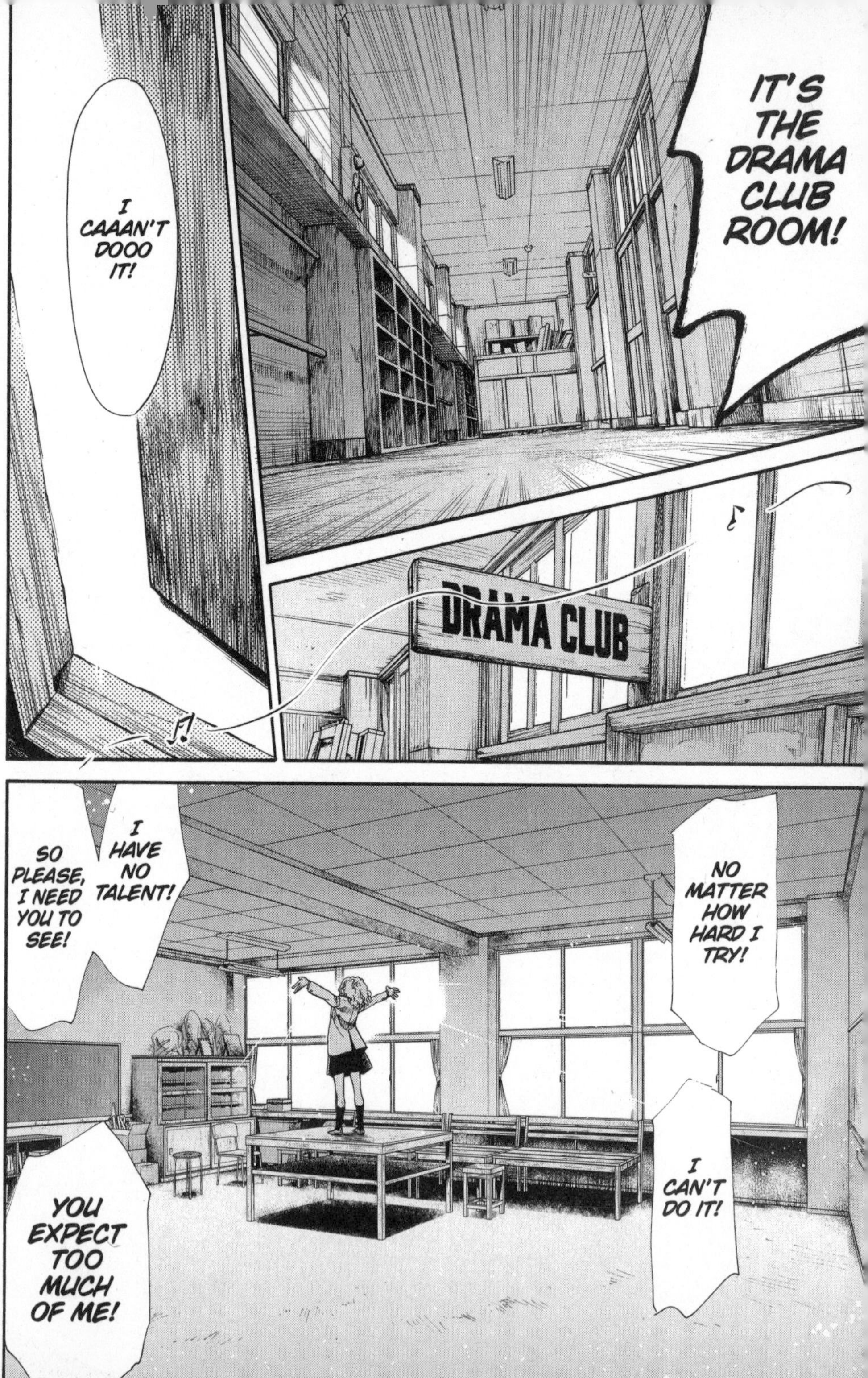
IT'S THE DRAMA CLUB ROOM!
DRAMA CLUB
I CAAAN'T DOOO IT!
NO MATTER HOW HARD I TRY!
I CAN'T DO IT!
I HAVE NO TALENT!
SO PLEASE, I NEED YOU TO SEE!
YOU EXPECT TOO MUCH OF ME!

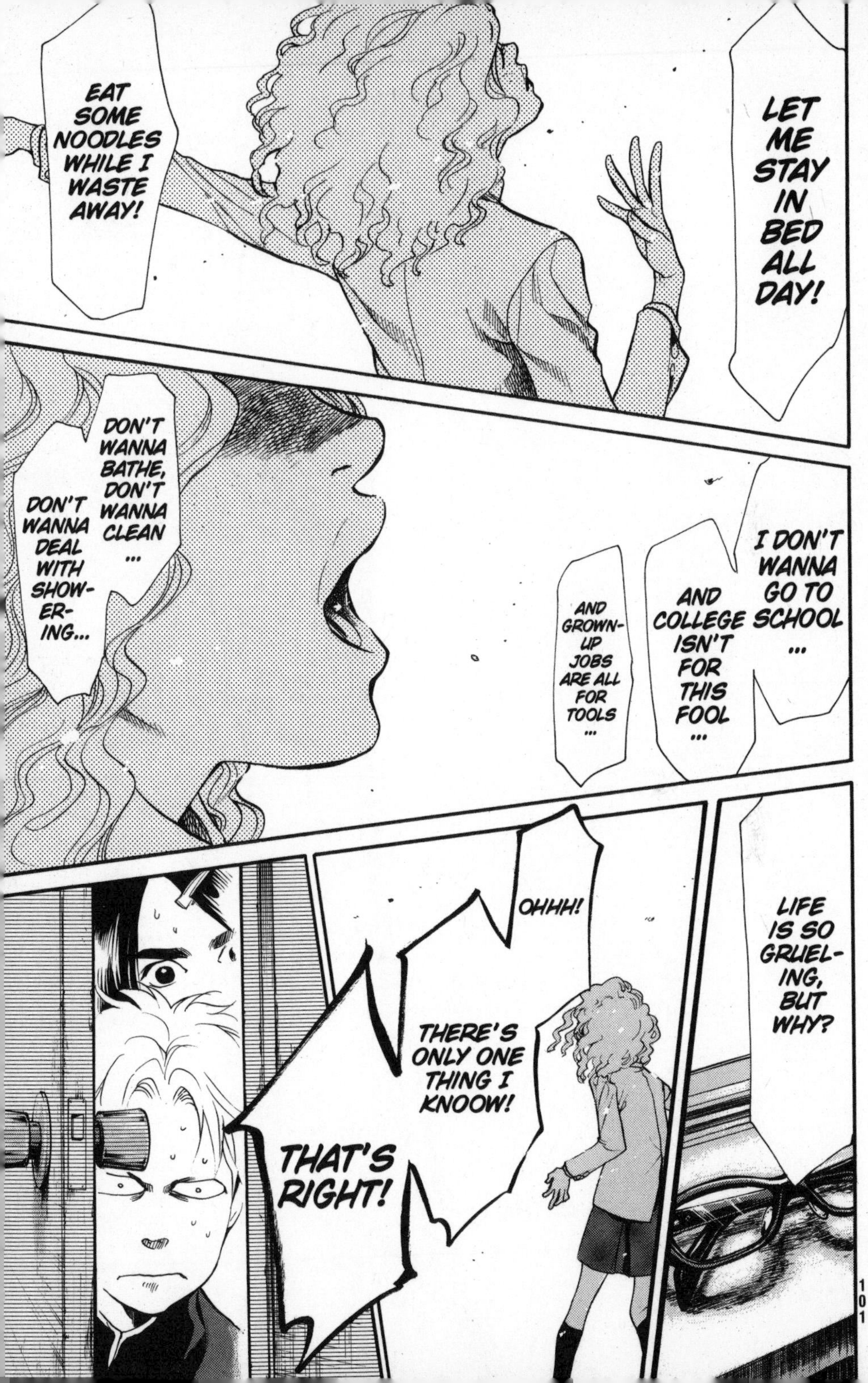
LET ME STAY IN BED ALL DAY!
EAT SOME NOODLES WHILE I WASTE AWAY!
I DON'T WANNA GO TO SCHOOL...
AND COLLEGE ISN'T FOR THIS FOOL...
AND GROWN-UP JOBS ARE ALL FOR TOOLS...
DON'T WANNA BATHE, DON'T WANNA CLEAN...
DON'T WANNA DEAL WITH SHOWER-ING...
LIFE IS SO GRUEL-ING, BUT WHY?
OHHH!
THERE'S ONLY ONE THING I KNOOW!
THAT'S RIGHT!

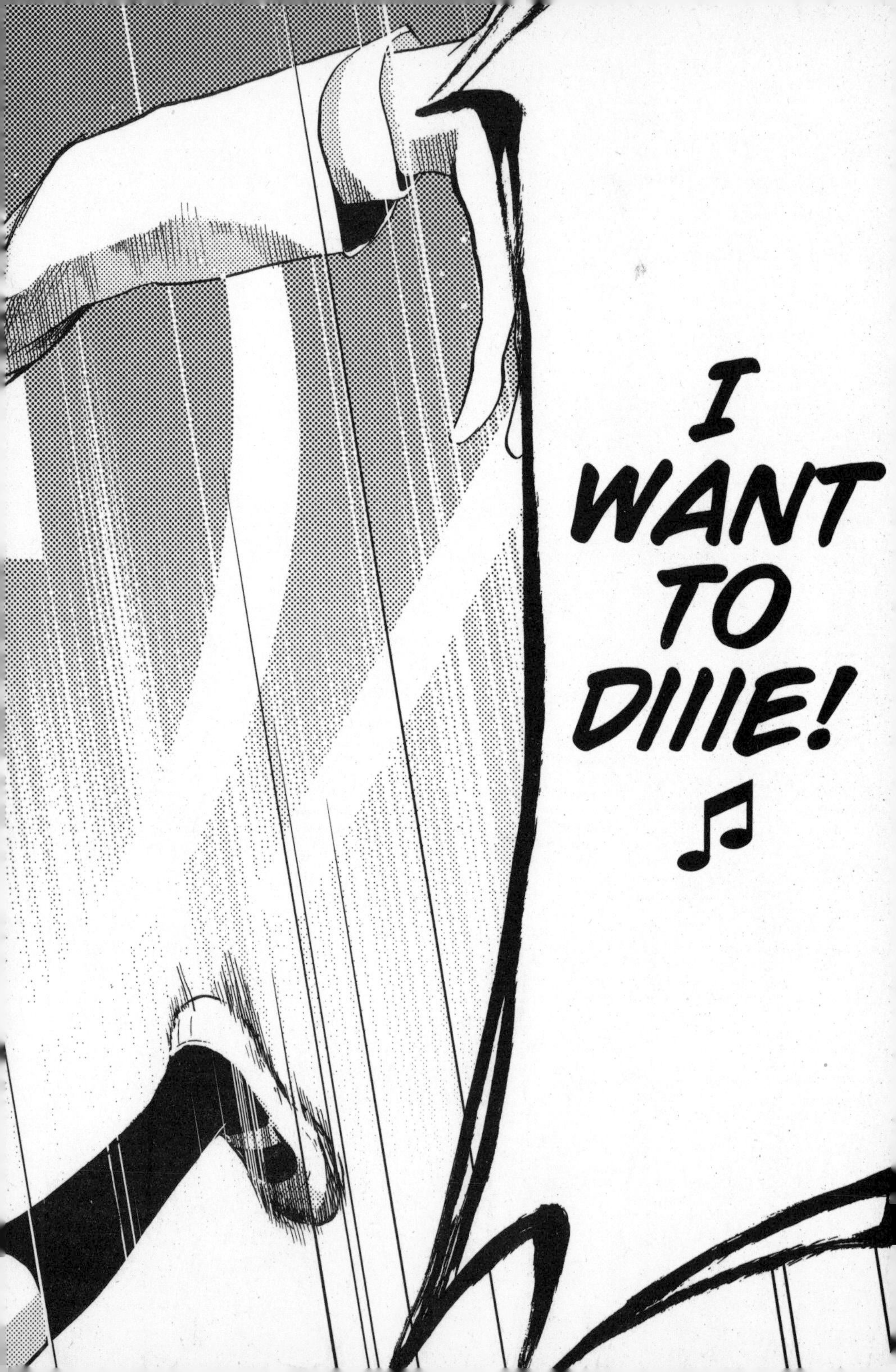
I WANT TO DIIIE! ♫

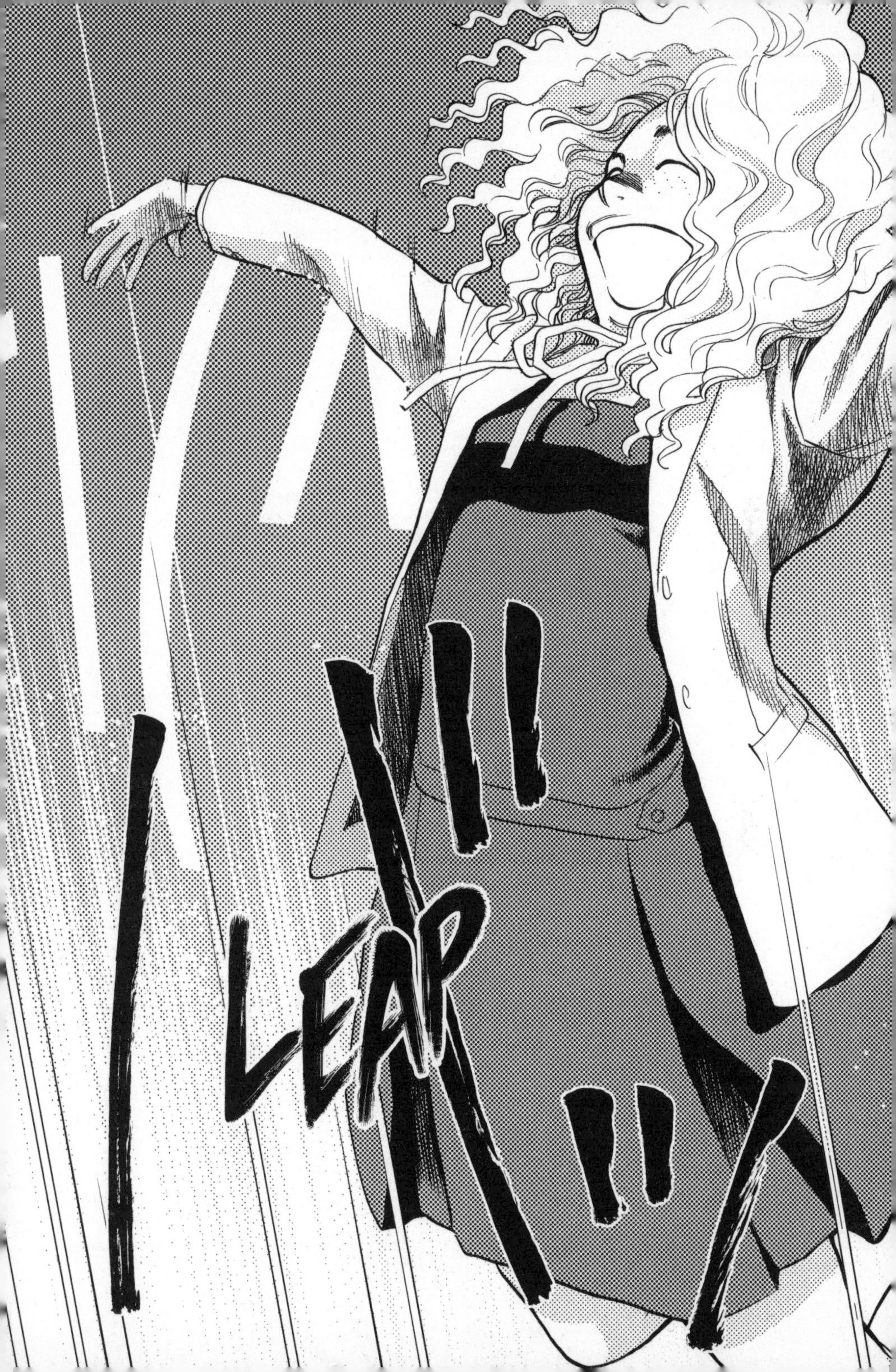
LEAP

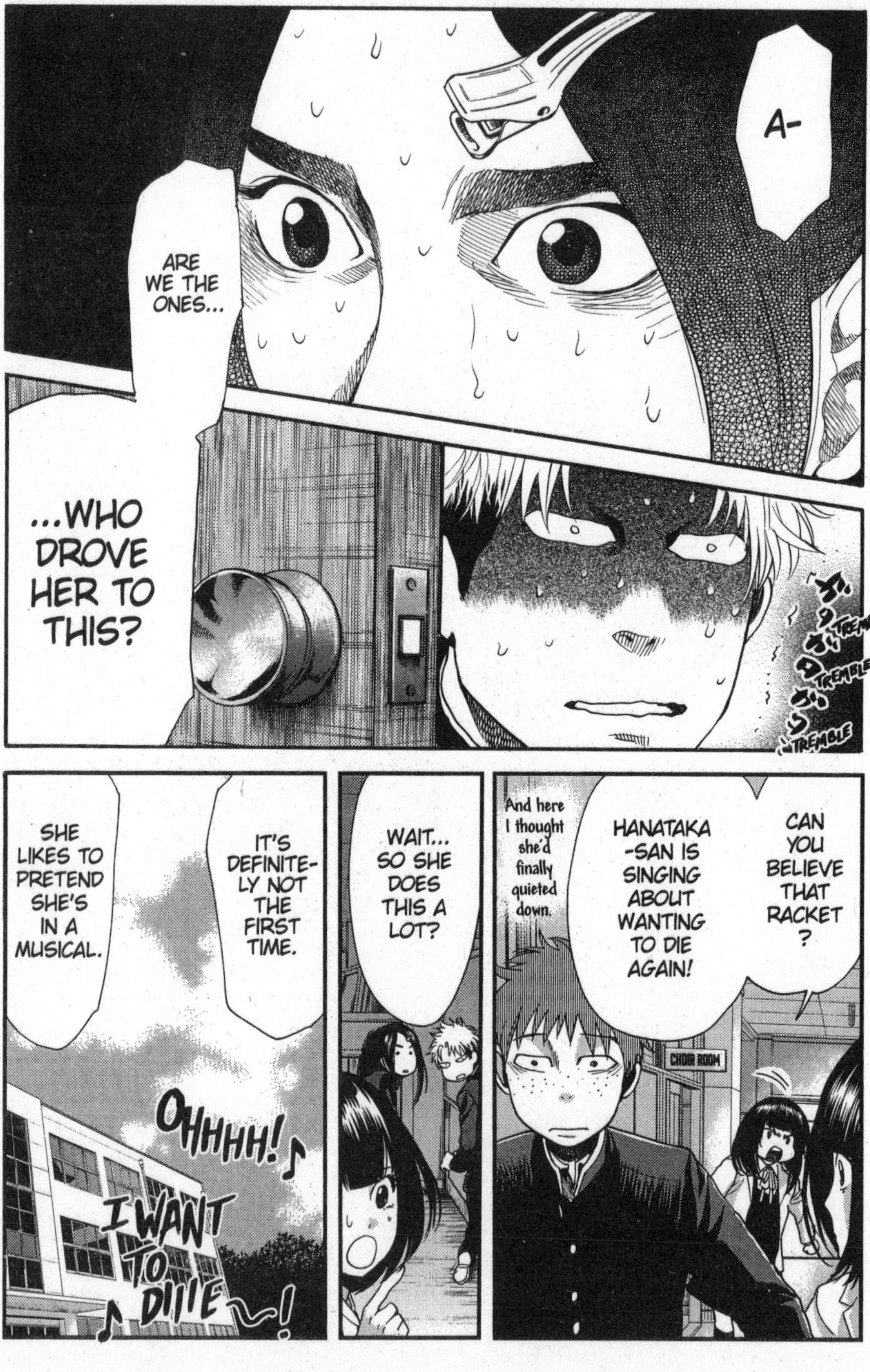
A-
ARE WE THE ONES...
TREMBLE
TREMBLE
TREMBLE
...WHO DROVE HER TO THIS?
CAN YOU BELIEVE THAT RACKET?
HANATAKA-SAN IS SINGING ABOUT WANTING TO DIE AGAIN!
And here I thought she'd finally quieted down.
CHOIR ROOM
WAIT... SO SHE DOES THIS A LOT?
IT'S DEFINITELY NOT THE FIRST TIME.
SHE LIKES TO PRETEND SHE'S IN A MUSICAL.
OHHHH! ♪
I WANT TO DIIIE~! ♪

Again!!

アゲイン!!

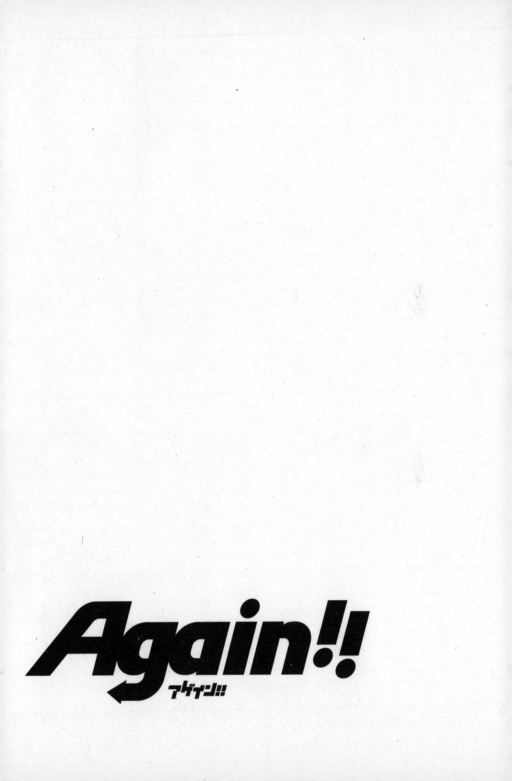

Again!!

アゲイン!!

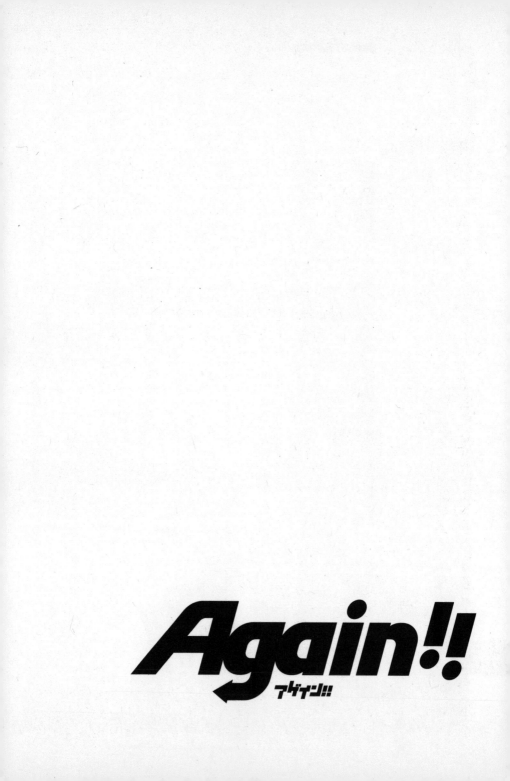

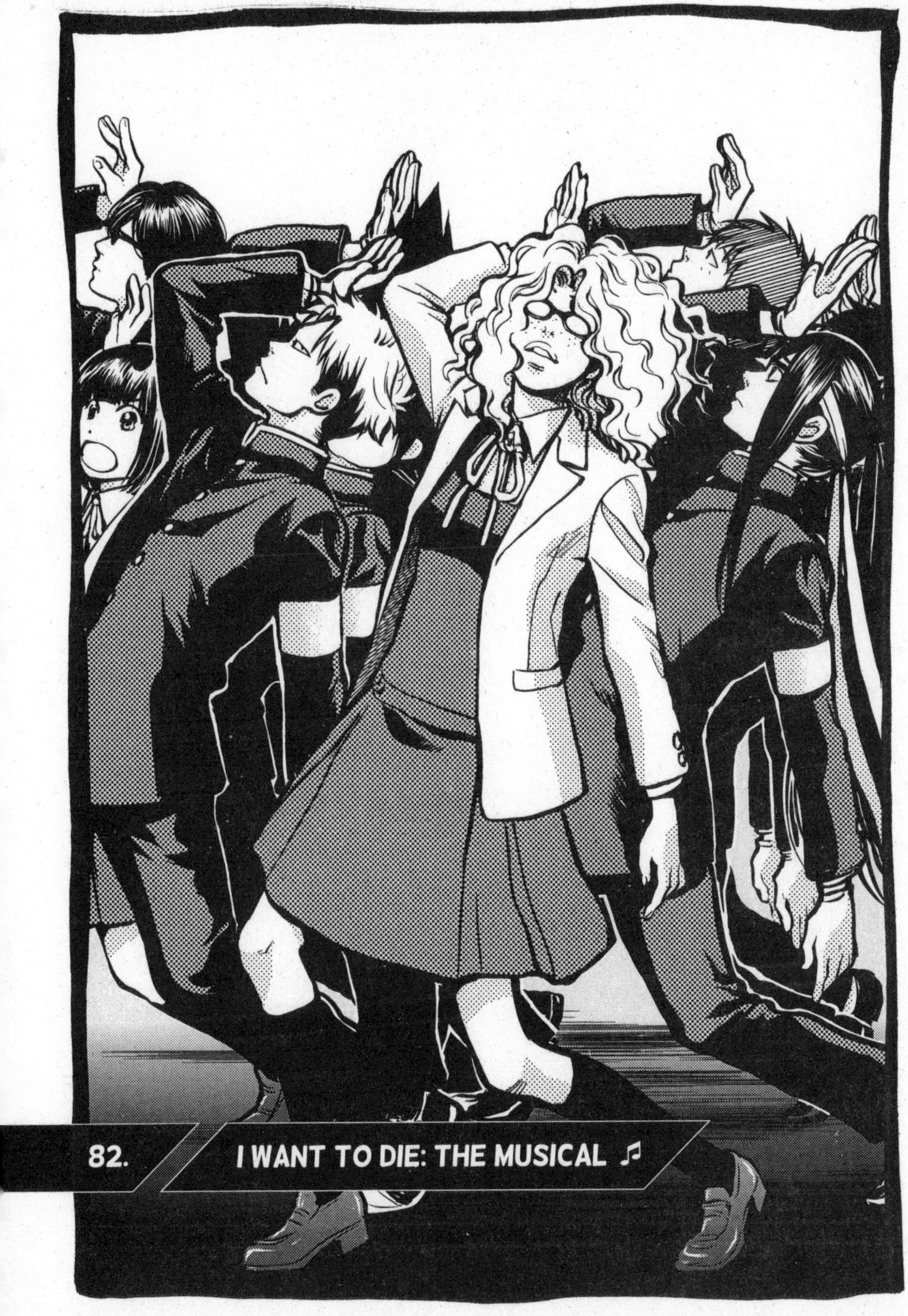
82.
I WANT TO DIE: THE MUSICAL ♫

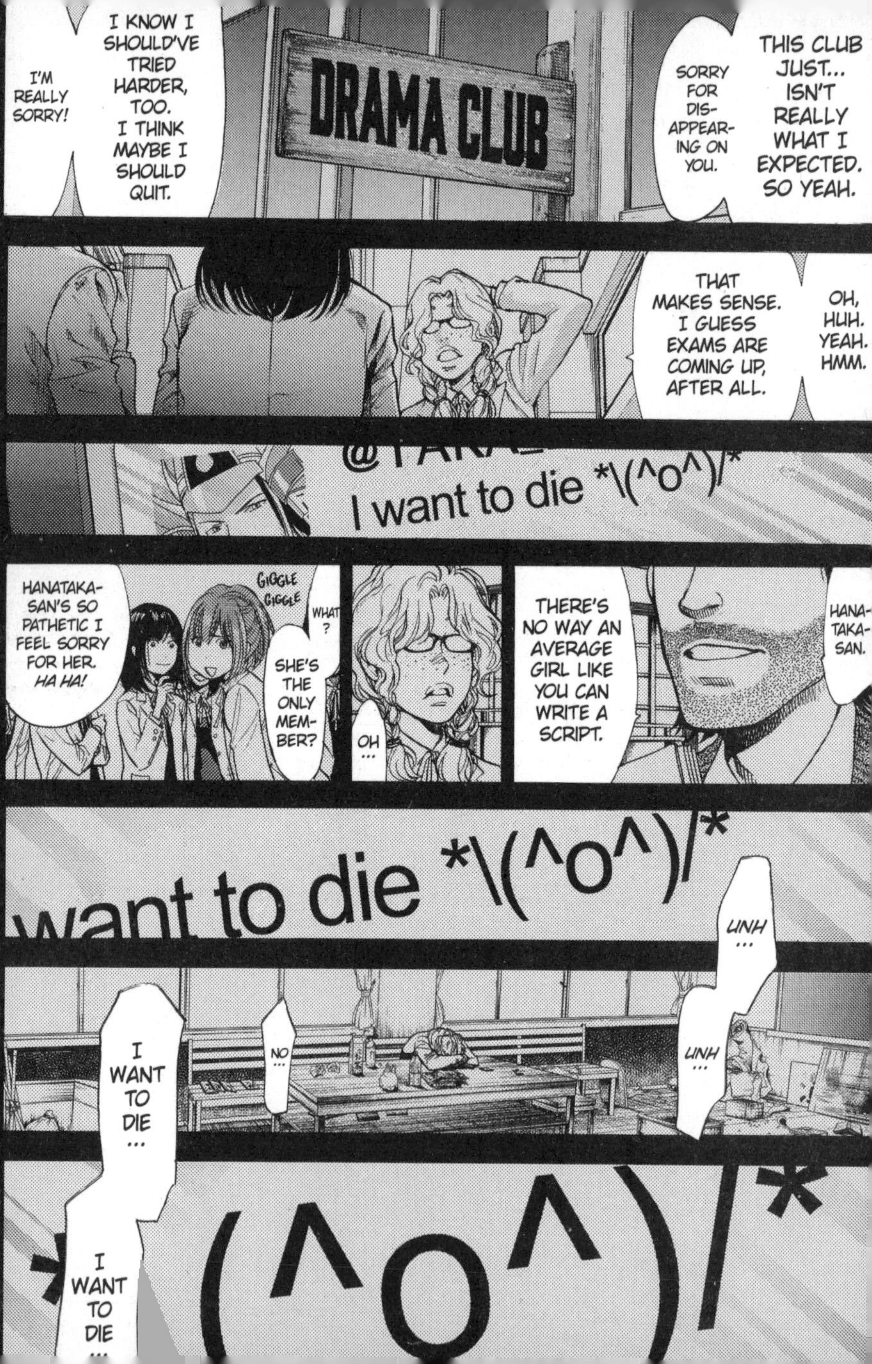
THIS CLUB JUST... ISN'T REALLY WHAT I EXPECTED. SO YEAH.
SORRY FOR DIS-APPEARING ON YOU.
DRAMA CLUB
I KNOW I SHOULD'VE TRIED HARDER, TOO. I THINK MAYBE I SHOULD QUIT.
I'M REALLY SORRY!
OH, HUH. YEAH. HMM.
THAT MAKES SENSE. I GUESS EXAMS ARE COMING UP, AFTER ALL.
I want to die *\(^o^)/*
HANA-TAKA-SAN.
THERE'S NO WAY AN AVERAGE GIRL LIKE YOU CAN WRITE A SCRIPT.
OH ...
WHAT ?
SHE'S THE ONLY MEM-BER?
GIGGLE GIGGLE
HANATAKA-SAN'S SO PATHETIC I FEEL SORRY FOR HER. HA HA!
want to die *\(^o^)/*
UNH ...
UNH ...
NO ...
I WANT TO DIE ...
I WANT TO DIE ...

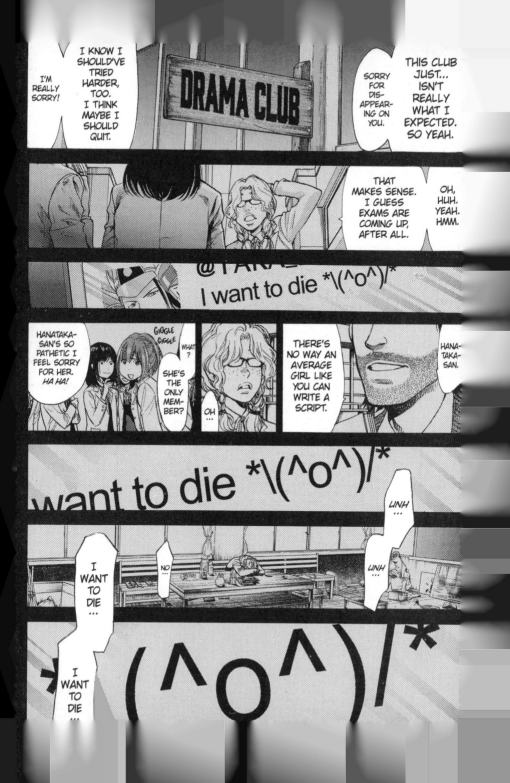

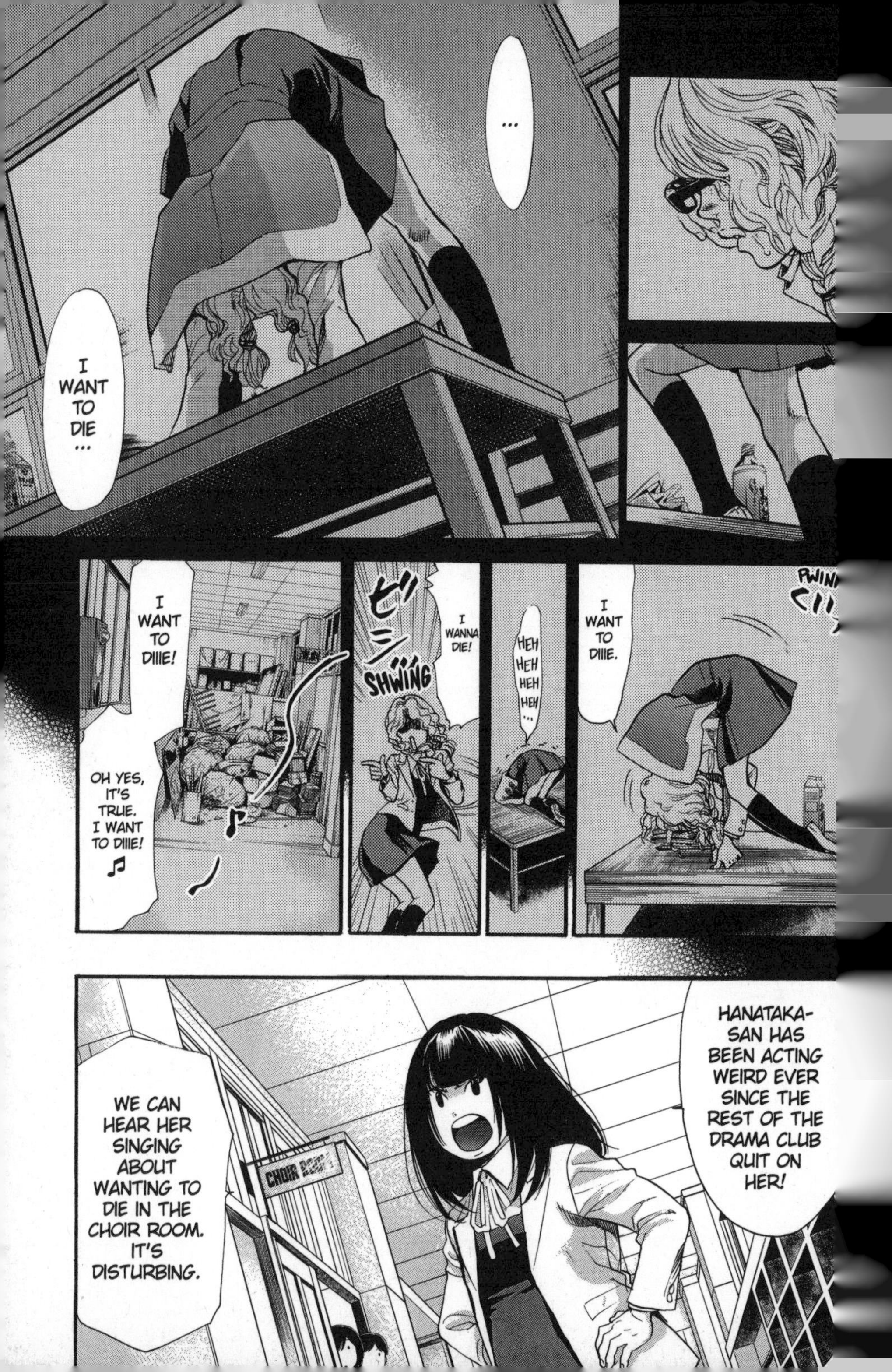
...
I WANT TO DIE ...
I WANT TO DIIIE.
HEH HEH HEH HEH ...
I WANNA DIE!
SHWING
I WANT TO DIIIE!
OH YES, IT'S TRUE. I WANT TO DIIIE! ♫
HANATAKA-SAN HAS BEEN ACTING WEIRD EVER SINCE THE REST OF THE DRAMA CLUB QUIT ON HER!
WE CAN HEAR HER SINGING ABOUT WANTING TO DIE IN THE CHOIR ROOM. IT'S DISTURBING.

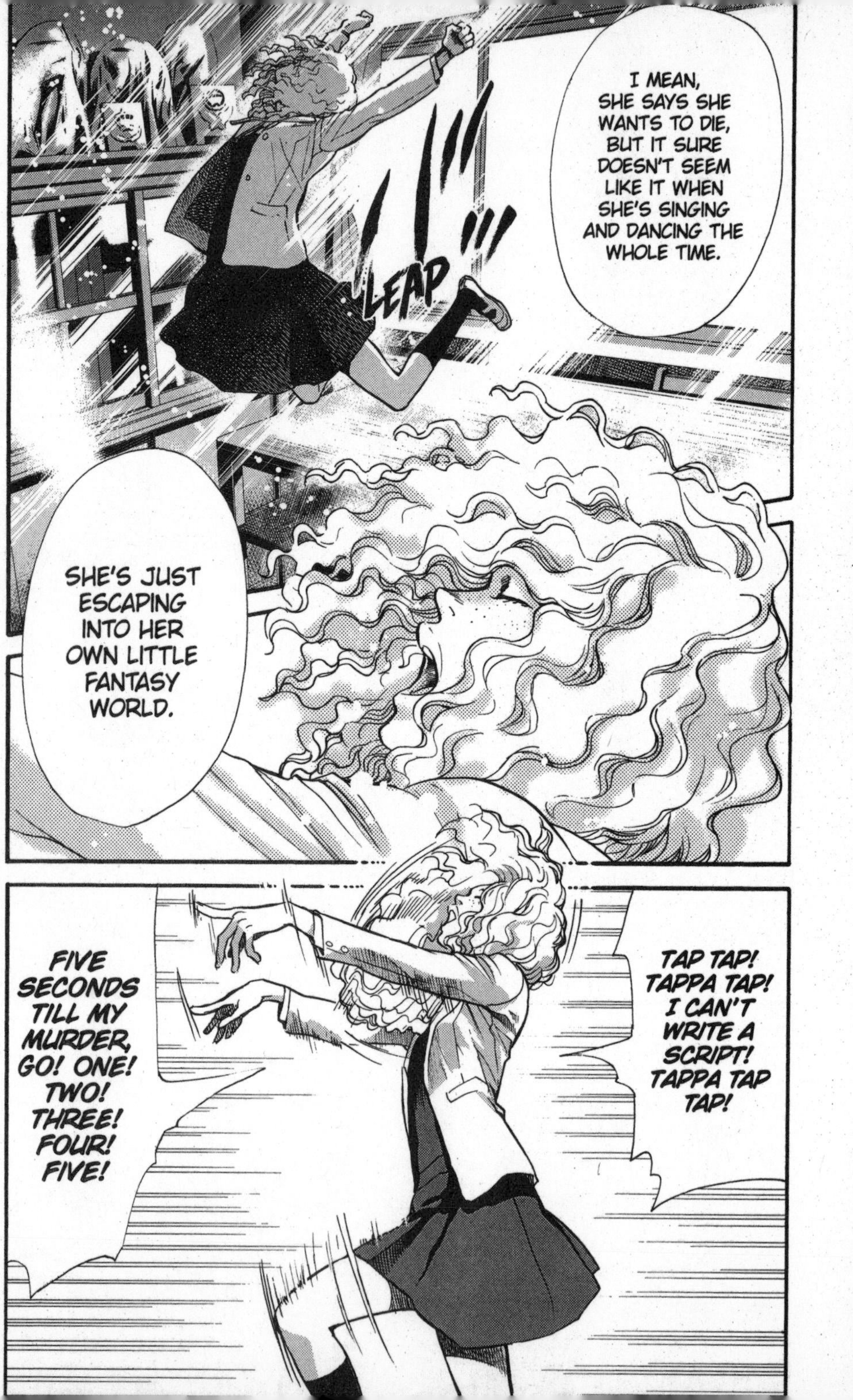
I MEAN, SHE SAYS SHE WANTS TO DIE, BUT IT SURE DOESN'T SEEM LIKE IT WHEN SHE'S SINGING AND DANCING THE WHOLE TIME.
LEAP
SHE'S JUST ESCAPING INTO HER OWN LITTLE FANTASY WORLD.
TAP TAP! TAPPA TAP! I CAN'T WRITE A SCRIPT! TAPPA TAP TAP TAP!
FIVE SECONDS TILL MY MURDER, GO! ONE! TWO! THREE! FOUR! FIVE!

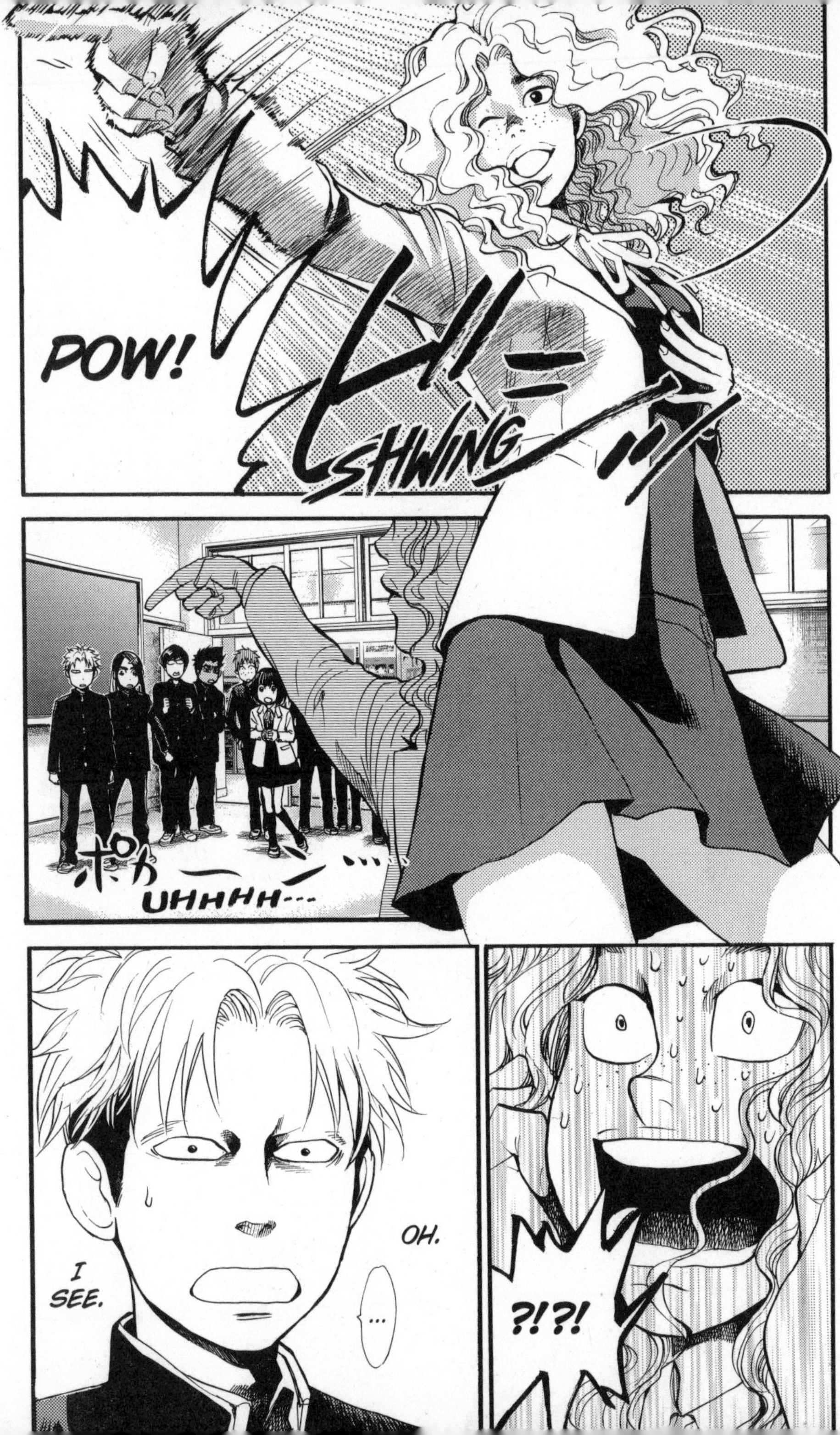
POW!
SHWING
ポカ——ン
UHHHH...
?!?!
OH.
...
I SEE.

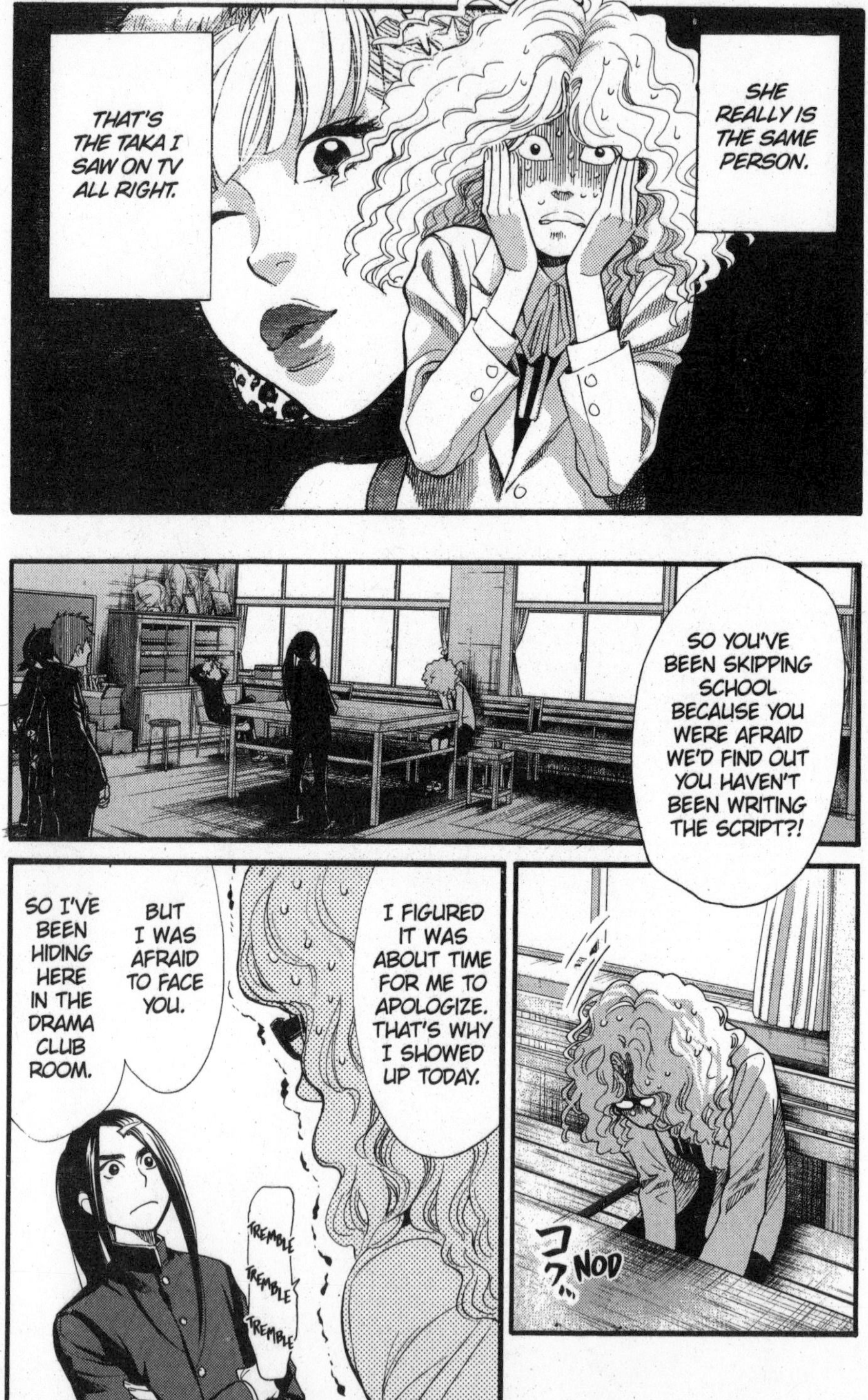
SHE REALLY IS THE SAME PERSON.
THAT'S THE TAKA I SAW ON TV ALL RIGHT.
SO YOU'VE BEEN SKIPPING SCHOOL BECAUSE YOU WERE AFRAID WE'D FIND OUT YOU HAVEN'T BEEN WRITING THE SCRIPT?!
コク NOD
I FIGURED IT WAS ABOUT TIME FOR ME TO APOLOGIZE. THAT'S WHY I SHOWED UP TODAY.
BUT I WAS AFRAID TO FACE YOU.
SO I'VE BEEN HIDING HERE IN THE DRAMA CLUB ROOM.
TREMBLE
TREMBLE
TREMBLE

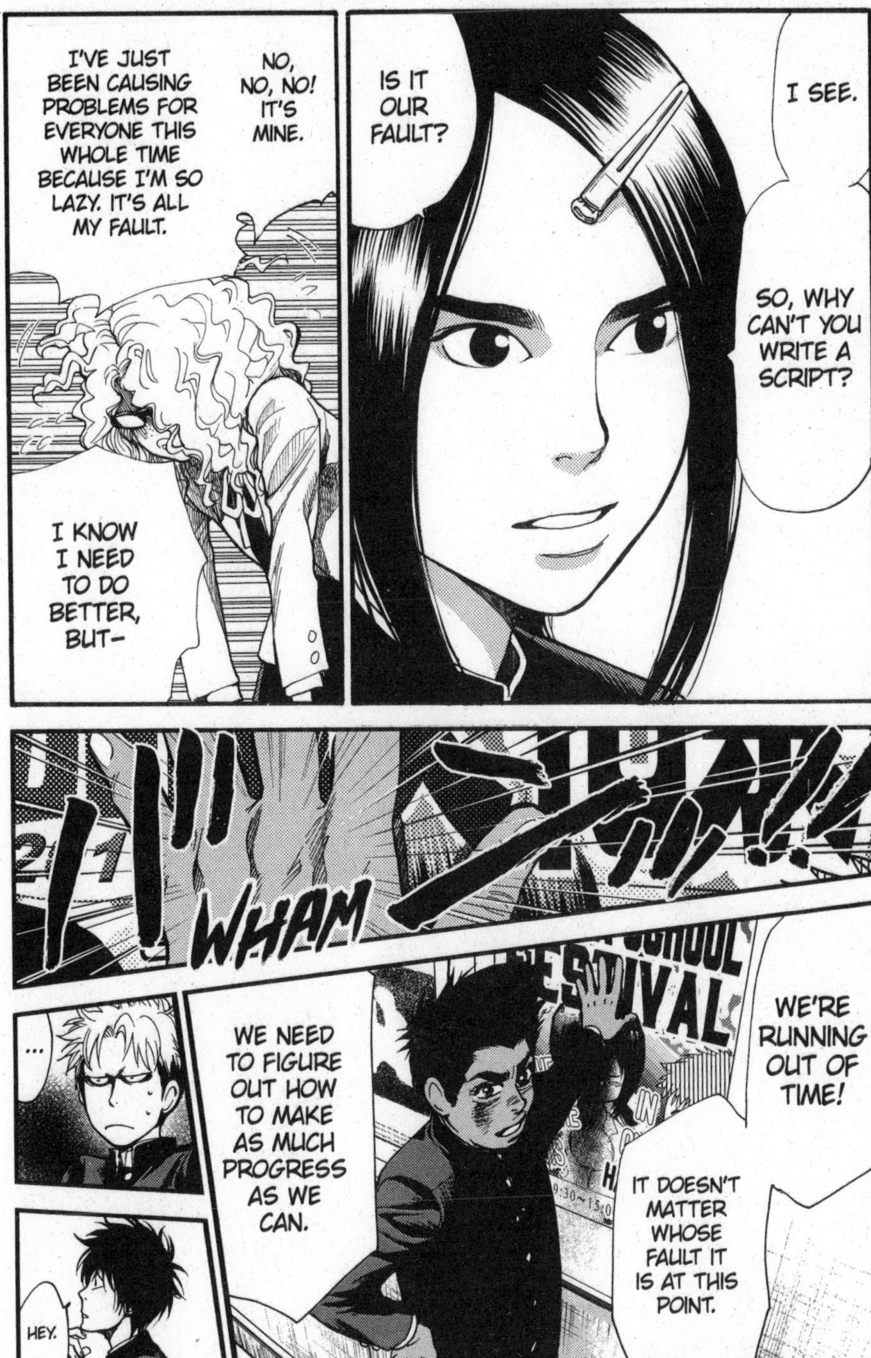
I SEE.
SO, WHY CAN'T YOU WRITE A SCRIPT?
IS IT OUR FAULT?
NO, NO, NO! IT'S MINE.
I'VE JUST BEEN CAUSING PROBLEMS FOR EVERYONE THIS WHOLE TIME BECAUSE I'M SO LAZY. IT'S ALL MY FAULT.
I KNOW I NEED TO DO BETTER, BUT-
WHAM
WE'RE RUNNING OUT OF TIME!
IT DOESN'T MATTER WHOSE FAULT IT IS AT THIS POINT.
WE NEED TO FIGURE OUT HOW TO MAKE AS MUCH PROGRESS AS WE CAN.
...
HEY.

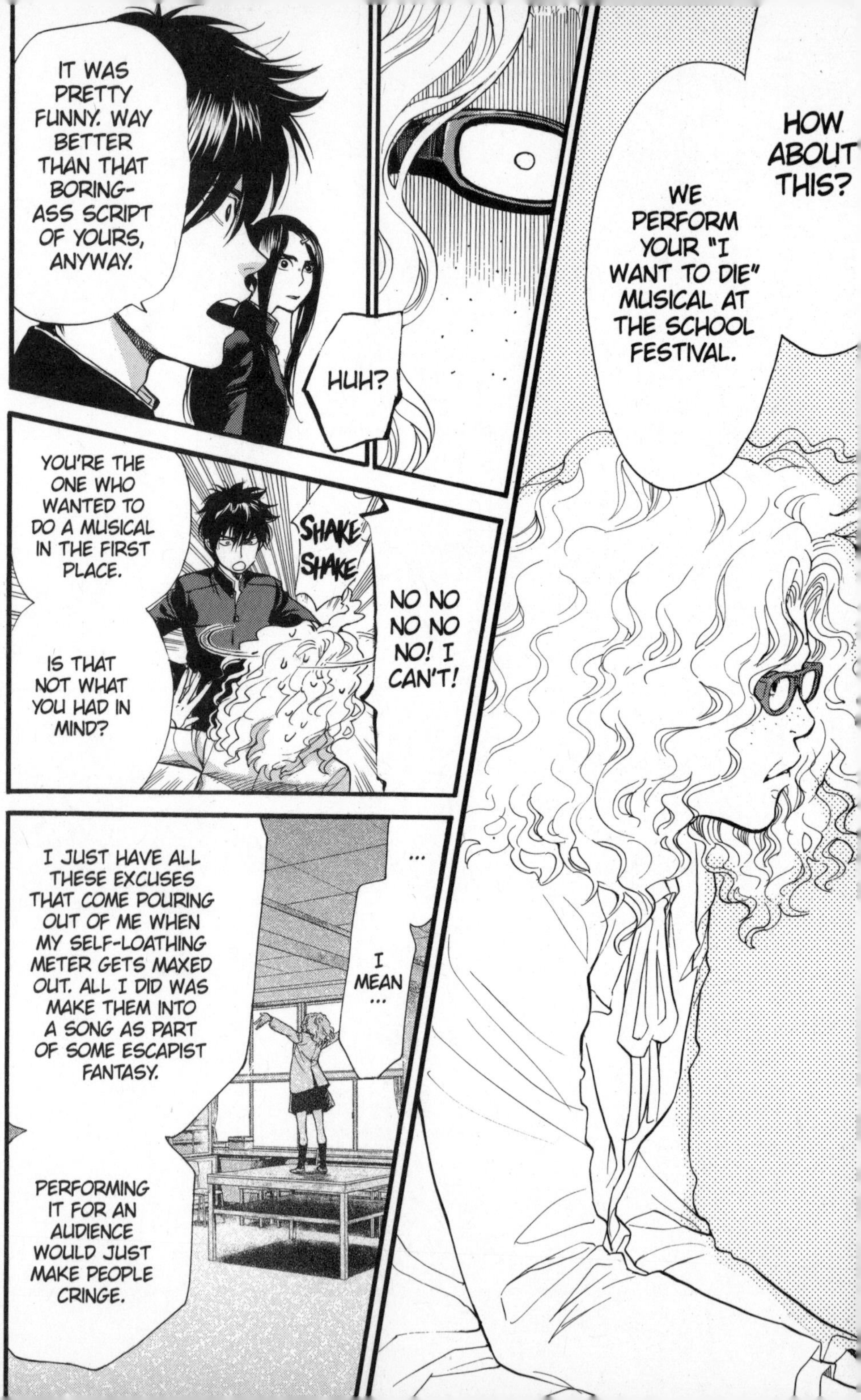
HOW ABOUT THIS?
WE PERFORM YOUR "I WANT TO DIE" MUSICAL AT THE SCHOOL FESTIVAL.
HUH?
IT WAS PRETTY FUNNY. WAY BETTER THAN THAT BORING-ASS SCRIPT OF YOURS, ANYWAY.
SHAKE SHAKE
NO NO NO NO NO! I CAN'T!
YOU'RE THE ONE WHO WANTED TO DO A MUSICAL IN THE FIRST PLACE.
IS THAT NOT WHAT YOU HAD IN MIND?
...
I MEAN...
I JUST HAVE ALL THESE EXCUSES THAT COME POURING OUT OF ME WHEN MY SELF-LOATHING METER GETS MAXED OUT. ALL I DID WAS MAKE THEM INTO A SONG AS PART OF SOME ESCAPIST FANTASY.
PERFORMING IT FOR AN AUDIENCE WOULD JUST MAKE PEOPLE CRINGE.

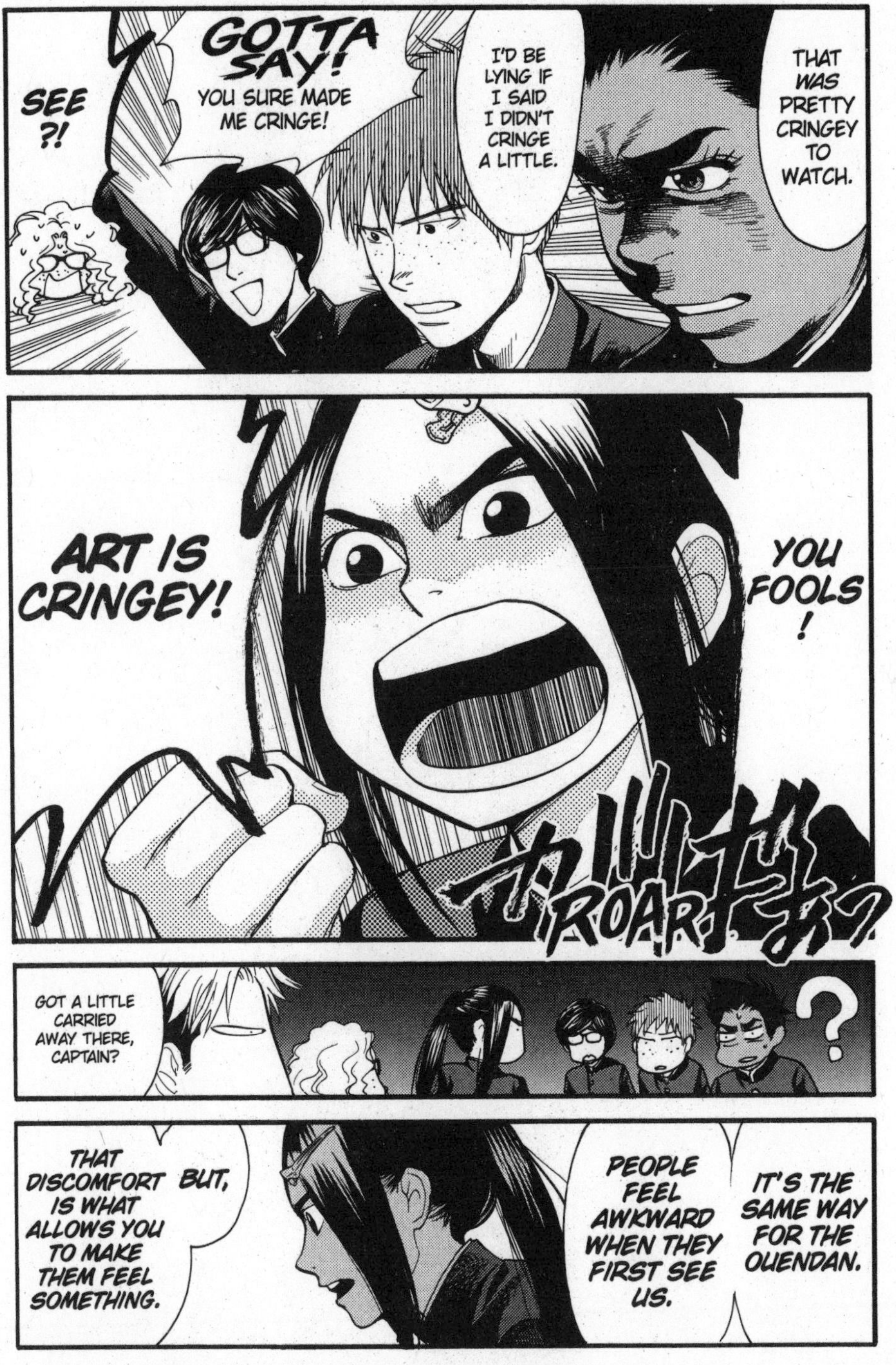
THAT WAS PRETTY CRINGEY TO WATCH.
I'D BE LYING IF I SAID I DIDN'T CRINGE A LITTLE.
GOTTA SAY! YOU SURE MADE ME CRINGE!
SEE?!
YOU FOOLS!
ART IS CRINGEY!
ROAR
?
GOT A LITTLE CARRIED AWAY THERE, CAPTAIN?
IT'S THE SAME WAY FOR THE OUENDAN.
PEOPLE FEEL AWKWARD WHEN THEY FIRST SEE US.
BUT,
THAT DISCOMFORT IS WHAT ALLOWS YOU TO MAKE THEM FEEL SOMETHING.

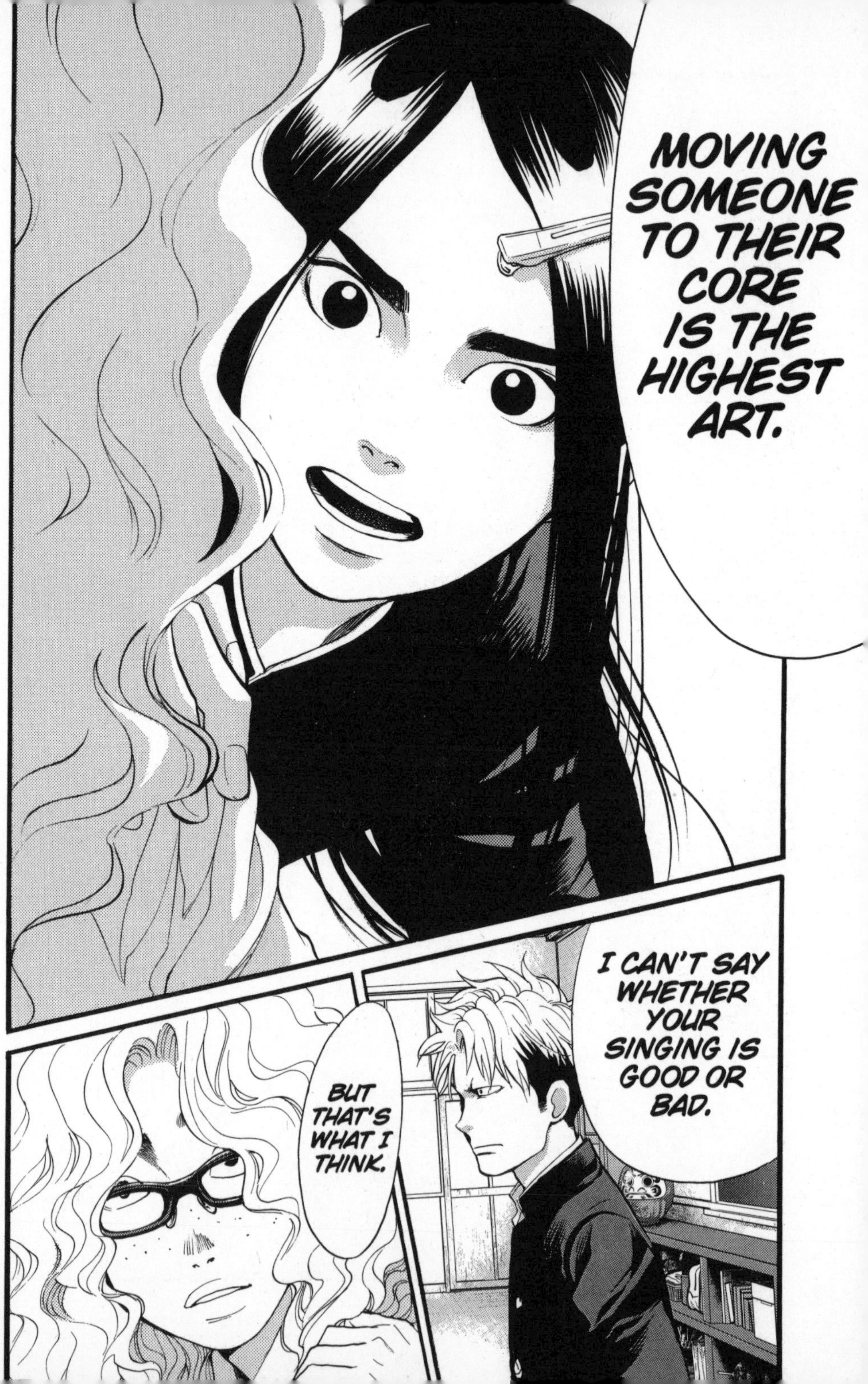
MOVING SOMEONE TO THEIR CORE IS THE HIGHEST ART.
I CAN'T SAY WHETHER YOUR SINGING IS GOOD OR BAD.
BUT THAT'S WHAT I THINK.

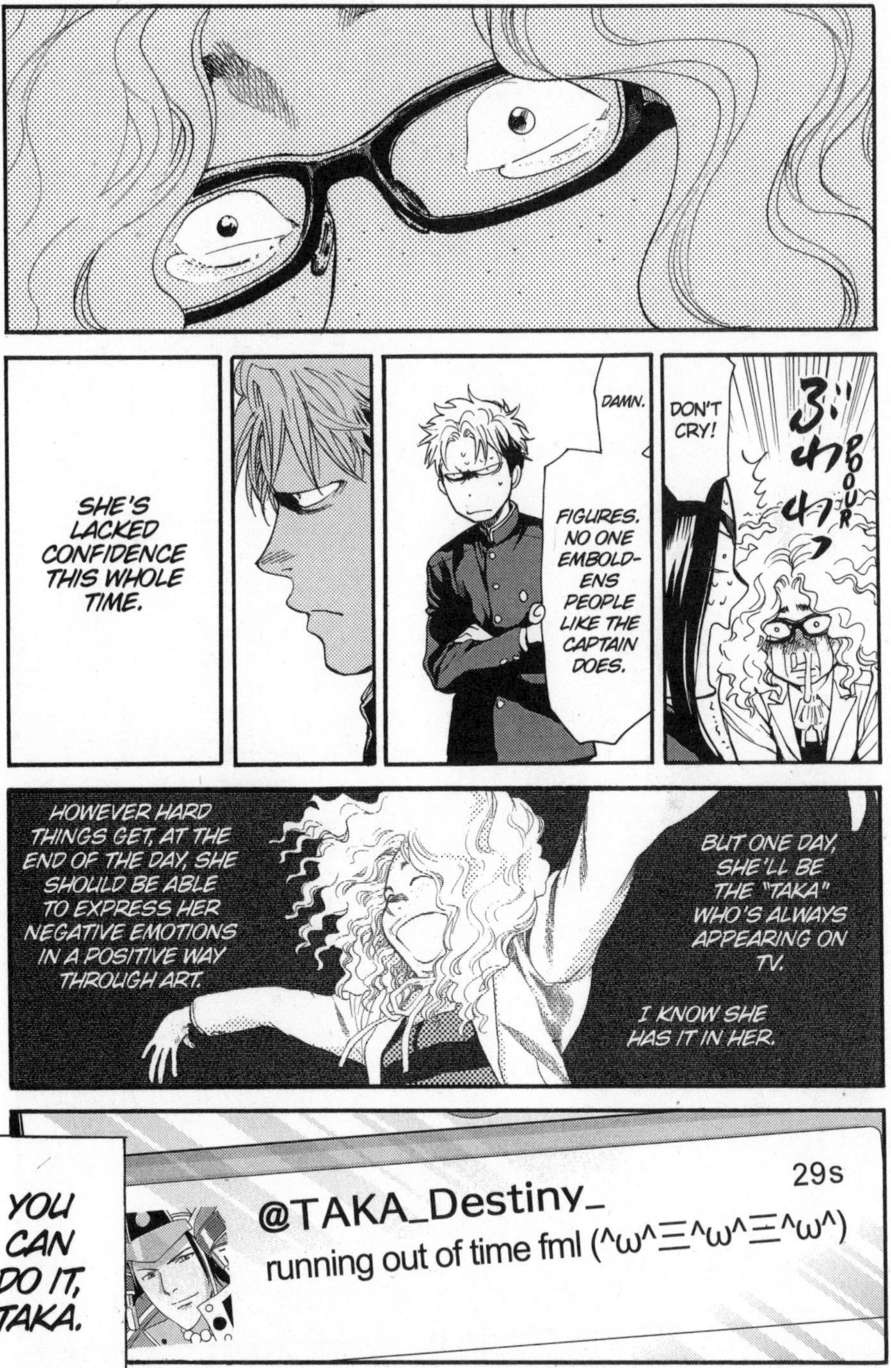
DON'T CRY!
ぶわわっ
POUR
DAMN.
FIGURES. NO ONE EMBOLDENS PEOPLE LIKE THE CAPTAIN DOES.
SHE'S LACKED CONFIDENCE THIS WHOLE TIME.
BUT ONE DAY, SHE'LL BE THE "TAKA" WHO'S ALWAYS APPEARING ON TV.
I KNOW SHE HAS IT IN HER.
HOWEVER HARD THINGS GET, AT THE END OF THE DAY, SHE SHOULD BE ABLE TO EXPRESS HER NEGATIVE EMOTIONS IN A POSITIVE WAY THROUGH ART.
29s
@TAKA_Destiny_
running out of time fml (^ω^三^ω^三^ω^)
YOU CAN DO IT, TAKA.

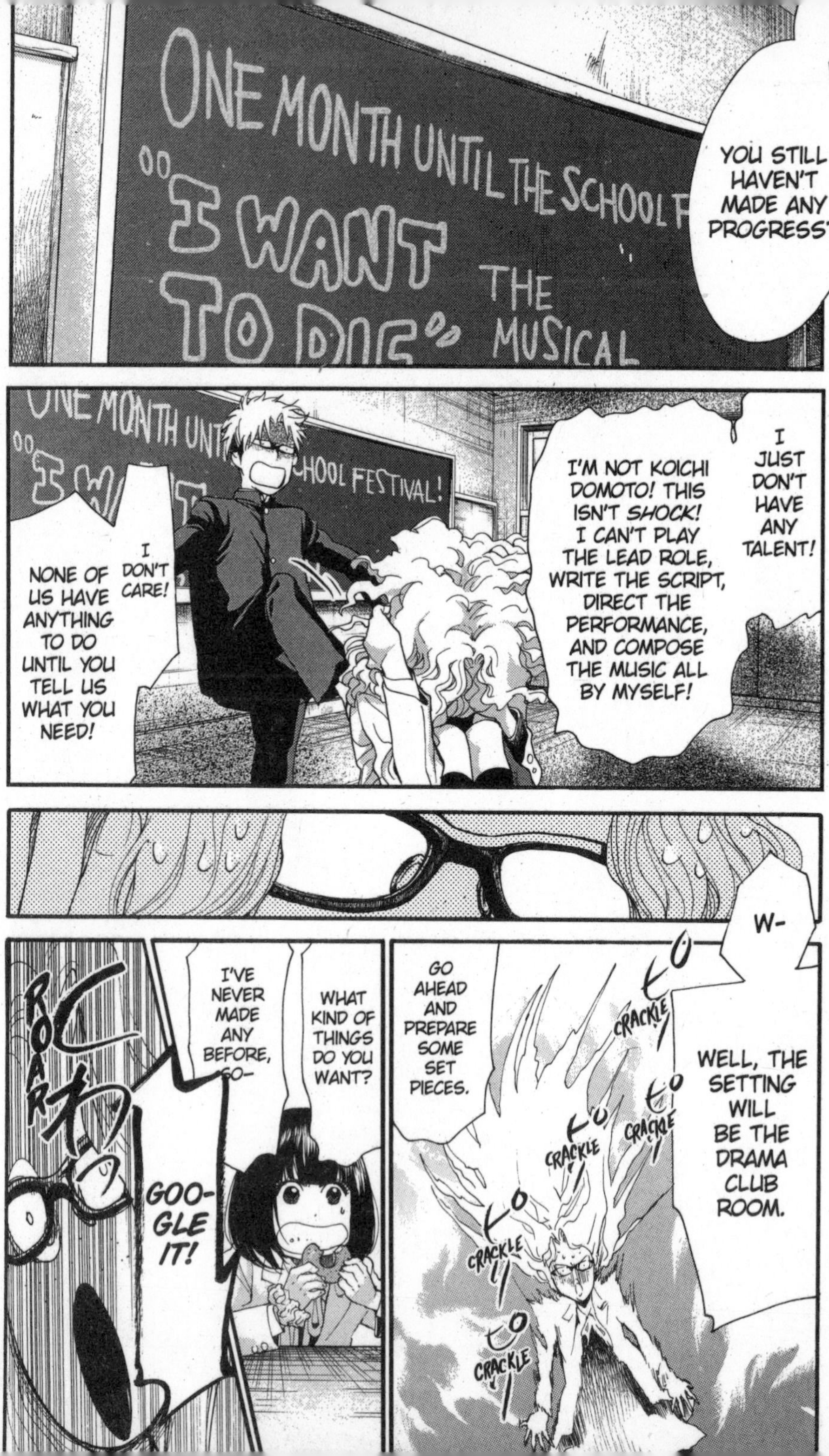
ONE MONTH UNTIL THE SCHOOL F
"I WANT TO DIE" THE MUSICAL
WHAT?
YOU STILL HAVEN'T MADE ANY PROGRESS?
I JUST DON'T HAVE ANY TALENT!
I'M NOT KOICHI DOMOTO! THIS ISN'T *SHOCK*! I CAN'T PLAY THE LEAD ROLE, WRITE THE SCRIPT, DIRECT THE PERFORMANCE, AND COMPOSE THE MUSIC ALL BY MYSELF!
SCHOOL FESTIVAL!
I DON'T CARE!
NONE OF US HAVE ANYTHING TO DO UNTIL YOU TELL US WHAT YOU NEED!
W-
WELL, THE SETTING WILL BE THE DRAMA CLUB ROOM.
CRACKLE
CRACKLE
CRACKLE
CRACKLE
CRACKLE
CRACKLE
GO AHEAD AND PREPARE SOME SET PIECES.
WHAT KIND OF THINGS DO YOU WANT?
I'VE NEVER MADE ANY BEFORE, SO-
GOOGLE IT!
ROAR

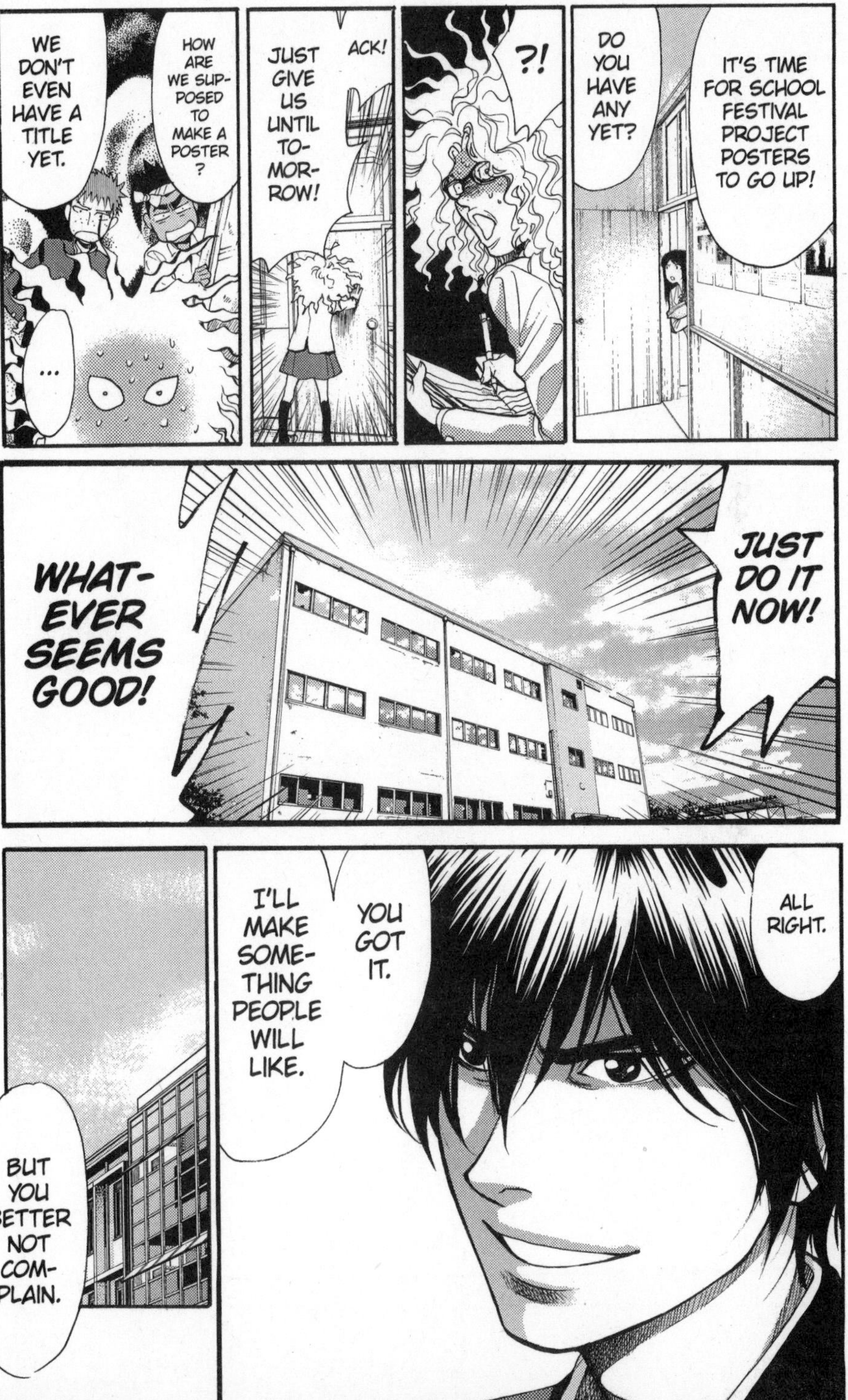

IT'S TIME FOR SCHOOL FESTIVAL PROJECT POSTERS TO GO UP!
DO YOU HAVE ANY YET?
?!
ACK!
JUST GIVE US UNTIL TO-MOR-ROW!
HOW ARE WE SUP-POSED TO MAKE A POSTER?
WE DON'T EVEN HAVE A TITLE YET.
...
JUST DO IT NOW!
WHAT-EVER SEEMS GOOD!
ALL RIGHT.
YOU GOT IT.
I'LL MAKE SOME-THING PEOPLE WILL LIKE.
BUT YOU BETTER NOT COM-PLAIN.

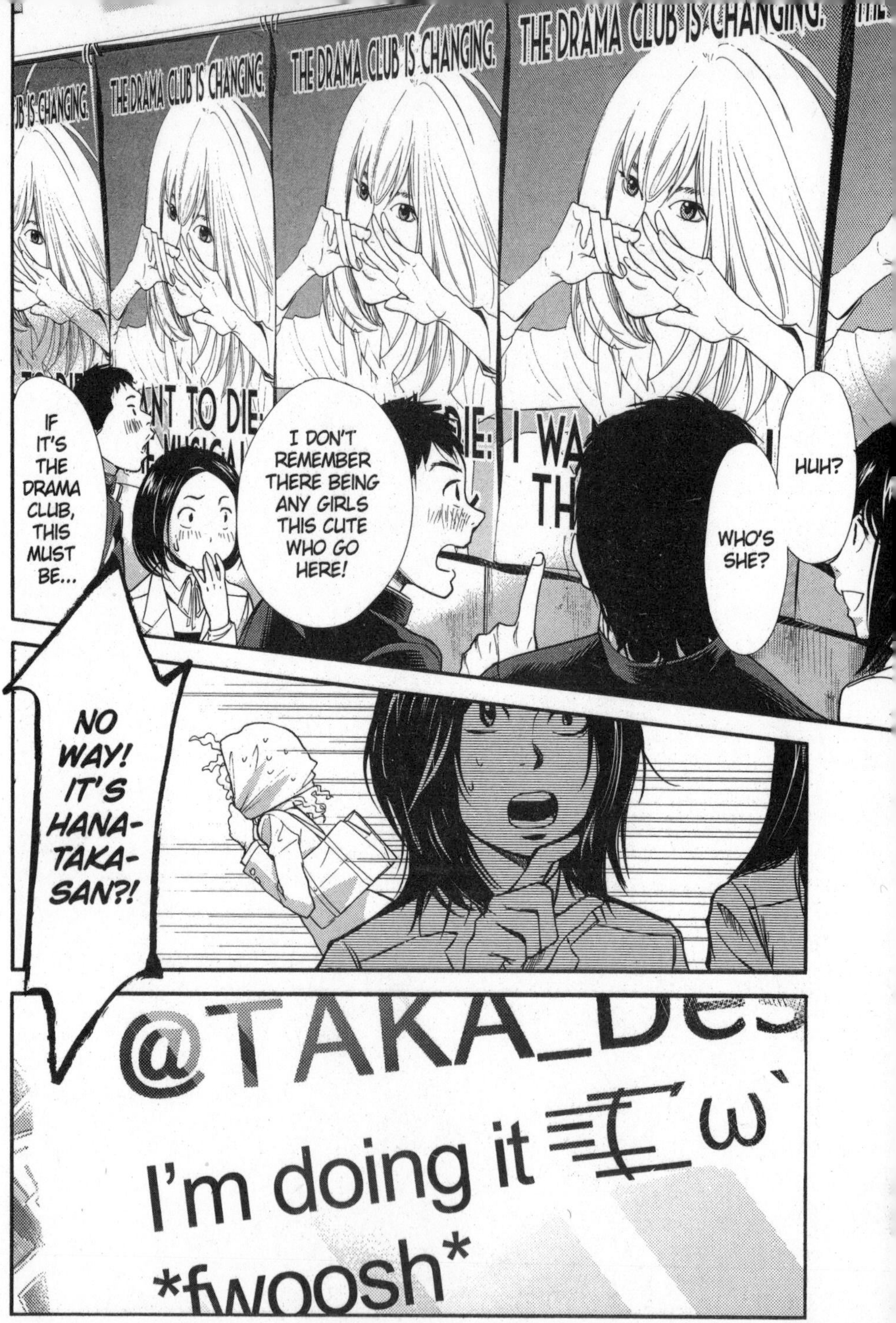
THE DRAMA CLUB IS CHANGING.
HUH?
WHO'S SHE?
I DON'T REMEMBER THERE BEING ANY GIRLS THIS CUTE WHO GO HERE!
IF IT'S THE DRAMA CLUB, THIS MUST BE...
NO WAY! IT'S HANA-TAKA-SAN?!
@TAKA_Des
I'm doing it
fwoosh

83. MY FAIR LADY

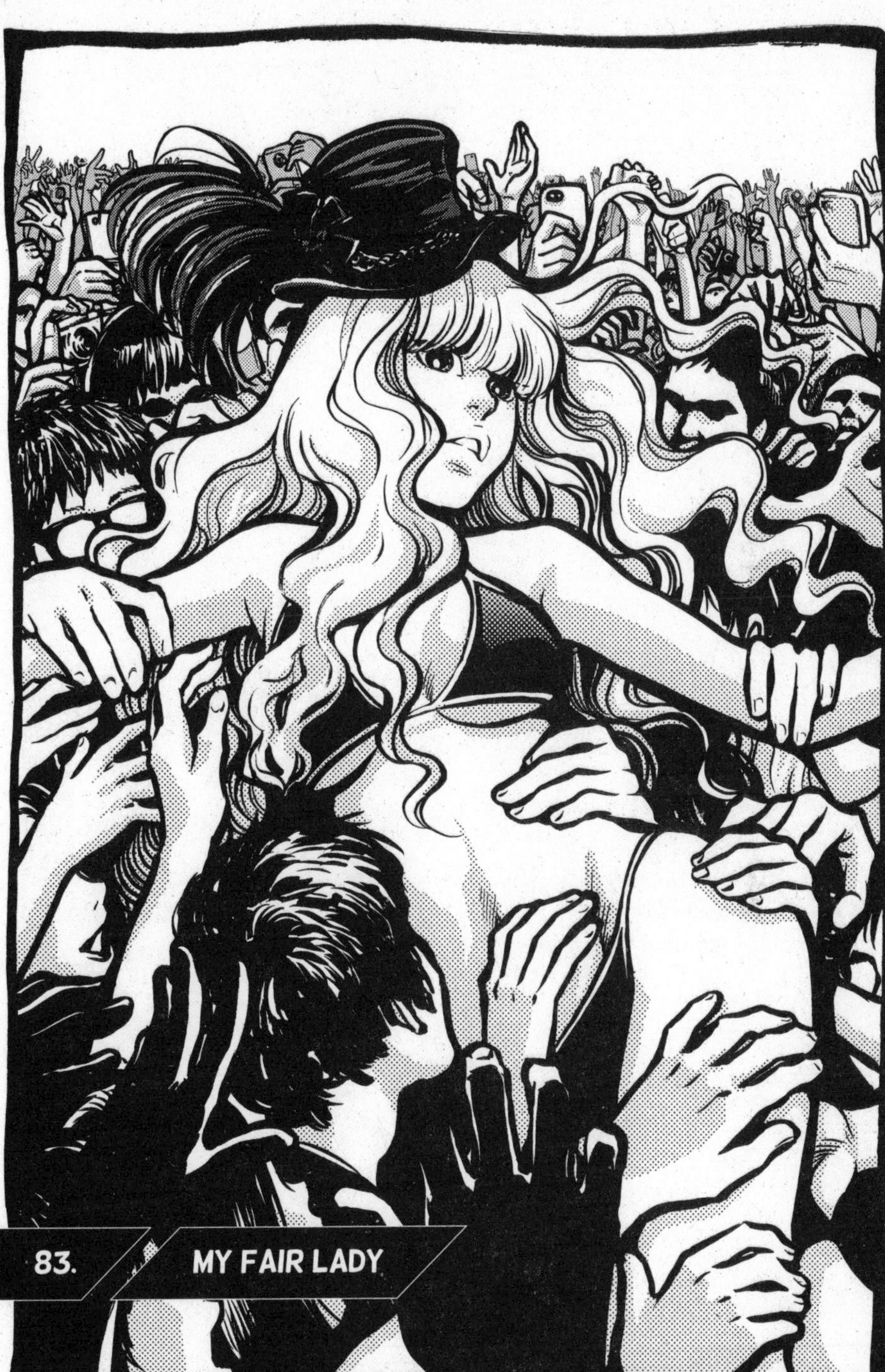

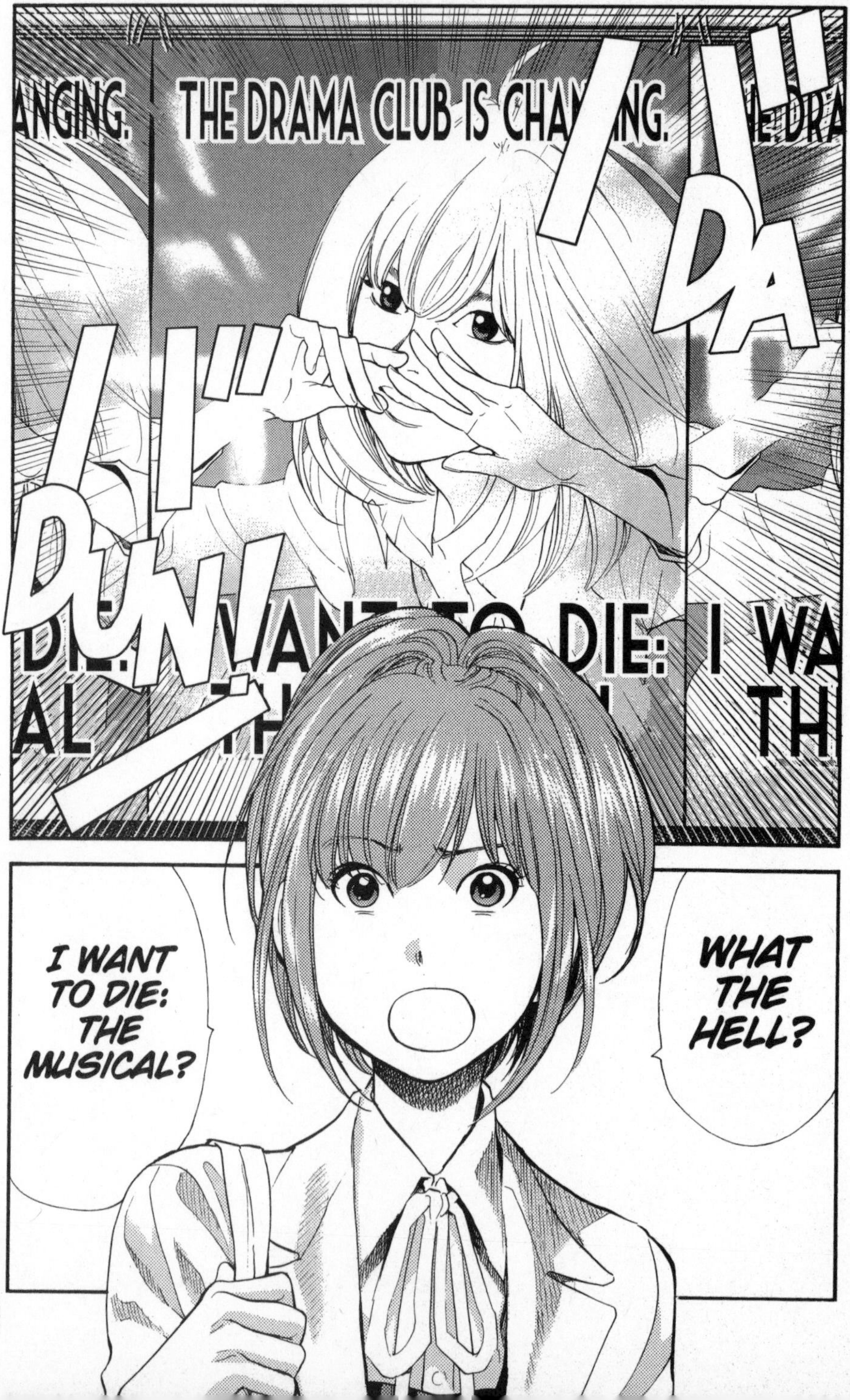
DA
THE DRAMA CLUB IS CHAN
DUN!
WANT TO DIE: I WA
WHAT THE HELL?
I WANT TO DIE: THE MUSICAL?

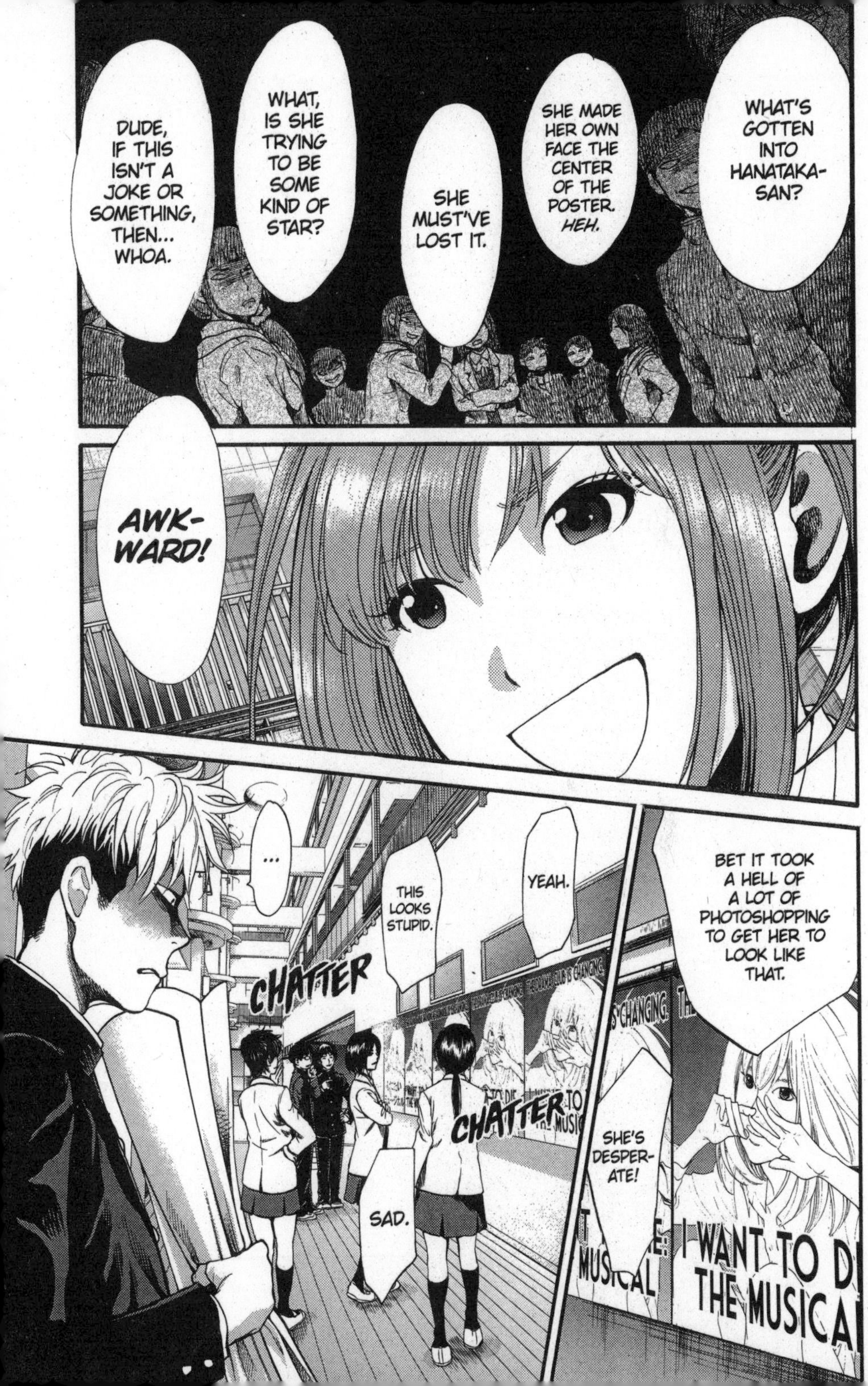
WHAT'S GOTTEN INTO HANATAKA-SAN?
SHE MADE HER OWN FACE THE CENTER OF THE POSTER. *HEH.*
SHE MUST'VE LOST IT.
WHAT, IS SHE TRYING TO BE SOME KIND OF STAR?
DUDE, IF THIS ISN'T A JOKE OR SOMETHING, THEN... WHOA.
AWK-WARD!
BET IT TOOK A HELL OF A LOT OF PHOTOSHOPPING TO GET HER TO LOOK LIKE THAT.
SHE'S DESPER-ATE!
YEAH.
THIS LOOKS STUPID.
...
CHATTER
CHATTER
SAD.

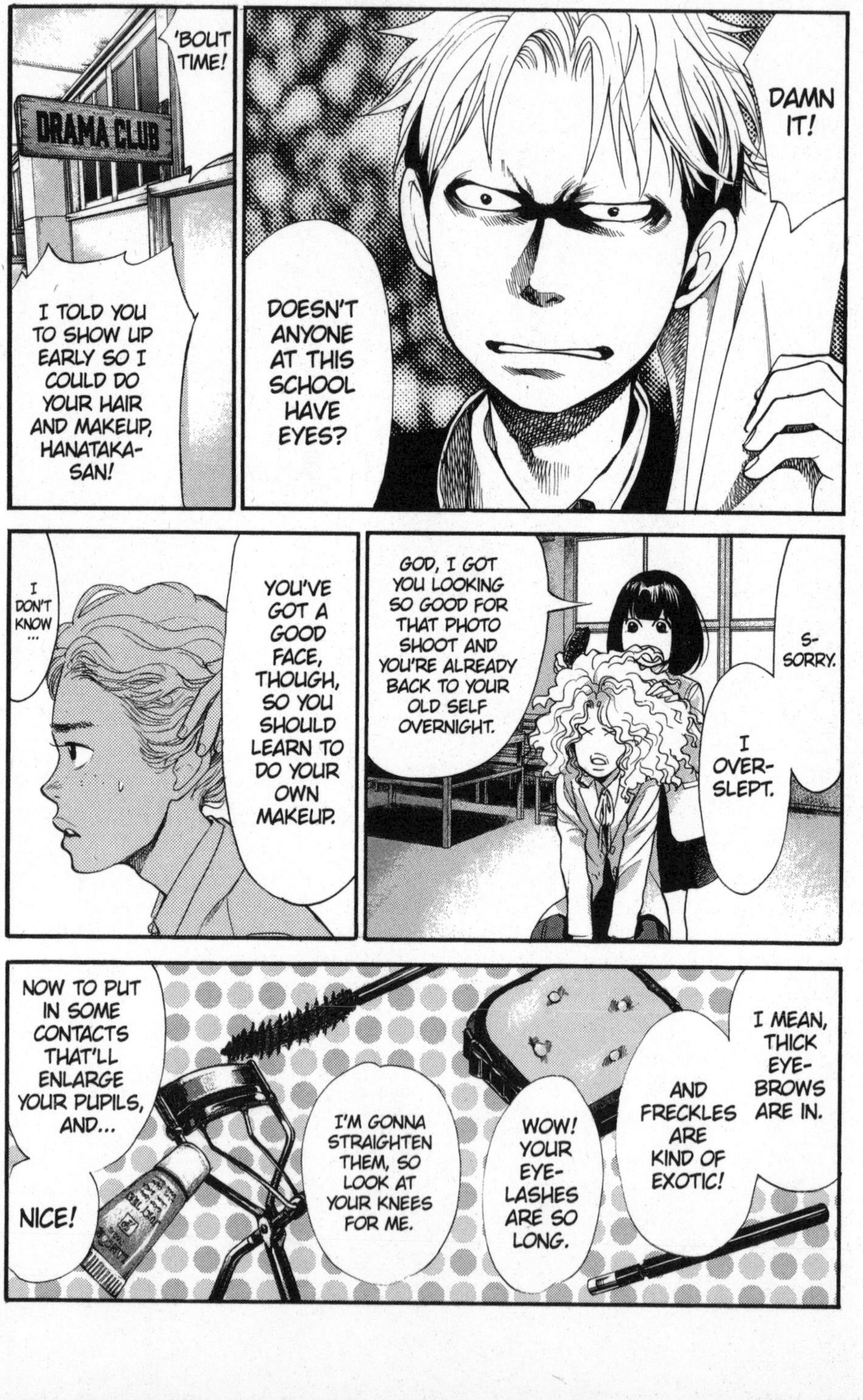
DAMN IT!
DOESN'T ANYONE AT THIS SCHOOL HAVE EYES?
'BOUT TIME!
DRAMA CLUB
I TOLD YOU TO SHOW UP EARLY SO I COULD DO YOUR HAIR AND MAKEUP, HANATAKA-SAN!
S-SORRY.
I OVER-SLEPT.
GOD, I GOT YOU LOOKING SO GOOD FOR THAT PHOTO SHOOT AND YOU'RE ALREADY BACK TO YOUR OLD SELF OVERNIGHT.
YOU'VE GOT A GOOD FACE, THOUGH, SO YOU SHOULD LEARN TO DO YOUR OWN MAKEUP.
I DON'T KNOW...
I MEAN, THICK EYE-BROWS ARE IN.
AND FRECKLES ARE KIND OF EXOTIC!
WOW! YOUR EYE-LASHES ARE SO LONG.
I'M GONNA STRAIGHTEN THEM, SO LOOK AT YOUR KNEES FOR ME.
NOW TO PUT IN SOME CONTACTS THAT'LL ENLARGE YOUR PUPILS, AND...
NICE!

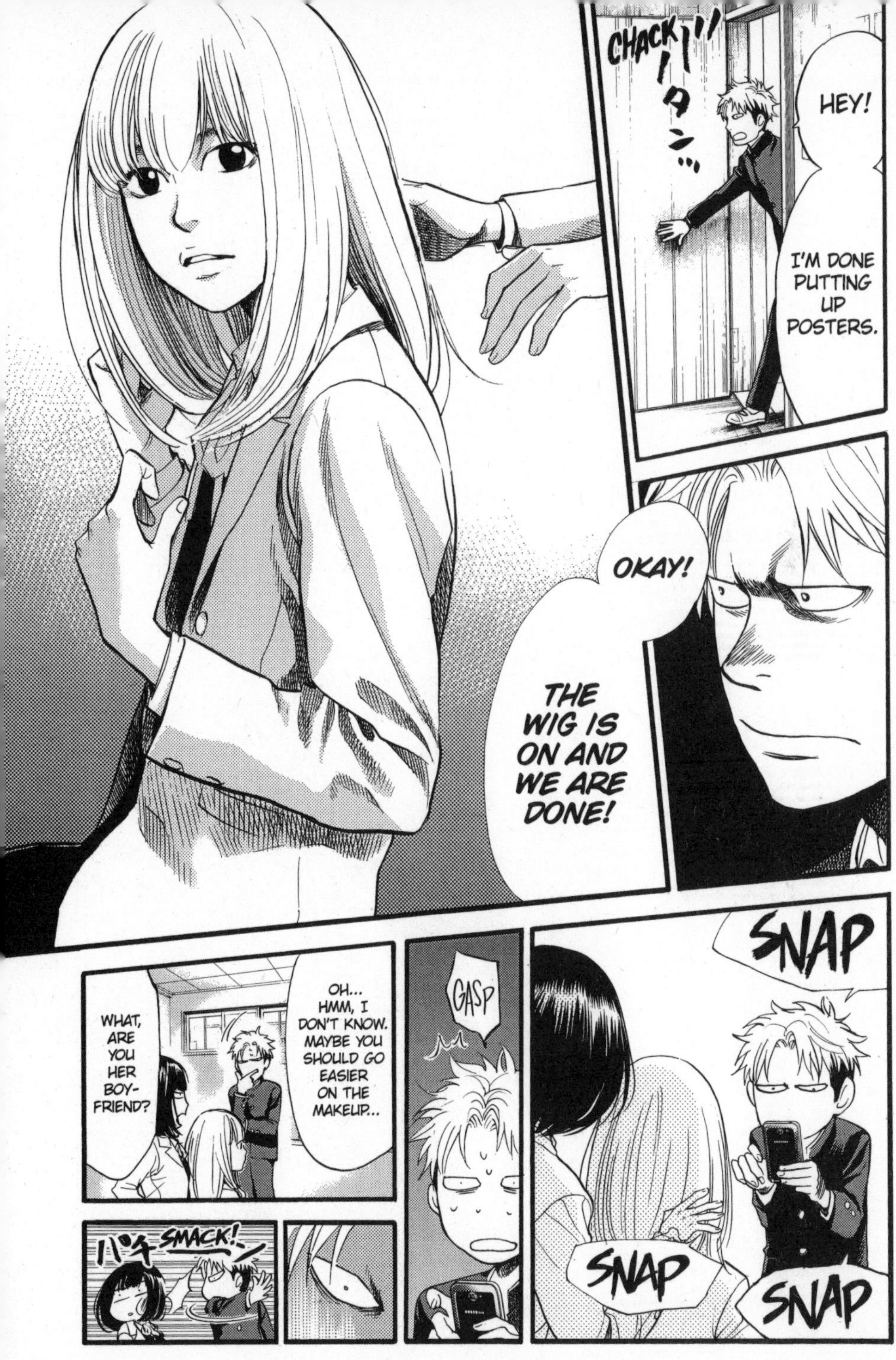
CHACK
HEY!
I'M DONE PUTTING UP POSTERS.
OKAY!
THE WIG IS ON AND WE ARE DONE!
SNAP
SNAP
SNAP
GASP
OH... HMM, I DON'T KNOW. MAYBE YOU SHOULD GO EASIER ON THE MAKEUP...
WHAT, ARE YOU HER BOY-FRIEND?
SMACK!

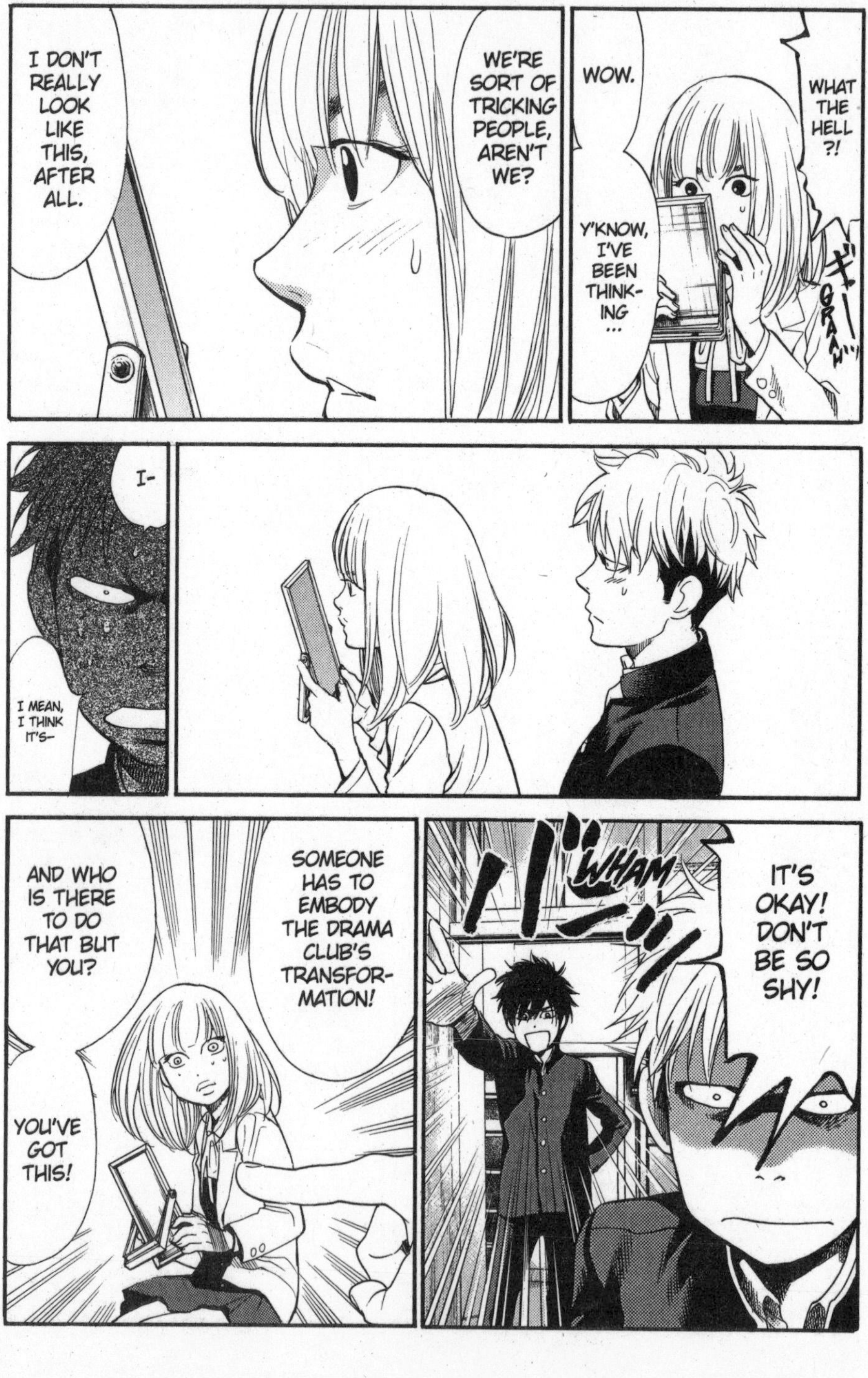
WHAT THE HELL?!
WOW.
Y'KNOW, I'VE BEEN THINKING...
GRAAH
WE'RE SORT OF TRICKING PEOPLE, AREN'T WE?
I DON'T REALLY LOOK LIKE THIS, AFTER ALL.
I-
I MEAN, I THINK IT'S—
IT'S OKAY! DON'T BE SO SHY!
WHAM
SOMEONE HAS TO EMBODY THE DRAMA CLUB'S TRANSFORMATION!
AND WHO IS THERE TO DO THAT BUT YOU?
YOU'VE GOT THIS!

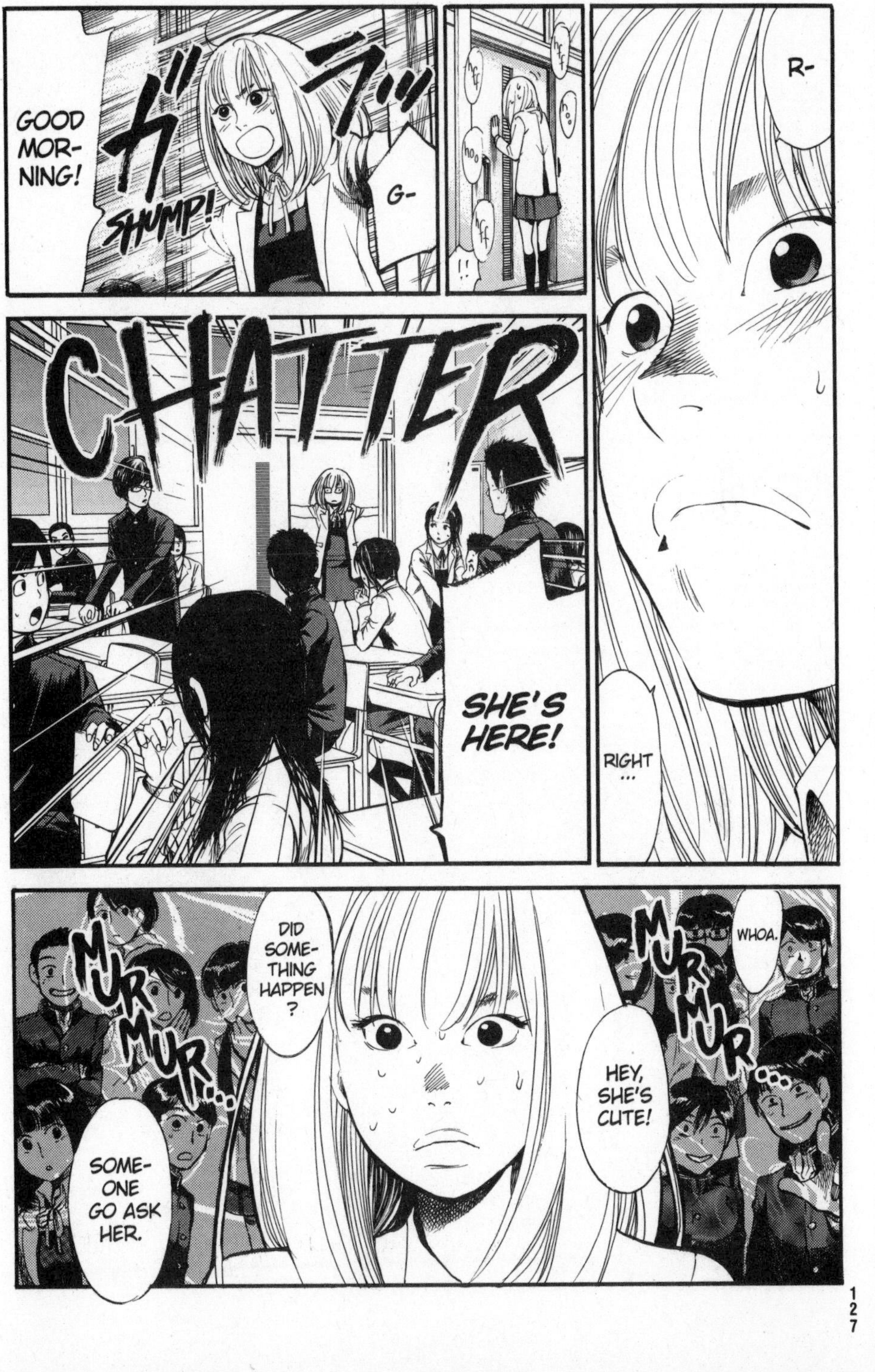
R-
RIGHT…
hnff
hoo
hoo
hnff
G-
!!
ガラッ
SHUMP!
GOOD MORNING!
CHATTER
SHE'S HERE!
MURMUR
WHOA.
HEY, SHE'S CUTE!
DID SOMETHING HAPPEN?
MURMUR…
SOMEONE GO ASK HER.

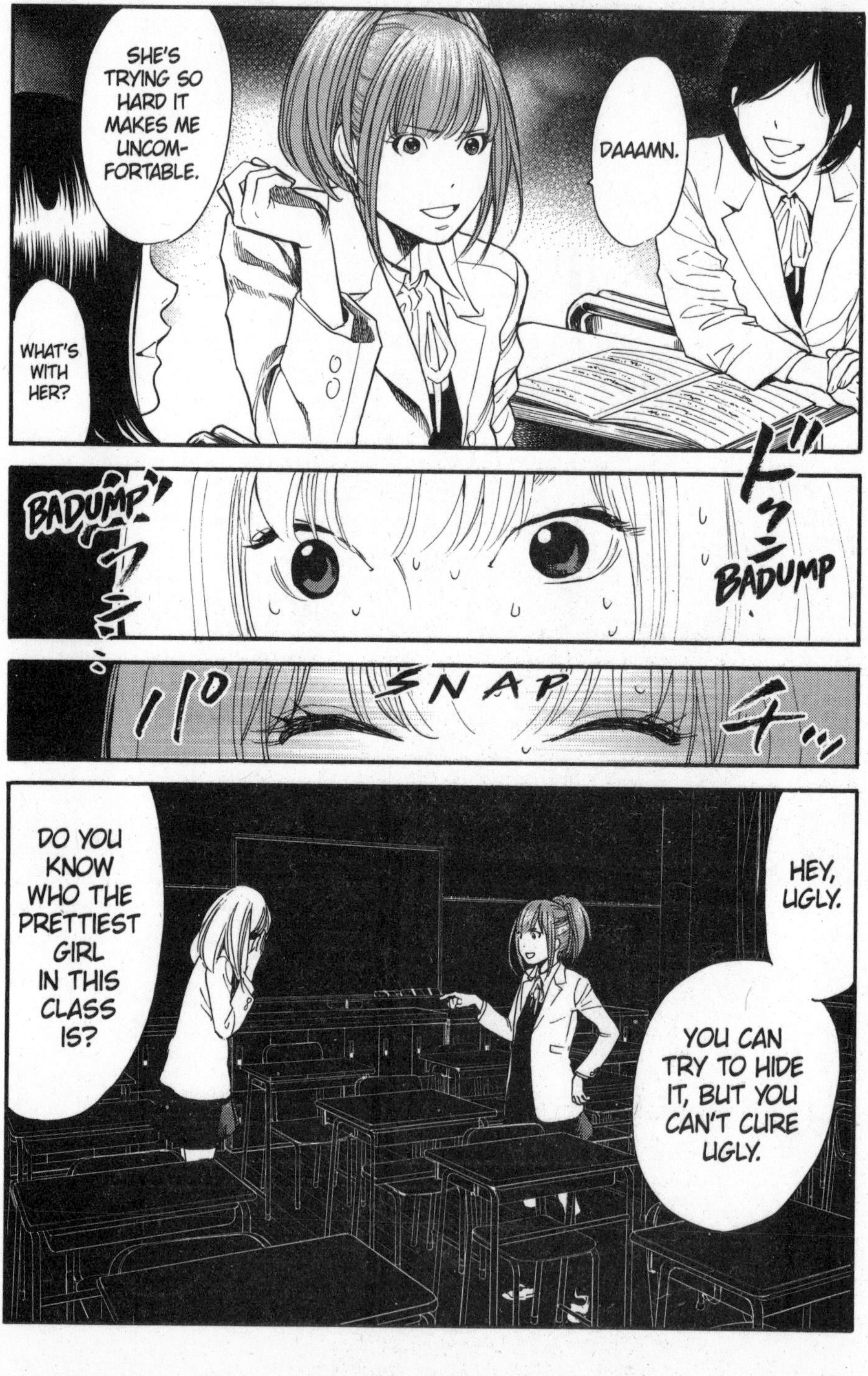
DAAAMN.
SHE'S TRYING SO HARD IT MAKES ME UNCOM-FORTABLE.
WHAT'S WITH HER?
BADUMP
BADUMP
SNAP
HEY, UGLY.
YOU CAN TRY TO HIDE IT, BUT YOU CAN'T CURE UGLY.
DO YOU KNOW WHO THE PRETTIEST GIRL IN THIS CLASS IS?

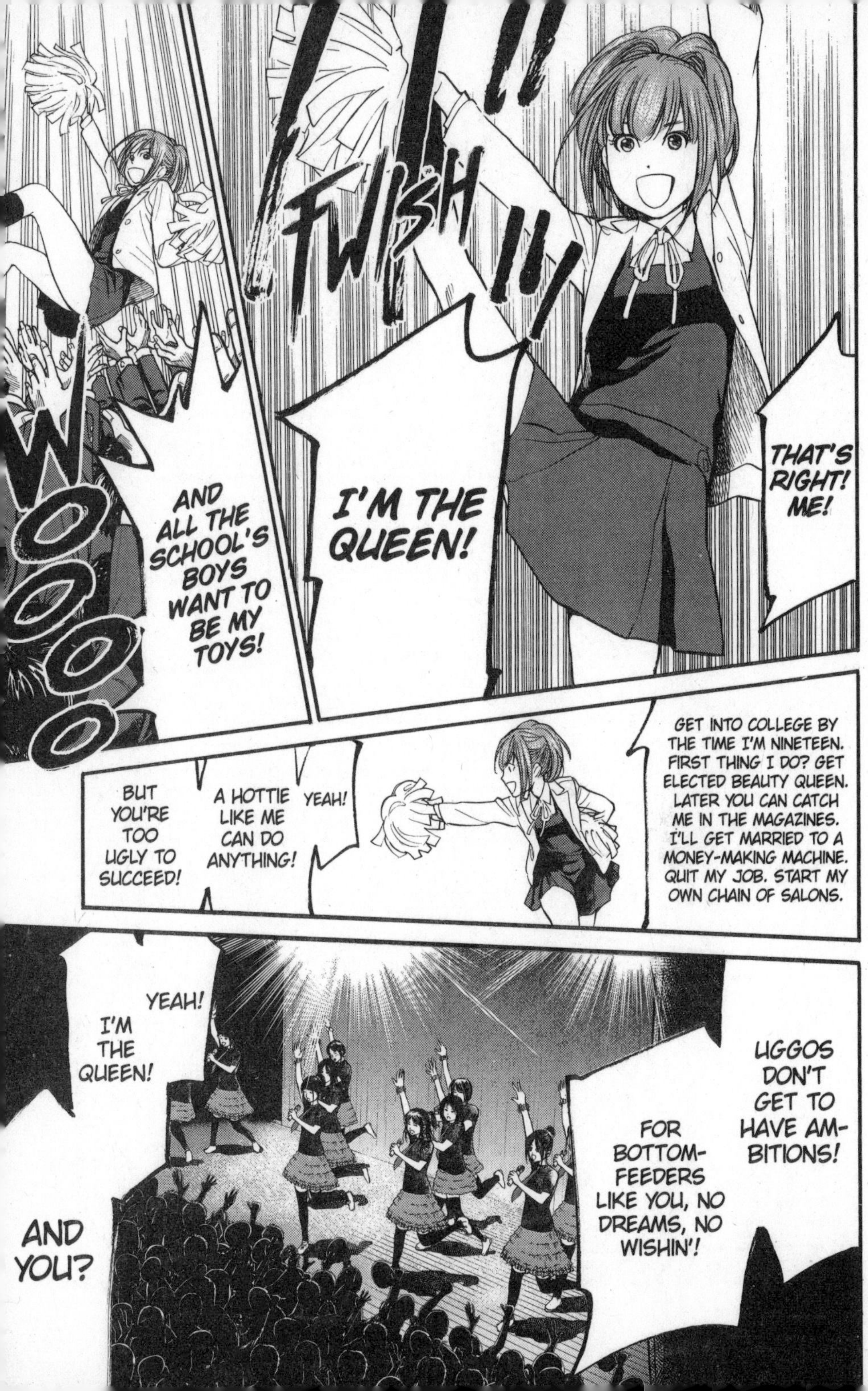
FWISH!!
THAT'S RIGHT! ME!
I'M THE QUEEN!
AND ALL THE SCHOOL'S BOYS WANT TO BE MY TOYS!
WOOOOO
GET INTO COLLEGE BY THE TIME I'M NINETEEN. FIRST THING I DO? GET ELECTED BEAUTY QUEEN. LATER YOU CAN CATCH ME IN THE MAGAZINES. I'LL GET MARRIED TO A MONEY-MAKING MACHINE. QUIT MY JOB. START MY OWN CHAIN OF SALONS.
YEAH!
A HOTTIE LIKE ME CAN DO ANYTHING!
BUT YOU'RE TOO UGLY TO SUCCEED!
UGGOS DON'T GET TO HAVE AMBITIONS!
FOR BOTTOM-FEEDERS LIKE YOU, NO DREAMS, NO WISHIN'!
YEAH! I'M THE QUEEN!
AND YOU?

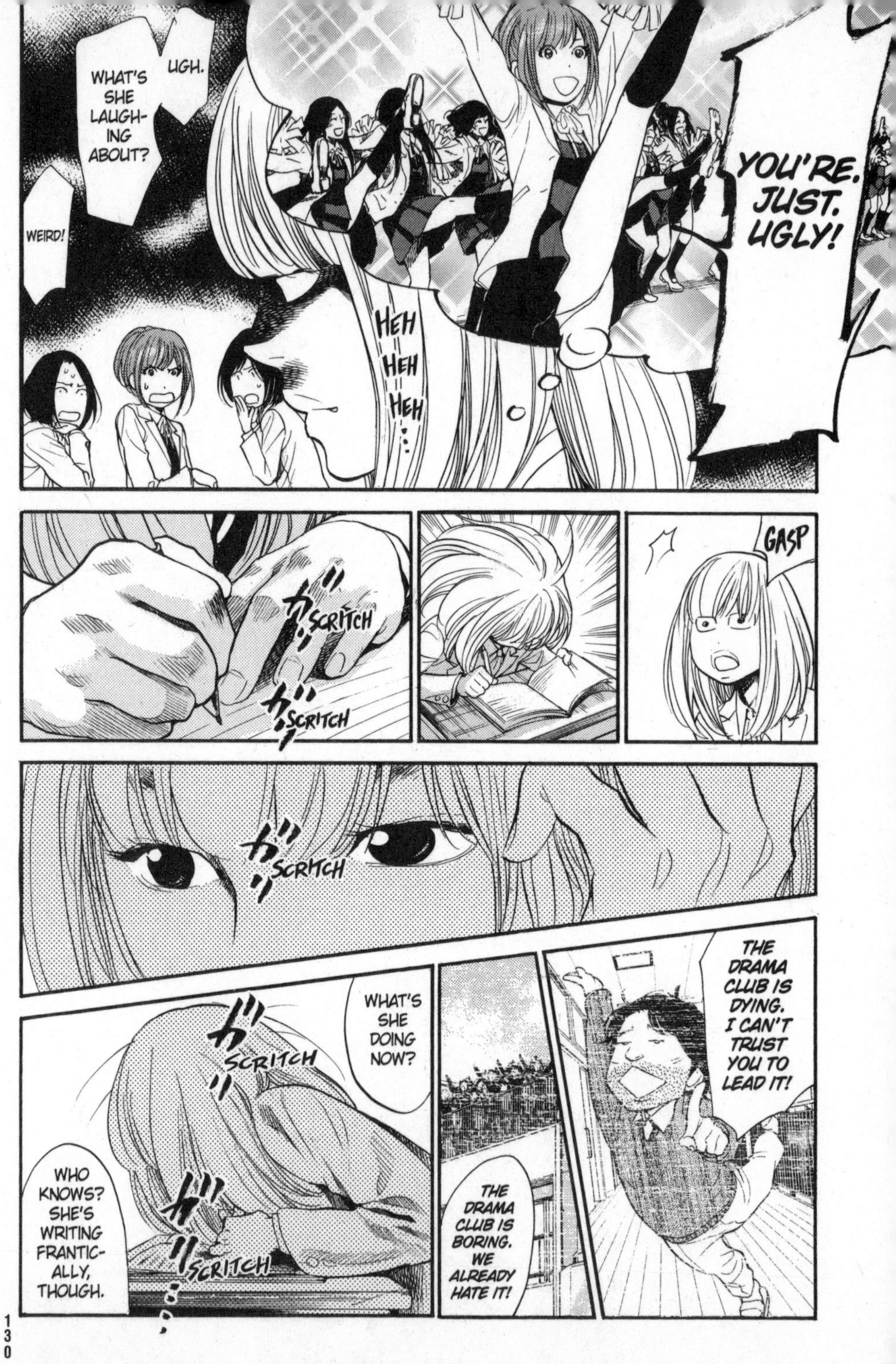
YOU'RE. JUST. UGLY!
UGH.
WHAT'S SHE LAUGHING ABOUT?
WEIRD!
HEH HEH HEH...
GASP
SCRITCH
SCRITCH
SCRITCH
THE DRAMA CLUB IS DYING. I CAN'T TRUST YOU TO LEAD IT!
THE DRAMA CLUB IS BORING. WE ALREADY HATE IT!
WHAT'S SHE DOING NOW?
SCRITCH
WHO KNOWS? SHE'S WRITING FRANTIC-ALLY, THOUGH.
SCRITCH

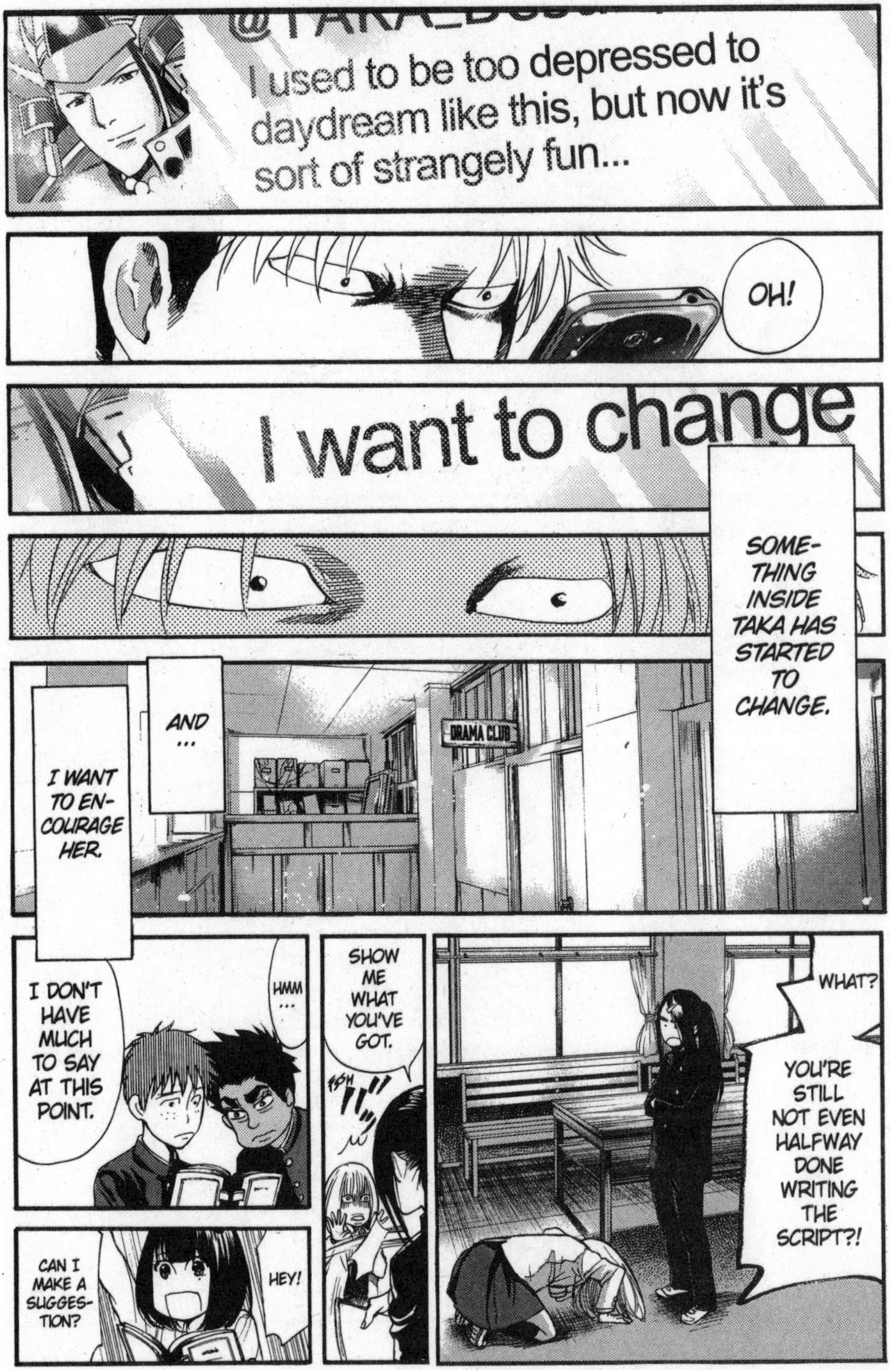

I used to be too depressed to daydream like this, but now it's sort of strangely fun...
OH!
I want to change
SOMETHING INSIDE TAKA HAS STARTED TO CHANGE.
AND ...
I WANT TO ENCOURAGE HER.
DRAMA CLUB
WHAT?
YOU'RE STILL NOT EVEN HALFWAY DONE WRITING THE SCRIPT?!
SHOW ME WHAT YOU'VE GOT.
HMM ...
I DON'T HAVE MUCH TO SAY AT THIS POINT.
HEY!
CAN I MAKE A SUGGESTION?

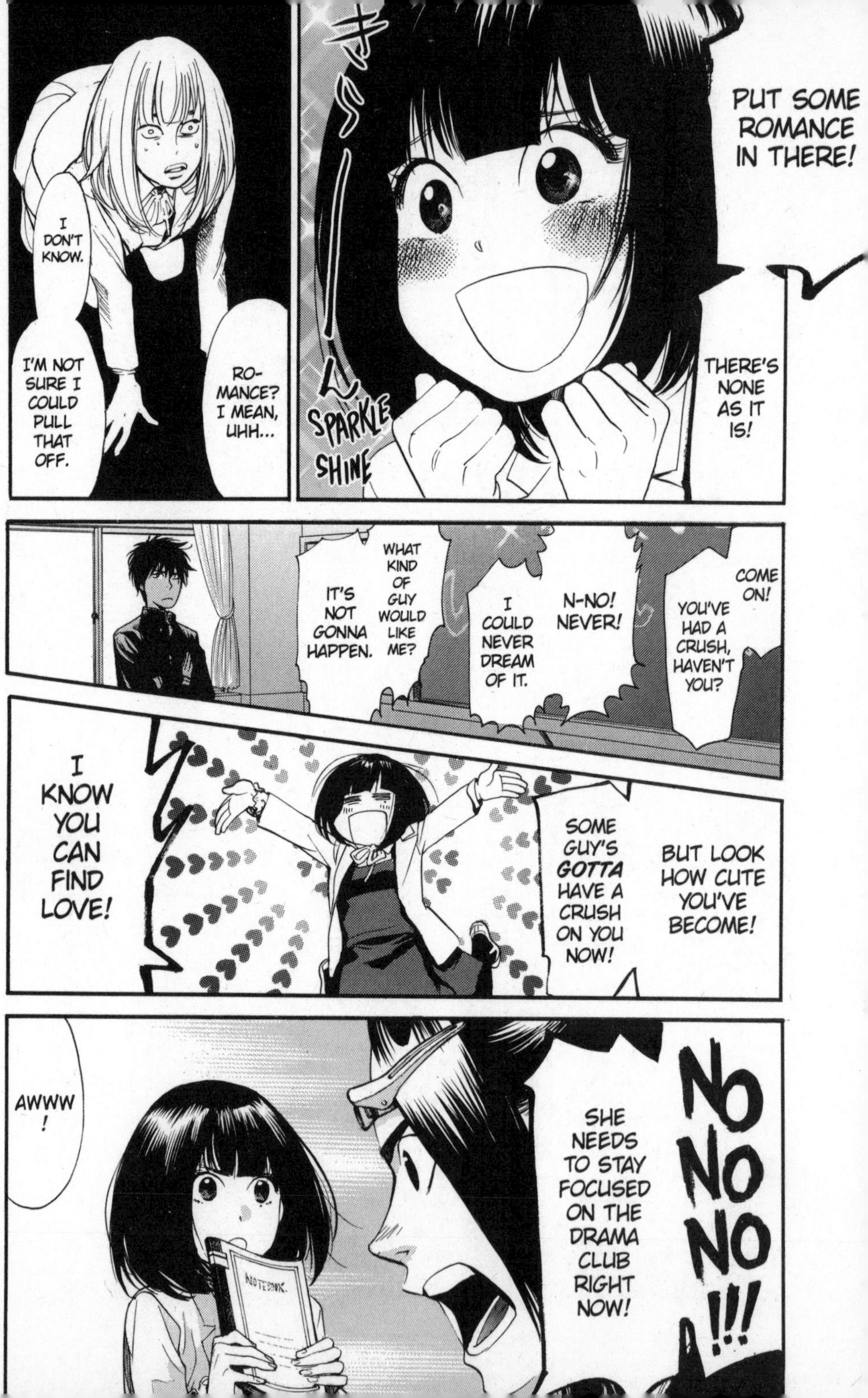
PUT SOME ROMANCE IN THERE!
THERE'S NONE AS IT IS!
SPARKLE SHINE
RO-MANCE? I MEAN, UHH...
I DON'T KNOW.
I'M NOT SURE I COULD PULL THAT OFF.
COME ON!
YOU'VE HAD A CRUSH, HAVEN'T YOU?
N-NO! NEVER!
I COULD NEVER DREAM OF IT.
WHAT KIND OF GUY WOULD LIKE ME?
IT'S NOT GONNA HAPPEN.
BUT LOOK HOW CUTE YOU'VE BECOME!
SOME GUY'S *GOTTA* HAVE A CRUSH ON YOU NOW!
I KNOW YOU CAN FIND LOVE!
NO NO NO!!!
SHE NEEDS TO STAY FOCUSED ON THE DRAMA CLUB RIGHT NOW!
AWWW!
NOTEBOOK.

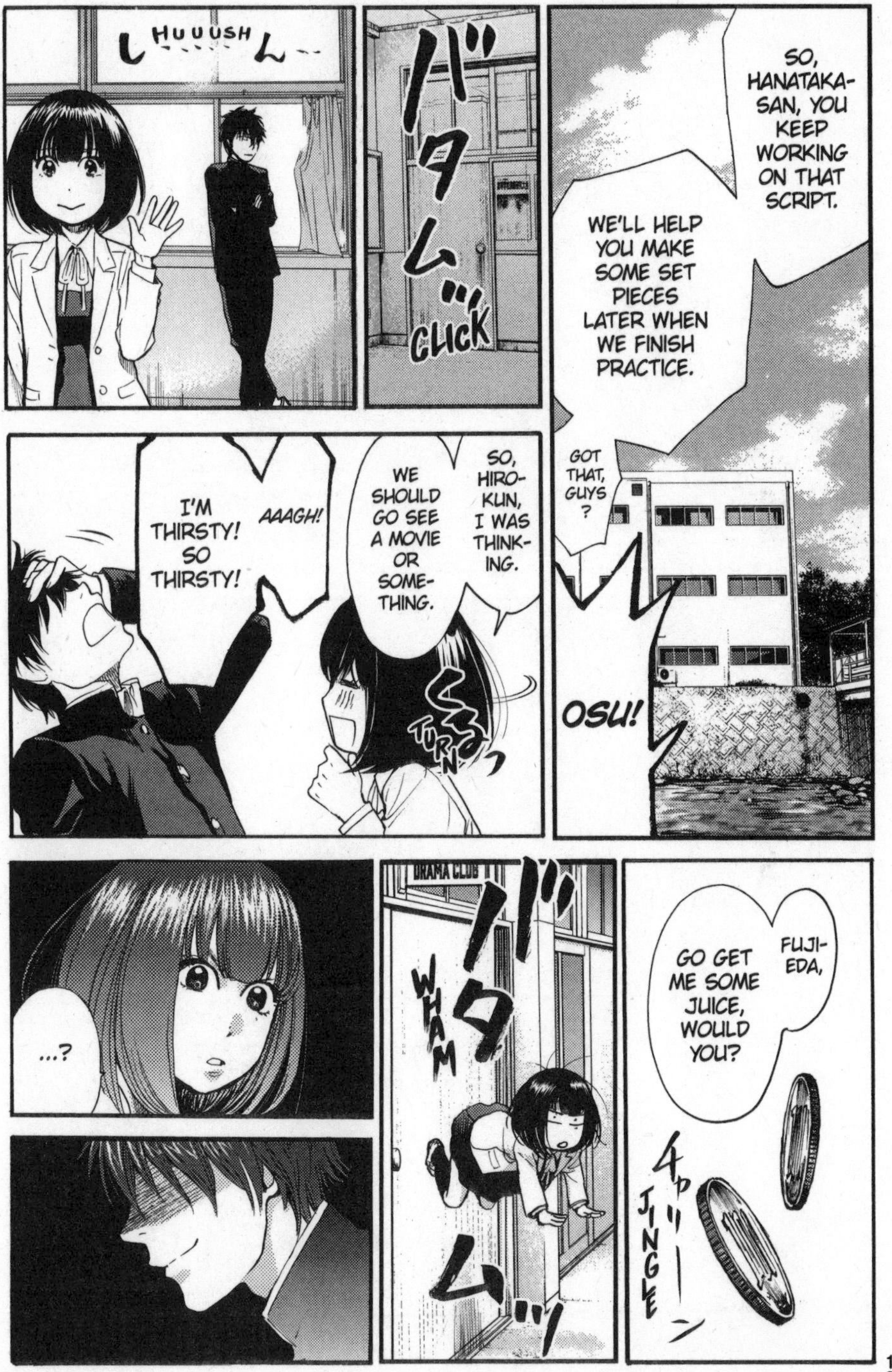
SO, HANATAKA-SAN, YOU KEEP WORKING ON THAT SCRIPT.
WE'LL HELP YOU MAKE SOME SET PIECES LATER WHEN WE FINISH PRACTICE.
GOT THAT, GUYS?
OSU!
CLICK
HUUUSH
SO, HIRO-KUN, I WAS THINKING.
WE SHOULD GO SEE A MOVIE OR SOMETHING.
TURN
AAAGH!
I'M THIRSTY! SO THIRSTY!
FUJI-EDA,
GO GET ME SOME JUICE, WOULD YOU?
JINGLE
DRAMA CLUB
WHAM
...?

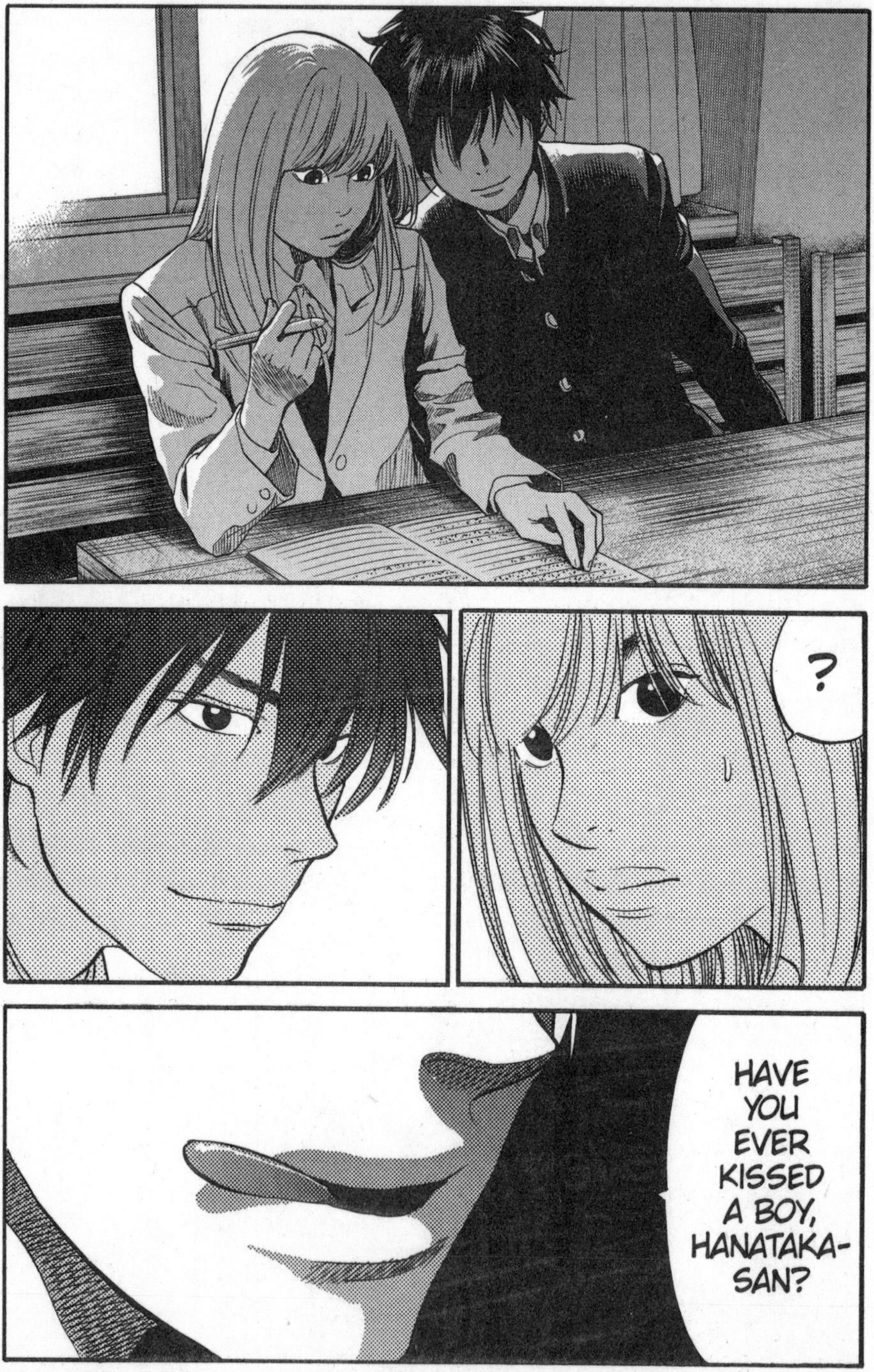
?
HAVE YOU EVER KISSED A BOY, HANATAKA-SAN?

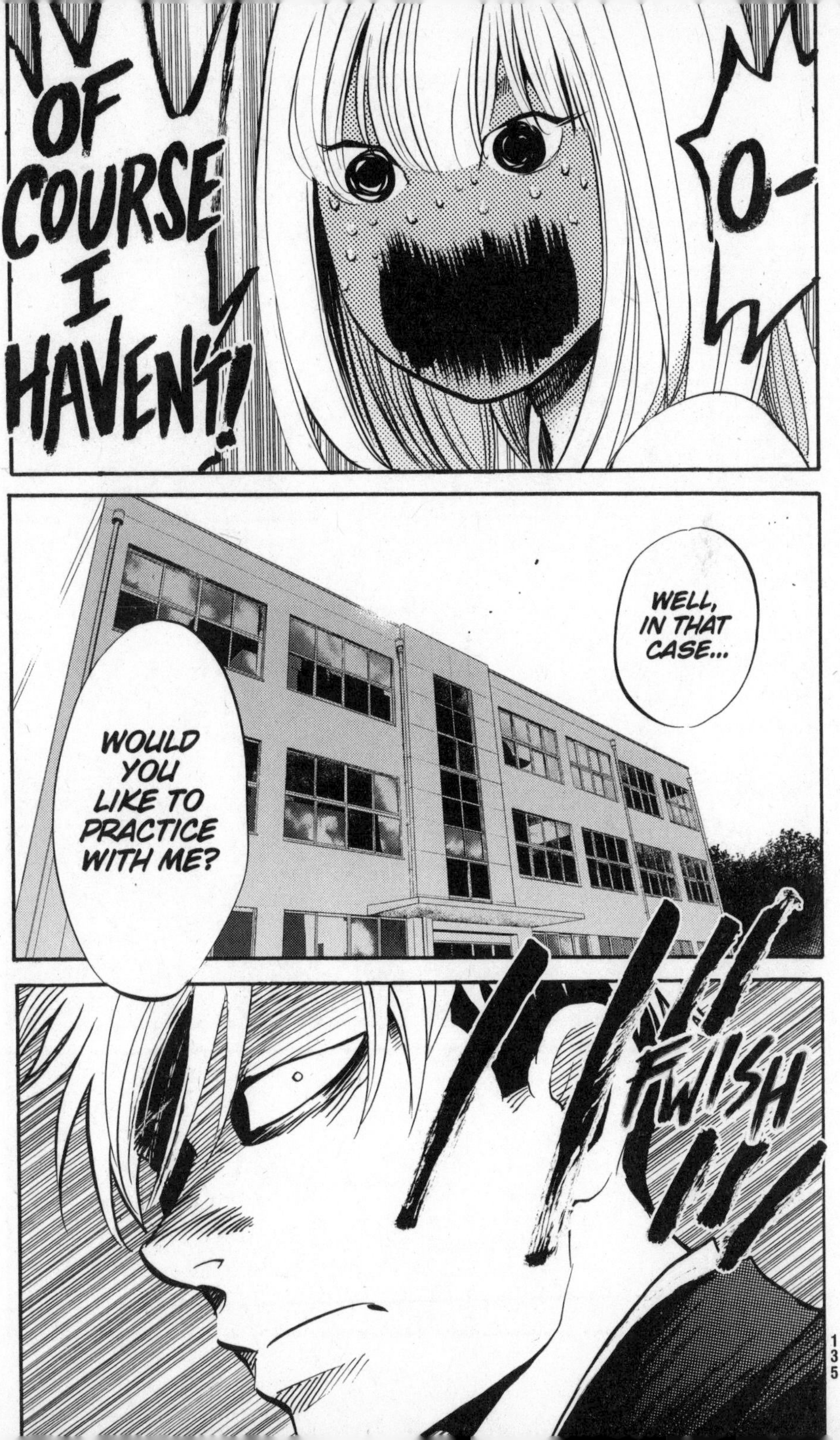
O-
OF COURSE I HAVEN'T!
WELL, IN THAT CASE...
WOULD YOU LIKE TO PRACTICE WITH ME?
FWISH

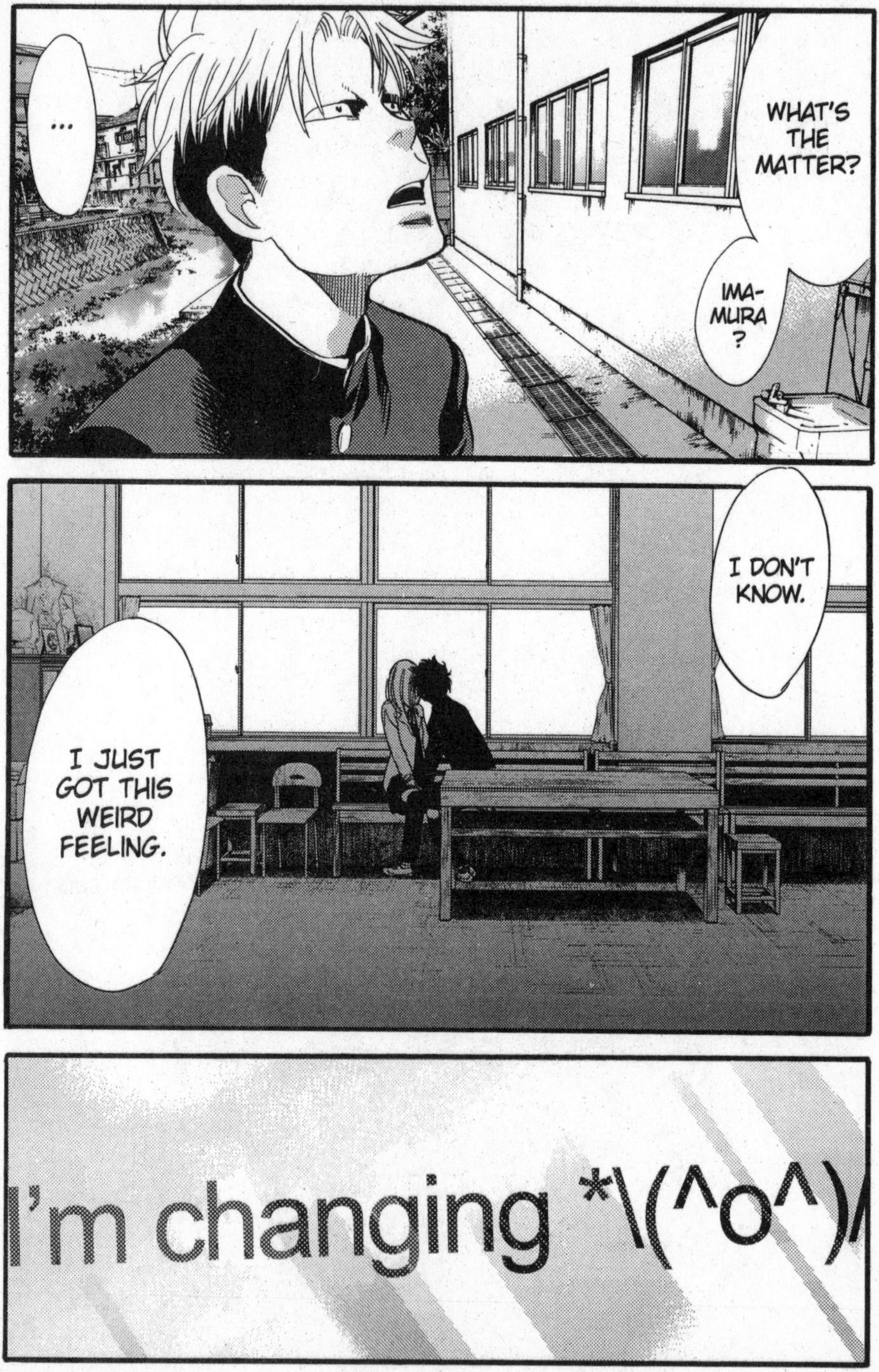
WHAT'S THE MATTER?
IMA-MURA?
...
I DON'T KNOW.
I JUST GOT THIS WEIRD FEELING.
I'm changing *\(^o^)/

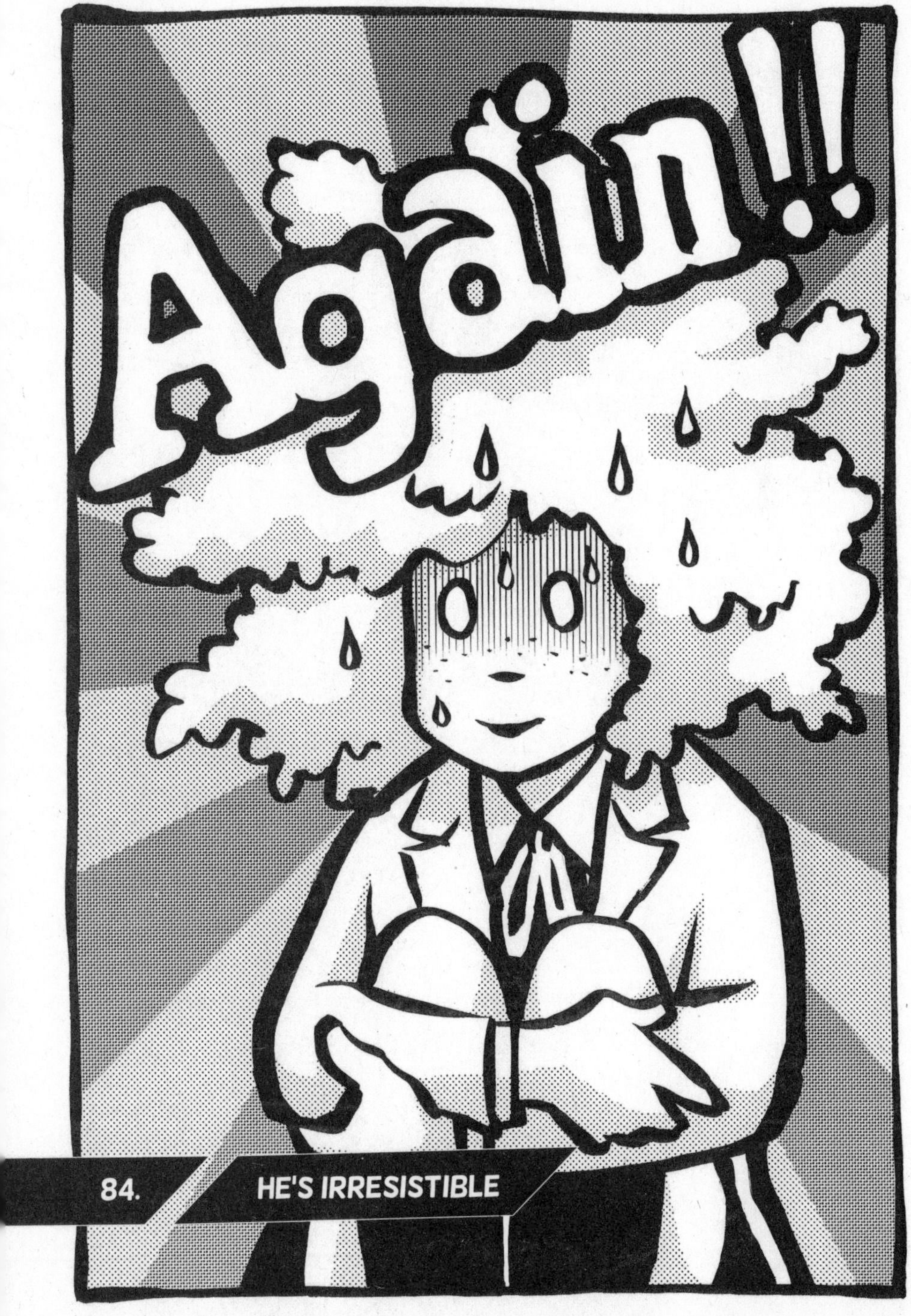
Again!!

84. HE'S IRRESISTIBLE

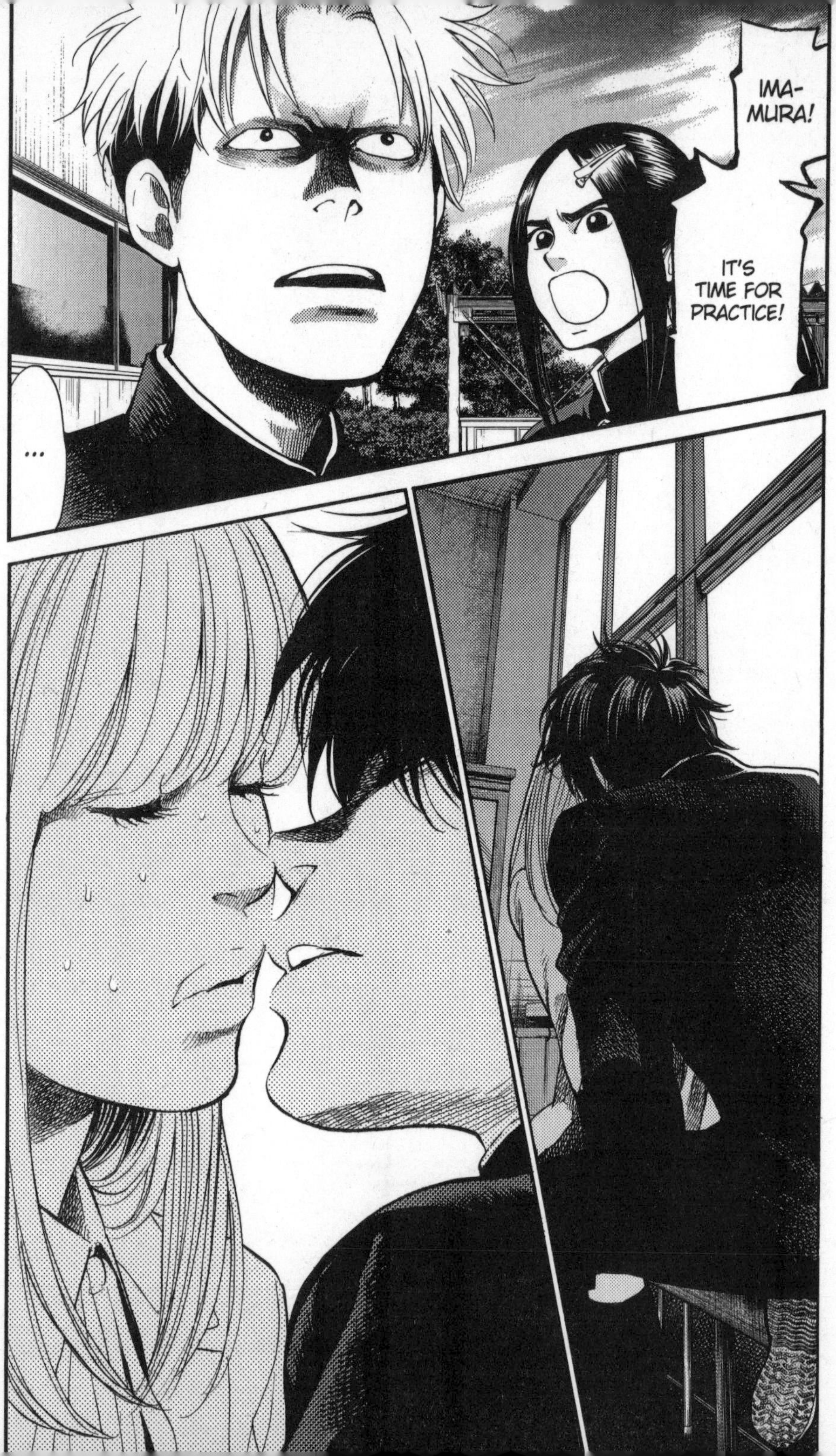
IMA-
MURA!
IT'S
TIME FOR
PRACTICE!
...

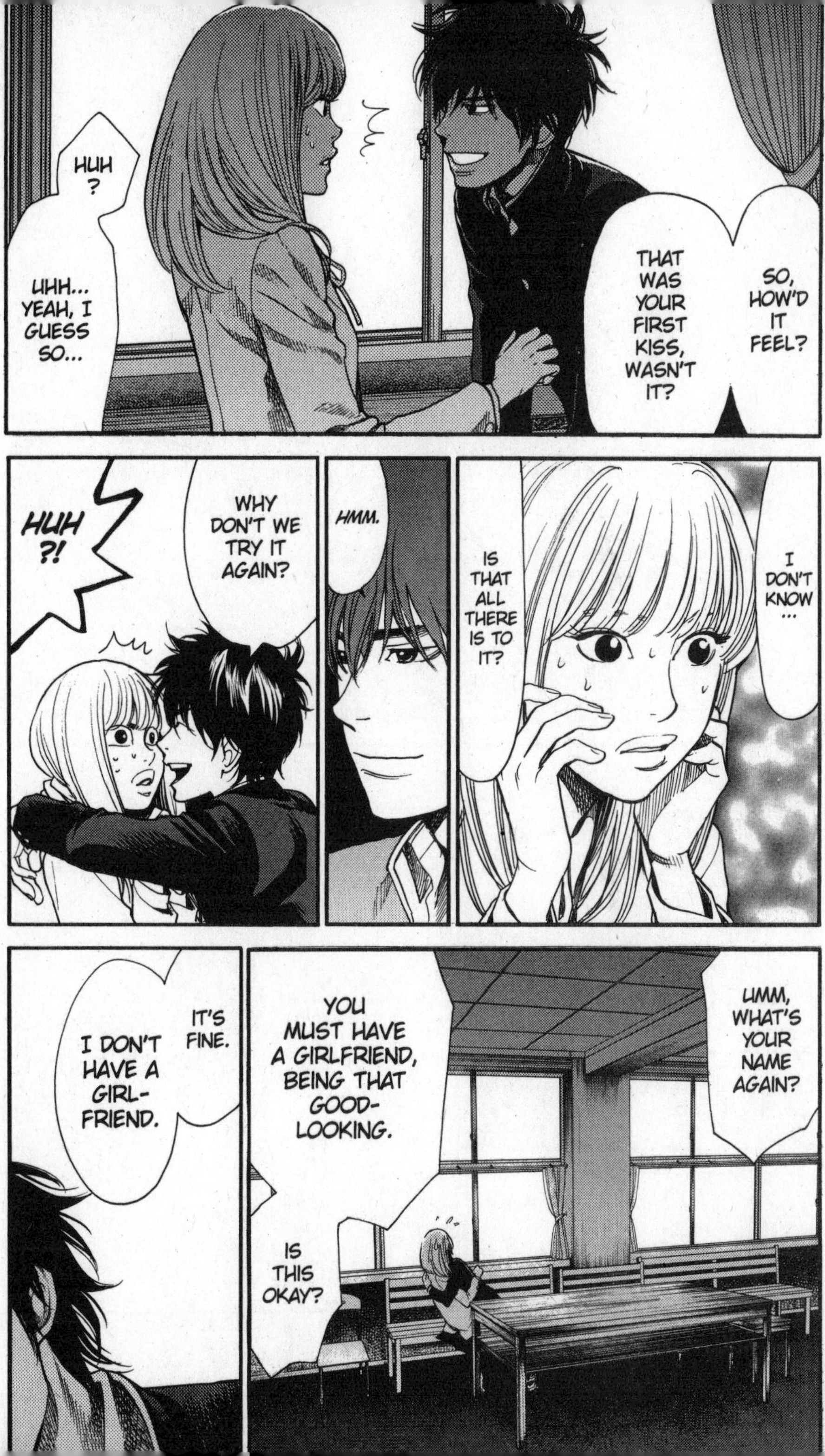
SO, HOW'D IT FEEL?
THAT WAS YOUR FIRST KISS, WASN'T IT?
HUH?
UHH... YEAH, I GUESS SO...
I DON'T KNOW...
IS THAT ALL THERE IS TO IT?
HMM.
WHY DON'T WE TRY IT AGAIN?
HUH?!
UMM, WHAT'S YOUR NAME AGAIN?
YOU MUST HAVE A GIRLFRIEND, BEING THAT GOOD-LOOKING.
IS THIS OKAY?
IT'S FINE.
I DON'T HAVE A GIRL-FRIEND.

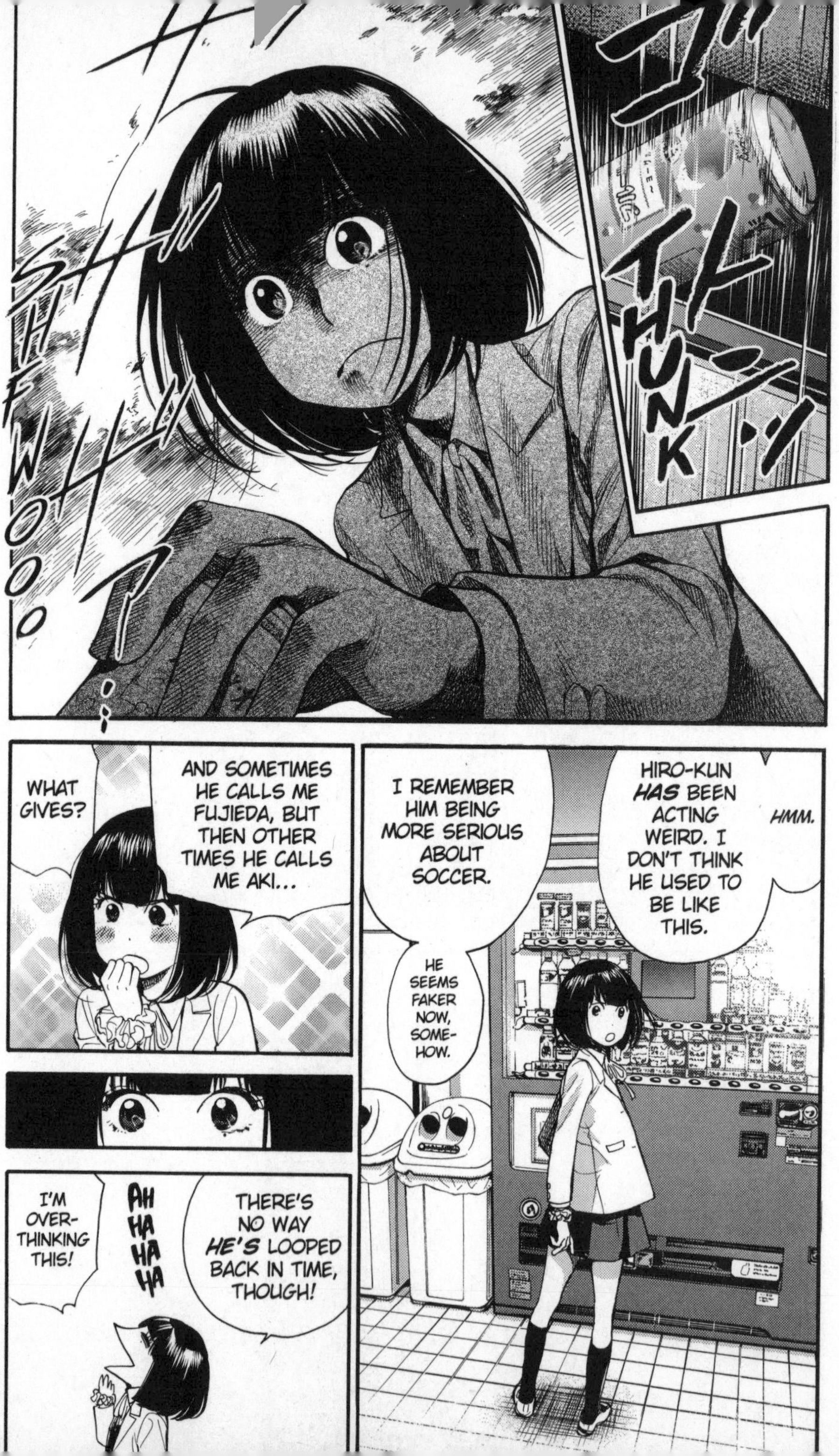
THUNK
SHFWOOOO
HMM.
HIRO-KUN *HAS* BEEN ACTING WEIRD. I DON'T THINK HE USED TO BE LIKE THIS.
I REMEMBER HIM BEING MORE SERIOUS ABOUT SOCCER.
HE SEEMS FAKER NOW, SOME-HOW.
AND SOMETIMES HE CALLS ME FUJIEDA, BUT THEN OTHER TIMES HE CALLS ME AKI...
WHAT GIVES?
THERE'S NO WAY *HE'S* LOOPED BACK IN TIME, THOUGH!
AH HA HA HA HA
I'M OVER-THINKING THIS!

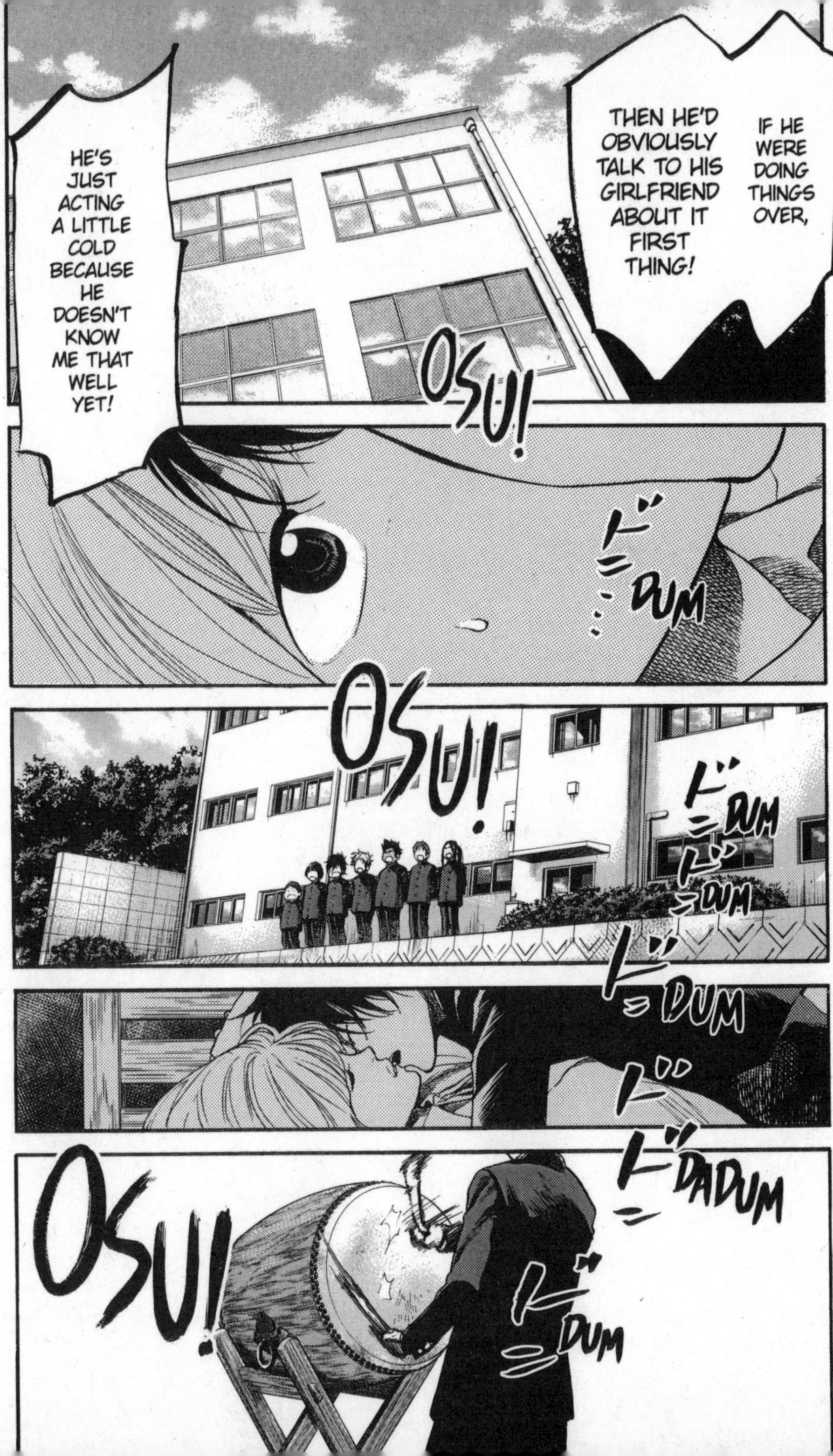
IF HE WERE DOING THINGS OVER,
THEN HE'D OBVIOUSLY TALK TO HIS GIRLFRIEND ABOUT IT FIRST THING!
HE'S JUST ACTING A LITTLE COLD BECAUSE HE DOESN'T KNOW ME THAT WELL YET!
OSU!
DUM
OSU!
DUM
DUM
DUM
DADUM
OSU!
DUM

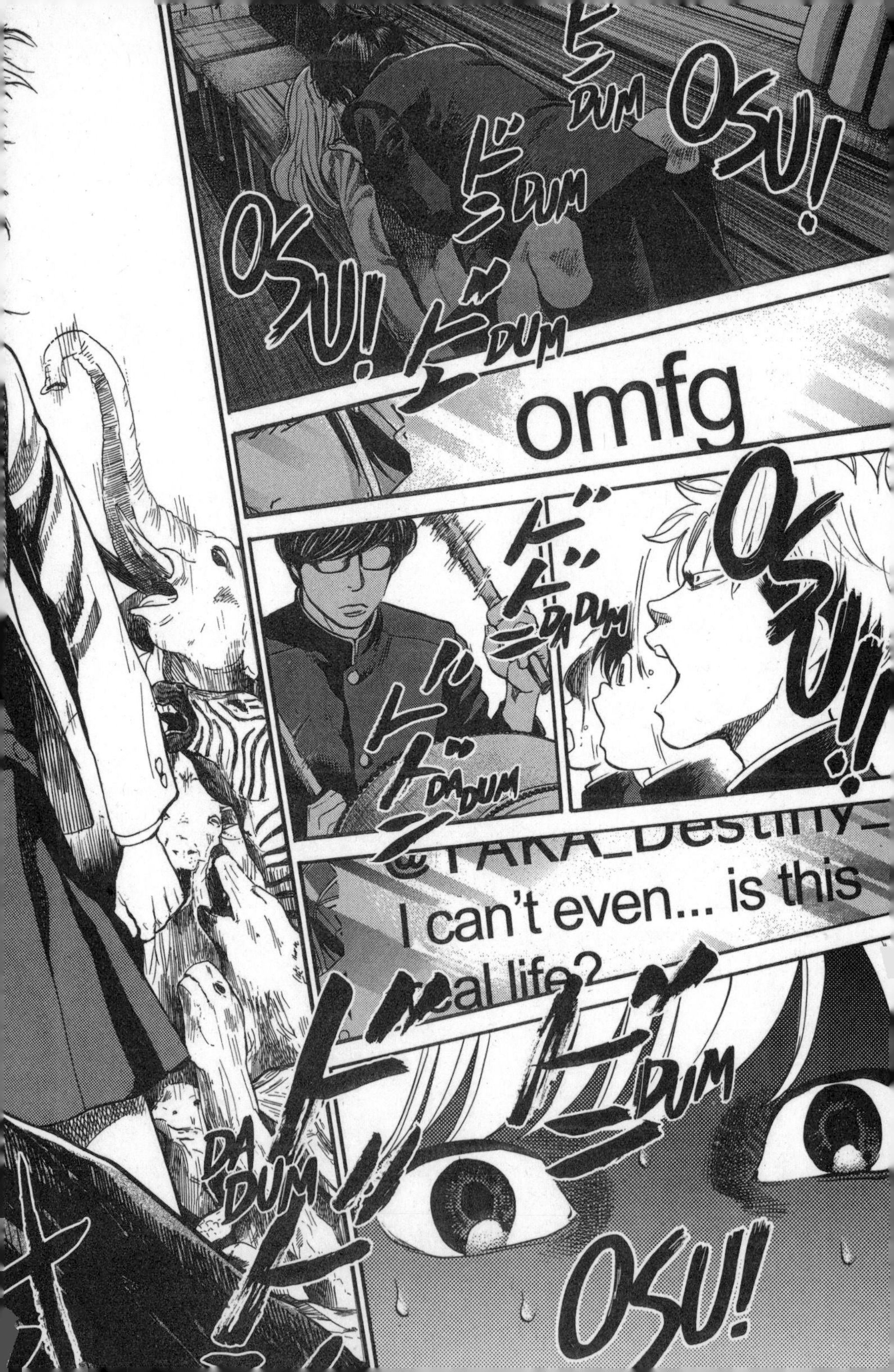
OSU!
DUM
DUM
OSU!
DUM
omfg
OSU!!
DADUM
DADUM
@TAKA_Destiny_
I can't even... is this real life?
DUM
DADUM
OSU!

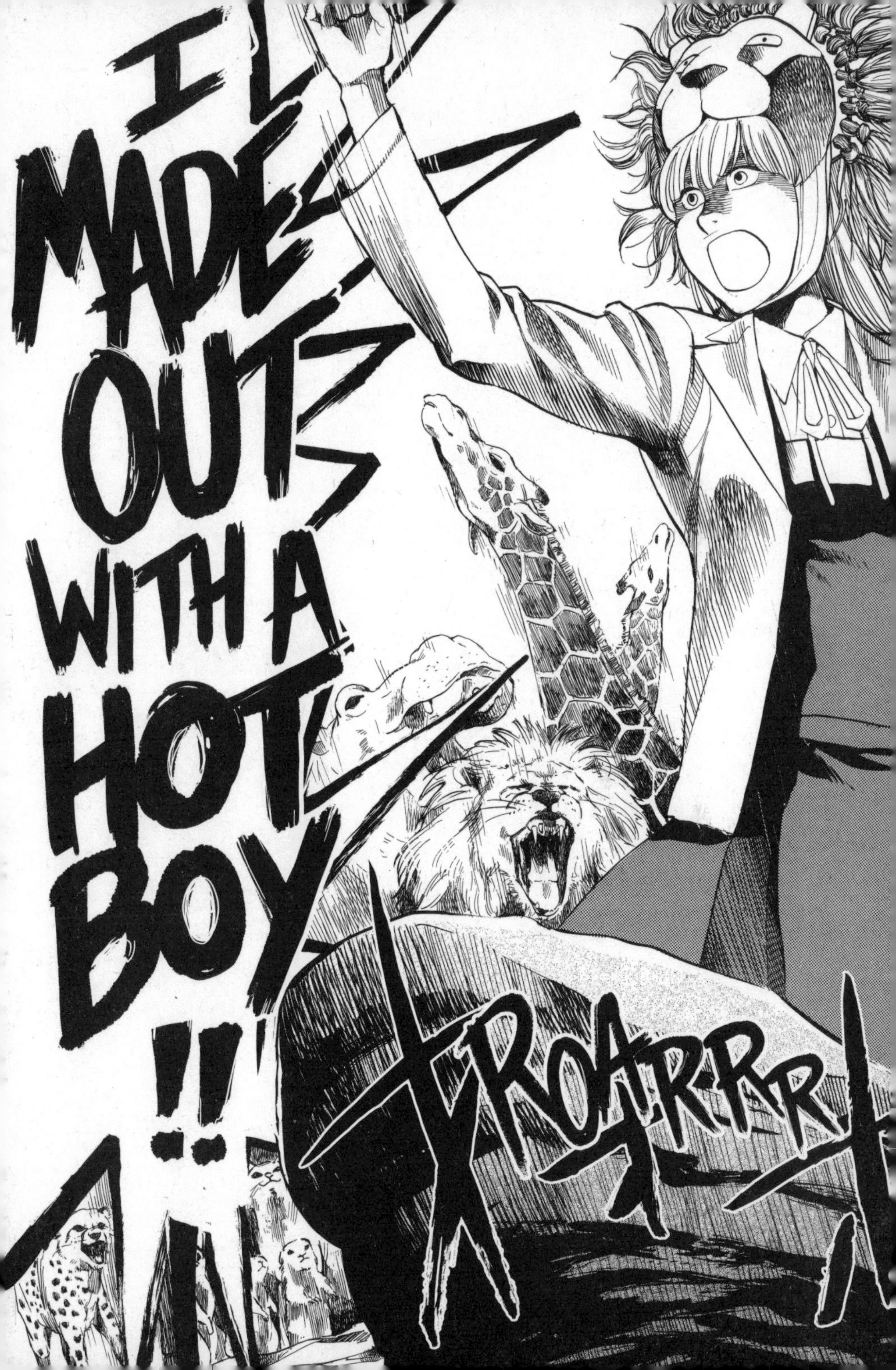
I MADE OUT WITH A HOT BOY!!
ROARRR

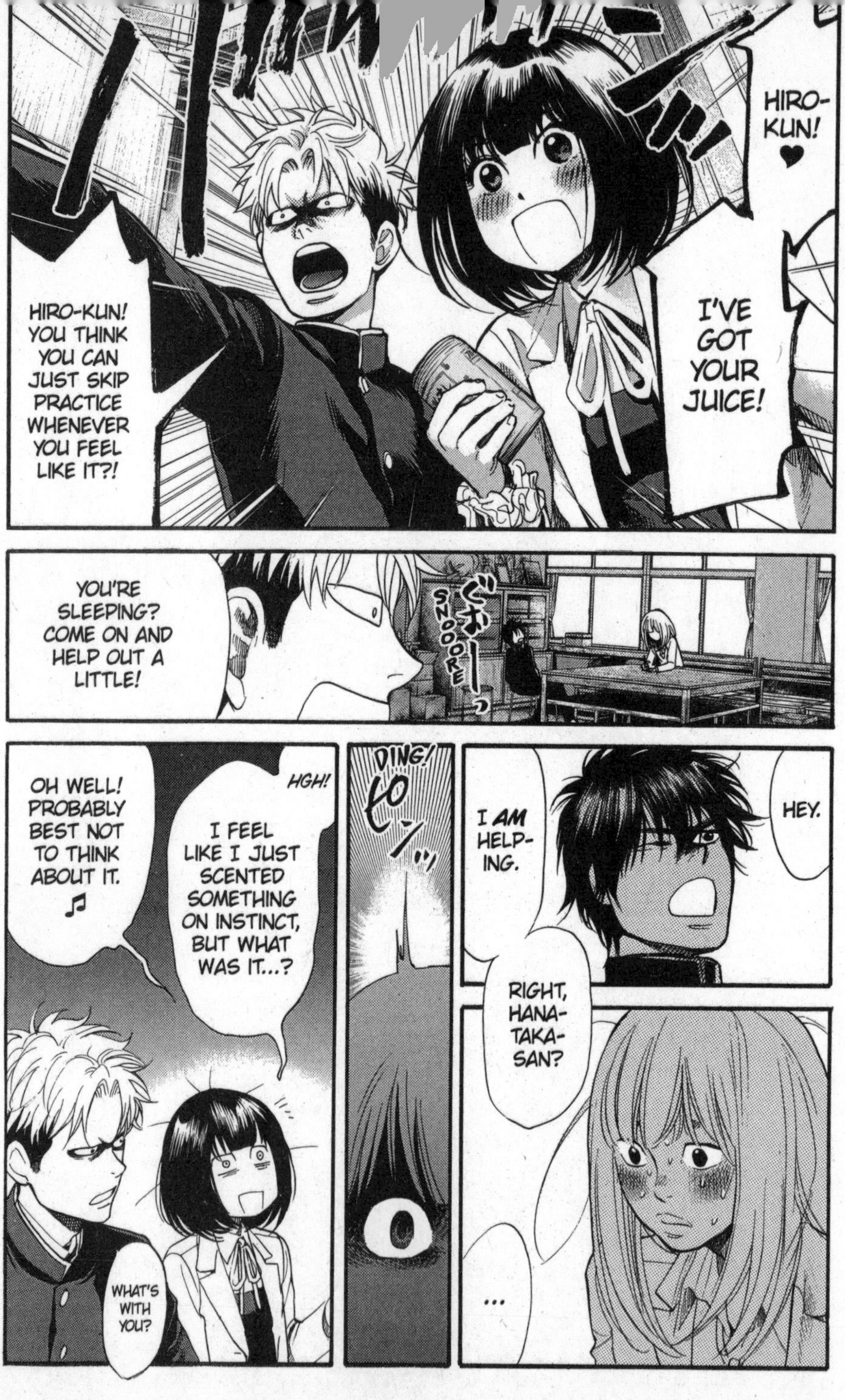
HIRO-KUN! ♥
I'VE GOT YOUR JUICE!
HIRO-KUN! YOU THINK YOU CAN JUST SKIP PRACTICE WHENEVER YOU FEEL LIKE IT?!
ぐおーっ
SNOOORE
YOU'RE SLEEPING? COME ON AND HELP OUT A LITTLE!
HEY.
I *AM* HELPING.
RIGHT, HANATAKA-SAN?
...
DING!
ピーン
HGH!
I FEEL LIKE I JUST SCENTED SOMETHING ON INSTINCT, BUT WHAT WAS IT...?
OH WELL! PROBABLY BEST NOT TO THINK ABOUT IT. ♫
WHAT'S WITH YOU?

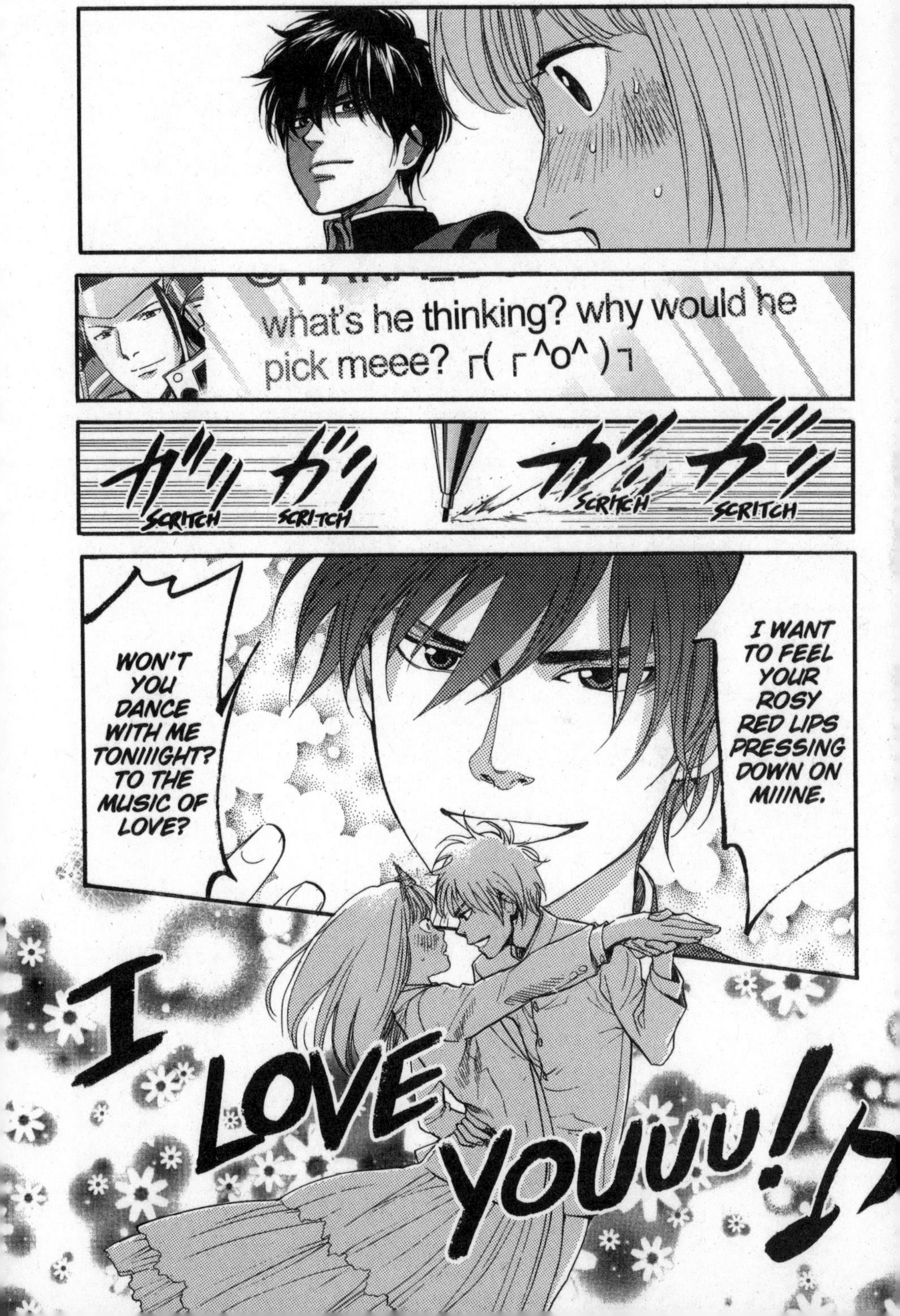
what's he thinking? why would he pick meee? ┌(┌^o^)┐
ガリ
SCRITCH
ガリ
SCRITCH
ガリ
SCRITCH
ガリ
SCRITCH
I WANT TO FEEL YOUR ROSY RED LIPS PRESSING DOWN ON MIIINE.
WON'T YOU DANCE WITH ME TONIIIGHT? TO THE MUSIC OF LOVE?
I LOVE YOUUU!♪

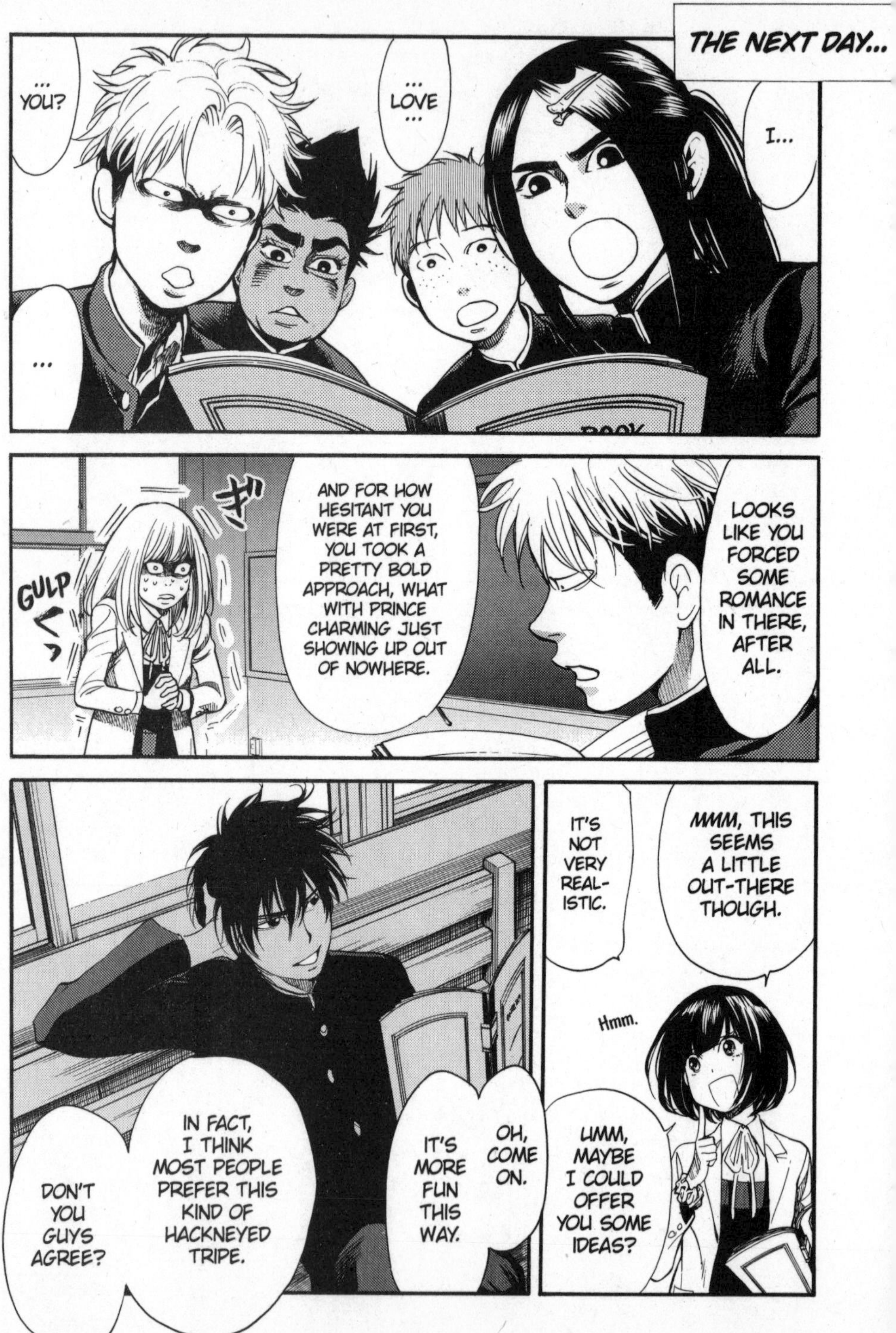
THE NEXT DAY...
I...
... LOVE ...
... YOU?
...
LOOKS LIKE YOU FORCED SOME ROMANCE IN THERE, AFTER ALL.
AND FOR HOW HESITANT YOU WERE AT FIRST, YOU TOOK A PRETTY BOLD APPROACH, WHAT WITH PRINCE CHARMING JUST SHOWING UP OUT OF NOWHERE.
ギ
GULP
MMM, THIS SEEMS A LITTLE OUT-THERE THOUGH.
IT'S NOT VERY REAL-ISTIC.
Hmm.
UMM, MAYBE I COULD OFFER YOU SOME IDEAS?
OH, COME ON.
IT'S MORE FUN THIS WAY.
IN FACT, I THINK MOST PEOPLE PREFER THIS KIND OF HACKNEYED TRIPE.
DON'T YOU GUYS AGREE?

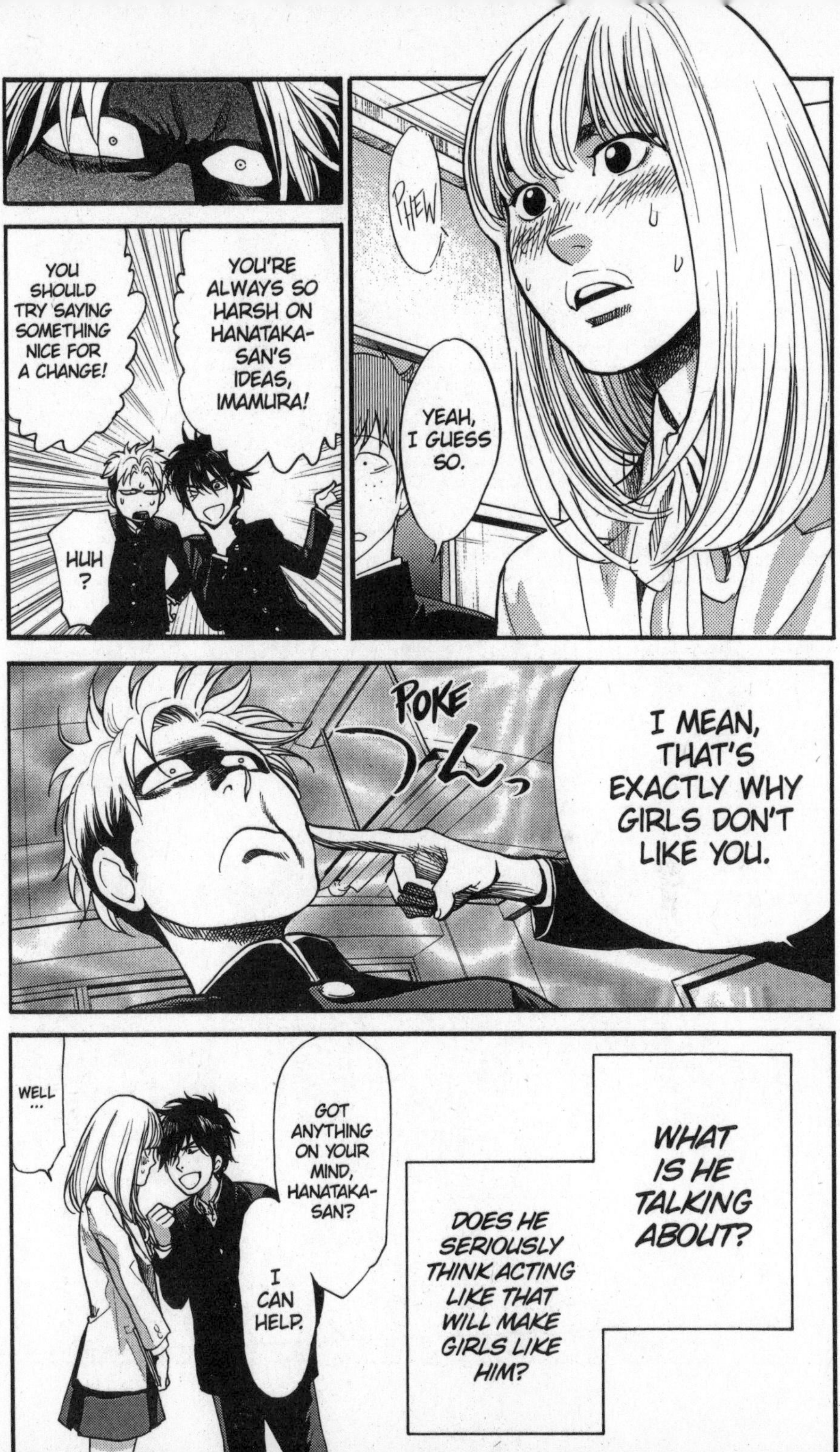
PHEW
YEAH, I GUESS SO.
YOU'RE ALWAYS SO HARSH ON HANATAKA-SAN'S IDEAS, IMAMURA!
YOU SHOULD TRY SAYING SOMETHING NICE FOR A CHANGE!
HUH?
I MEAN, THAT'S EXACTLY WHY GIRLS DON'T LIKE YOU.
POKE
WHAT IS HE TALKING ABOUT?
DOES HE SERIOUSLY THINK ACTING LIKE THAT WILL MAKE GIRLS LIKE HIM?
GOT ANYTHING ON YOUR MIND, HANATAKA-SAN?
I CAN HELP.
WELL...

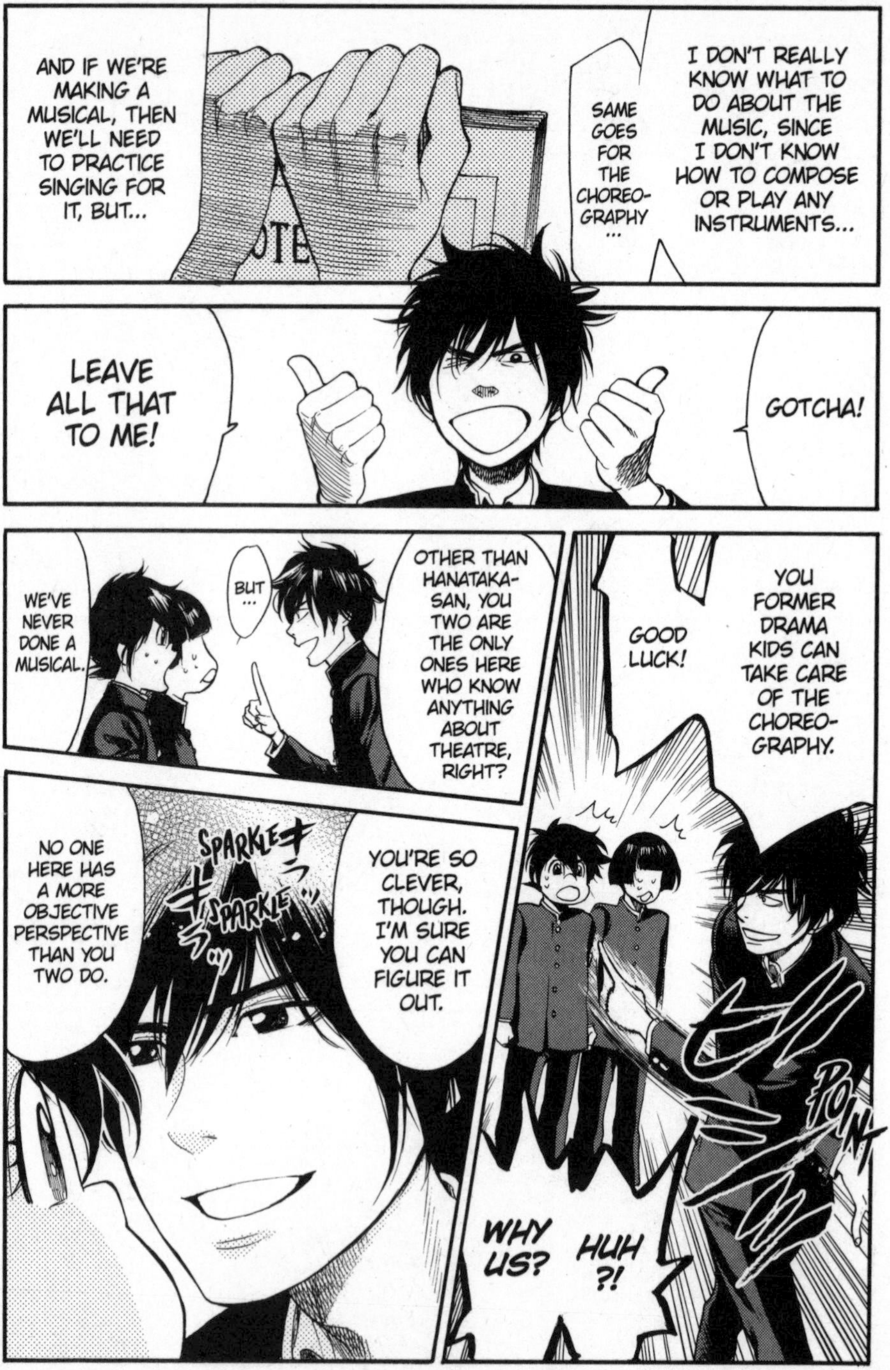
I DON'T REALLY KNOW WHAT TO DO ABOUT THE MUSIC, SINCE I DON'T KNOW HOW TO COMPOSE OR PLAY ANY INSTRUMENTS...
SAME GOES FOR THE CHOREOGRAPHY...
AND IF WE'RE MAKING A MUSICAL, THEN WE'LL NEED TO PRACTICE SINGING FOR IT, BUT...
GOTCHA!
LEAVE ALL THAT TO ME!
YOU FORMER DRAMA KIDS CAN TAKE CARE OF THE CHOREOGRAPHY.
GOOD LUCK!
POINT
HUH ?!
WHY US?
OTHER THAN HANATAKA-SAN, YOU TWO ARE THE ONLY ONES HERE WHO KNOW ANYTHING ABOUT THEATRE, RIGHT?
BUT ...
WE'VE NEVER DONE A MUSICAL.
YOU'RE SO CLEVER, THOUGH. I'M SURE YOU CAN FIGURE IT OUT.
SPARKLE
SPARKLE
NO ONE HERE HAS A MORE OBJECTIVE PERSPECTIVE THAN YOU TWO DO.

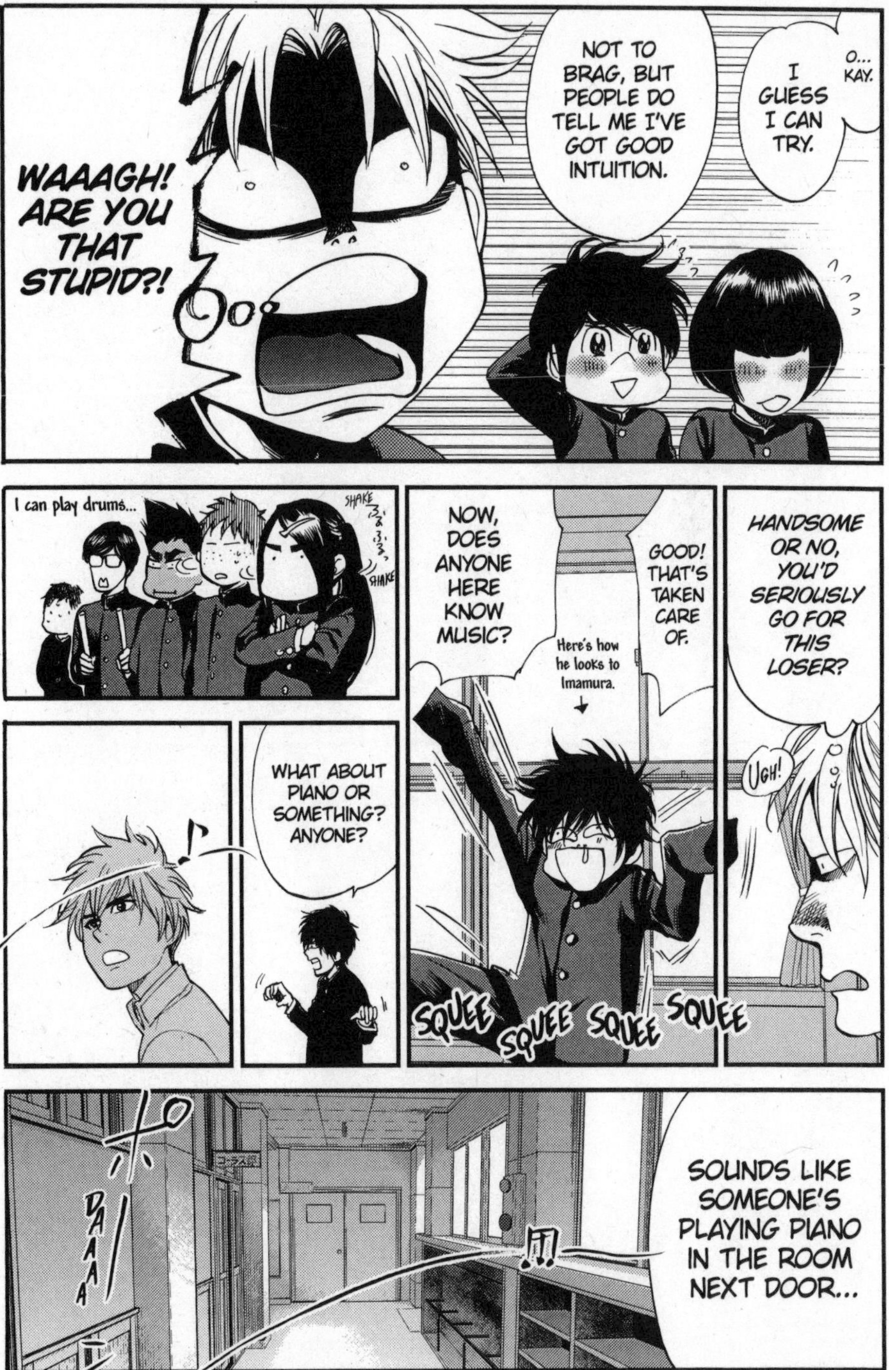

O... KAY.
I GUESS I CAN TRY.
NOT TO BRAG, BUT PEOPLE DO TELL ME I'VE GOT GOOD INTUITION.
WAAAGH! ARE YOU THAT STUPID?!
HANDSOME OR NO, YOU'D SERIOUSLY GO FOR THIS LOSER?
UGH!
GOOD! THAT'S TAKEN CARE OF.
NOW, DOES ANYONE HERE KNOW MUSIC?
Here's how he looks to Imamura.
SQUEE SQUEE SQUEE SQUEE
SHAKE SHAKE
I can play drums...
WHAT ABOUT PIANO OR SOMETHING? ANYONE?
!
SOUNDS LIKE SOMEONE'S PLAYING PIANO IN THE ROOM NEXT DOOR...
DAAAA

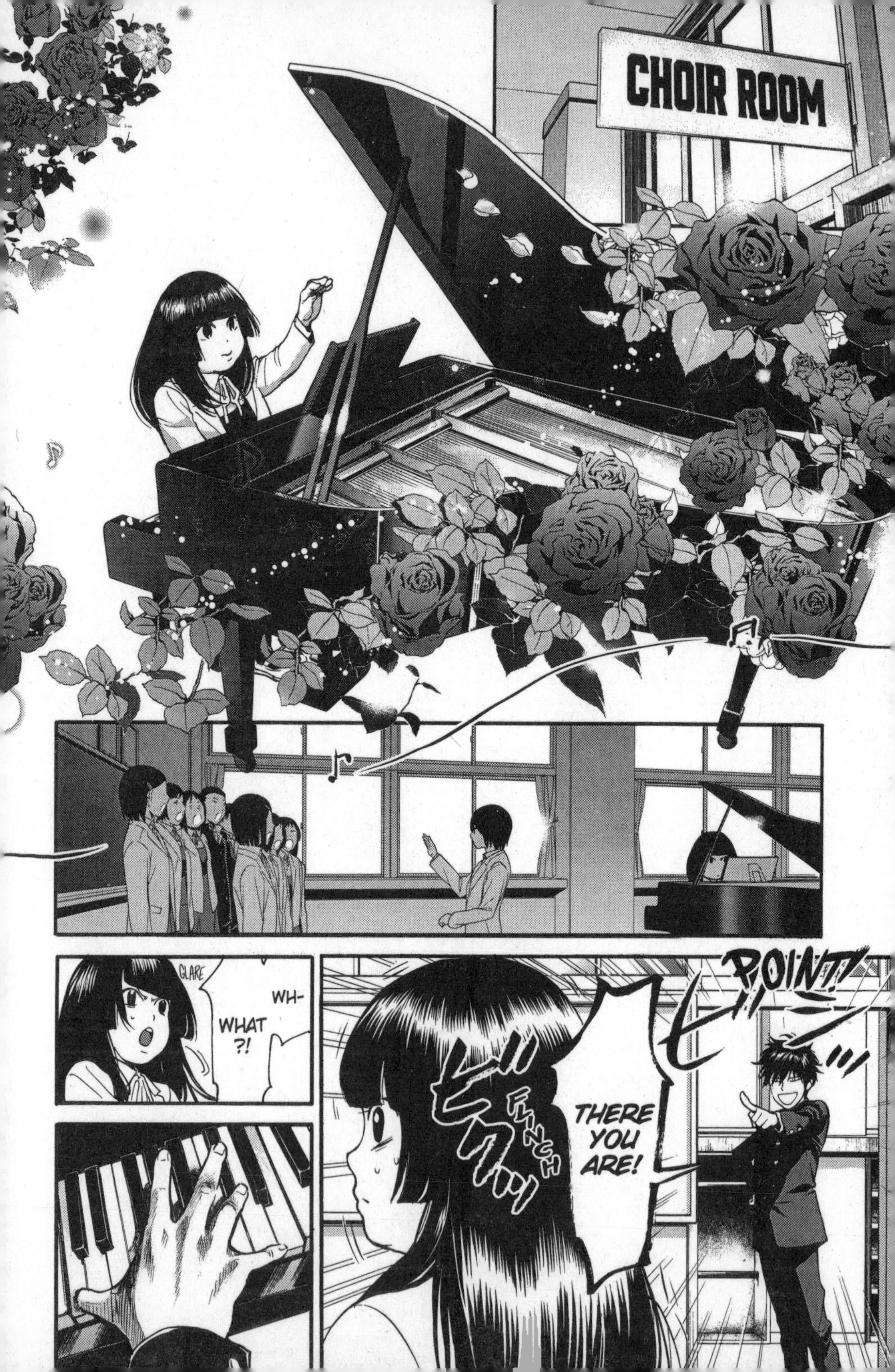
CHOIR ROOM
POINT!
THERE YOU ARE!
FLINCH
GLARE
WH- WHAT ?!

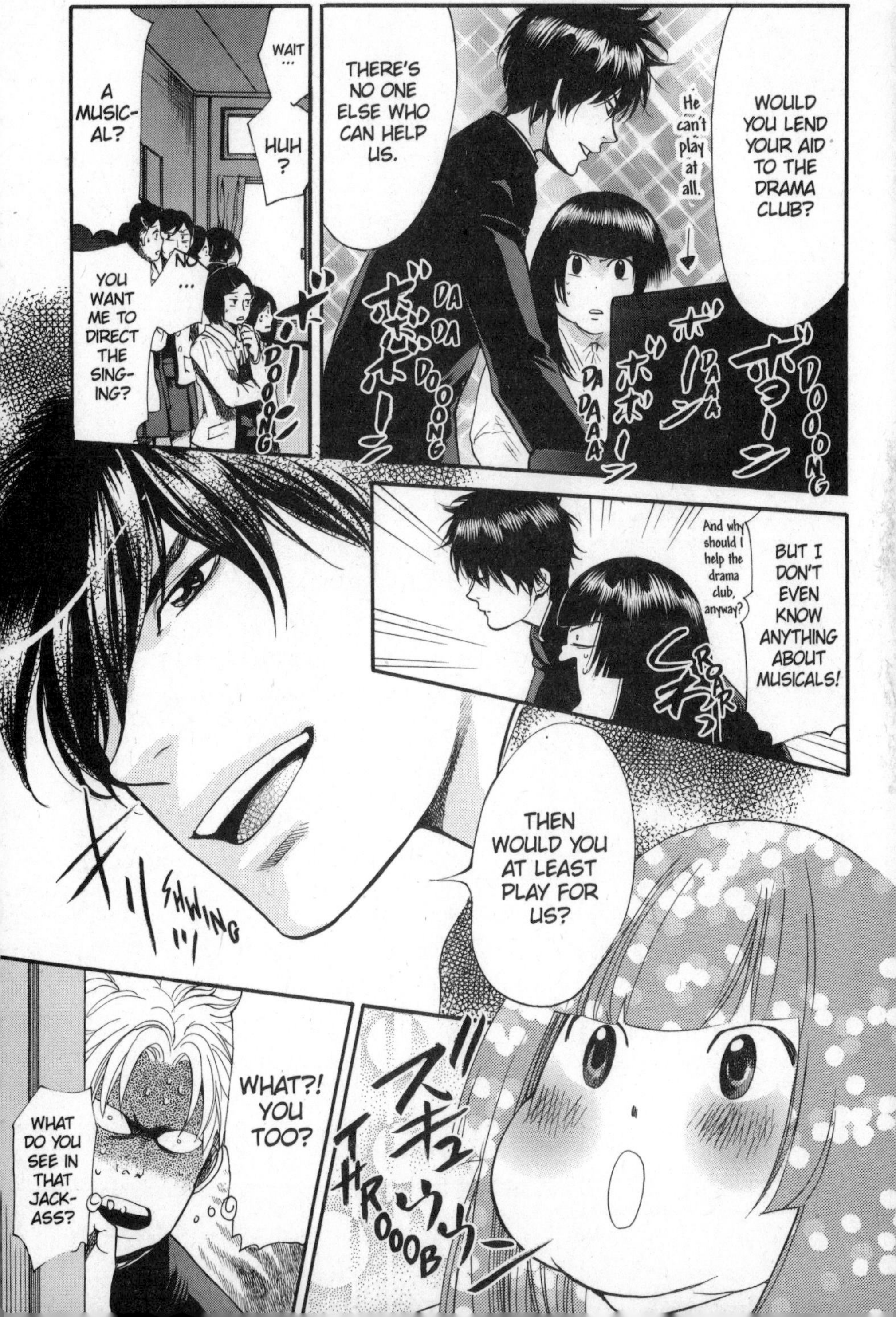
WOULD YOU LEND YOUR AID TO THE DRAMA CLUB?
He can't play at all.
DOOOONG
DAAA
DA DAAA
THERE'S NO ONE ELSE WHO CAN HELP US.
DA DA DOOOONG
WAIT ...
HUH ?
A MUSICAL?
NO ...
YOU WANT ME TO DIRECT THE SINGING?
DOOOONG
BUT I DON'T EVEN KNOW ANYTHING ABOUT MUSICALS!
And why should I help the drama club, anyway?
ROAR
THEN WOULD YOU AT LEAST PLAY FOR US?
SHWING
THROOOB
WHAT?! YOU TOO?
WHAT DO YOU SEE IN THAT JACKASS?

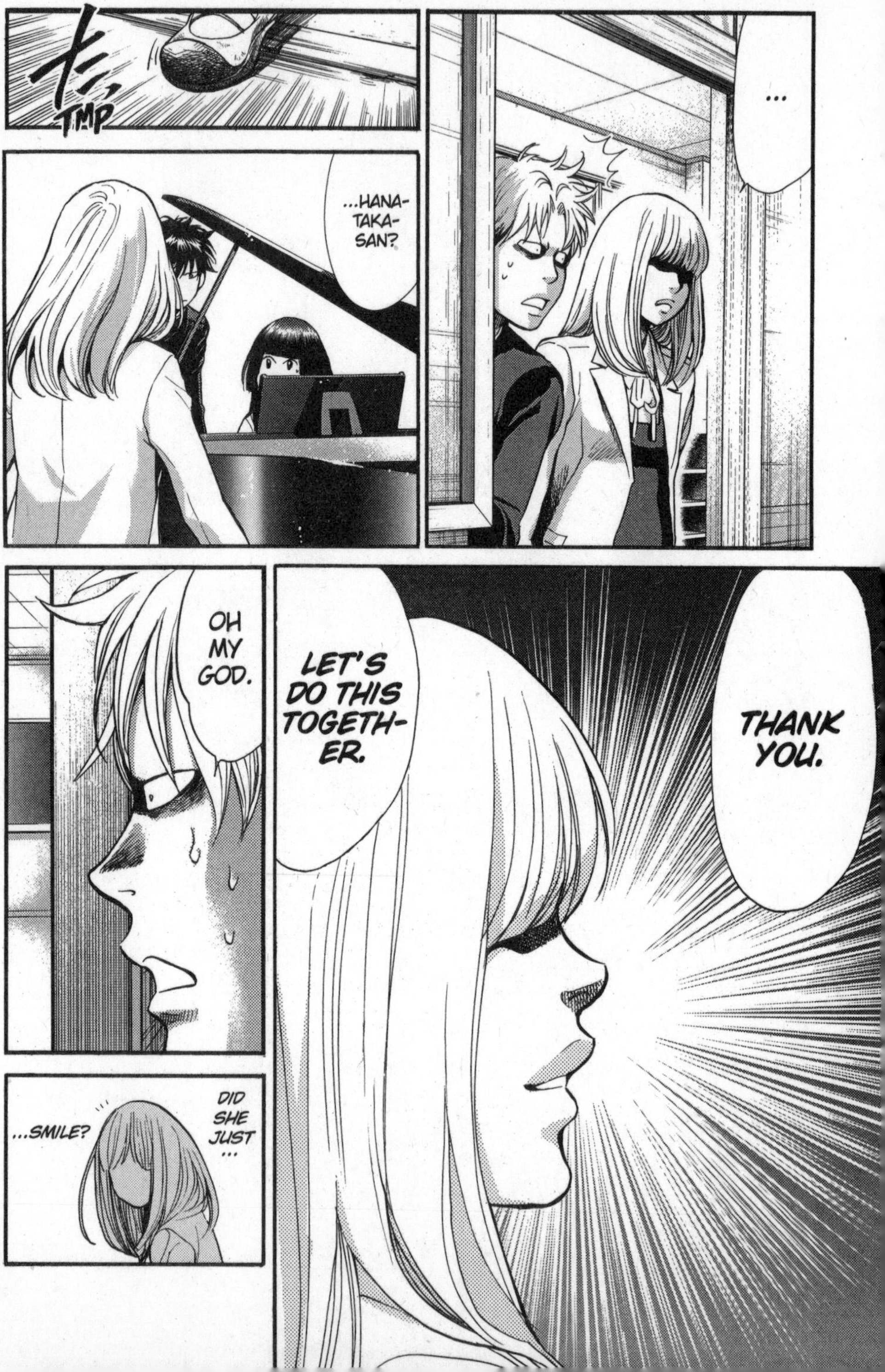
...
TMP
...HANA-TAKA-SAN?
THANK YOU.
LET'S DO THIS TOGETH-ER.
OH MY GOD.
DID SHE JUST ...
...SMILE?

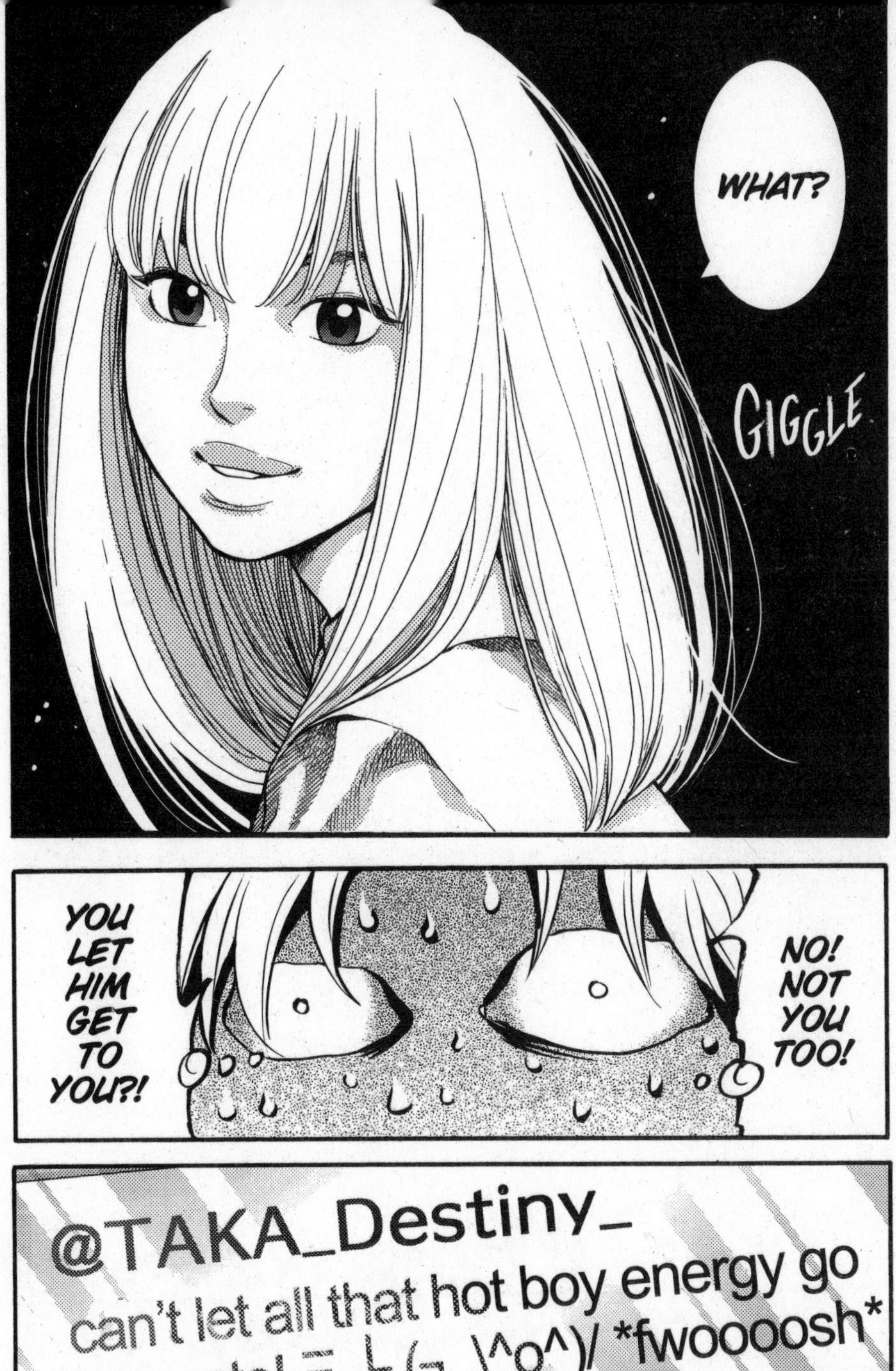
WHAT?
GIGGLE
NO! NOT YOU TOO!
YOU LET HIM GET TO YOU?!
@TAKA_Destiny_
can't let all that hot boy energy go to waste! ≡ └(┐ \^o^)/ *fwoooosh*

Again!!
アゲイン!!

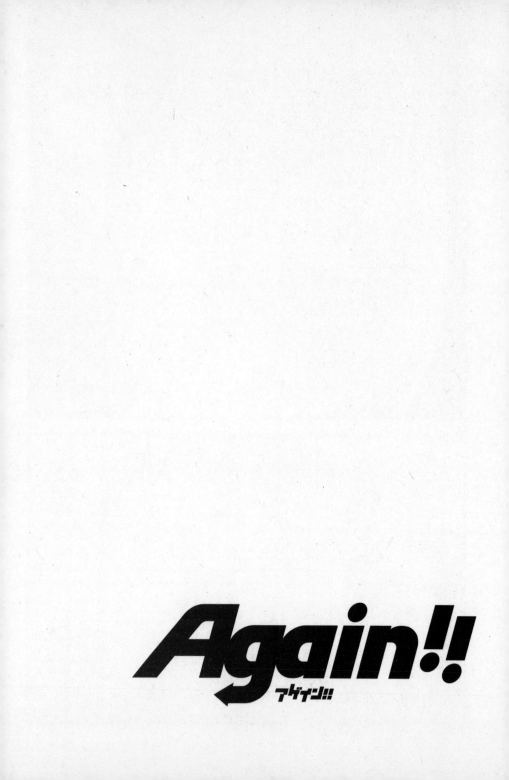

85. BEAUTIFUL POWER

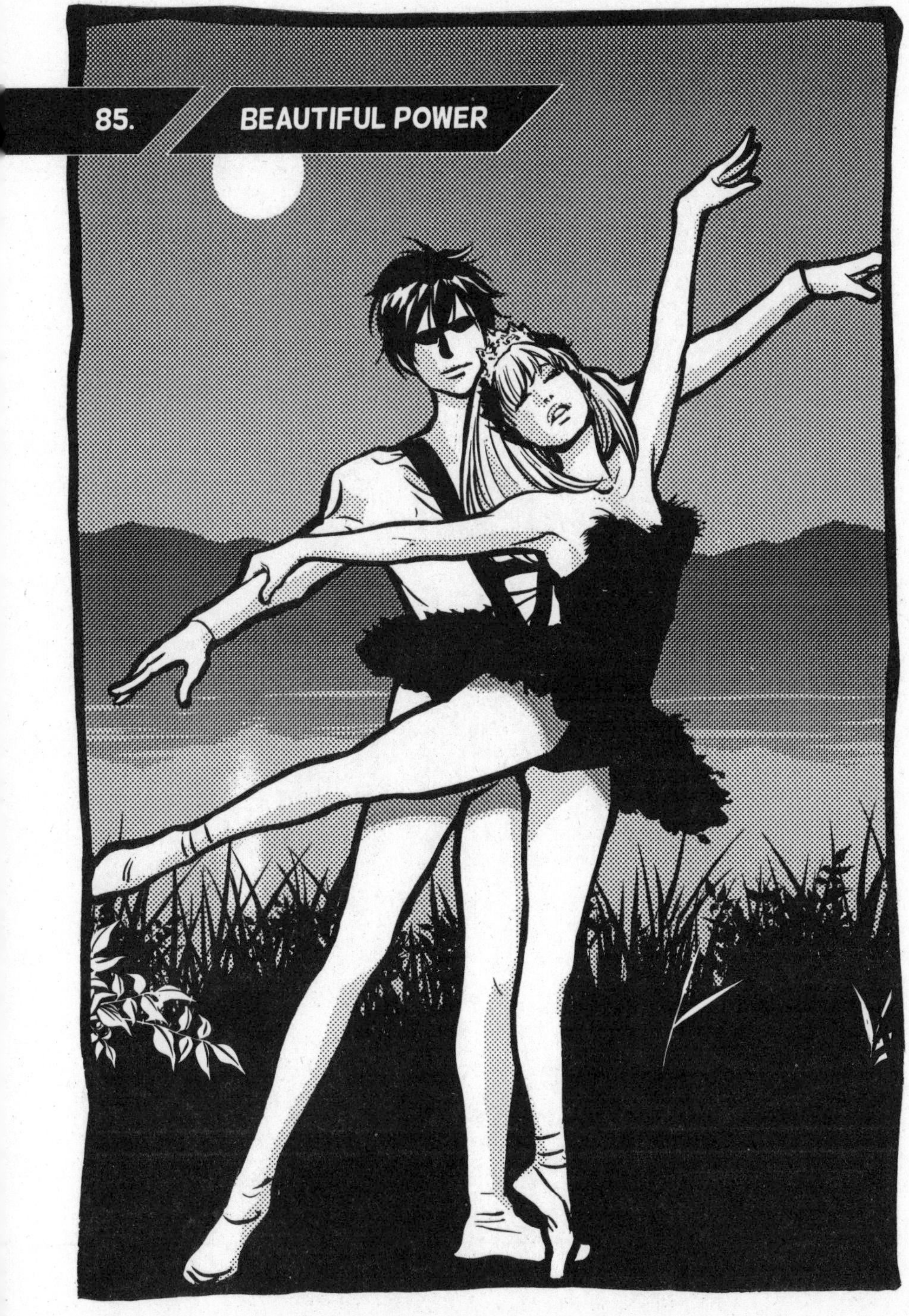

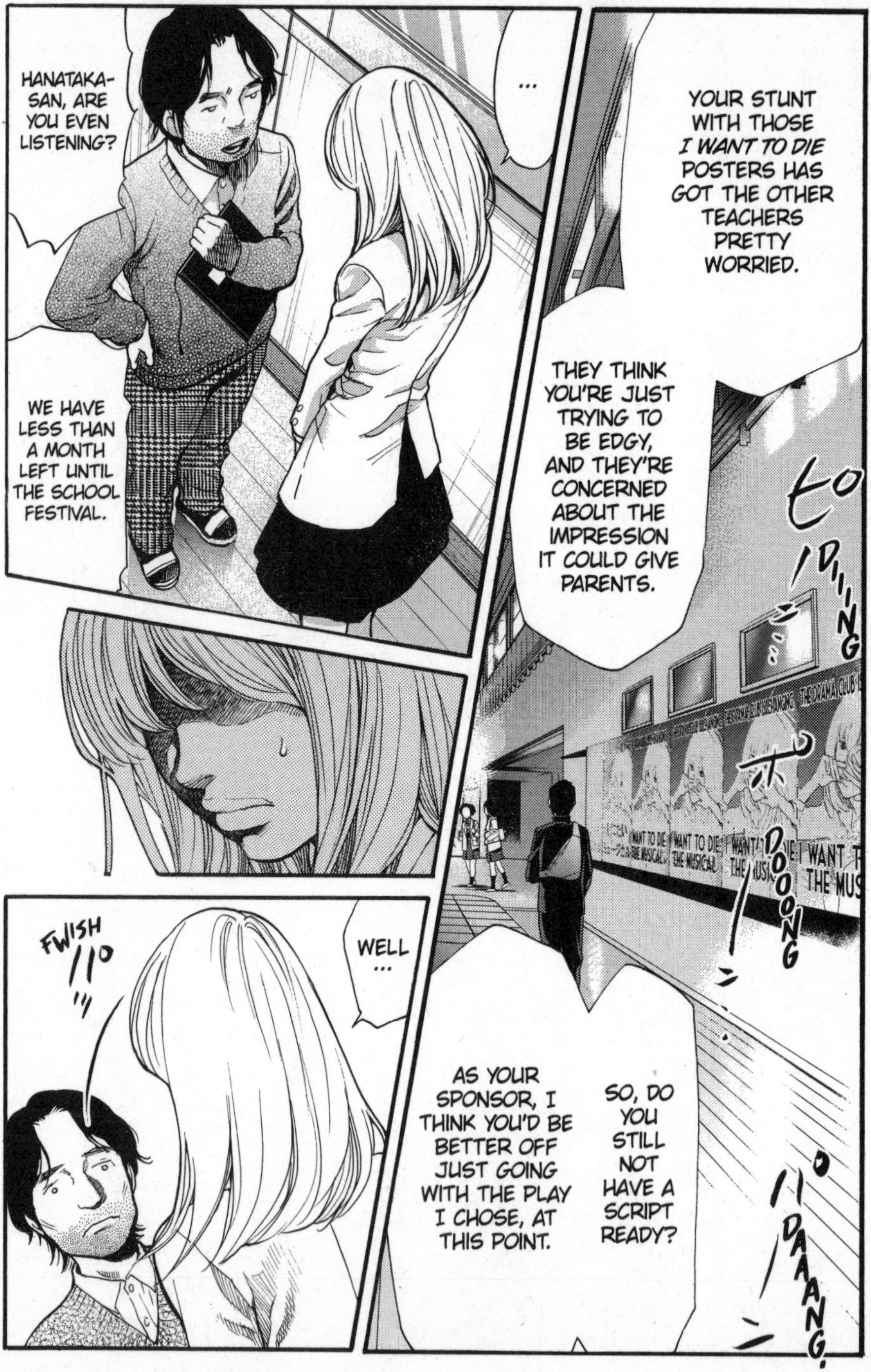
YOUR STUNT WITH THOSE *I WANT TO DIE* POSTERS HAS GOT THE OTHER TEACHERS PRETTY WORRIED.
THEY THINK YOU'RE JUST TRYING TO BE EDGY, AND THEY'RE CONCERNED ABOUT THE IMPRESSION IT COULD GIVE PARENTS.
DIIING
I WANT TO DIE THE MUSICAL
DOOOONG
SO, DO YOU STILL NOT HAVE A SCRIPT READY?
AS YOUR SPONSOR, I THINK YOU'D BE BETTER OFF JUST GOING WITH THE PLAY I CHOSE, AT THIS POINT.
DAAANG...
...
HANATAKA-SAN, ARE YOU EVEN LISTENING?
WE HAVE LESS THAN A MONTH LEFT UNTIL THE SCHOOL FESTIVAL.
WELL ...
FWISH

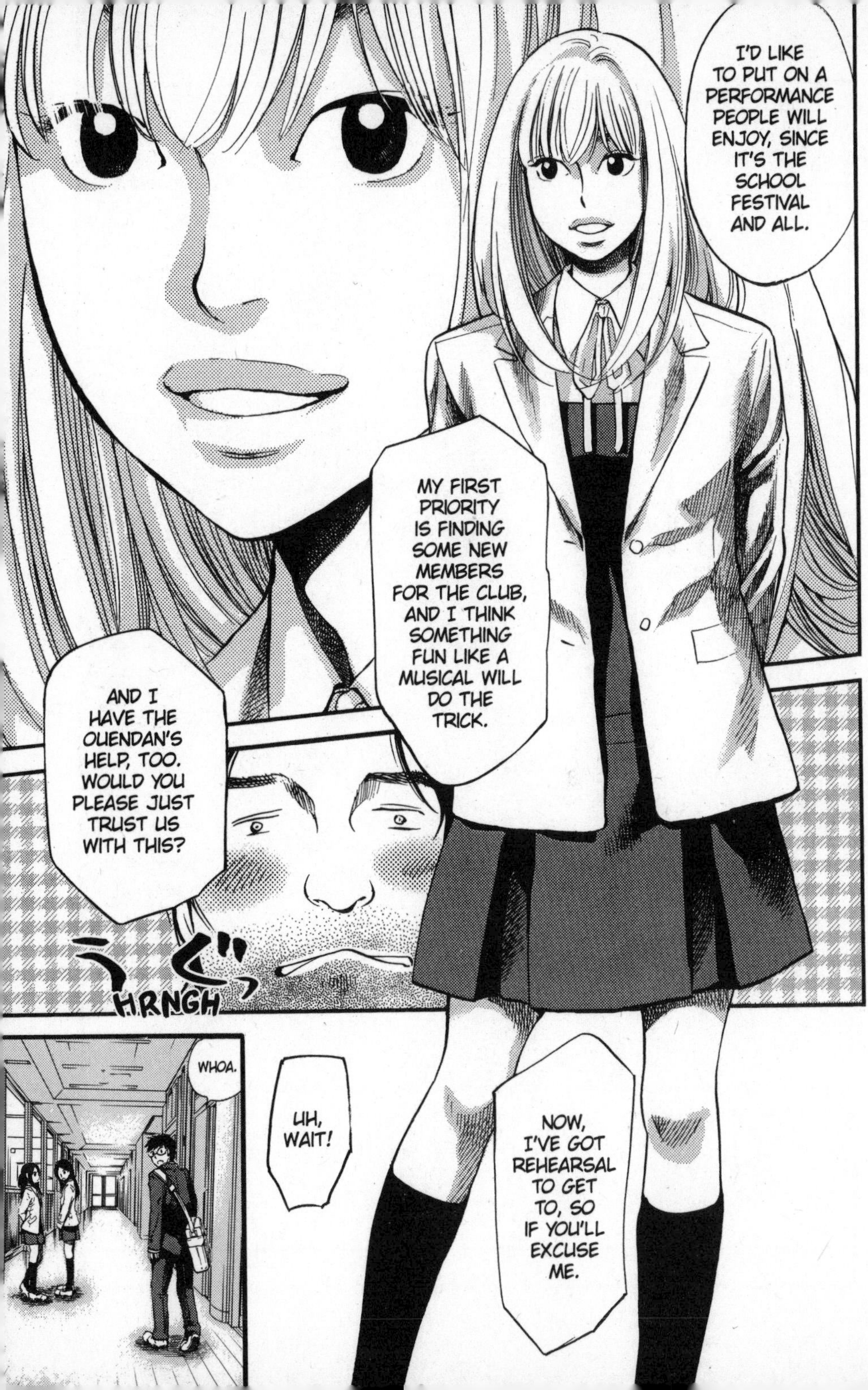
I'D LIKE TO PUT ON A PERFORMANCE PEOPLE WILL ENJOY, SINCE IT'S THE SCHOOL FESTIVAL AND ALL.
MY FIRST PRIORITY IS FINDING SOME NEW MEMBERS FOR THE CLUB, AND I THINK SOMETHING FUN LIKE A MUSICAL WILL DO THE TRICK.
AND I HAVE THE OUENDAN'S HELP, TOO. WOULD YOU PLEASE JUST TRUST US WITH THIS?
HRNGH
NOW, I'VE GOT REHEARSAL TO GET TO, SO IF YOU'LL EXCUSE ME.
UH, WAIT!
WHOA.

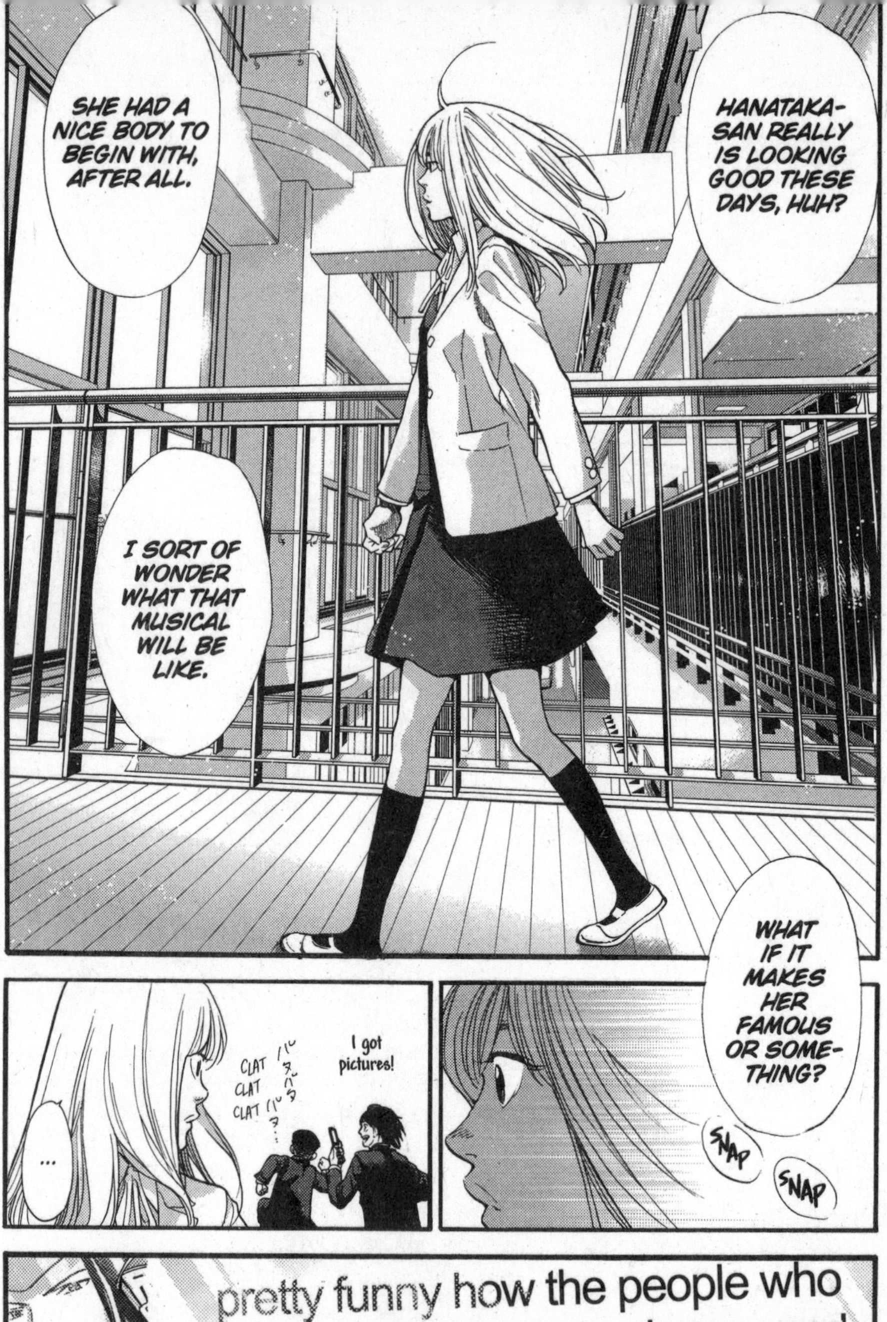
HANATAKA-SAN REALLY IS LOOKING GOOD THESE DAYS, HUH?
SHE HAD A NICE BODY TO BEGIN WITH, AFTER ALL.
I SORT OF WONDER WHAT THAT MUSICAL WILL BE LIKE.
WHAT IF IT MAKES HER FAMOUS OR SOME-THING?
SNAP
SNAP
I got pictures!
CLAT CLAT CLAT
...
pretty funny how the people who used to say I was so gloomy and ugly have changed their tune lmac

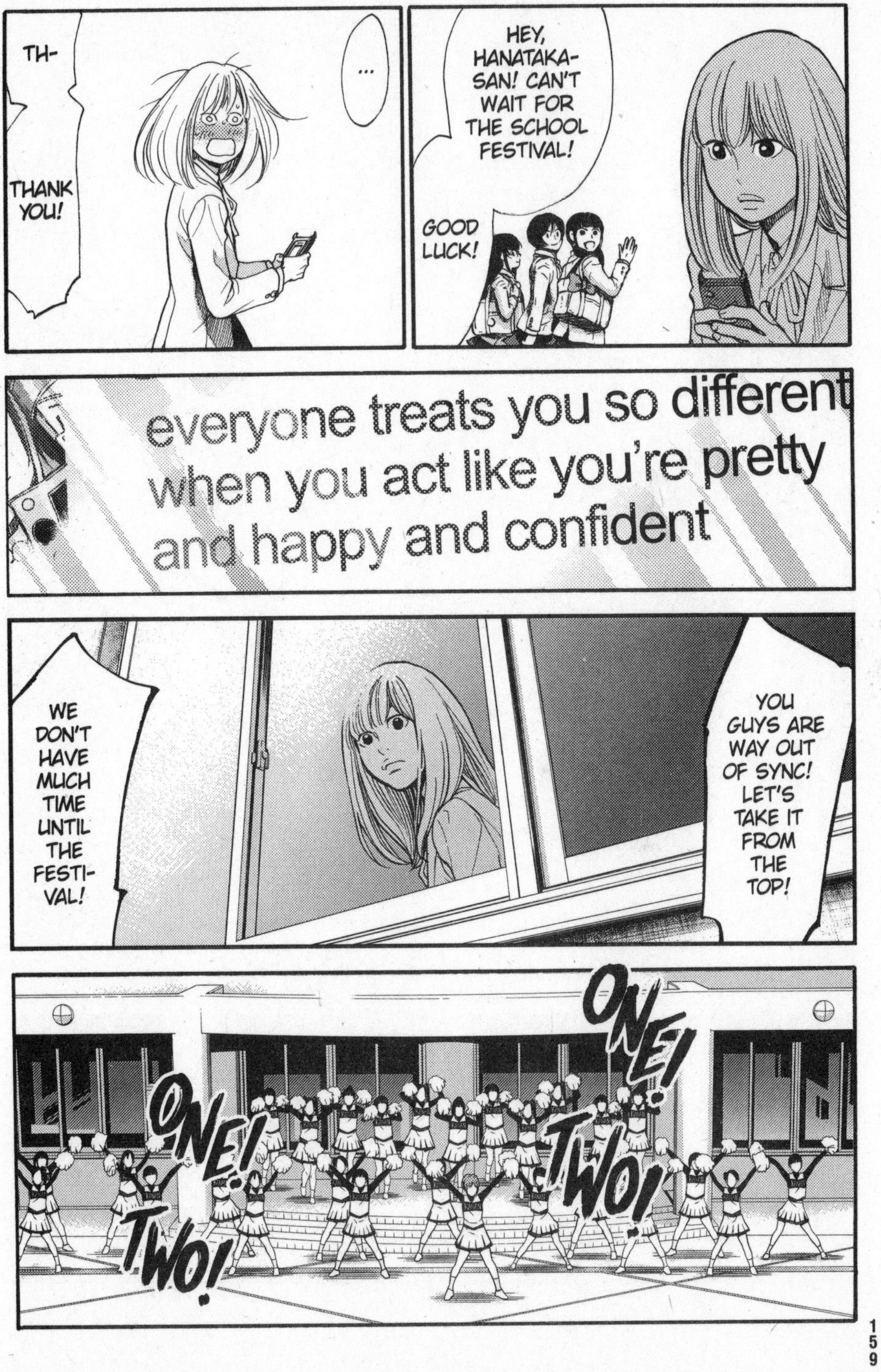
HEY, HANATAKA-SAN! CAN'T WAIT FOR THE SCHOOL FESTIVAL!
GOOD LUCK!
...
TH-
THANK YOU!
everyone treats you so different when you act like you're pretty and happy and confident
YOU GUYS ARE WAY OUT OF SYNC! LET'S TAKE IT FROM THE TOP!
WE DON'T HAVE MUCH TIME UNTIL THE FESTI-VAL!
ONE! TWO!
ONE! TWO!

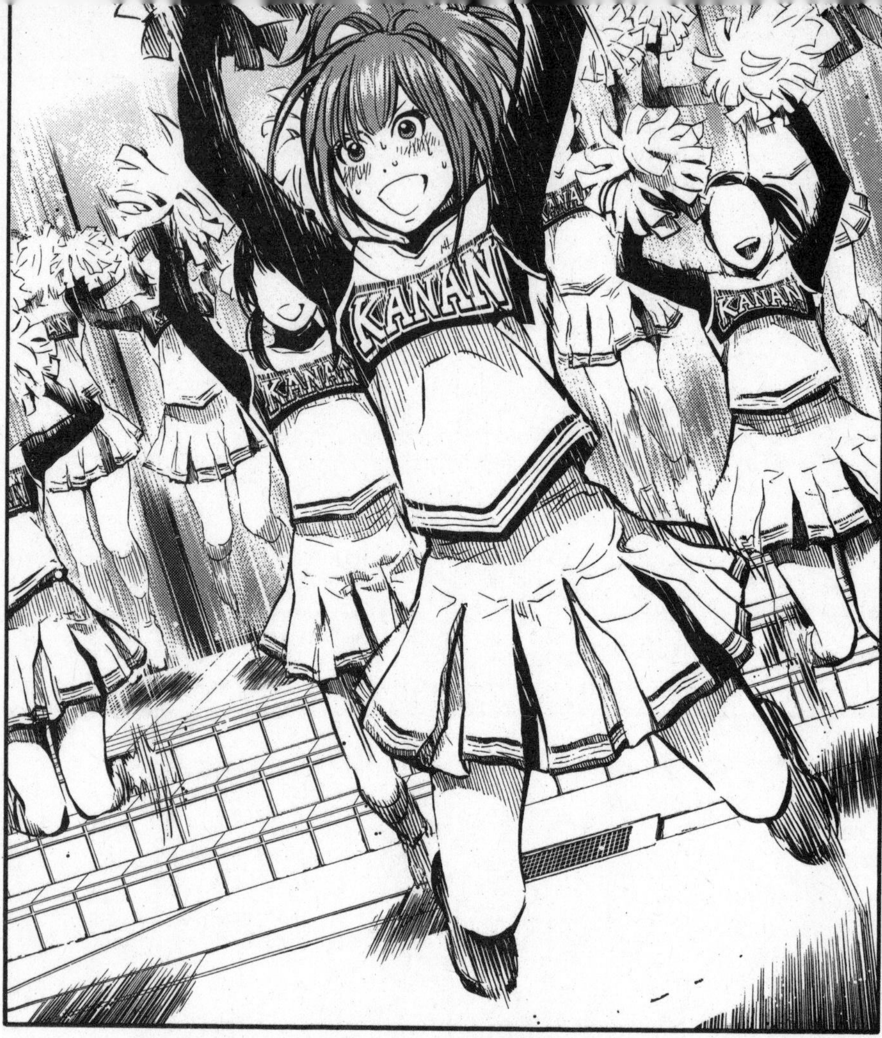
KANAN
KANAN
KANAN
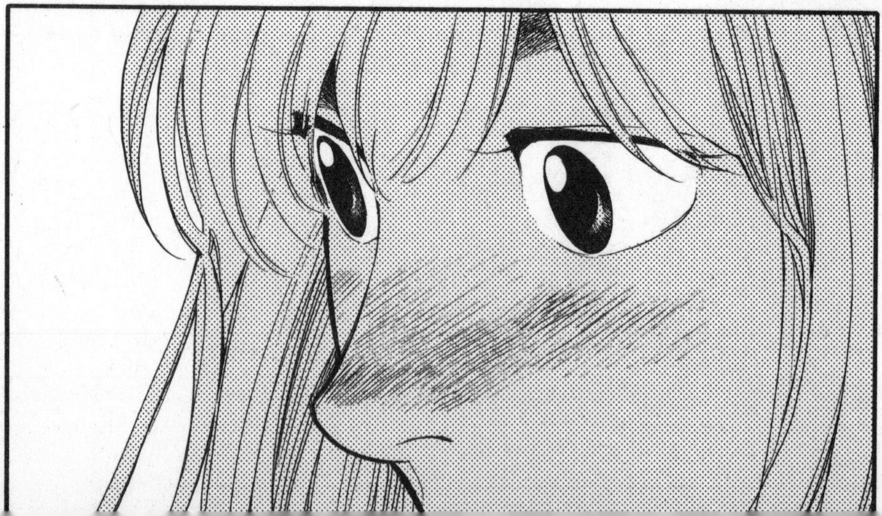

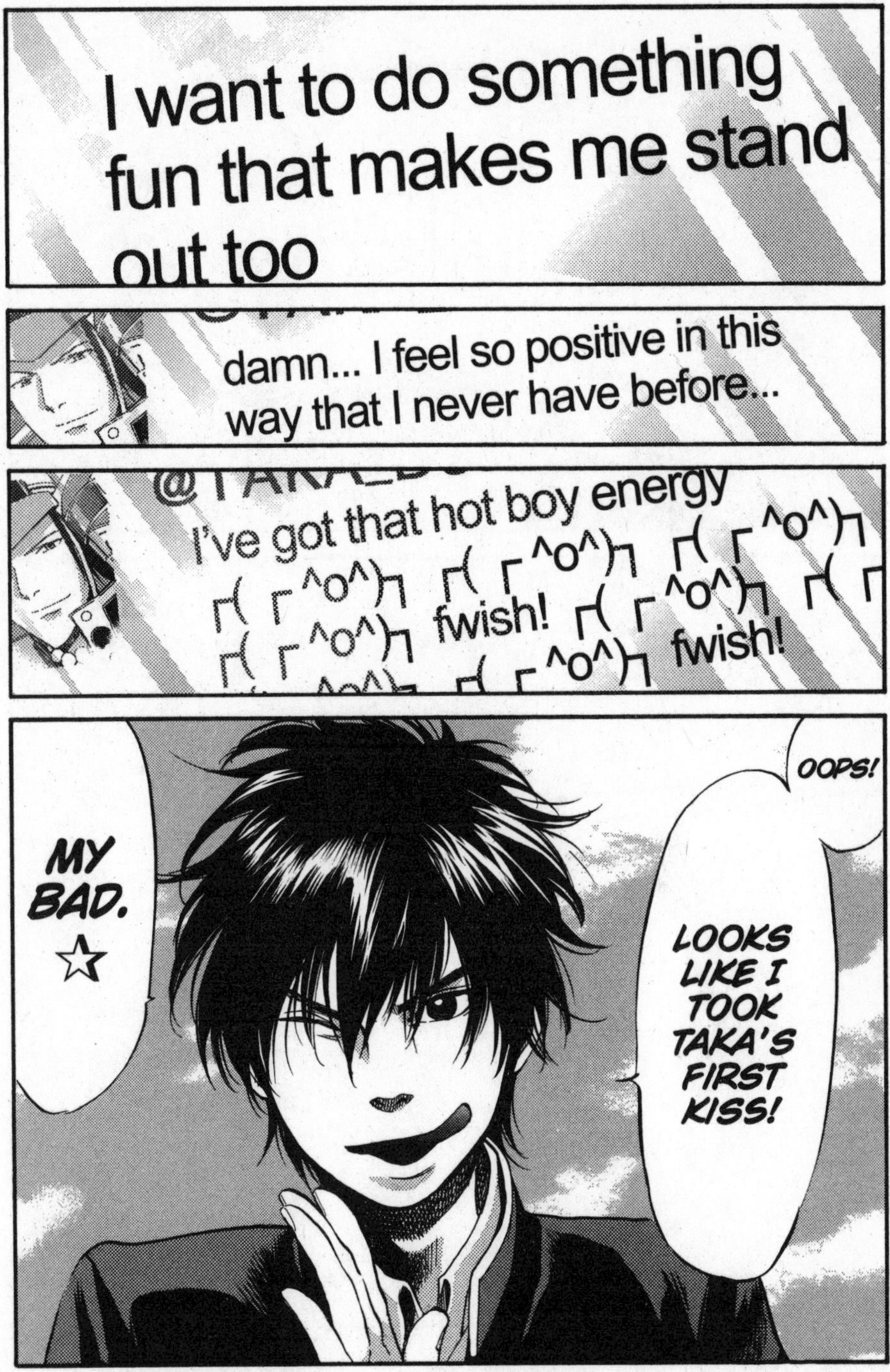
I want to do something fun that makes me stand out too
damn... I feel so positive in this way that I never have before...
I've got that hot boy energy
┌(┌^o^)┐ ┌(┌^o^)┐ ┌(┌^o^)┐
┌(┌^o^)┐ ┌(┌^o^)┐ fwish! ┌(┌^o^)┐ fwish!
OOPS!
LOOKS LIKE I TOOK TAKA'S FIRST KISS!
MY BAD. ☆

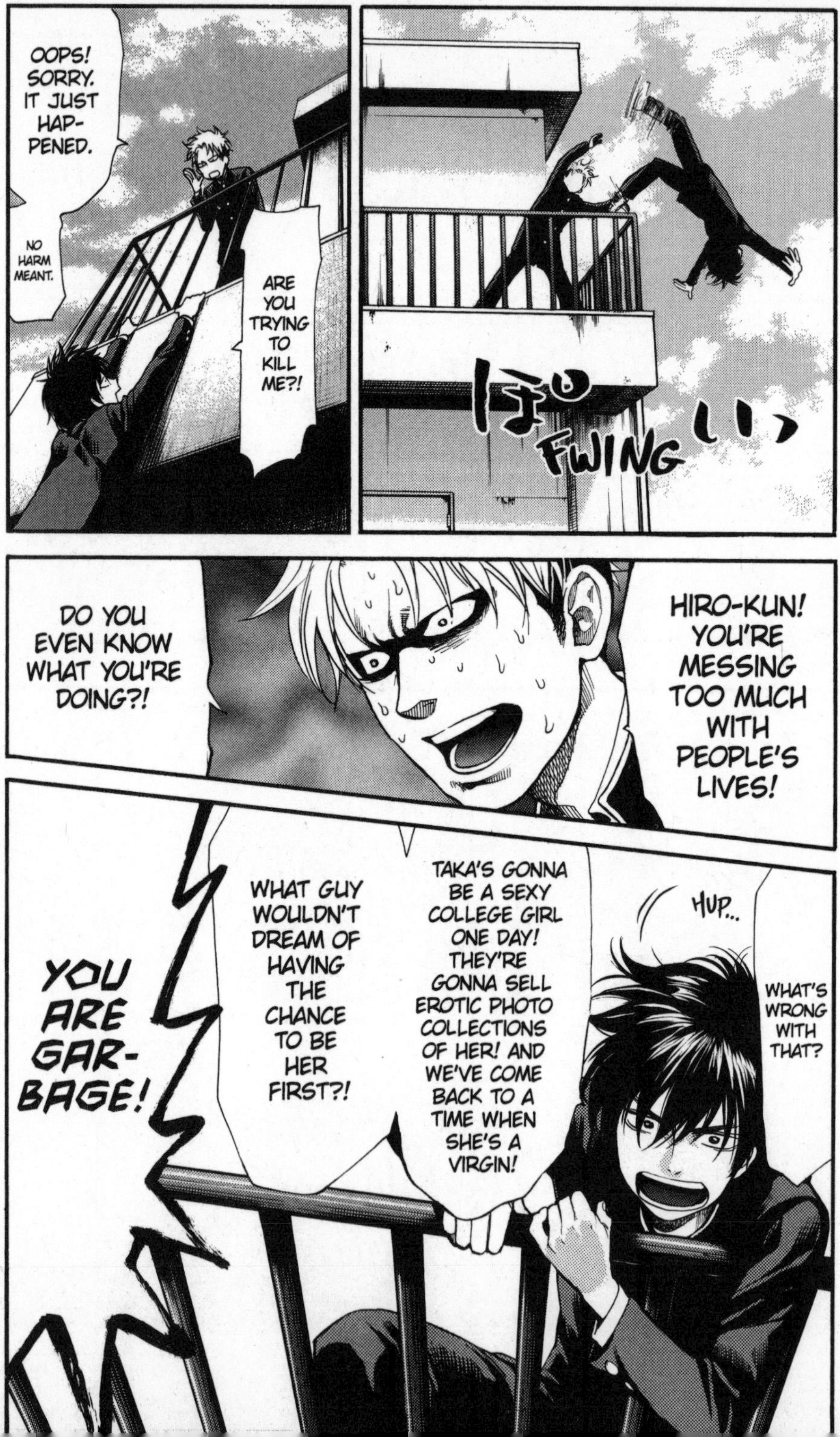
ぽいっ
FWING
ARE YOU TRYING TO KILL ME?!
OOPS! SORRY. IT JUST HAP-PENED.
NO HARM MEANT.
HIRO-KUN! YOU'RE MESSING TOO MUCH WITH PEOPLE'S LIVES!
DO YOU EVEN KNOW WHAT YOU'RE DOING?!
HUP...
WHAT'S WRONG WITH THAT?
TAKA'S GONNA BE A SEXY COLLEGE GIRL ONE DAY! THEY'RE GONNA SELL EROTIC PHOTO COLLECTIONS OF HER! AND WE'VE COME BACK TO A TIME WHEN SHE'S A VIRGIN!
WHAT GUY WOULDN'T DREAM OF HAVING THE CHANCE TO BE HER FIRST?!
YOU ARE GAR-BAGE!

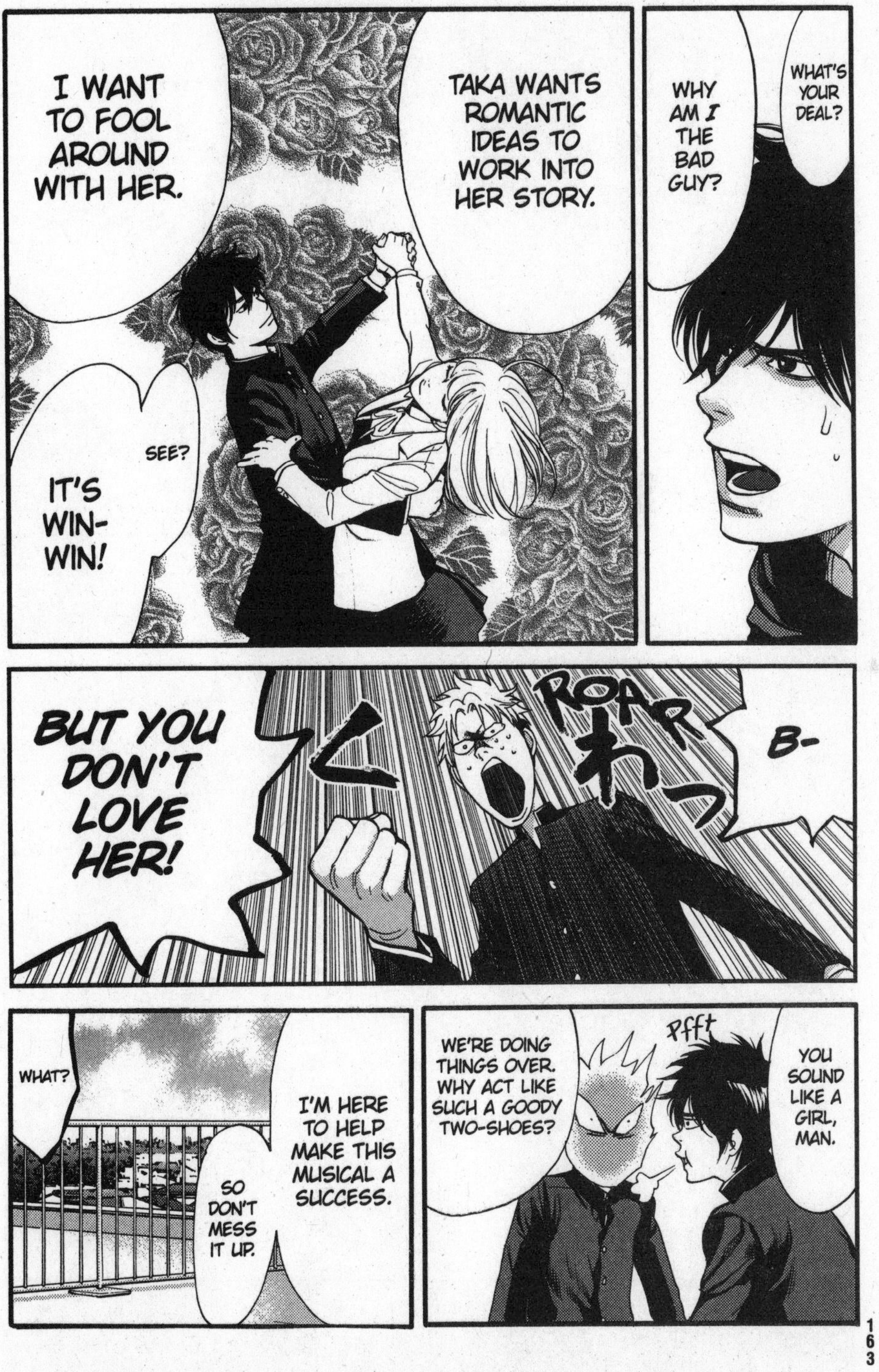

WHAT'S YOUR DEAL?
WHY AM I THE BAD GUY?
TAKA WANTS ROMANTIC IDEAS TO WORK INTO HER STORY.
I WANT TO FOOL AROUND WITH HER.
SEE?
IT'S WIN-WIN!
B-
ROAR
わっ
BUT YOU DON'T LOVE HER!
YOU SOUND LIKE A GIRL, MAN.
Pfft
WE'RE DOING THINGS OVER. WHY ACT LIKE SUCH A GOODY TWO-SHOES?
I'M HERE TO HELP MAKE THIS MUSICAL A SUCCESS.
SO DON'T MESS IT UP.
WHAT?

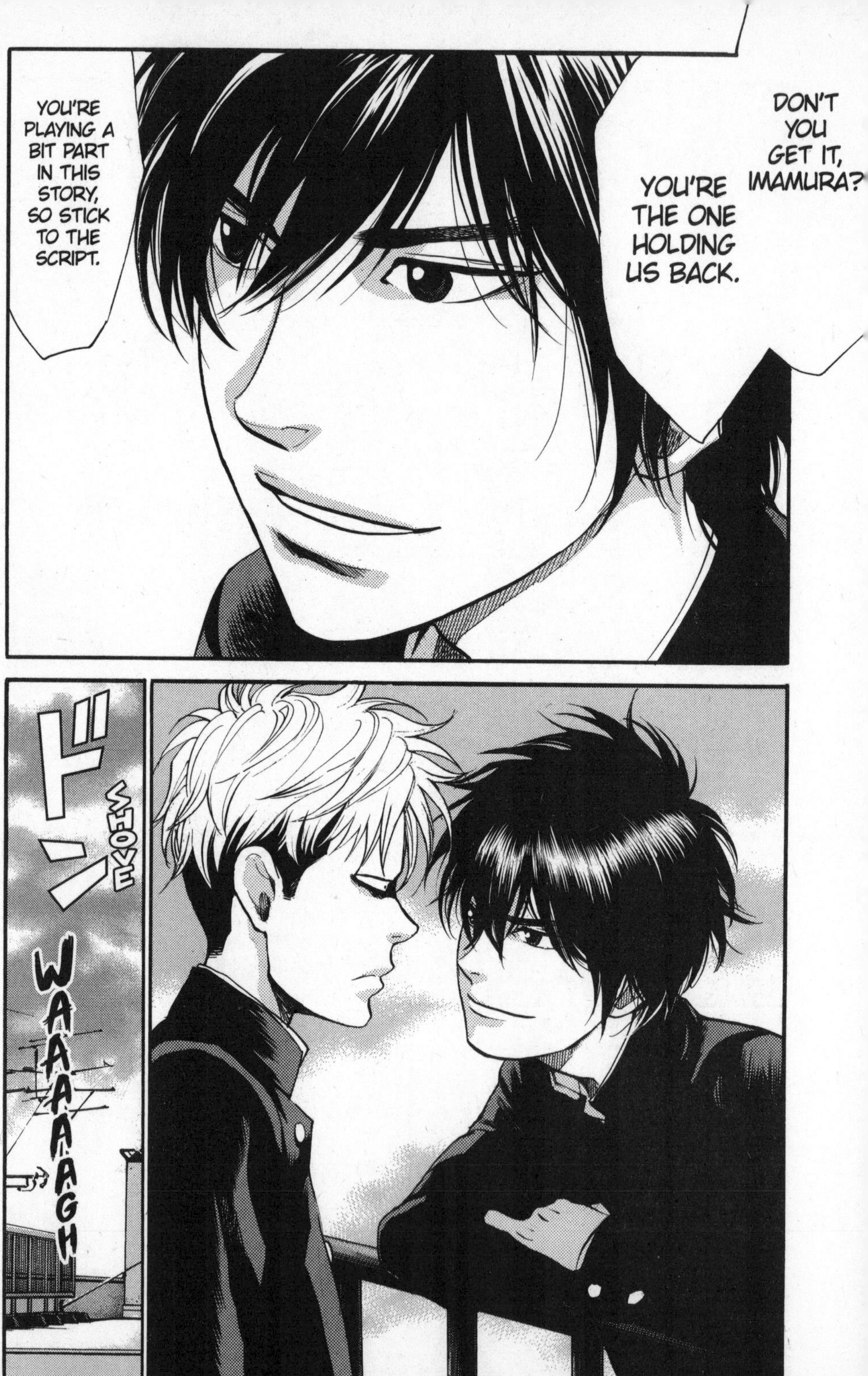
DON'T YOU GET IT, IMAMURA?
YOU'RE THE ONE HOLDING US BACK.
YOU'RE PLAYING A BIT PART IN THIS STORY, SO STICK TO THE SCRIPT.
ドン
SHOVE
WAAAAAAGH

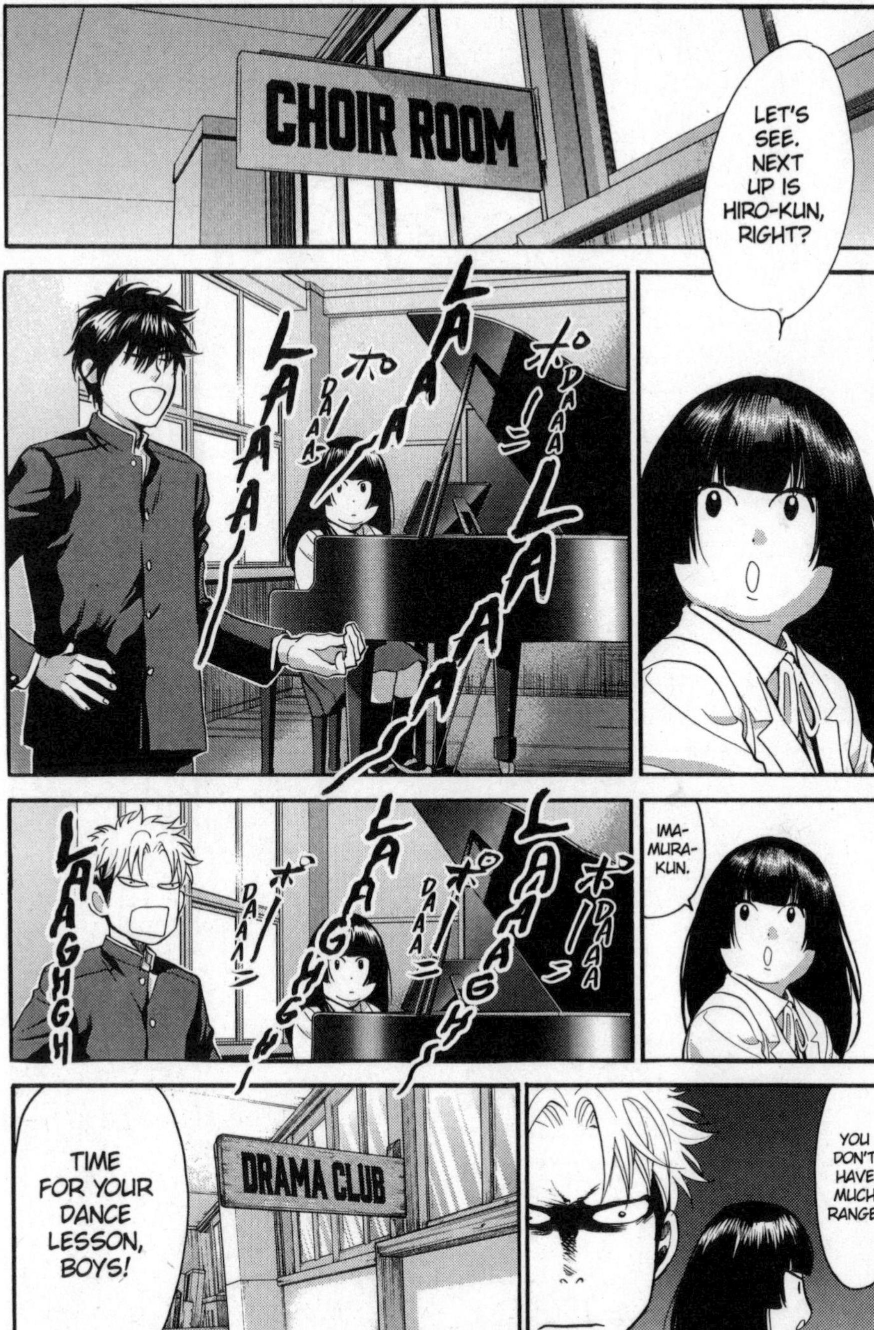
CHOIR ROOM
LET'S SEE. NEXT UP IS HIRO-KUN, RIGHT?
DAAAA
DAAAA
LAAAA
LAAAAA
LAAAAAA
IMAMURA-KUN.
DAAAA
DAAAA
LAAAGHGH
LAAAGHGH
LAAGHGH
YOU DON'T HAVE MUCH RANGE.
DRAMA CLUB
TIME FOR YOUR DANCE LESSON, BOYS!

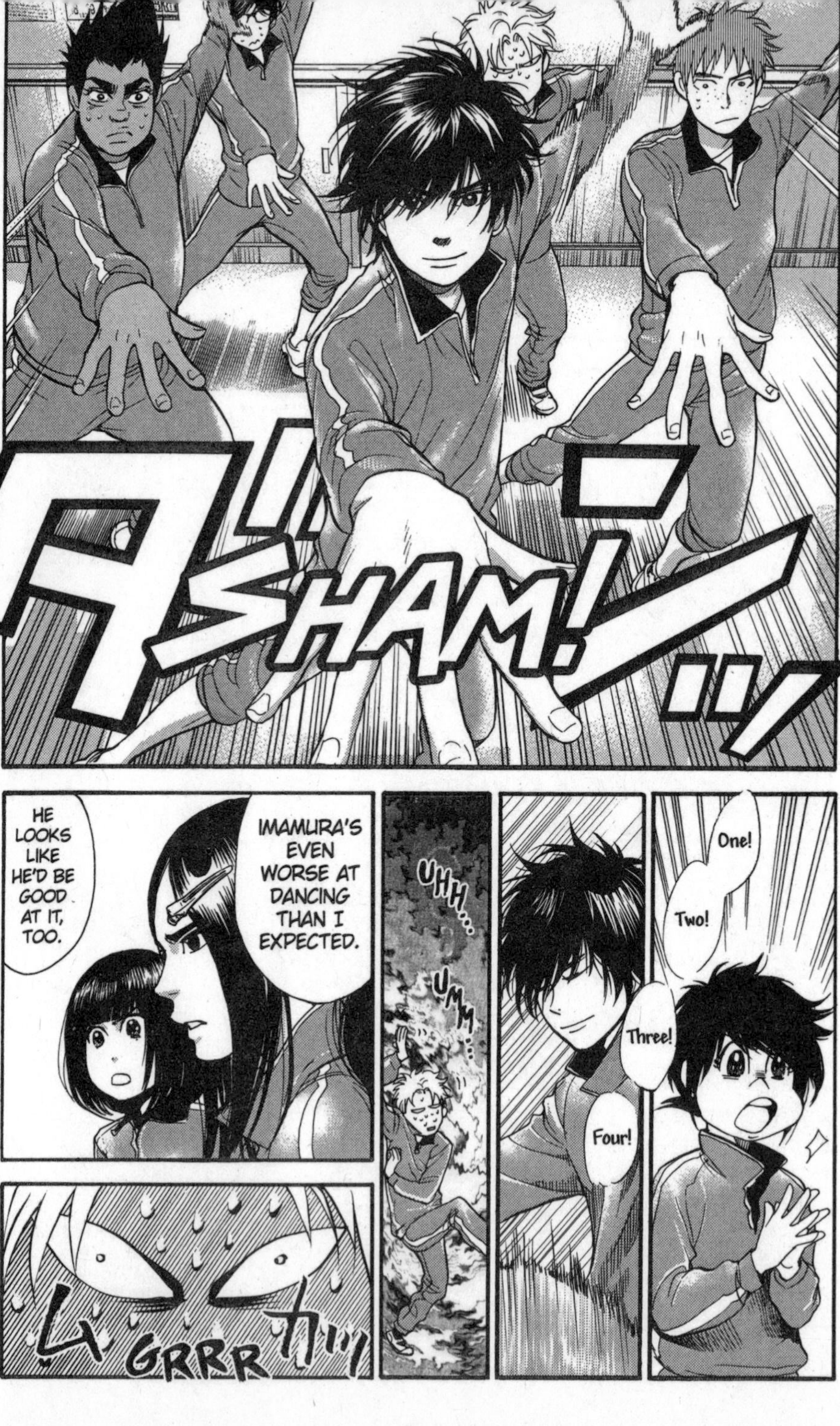
SHAM!
One!
Two!
Three!
Four!
UHH...
UMM...
IMAMURA'S EVEN WORSE AT DANCING THAN I EXPECTED.
HE LOOKS LIKE HE'D BE GOOD AT IT, TOO.
GRRR

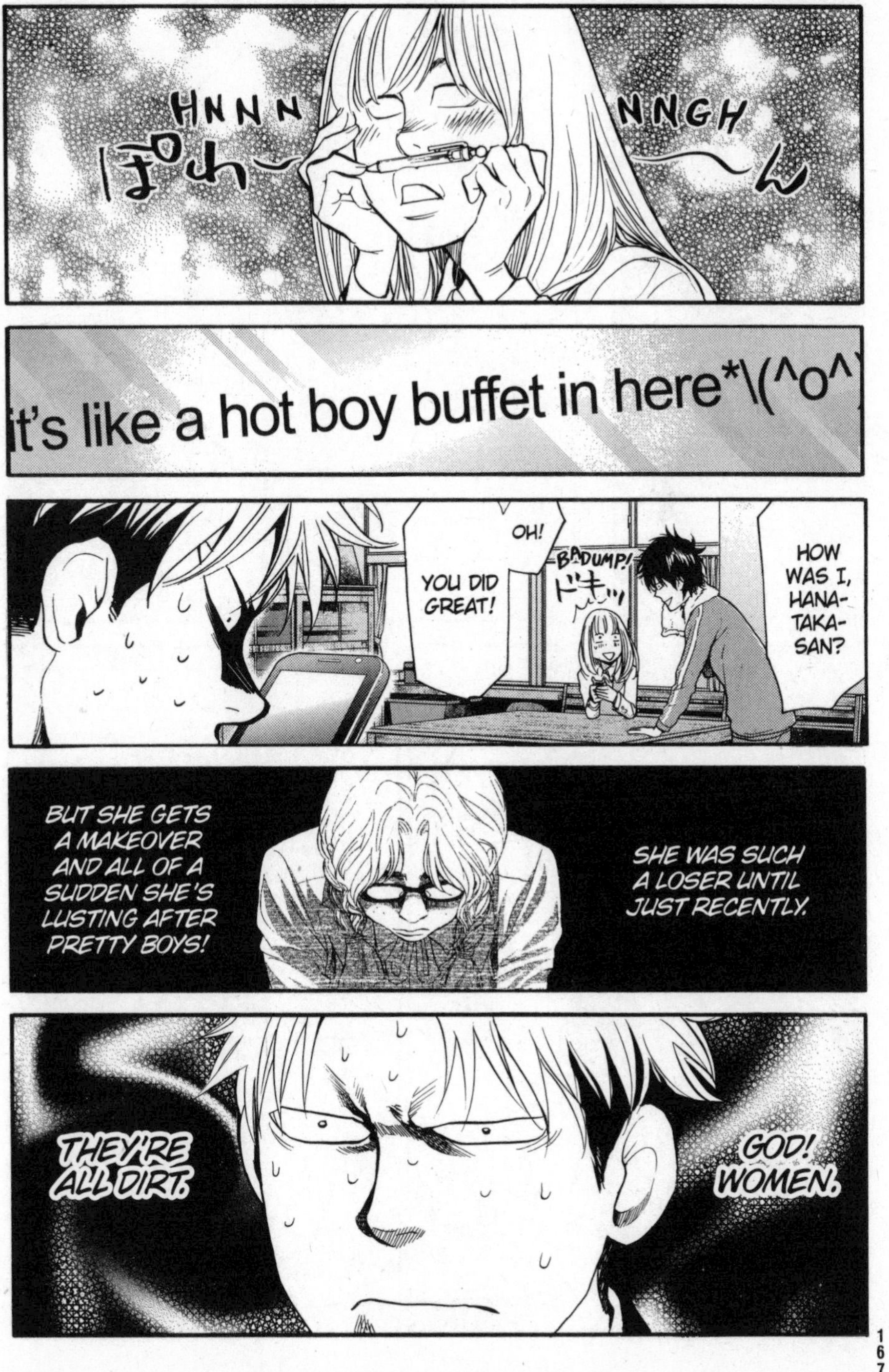
HNNN
NNGH
ぽわ〜〜ん
it's like a hot boy buffet in here*\(^o^)
HOW WAS I, HANA-TAKA-SAN?
BADUMP!
ドキッ
OH!
YOU DID GREAT!
SHE WAS SUCH A LOSER UNTIL JUST RECENTLY.
BUT SHE GETS A MAKEOVER AND ALL OF A SUDDEN SHE'S LUSTING AFTER PRETTY BOYS!
GOD! WOMEN.
THEY'RE ALL DIRT.

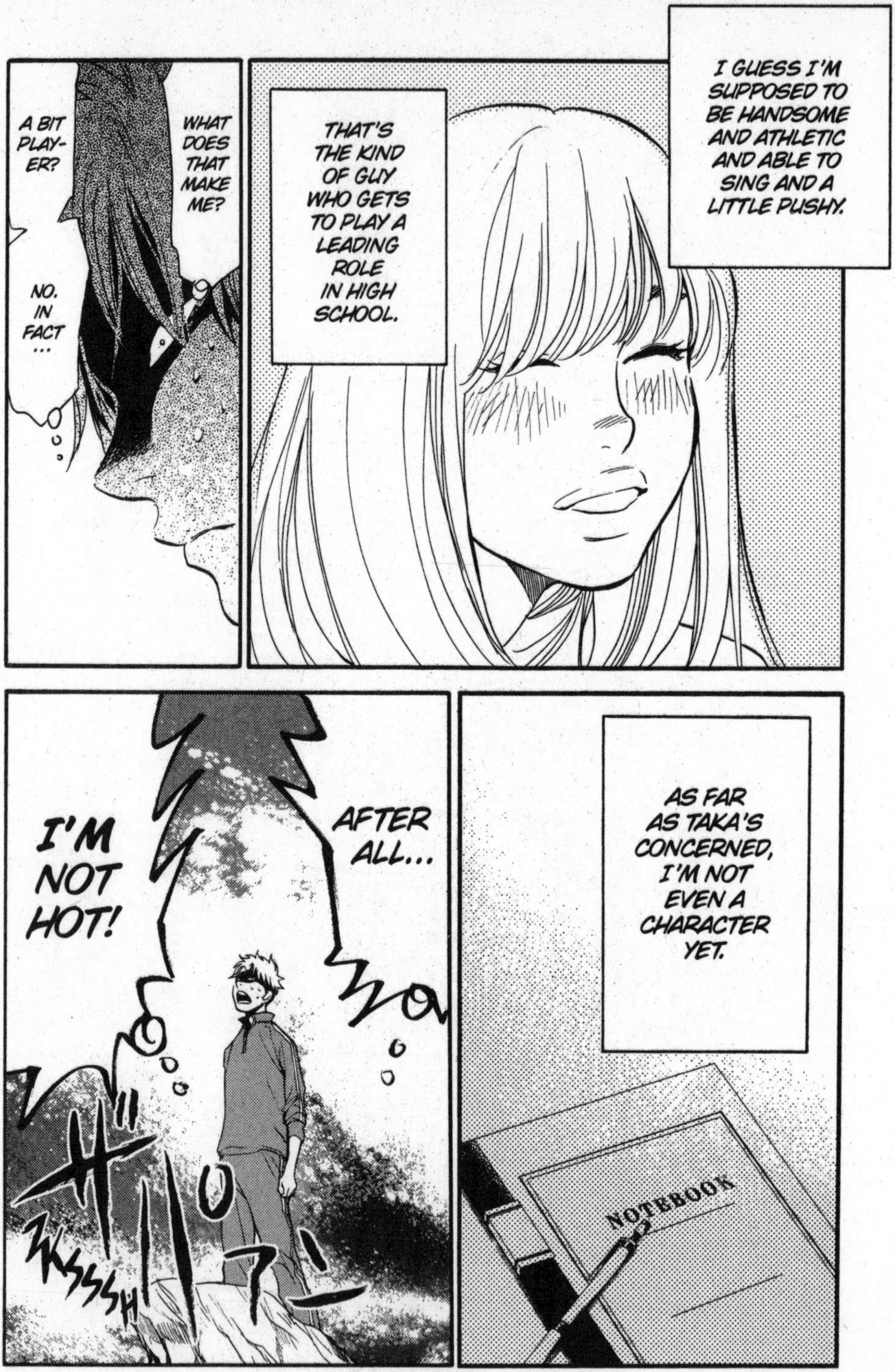
I GUESS I'M SUPPOSED TO BE HANDSOME AND ATHLETIC AND ABLE TO SING AND A LITTLE PUSHY.
THAT'S THE KIND OF GUY WHO GETS TO PLAY A LEADING ROLE IN HIGH SCHOOL.
WHAT DOES THAT MAKE ME?
A BIT PLAYER?
NO. IN FACT...
AS FAR AS TAKA'S CONCERNED, I'M NOT EVEN A CHARACTER YET.
NOTEBOOK
AFTER ALL...
I'M NOT HOT!
ZKSSSSH

Again!!

アゲイン!!

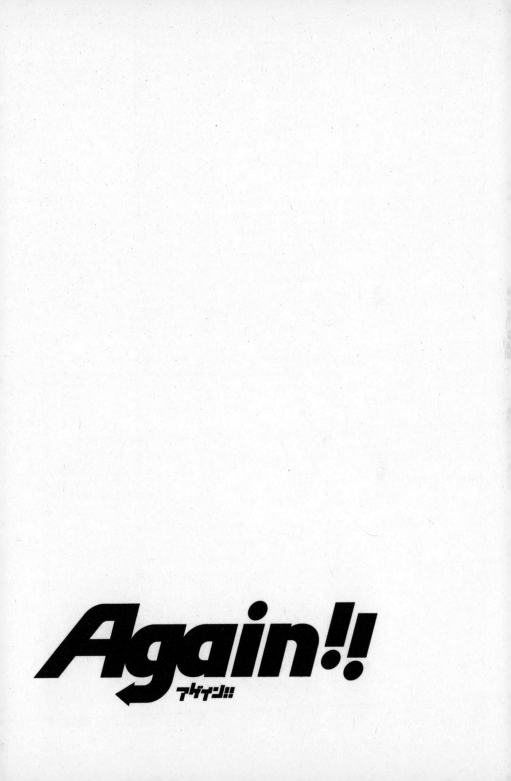

Again!!

アゲイン!!

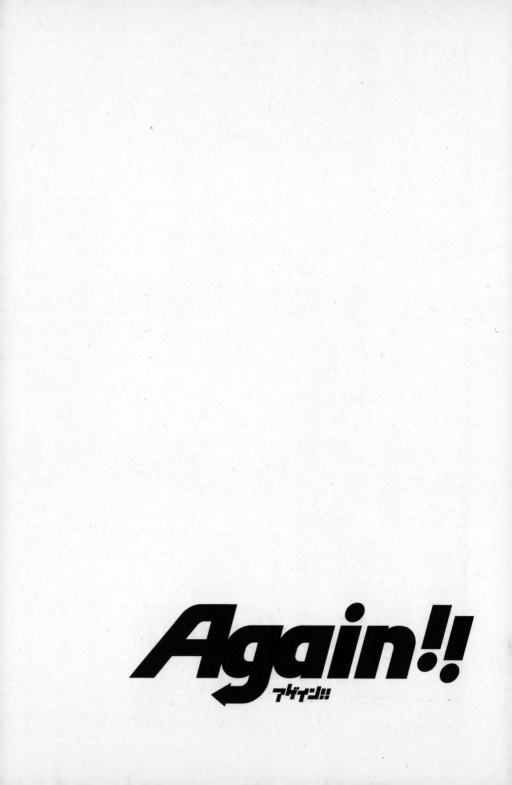

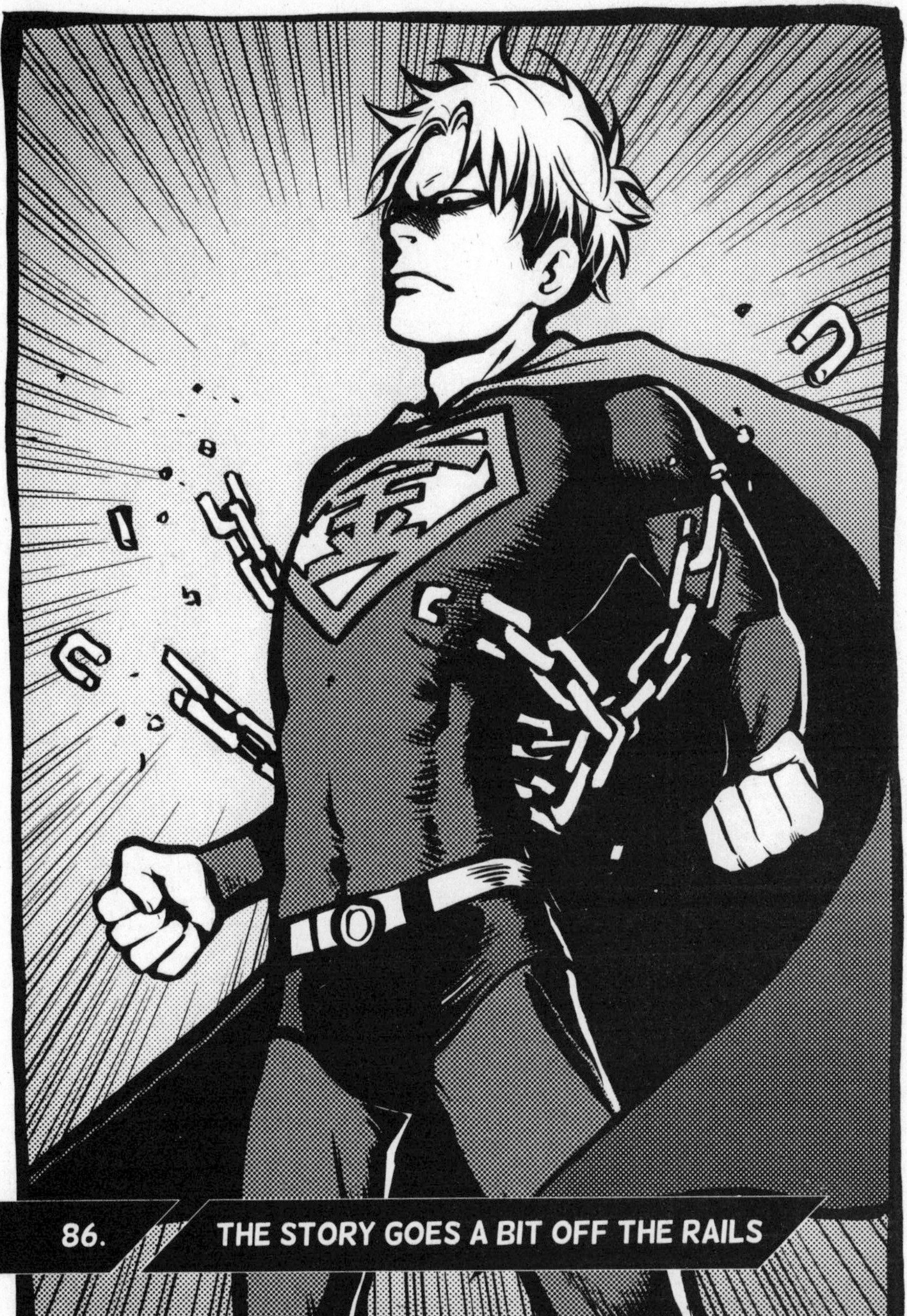

86. THE STORY GOES A BIT OFF THE RAILS

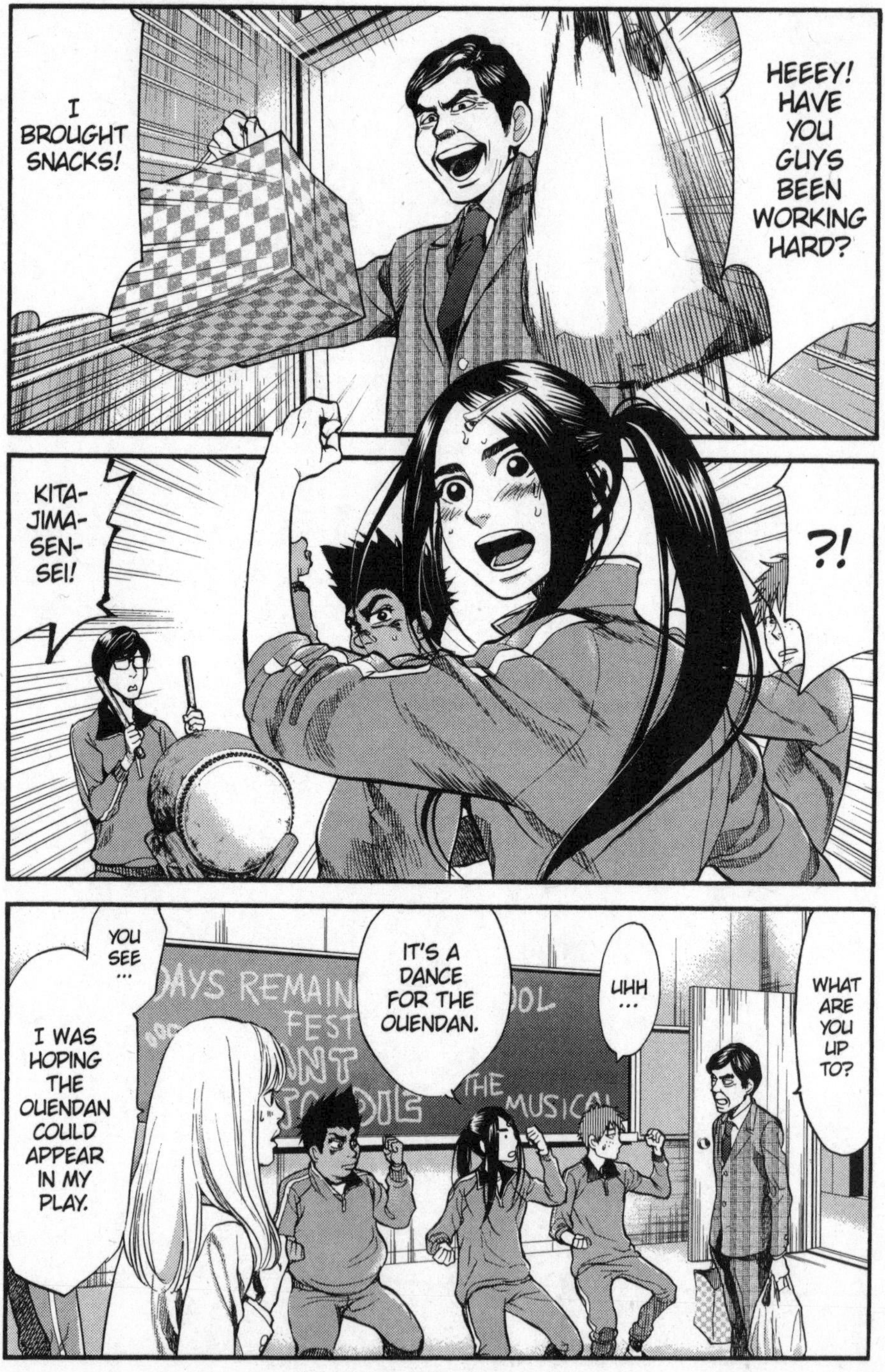
HEEEY! HAVE YOU GUYS BEEN WORKING HARD?
I BROUGHT SNACKS!
?!
KITA-JIMA-SEN-SEI!
WHAT ARE YOU UP TO?
UHH ...
IT'S A DANCE FOR THE OUENDAN.
THE MUSICAL
YOU SEE ...
I WAS HOPING THE OUENDAN COULD APPEAR IN MY PLAY.

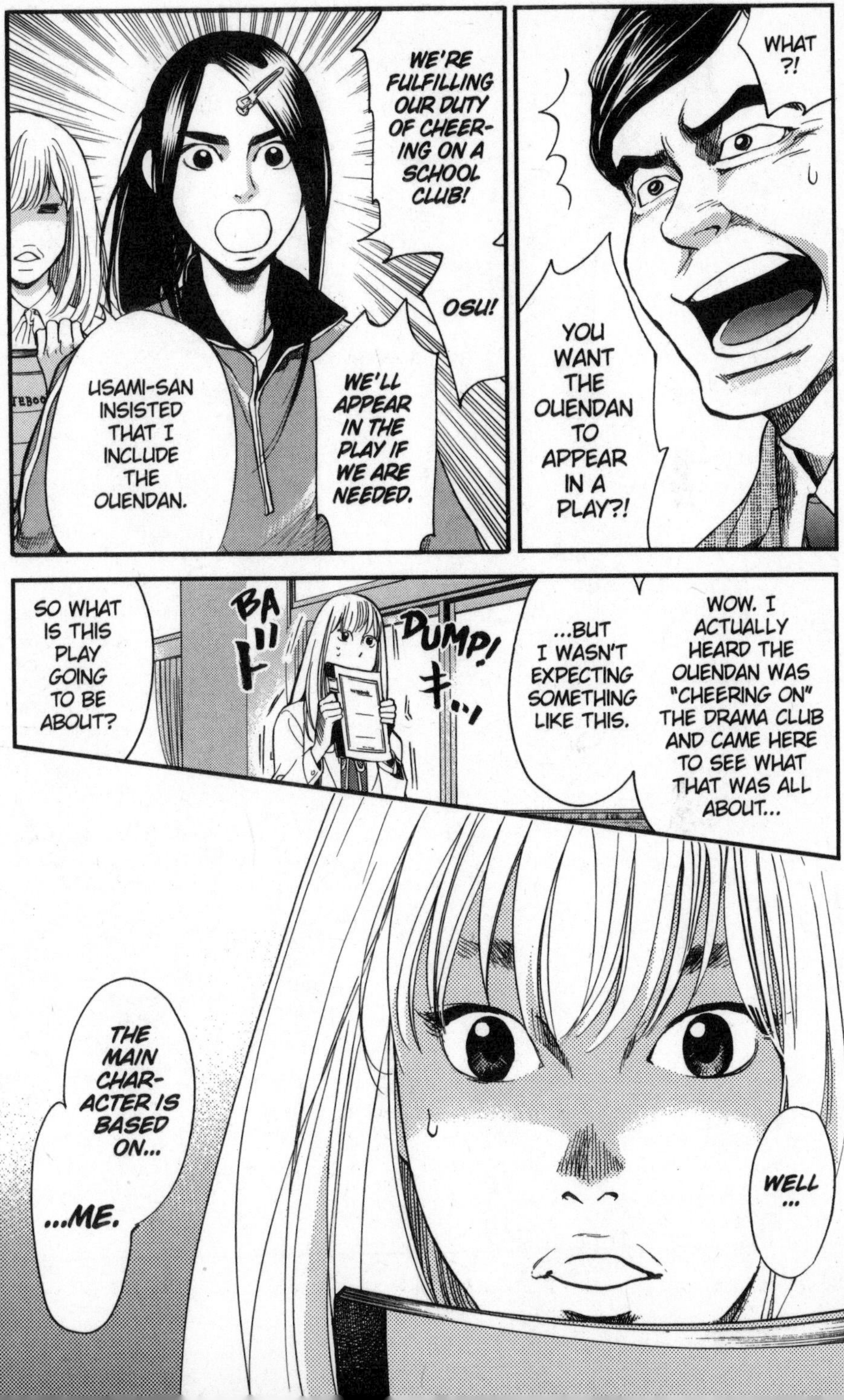
WHAT ?!
YOU WANT THE OUENDAN TO APPEAR IN A PLAY?!
WE'RE FULFILLING OUR DUTY OF CHEER-ING ON A SCHOOL CLUB!
OSU!
WE'LL APPEAR IN THE PLAY IF WE ARE NEEDED.
USAMI-SAN INSISTED THAT I INCLUDE THE OUENDAN.
WOW. I ACTUALLY HEARD THE OUENDAN WAS "CHEERING ON" THE DRAMA CLUB AND CAME HERE TO SEE WHAT THAT WAS ALL ABOUT...
...BUT I WASN'T EXPECTING SOMETHING LIKE THIS.
DUMP! キッ
BA ド
SO WHAT IS THIS PLAY GOING TO BE ABOUT?
WELL ...
THE MAIN CHAR-ACTER IS BASED ON...
...ME.

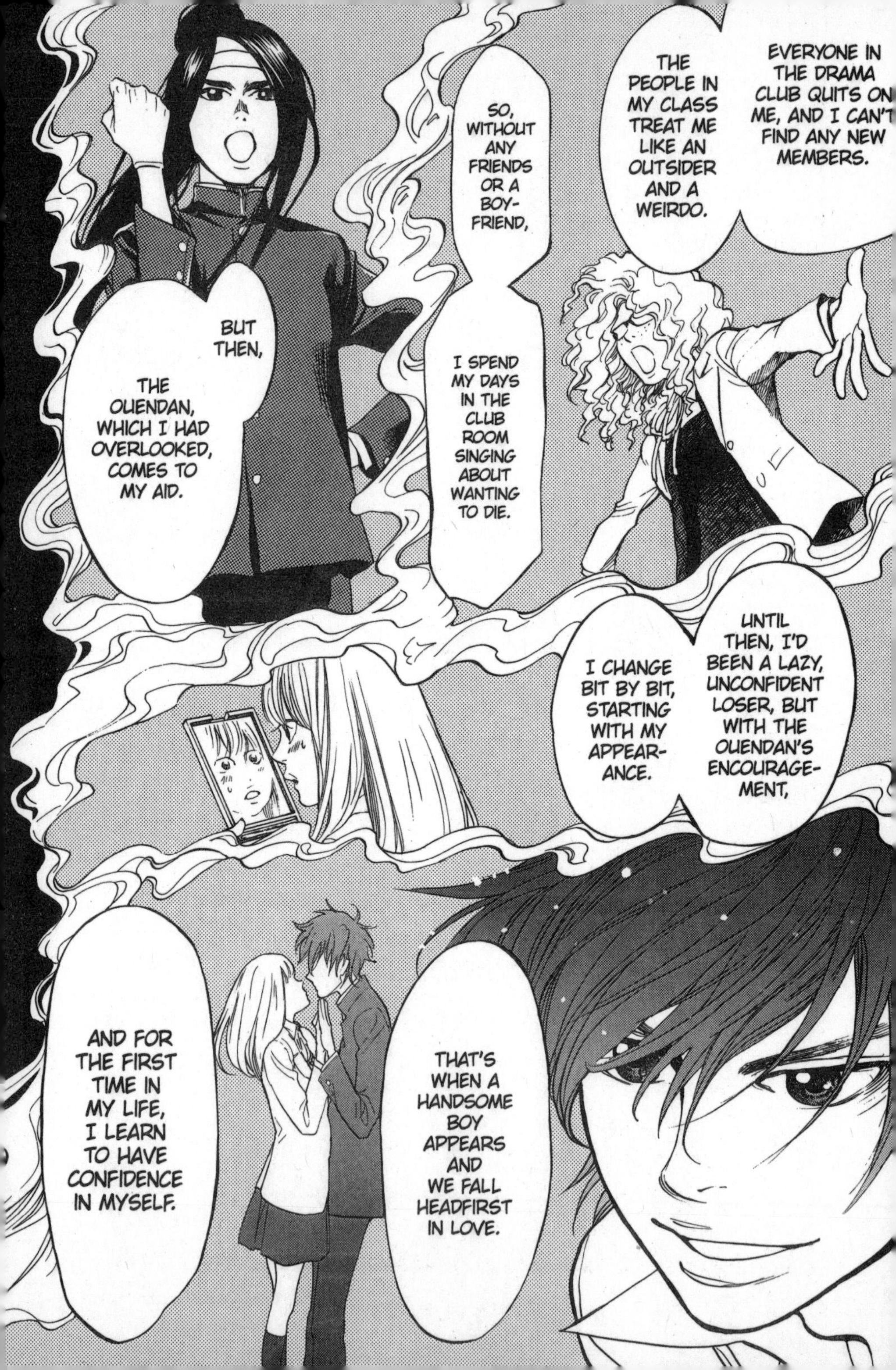
EVERYONE IN THE DRAMA CLUB QUITS ON ME, AND I CAN'T FIND ANY NEW MEMBERS.
THE PEOPLE IN MY CLASS TREAT ME LIKE AN OUTSIDER AND A WEIRDO.
SO, WITHOUT ANY FRIENDS OR A BOY-FRIEND,
I SPEND MY DAYS IN THE CLUB ROOM SINGING ABOUT WANTING TO DIE.
BUT THEN,
THE OUENDAN, WHICH I HAD OVERLOOKED, COMES TO MY AID.
UNTIL THEN, I'D BEEN A LAZY, UNCONFIDENT LOSER, BUT WITH THE OUENDAN'S ENCOURAGE-MENT,
I CHANGE BIT BY BIT, STARTING WITH MY APPEAR-ANCE.
THAT'S WHEN A HANDSOME BOY APPEARS AND WE FALL HEADFIRST IN LOVE.
AND FOR THE FIRST TIME IN MY LIFE, I LEARN TO HAVE CONFIDENCE IN MYSELF.

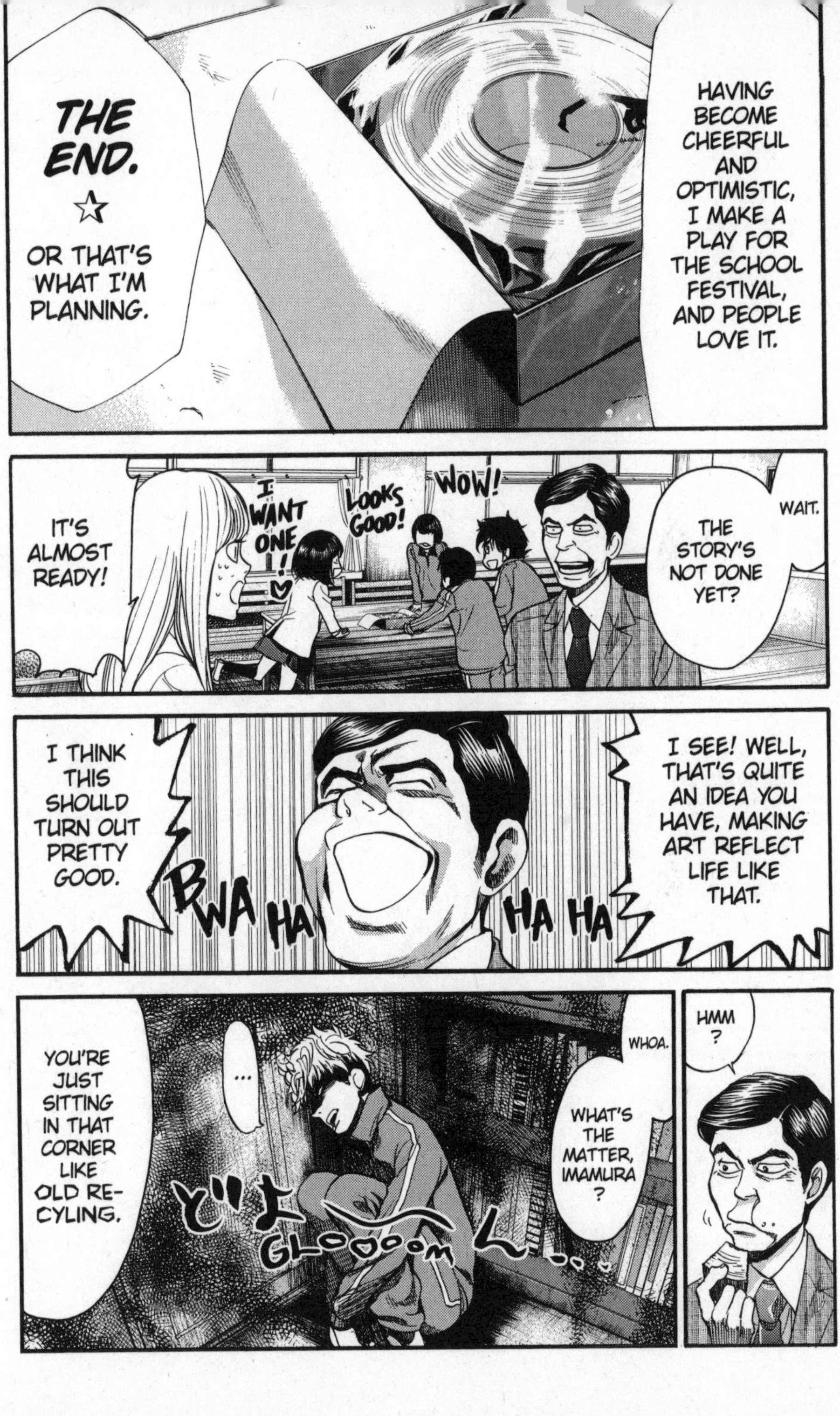
HAVING BECOME CHEERFUL AND OPTIMISTIC, I MAKE A PLAY FOR THE SCHOOL FESTIVAL, AND PEOPLE LOVE IT.
THE END. ☆
OR THAT'S WHAT I'M PLANNING.
WAIT.
THE STORY'S NOT DONE YET?
WOW!
LOOKS GOOD!
I WANT ONE! ♥
IT'S ALMOST READY!
I SEE! WELL, THAT'S QUITE AN IDEA YOU HAVE, MAKING ART REFLECT LIFE LIKE THAT.
BWA HA HA HA
I THINK THIS SHOULD TURN OUT PRETTY GOOD.
HMM?
WHOA.
WHAT'S THE MATTER, IMAMURA?
...
YOU'RE JUST SITTING IN THAT CORNER LIKE OLD RE-CYLING.
どよ〜ん
GLOOOOM

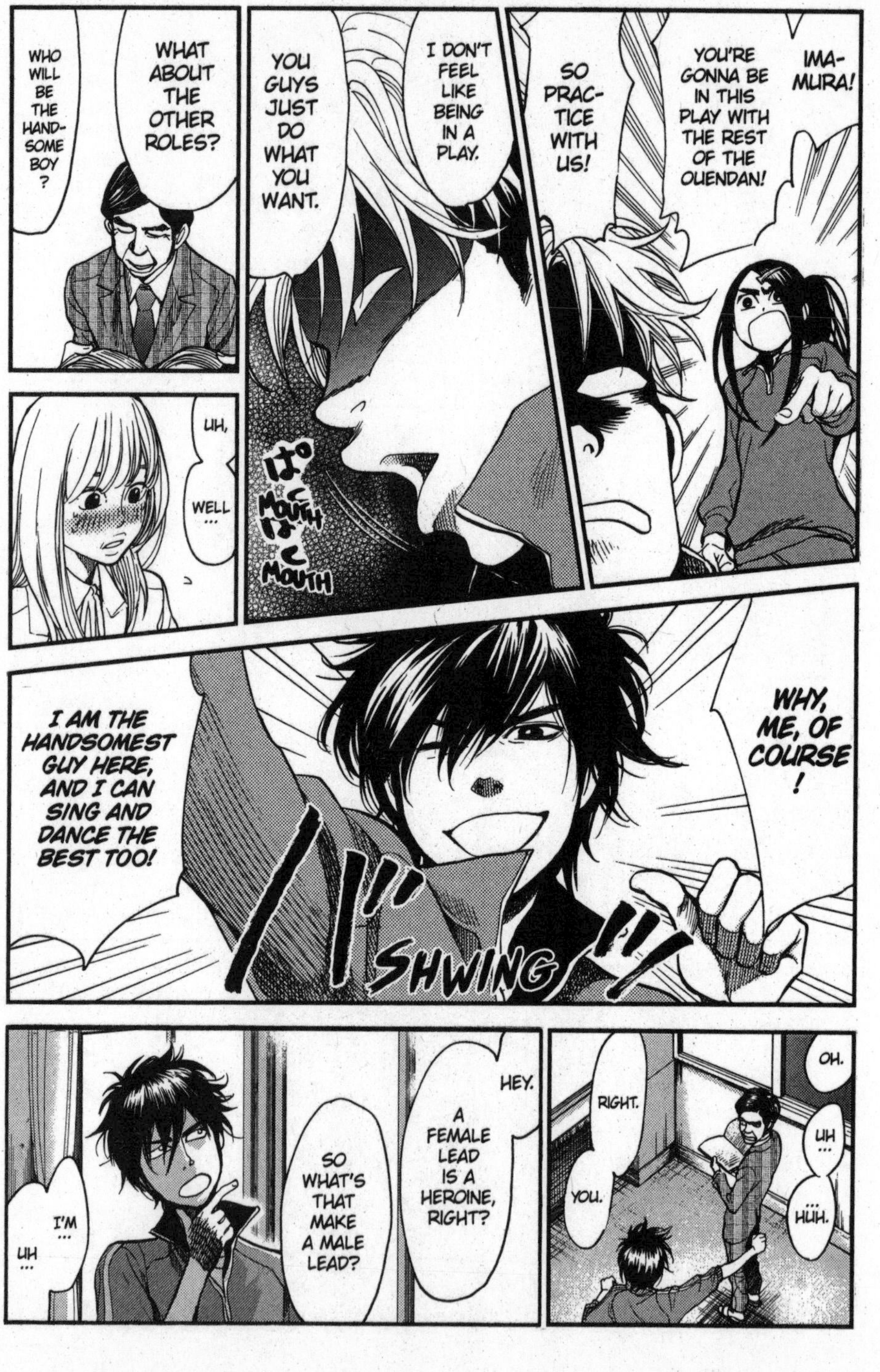
IMA-MURA!
YOU'RE GONNA BE IN THIS PLAY WITH THE REST OF THE OUENDAN!
SO PRAC-TICE WITH US!
I DON'T FEEL LIKE BEING IN A PLAY.
YOU GUYS JUST DO WHAT YOU WANT.
ぱく MOUTH ぱく MOUTH
WHAT ABOUT THE OTHER ROLES?
WHO WILL BE THE HAND-SOME BOY?
UH,
WELL...
WHY, ME, OF COURSE!
I AM THE HANDSOMEST GUY HERE, AND I CAN SING AND DANCE THE BEST TOO!
SHWING
OH.
UH...
...HUH.
RIGHT.
YOU.
HEY.
A FEMALE LEAD IS A HEROINE, RIGHT?
SO WHAT'S THAT MAKE A MALE LEAD?
I'M...
UH...

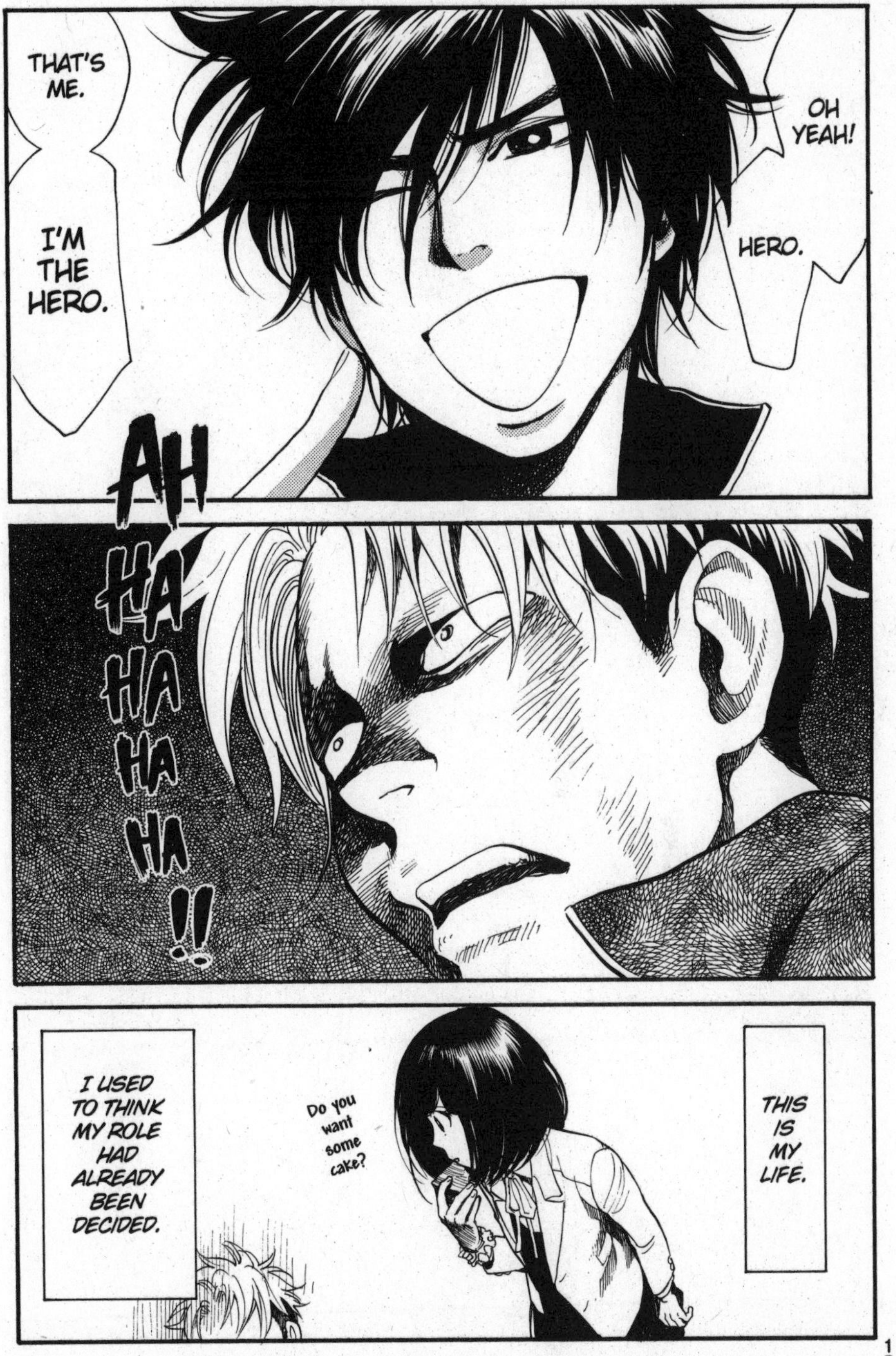
OH YEAH!
HERO.
THAT'S ME.
I'M THE HERO.
AH HA HA HA HA HA!!
THIS IS MY LIFE.
Do you want some cake?
I USED TO THINK MY ROLE HAD ALREADY BEEN DECIDED.

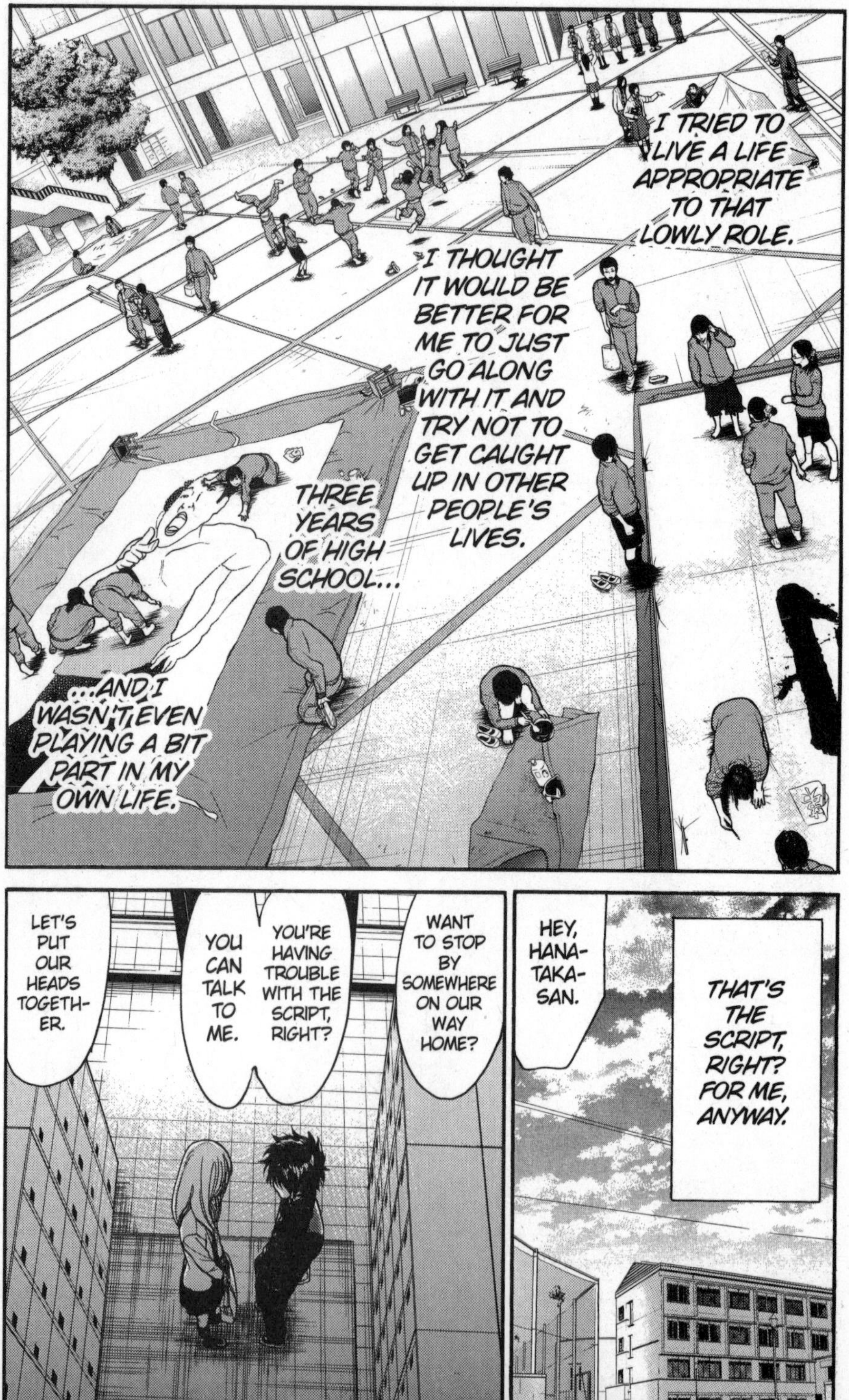
I TRIED TO LIVE A LIFE APPROPRIATE TO THAT LOWLY ROLE.
I THOUGHT IT WOULD BE BETTER FOR ME TO JUST GO ALONG WITH IT AND TRY NOT TO GET CAUGHT UP IN OTHER PEOPLE'S LIVES.
THREE YEARS OF HIGH SCHOOL...
...AND I WASN'T EVEN PLAYING A BIT PART IN MY OWN LIFE.
THAT'S THE SCRIPT, RIGHT? FOR ME, ANYWAY.
HEY, HANA-TAKA-SAN.
WANT TO STOP BY SOMEWHERE ON OUR WAY HOME?
YOU'RE HAVING TROUBLE WITH THE SCRIPT, RIGHT?
YOU CAN TALK TO ME.
LET'S PUT OUR HEADS TOGETH-ER.

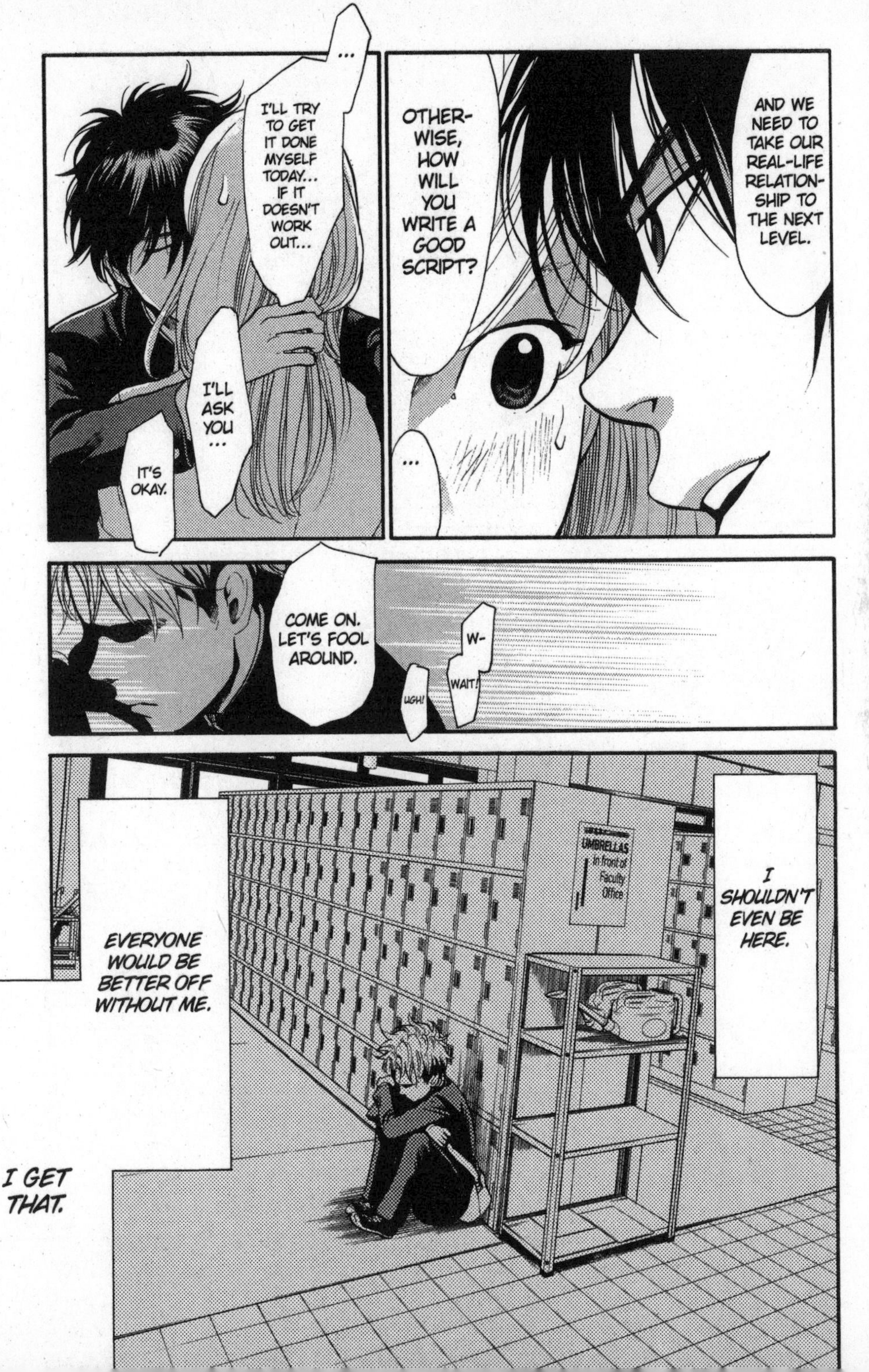
AND WE NEED TO TAKE OUR REAL-LIFE RELATIONSHIP TO THE NEXT LEVEL.
OTHER-WISE, HOW WILL YOU WRITE A GOOD SCRIPT?
...
...
I'LL TRY TO GET IT DONE MYSELF TODAY... IF IT DOESN'T WORK OUT...
I'LL ASK YOU ...
IT'S OKAY.
COME ON. LET'S FOOL AROUND.
W- WAIT!
UGH!
I SHOULDN'T EVEN BE HERE.
UMBRELLAS in front of Faculty Office
EVERYONE WOULD BE BETTER OFF WITHOUT ME.
I GET THAT.

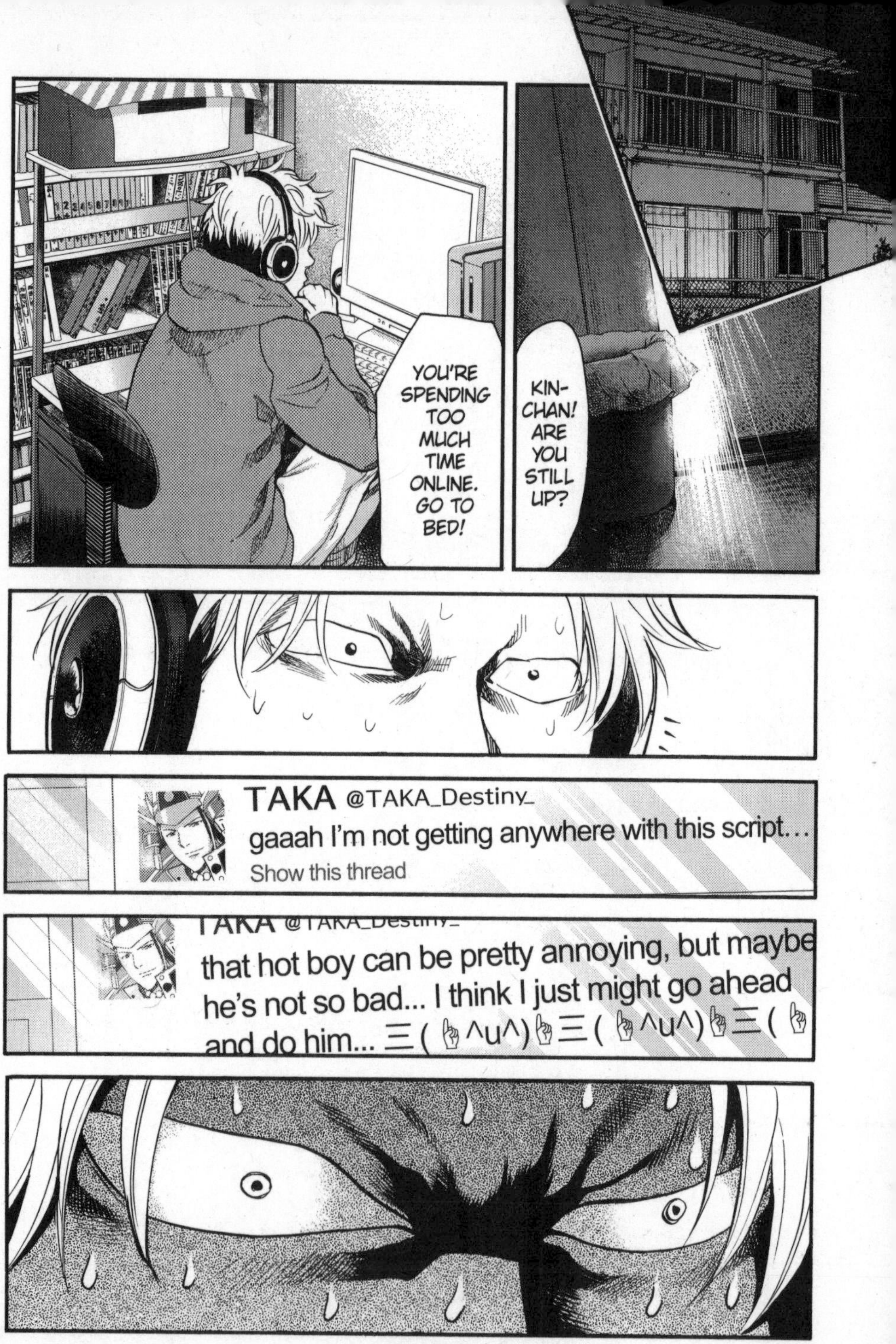
KIN-CHAN! ARE YOU STILL UP?
YOU'RE SPENDING TOO MUCH TIME ONLINE. GO TO BED!
TAKA @TAKA_Destiny_
gaaah I'm not getting anywhere with this script…
Show this thread
that hot boy can be pretty annoying, but maybe he's not so bad... I think I just might go ahead and do him... 三(☝^u^)☝三(☝^u^)☝三(☝

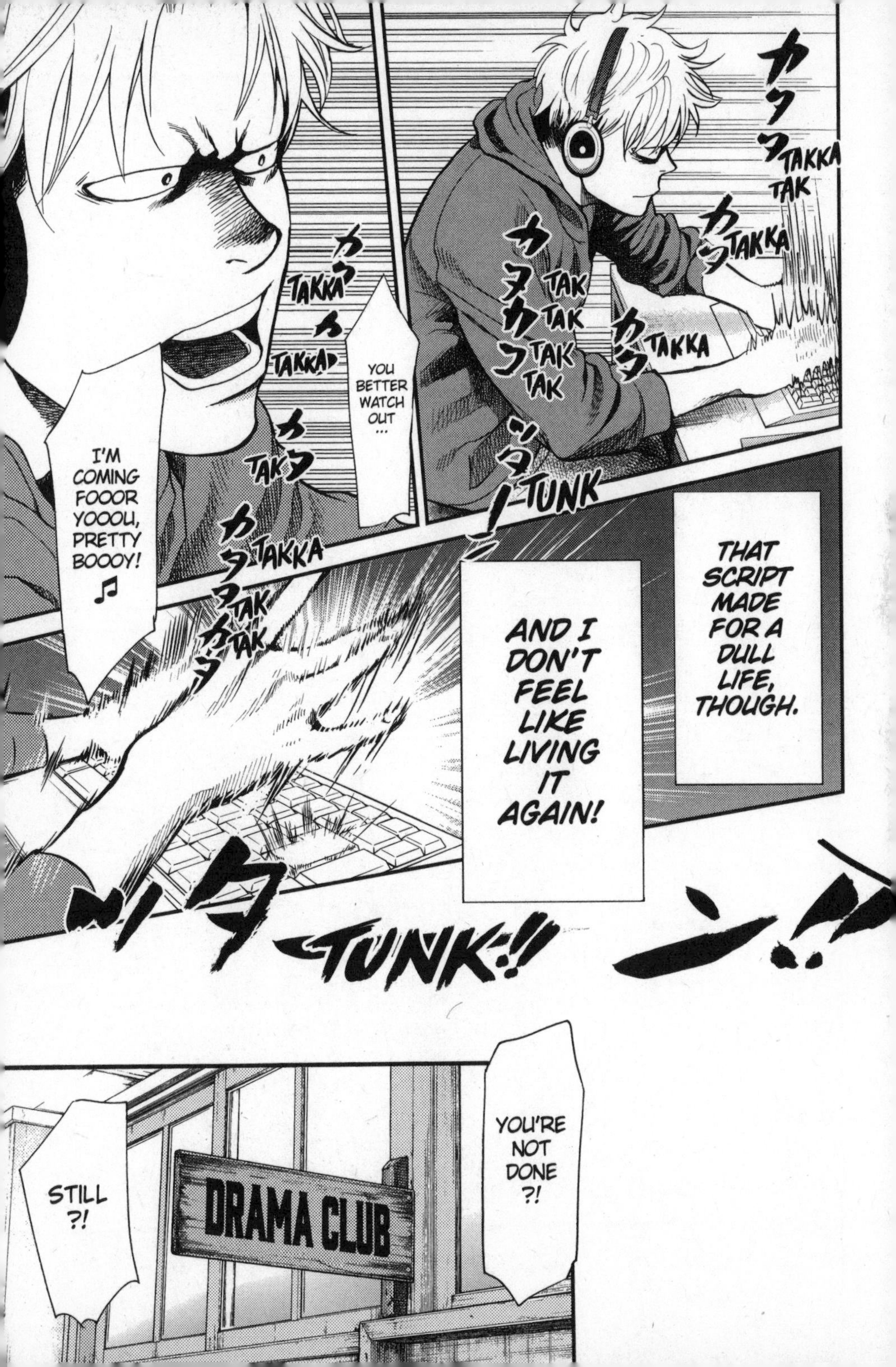

TAKKA TAK
TAKKA
TAK TAK TAK TAK
TAKKA
TUNK
YOU BETTER WATCH OUT...
I'M COMING FOOOR YOOOU, PRETTY BOOOY! ♪
TAKKA
TAKKA
TAKA
TAKKA TAK TAK
THAT SCRIPT MADE FOR A DULL LIFE, THOUGH.
AND I DON'T FEEL LIKE LIVING IT AGAIN!
TUNK!!
YOU'RE NOT DONE ?!
STILL ?!
DRAMA CLUB

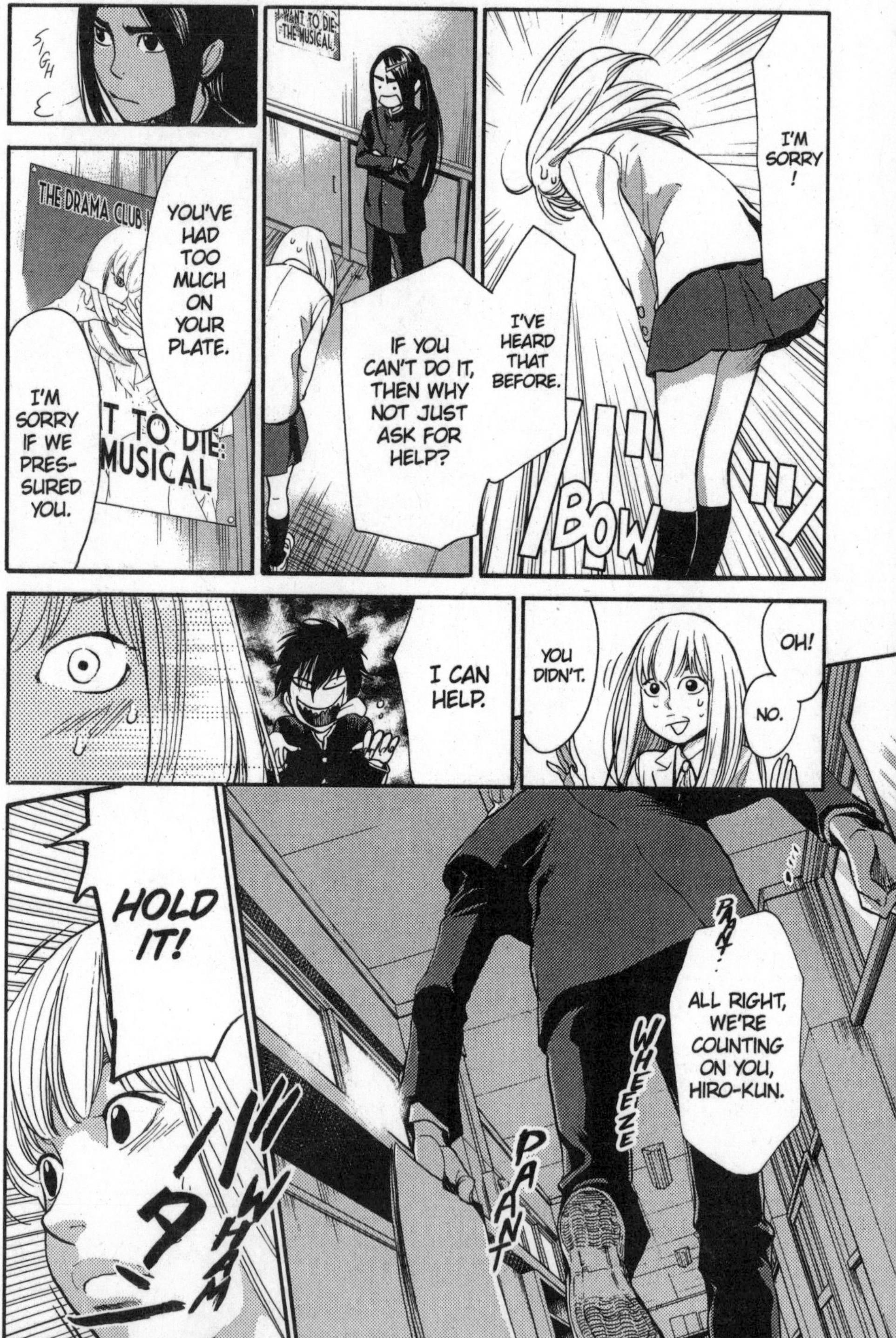
I'M SORRY!
BOW
WANT TO DIE: THE MUSICAL
I'VE HEARD THAT BEFORE.
IF YOU CAN'T DO IT, THEN WHY NOT JUST ASK FOR HELP?
SIGH
THE DRAMA CLUB
YOU'VE HAD TOO MUCH ON YOUR PLATE.
I'M SORRY IF WE PRES-SURED YOU.
T TO DIE: MUSICAL
OH!
NO.
YOU DIDN'T.
I CAN HELP.
PANT
ALL RIGHT, WE'RE COUNTING ON YOU, HIRO-KUN.
WHEEZE
PAANT
HOLD IT!
WHAM

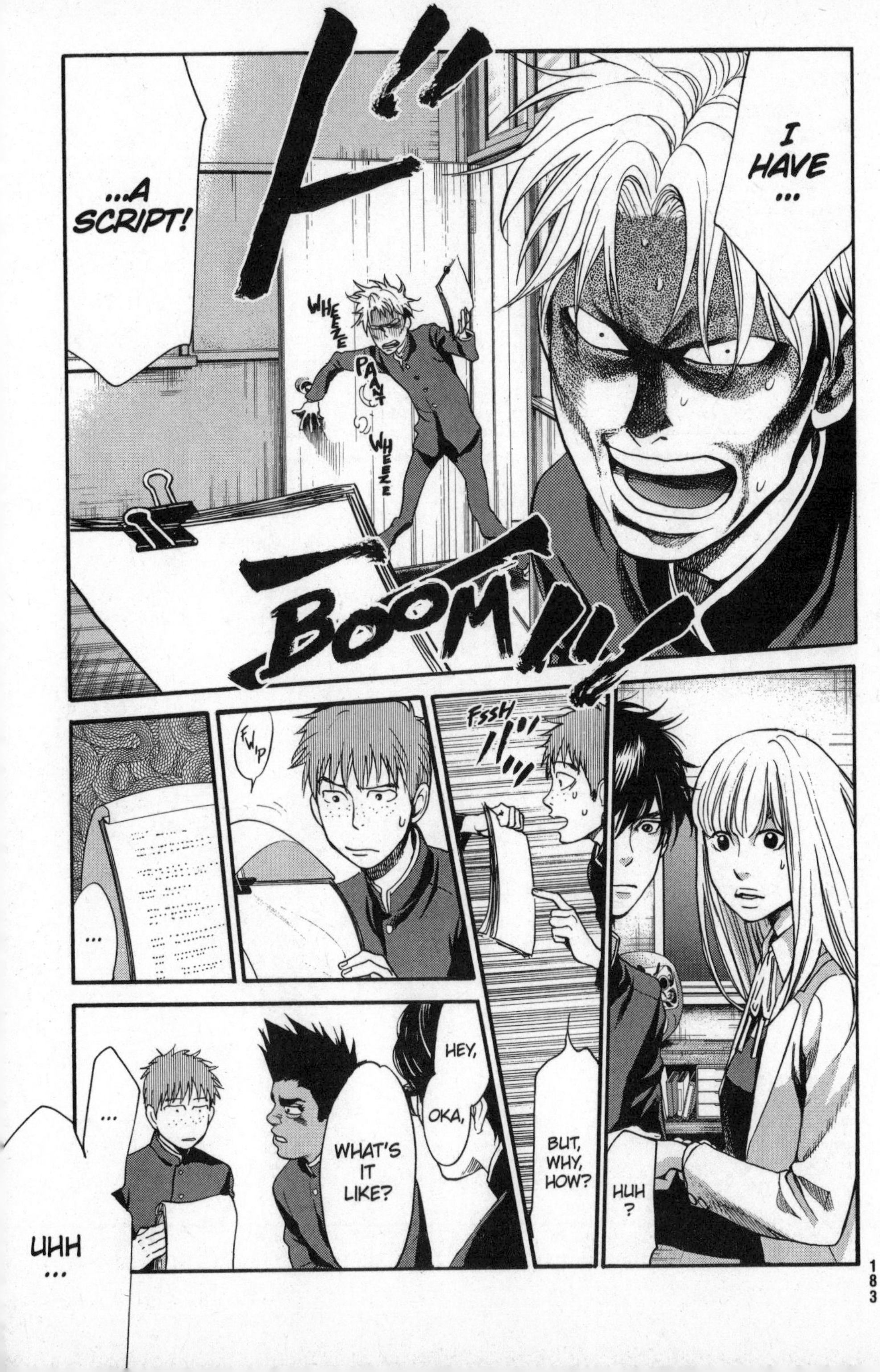
I HAVE ...
...A SCRIPT!
WHEEZE
PAANT
WHEEZE
BOOM!!!
HUH ?
FSSH
FWIP
...
BUT, WHY, HOW?
HEY, OKA, WHAT'S IT LIKE?
...
UHH ...

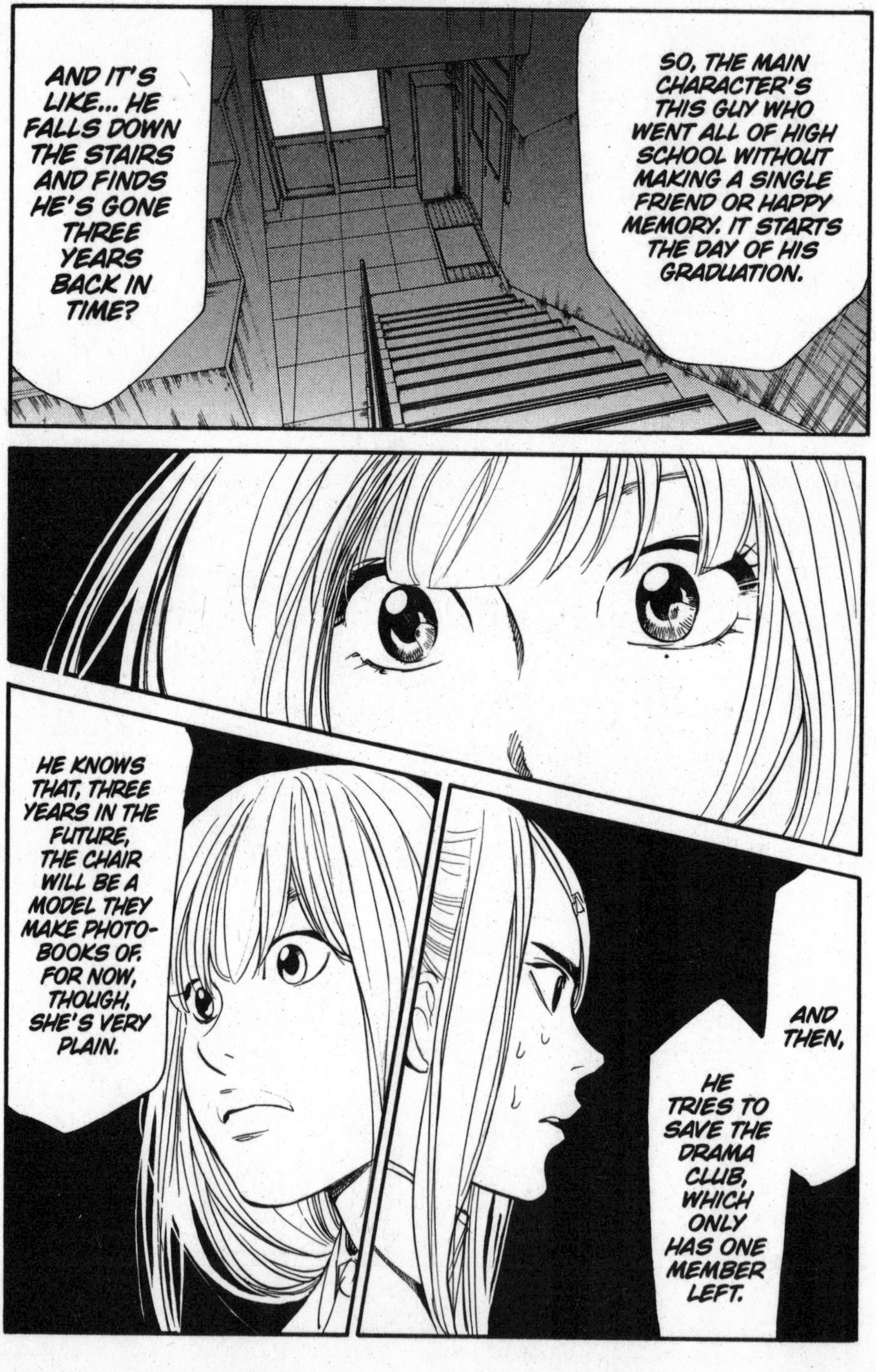
SO, THE MAIN CHARACTER'S THIS GUY WHO WENT ALL OF HIGH SCHOOL WITHOUT MAKING A SINGLE FRIEND OR HAPPY MEMORY. IT STARTS THE DAY OF HIS GRADUATION.
AND IT'S LIKE... HE FALLS DOWN THE STAIRS AND FINDS HE'S GONE THREE YEARS BACK IN TIME?
HE KNOWS THAT, THREE YEARS IN THE FUTURE, THE CHAIR WILL BE A MODEL THEY MAKE PHOTO-BOOKS OF. FOR NOW, THOUGH, SHE'S VERY PLAIN.
AND THEN,
HE TRIES TO SAVE THE DRAMA CLUB, WHICH ONLY HAS ONE MEMBER LEFT.

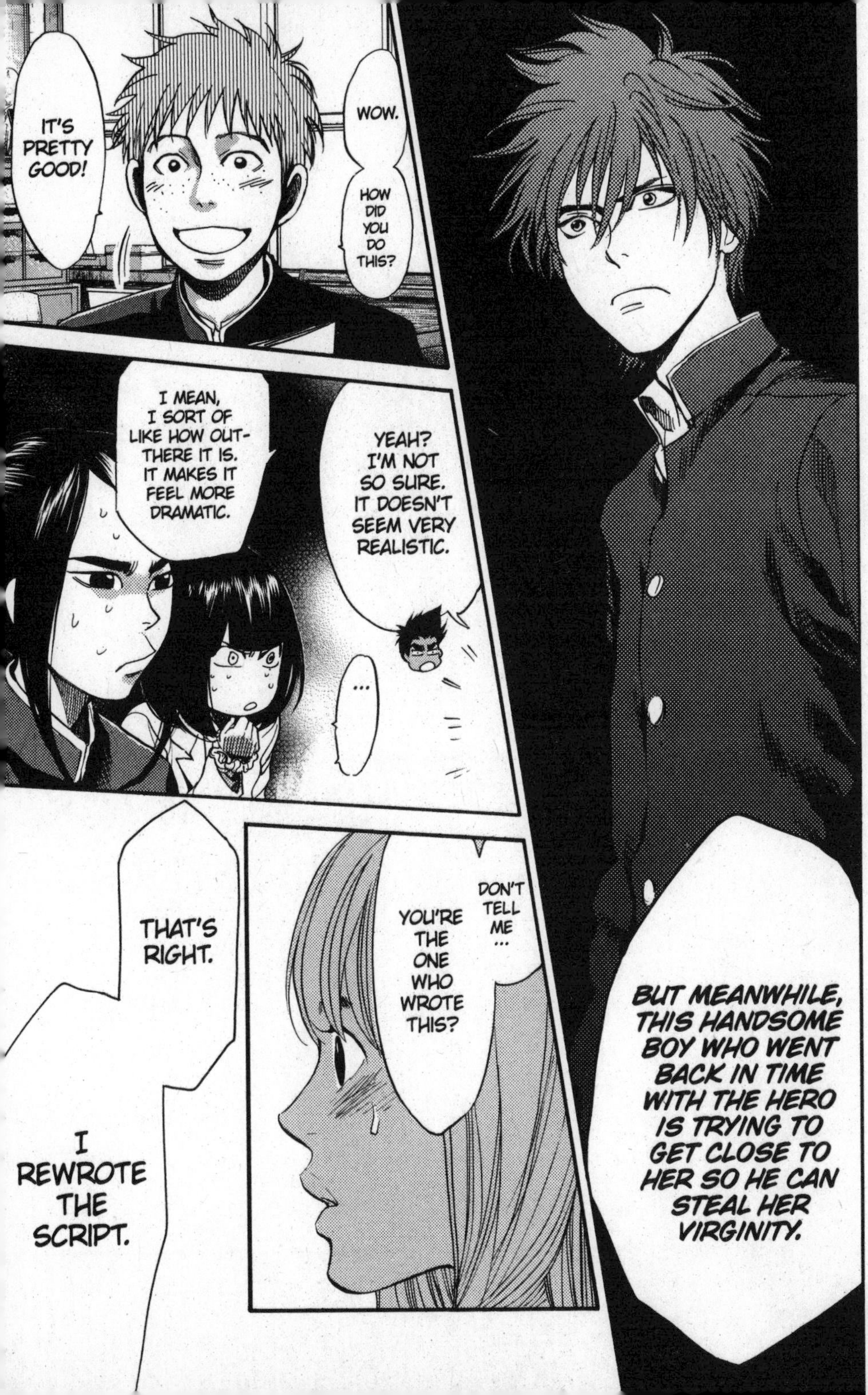
BUT MEANWHILE, THIS HANDSOME BOY WHO WENT BACK IN TIME WITH THE HERO IS TRYING TO GET CLOSE TO HER SO HE CAN STEAL HER VIRGINITY.
WOW.
HOW DID YOU DO THIS?
IT'S PRETTY GOOD!
YEAH? I'M NOT SO SURE. IT DOESN'T SEEM VERY REALISTIC.
I MEAN, I SORT OF LIKE HOW OUT-THERE IT IS. IT MAKES IT FEEL MORE DRAMATIC.
...
DON'T TELL ME ...
YOU'RE THE ONE WHO WROTE THIS?
THAT'S RIGHT.
I REWROTE THE SCRIPT.

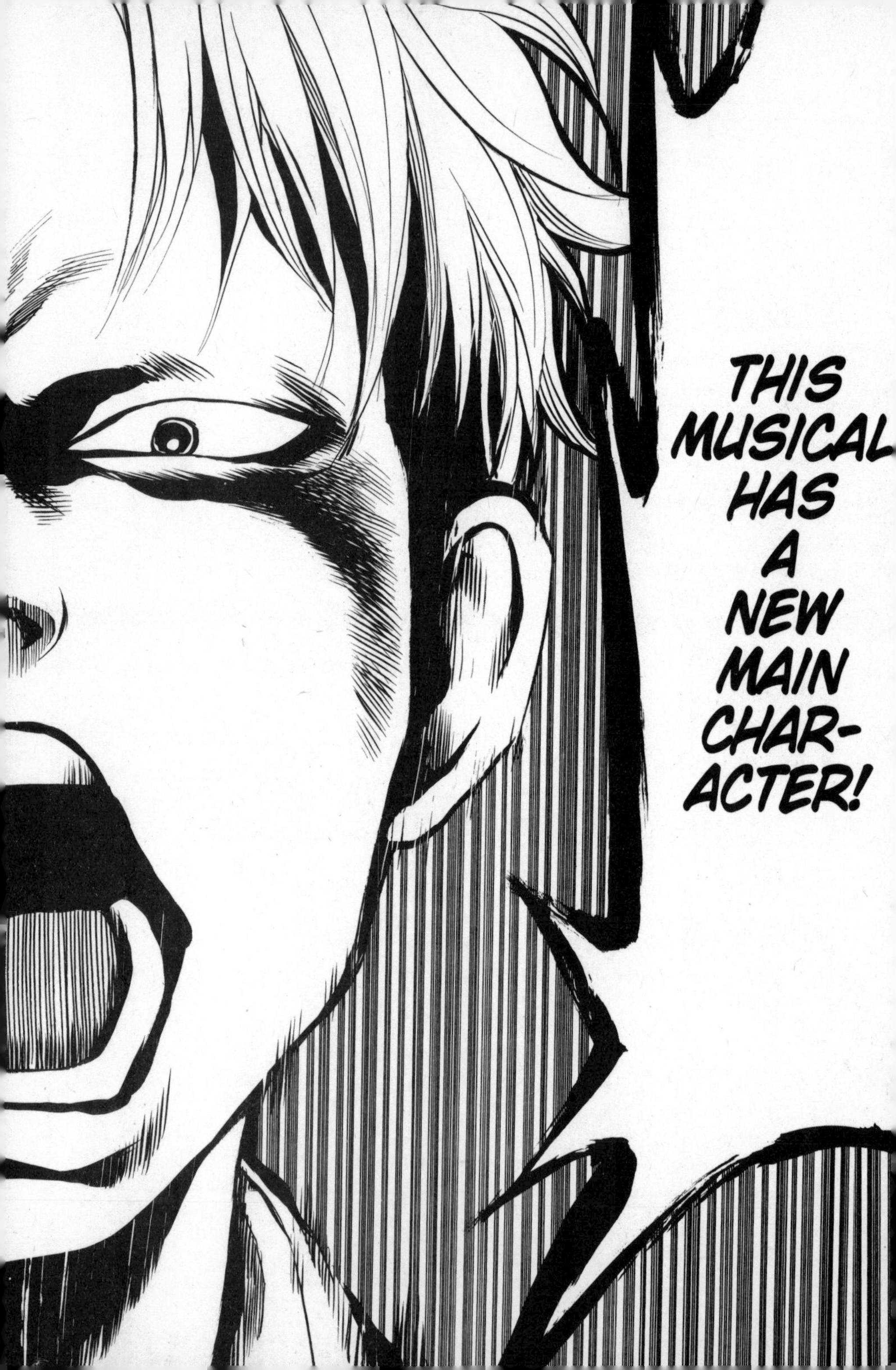
THIS MUSICAL HAS A NEW MAIN CHAR-ACTER!

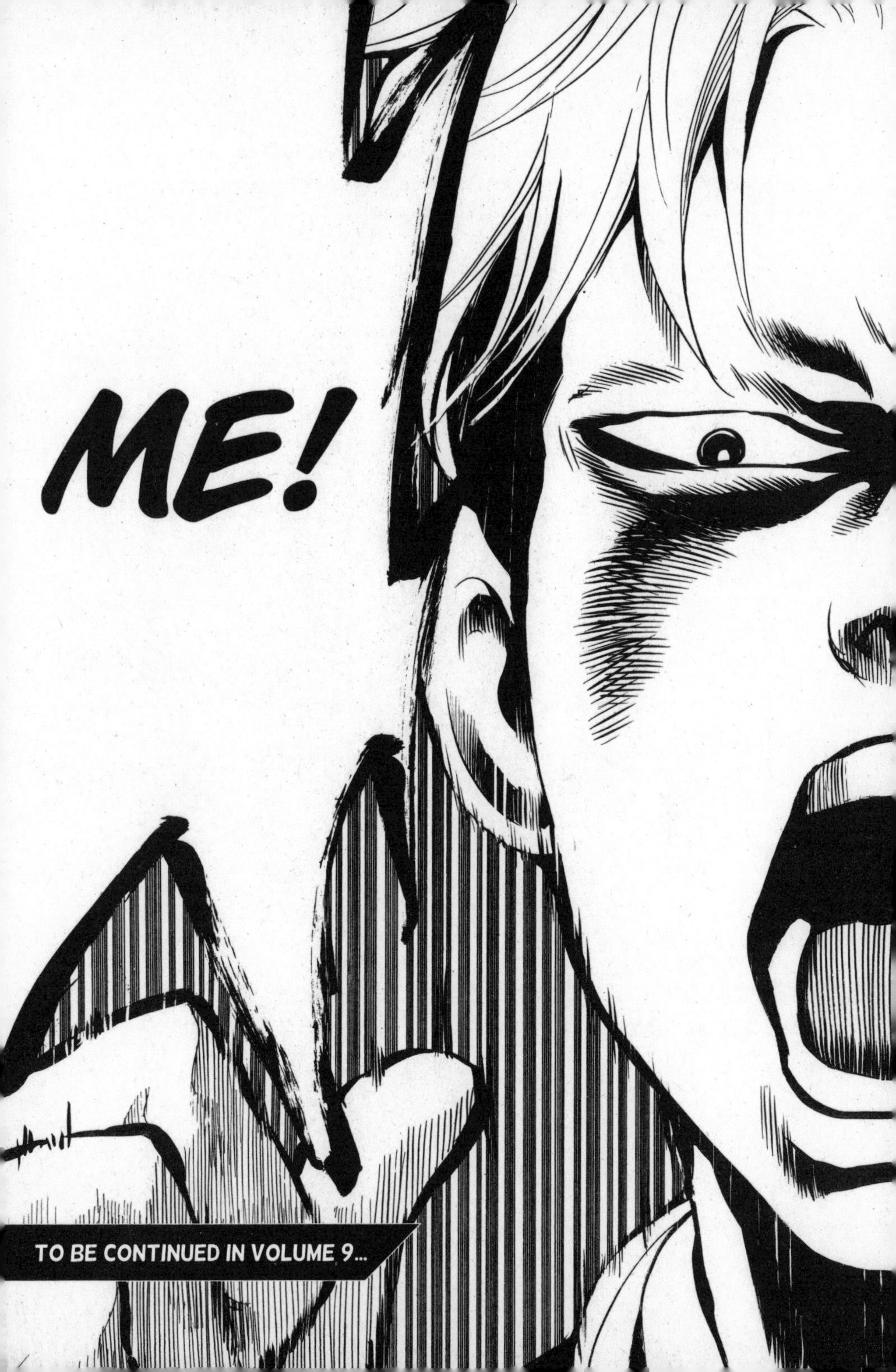
ME!
TO BE CONTINUED IN VOLUME 9...

*There's a mistake on this version of chapter 86's cover. I explain it on the next page.

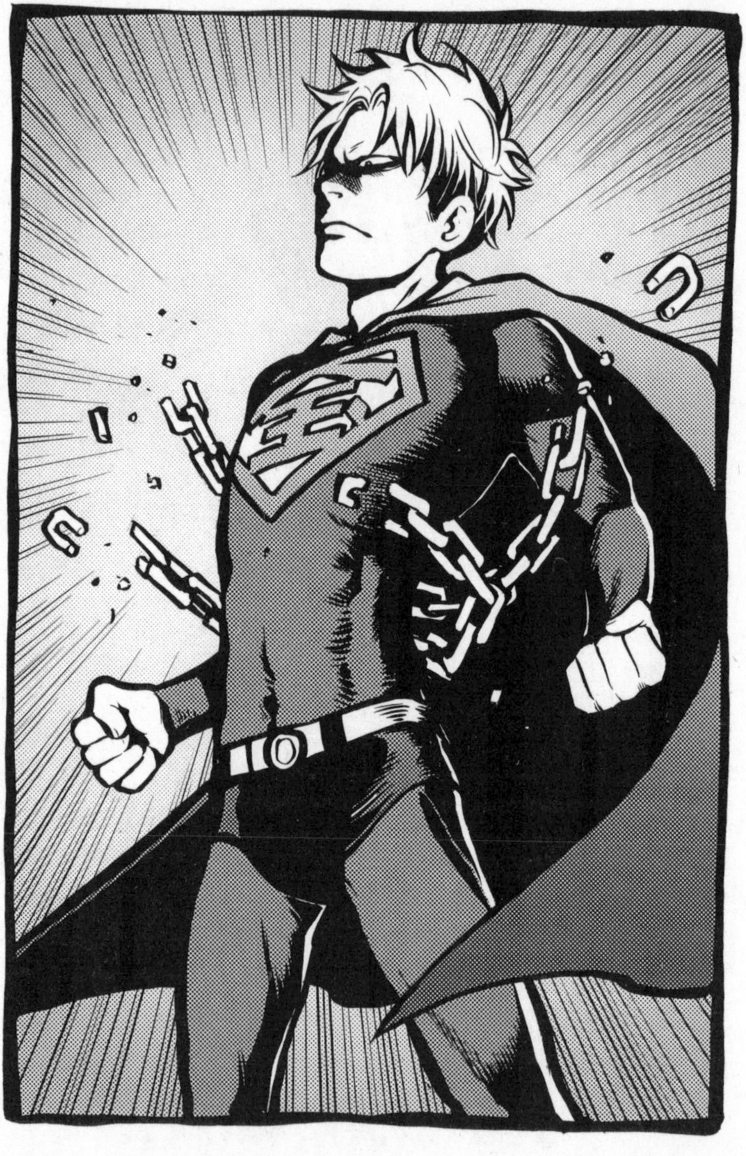

This is the AFTERWORD!

The mistake on the previous page is that I wrote the first character of Kinichiro's name wrong. I guess I was pretty tired...
     The stuff I'm putting in the drama club arc isn't anything like what the drama club was like for me in high school. It's really fun to be able to do in the manga what I couldn't back then.

Mitsurou Kubo, April 2013 ☆

☆ My Agent: Hiromi Sakitani

☆ My Assistants: Shunsuke Ono
                 Youko Mikuni
                 Hiromu Kitano
                 Koushi Tezuka
                 Kouhei Mihara
                 Rana Satou

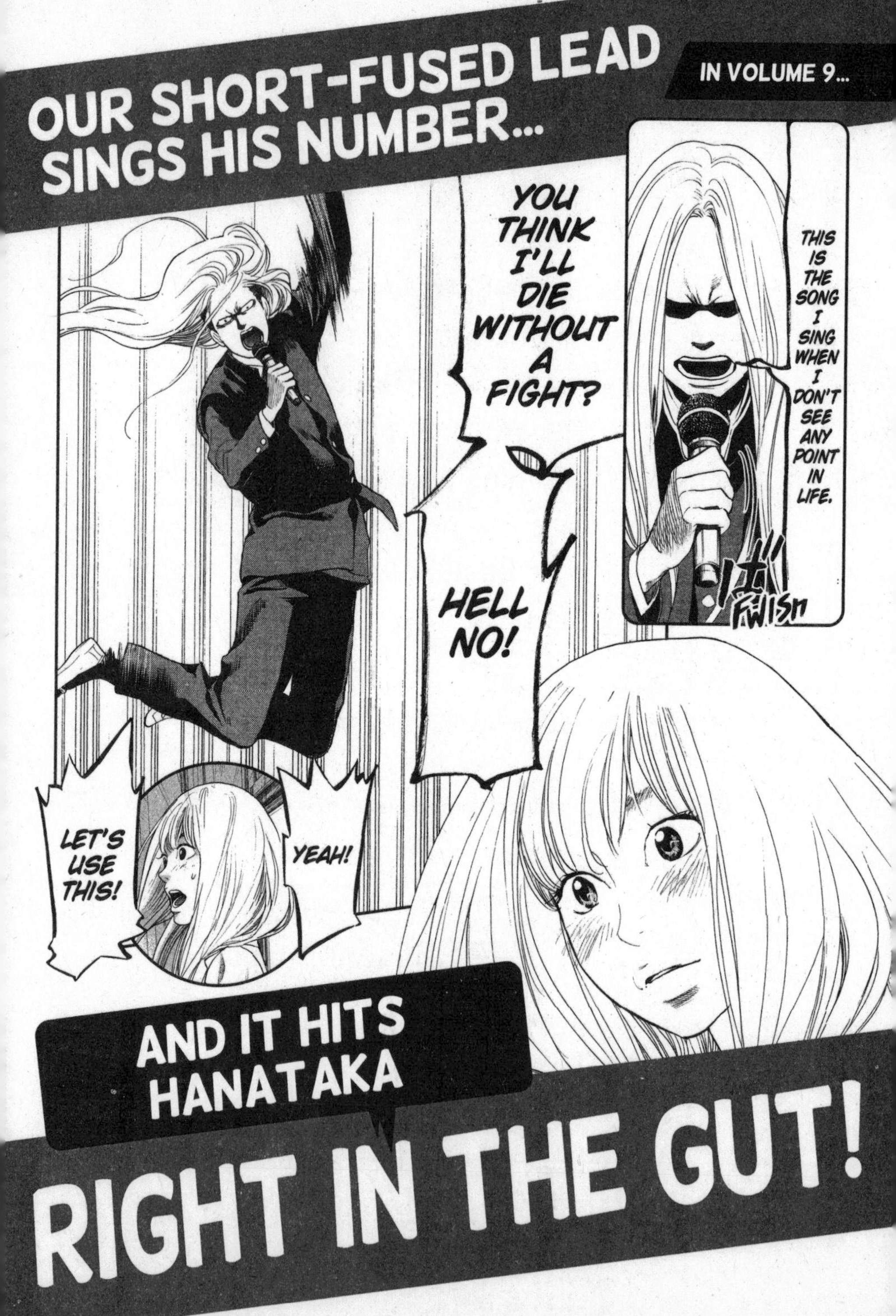
OUR SHORT-FUSED LEAD SINGS HIS NUMBER...
IN VOLUME 9...
THIS IS THE SONG I SING WHEN I DON'T SEE ANY POINT IN LIFE.
FWISH
YOU THINK I'LL DIE WITHOUT A FIGHT?
HELL NO!
YEAH!
LET'S USE THIS!
AND IT HITS HANATAKA
RIGHT IN THE GUT!

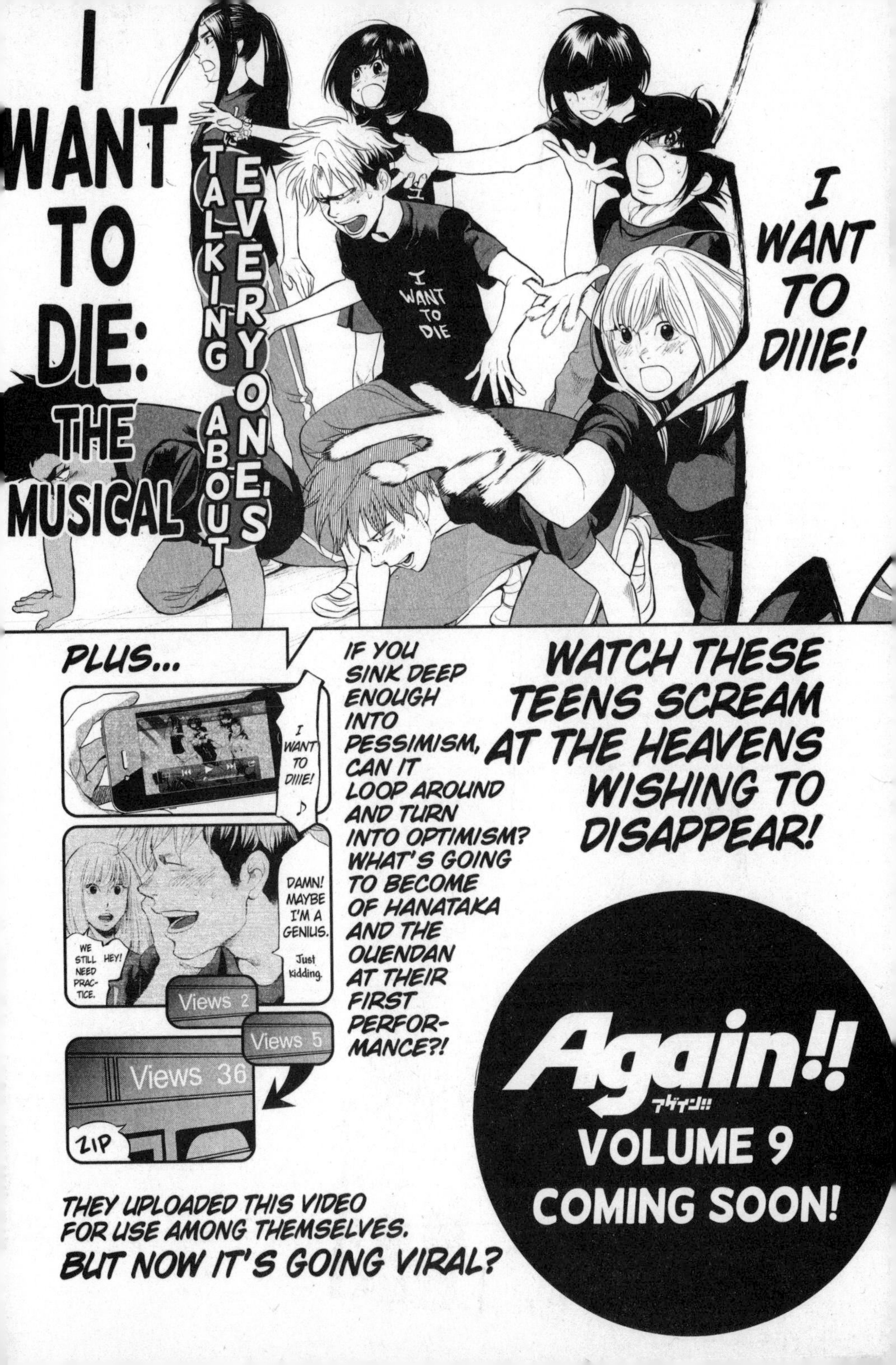
EVERYONE'S TALKING ABOUT
I WANT TO DIE: THE MUSICAL
I WANT TO DIIIE!
I WANT TO DIE
WATCH THESE TEENS SCREAM AT THE HEAVENS WISHING TO DISAPPEAR!
IF YOU SINK DEEP ENOUGH INTO PESSIMISM, CAN IT LOOP AROUND AND TURN INTO OPTIMISM? WHAT'S GOING TO BECOME OF HANATAKA AND THE OUENDAN AT THEIR FIRST PERFORMANCE?!
PLUS...
I WANT TO DIIIE! ♪
DAMN! MAYBE I'M A GENIUS.
Just kidding.
HEY!
WE STILL NEED PRAC-TICE.
Views 2
Views 5
Views 36
ZIP
Again!!
アゲイン!!
VOLUME 9
COMING SOON!
THEY UPLOADED THIS VIDEO FOR USE AMONG THEMSELVES.
BUT NOW IT'S GOING VIRAL?

Again!! volume 8 is a work of fiction. Names, characters, places, and incidents are the products of the author's imagination or are used fictitiously. Any resemblance to actual events, locales, or persons, living or dead, is entirely coincidental.

A Kodansha Comics Trade Paperback Original.

Published in the United States by Kodansha Comics, an imprint of Kodansha USA Publishing, LLC, New York.

Publication rights for this English edition arranged through Kodansha Ltd., Tokyo.

First published in Japan in 2013 by Kodansha Ltd., Tokyo, as *Agein!!* volume 8.

ISBN 978-1-63236-714-3

Printed in the United States of America.

www.kodanshacomics.com

9 8 7 6 5 4 3 2 1

Translator: Rose Padgett
Lettering: E. K. Weaver
Editing: Paul Starr
Editorial Assistance: Tiff Ferentini
Kodansha Comics edition cover design by Phil Balsman